Praise for *Real Estate Success in 5 Minutes a Day*

"Just like a daily spiritual or motivational devotional, "Real Estate Success in 5 Minutes a Day" readings are full of information and inspiration. By investing just 5 minutes a day, one can achieve success at a higher level in business and life. Use it to help you create your bigger brighter future."

> Linda McKissack
> Author of "Hold" and "Presentation Mastery for Realtors", Speaker and Business Coach with 25 plus years experience in real estate

"I followed Karen's suggestions each morning for seven days. By day eight I was excited to keep up my new habits because I was getting results. It was fast, easy, and fun—like getting a present every morning. I couldn't wait to read the day's success tip while drinking my morning coffee. Karen's approach is easy to follow and I'm already seeing results in a week!"

> Moira Lethbridge, M.Ed.
> Trainer, coach, and creator of Take the Leap to Success™ coaching program

"Karen Briscoe is force to be reckoned with in the real estate world. She has been through so many ups and downs and has emerged victorious when so many other agents would have quit. This book is so needed in this industry!"

> Pat Hiban
> International best-selling author of *6 Steps to 7 Figures—A Real Estate Practitioner's Guide to Building Wealth and Creating Your Destiny*

"Karen shows you how to prioritize the important aspects of your business—and life. By doing one simple thing a day for 365 days, imagine where you can be in one year!"

> Tony Giordano
> Author of *'the social agent'* and Founder of www.Giordano.Global

"Every professional real estate agent should take a few minutes every day to capture some of the knowledge and wisdom Karen delivers in *Real Estate Success in 5 Minutes a Day*. Each of her daily vignettes offers a nugget or two of practical advice that have helped make her one of the most successful real estate agents in the country. Brokers should give every one of their agents this book to help them boost their productivity and become more sensitive their clients' needs. It's a must-read."

> Ron Cathell
> Principal broker
> Keller Williams Realty
> McLean, Virginia

"If success was easy, we could all do it—and now, thanks to Karen, we can! In *Real Estate Success in 5 Minutes a Day* she gives us the opportunity to pick up daily habits that will be the foundation of a growing business. Don't miss the chance for a great journey to financial freedom from the industry's biggest star!"

> Liz Trocchio Smith
> Founder and CEO
> The Trocchio Advantage, LLC
> Certified executive business coach, trusted advisor,
> corporate consultant, and best-selling author

"*Real Estate Success in 5 Minutes a Day* was made for REAL estate agents. Whether you are new to the industry or a seasoned professional, Karen Briscoe provides the tools for excellence. As the leader of one of the country's top real estate groups, Karen has the knowledge to further expand your career. This book provides the keys; all you have to do is open it up!"

> Amina Basic
> CEO/team leader
> Keller Williams McLean/Great Falls
> #1 real estate company in the world
> #1 real estate training company in the world
> Certified John Maxwell teacher
> Trainer, coach, and speaker

REAL ESTATE
SUCCESS
IN 5 MINUTES A DAY

— SECRETS OF A TOP AGENT REVEALED —

KAREN BRISCOE

ISBN 978-1-936961-27-6

Books are available for special promotions and premiums.

For details, contact:

Special Markets
5 Minute Press
6820 Elm Street
McLean, VA 22101

E-mail: specialmarkets@5minutepress.com
Published by 5 Minute Press

DEDICATION

This book is dedicated to:

My dad and mom, who were my first cheerleaders and role
models of what success looks like.

My husband, Andy, who has encouraged me to achieve success
in all areas of my life and work.

Our children, Drew and Callie, who have brought both joy and challenge
to my life beyond what I ever dreamed possible.

And to you, the reader: Here's to your success!

TABLE OF CONTENTS

JANUARY

FEBRUARY

MARCH

APRIL

MAY

JUNE

JULY

AUGUST

SEPTEMBER

OCTOBER

NOVEMBER

DECEMBER

Introduction
SECRETS TO MY SUCCESS

Hi, Karen here. Like many of us who become real estate agents, I entered the profession because I like people and houses and thought it would be a perfect combination. The scary part was that I didn't really want to be a salesperson. Immediately out of college I found myself in sales in the financial services industry (code for life insurance) and was honestly turned off by it, even though I was good at it. In order to be successful in sales, I had the perception that a person had to be pushy. Combine that with a strong fear of rejection, and looking back I still find it surprising that I was successful so quickly.

So what did I do to overcome my aversion to sales and rejection? My first secret was I embraced the approach of being helpful to people, to act as a consultant. In addition to having a strong head for business, I also have a heart for ministry. Instead of "selling" me and my services, I gave freely of my time and resources. I found that people were attracted to my low-key approach. To this day I embrace this philosophy—that the relationship needs to be win-win or no deal. I want people to work with me because they want to.

The next challenge I faced was how to let people know I was a real estate agent in such a way that they wouldn't feel like I was being "salesy." The old saying, "Don't be a secret agent," really hit home in real estate. So I started a database that included everyone I knew. I decided that if I added ten names each week, in one year I would have 520 contacts. That assured I was out meeting people, since I had to come up with ten names. This secret turned out to be a key aspect of success in sales of any kind! This was before e-mail and the Internet, so I chose the old-fashioned marketing platform of postcards. The postcards became conversation pieces in and of themselves, which made it easier for me to talk with people about real estate, because they brought up the subject!

This led to my secret of "touching" people. I tracked in a notebook everyone I talked to or wrote a note to about real estate (again, this was before the Internet and e-mail). Sometimes it was as simple as a birthday card and other times more complex, like a market study. I still have all those records, so I guess that this type of tracking is a secret of success too. My success activities consisted of touching twenty-five people every week or five people each "working day."

As more and more people found out I was in real estate, they would ask me about houses in their neighborhoods. True story: at a book club, one of my friends was better informed about a home in her neighborhood than I was. Boy, did I feel convicted. What kind of professional doesn't even know the product she is selling? That's when I discovered my next secret: know the inventory. A real estate agent is licensed to not only sell houses but also to see houses. So I started a systematic program to view houses, which I continue to do even today!

At this juncture I had reached a nice level of success, yet I felt there was more and I just didn't know how to achieve it. That's when I reached out to the best Realtor® I knew in the market. Sue Huckaby attended the same church as our family. Associating with a top agent was the secret of how I went from being a good agent to becoming a partner with Sue's top team in 2006.

Sadly, Sue passed away in September 2008, the same month that the financial markets crashed. Running the company alone was very hard in a very difficult market. After living in Texas in the 1980s during the savings and loan crisis, I had some experience with challenging real estate markets. My next secret was recognizing the market signs and quickly making the changes necessary to first survive and then thrive.

These changes included moving the team from a regional brokerage to Keller Williams International, which offered me a bigger platform to rebuild on. KW was and still is on the cutting edge in training and technology, key factors to being successful in this fast-changing business. At the same time, I focused on being lean, recognizing that I was operating a business and as such it had to make money. I worked hard to boost the bottom line. That meant cutting expenses such as heavy advertising, which was the backbone of the Sue Huckaby business, as well as making staff changes. No secret here—all of these were very hard decisions. And the market wasn't getting any better.

In 2009, Lizzy Conroy joined me as a partner. Lizzy was a past client and also a friend from church. She truly came along just in time, as I was becoming very discouraged operating the business alone. Thus, my next secret was that I recognized that I would rather be part of a team than a lone agent. The philosophy of "together everyone achieves more" really resonates with me. Lizzy is a fantastic partner with whom to share the triumphs and trials of running a business. Our partnership also allows each of us to have a life in addition to a business, which has been one of my best and greatest secrets.

The journey is much sweeter for me when it is shared. We are grateful to have an amazing support staff and the best agents around who work with our clients to provide top-notch service. And who could forget all the clients through the years whom we have served—many have become dear friends.

There are great rewards in achieving personal and professional success. I've found even greater rewards in helping others achieve success, which to me is the ultimate secret. It is similar to raising children—parents often cherish their children's accomplishments more than their own. It is the same when I coach and train an agent to success. It shows that my secrets to achieving success in real estate can be followed by others. It leaves a legacy. Training, coaching, and inspiring agents to achieve their highest success is my gift.

So that brings me to this final secret: there are more secrets in the book! These stories are what I've been telling clients and agents throughout my career. They are "sticky" for a reason—you will be more likely to remember them. What good is an application or story if you never think of it again?

I hope you enjoy these secrets revealed by a top agent—me!

Real Estate Success in 5 Minutes a Day
BREAKFAST OF CHAMPIONS

The advertising slogan "Breakfast of Champions," first made popular by Wheaties cereal in the 1930s, is about feeding your body healthy food to ensure top performance. I have found that the true breakfast of champions includes feeding your mind, as well.

Hal Elrod's *The Miracle Morning for Real Estate Agents* advocates ten to fifteen minutes of reading each day as the fast track to transformation in one's life and business. Many masters and experts have shared their wisdom through words. Learning from these experienced leaders by reading their words is how you, too, can achieve transformation. Success is achieved by getting into action immediately and applying the principles learned. Applied knowledge leads to success.

That is the beauty of this book and program, *Real Estate Success in 5 Minutes a Day*. You truly only have to invest five minutes a day to achieve amazing results. If I can do it—you can too!

Incorporate the habit of reading *Real Estate Success* for inspiration in the first five minutes of your day. One of the easiest ways I've found to develop a new habit is to attach it to an existing habit. The new activity is particularly "sticky" when combined with one I enjoy. So I pair my inspirational reading for the day with my morning cup of coffee. By combining a new behavior with an already established habit, the established habit becomes the reminder. Then I don't even have to think about it. The new habit becomes effortless, as there is the automatic reward associated with it.

Make the decision now to become a lifelong learner and you will become one. Commit to the habit of reading *Real Estate Success in 5 Minutes a Day* first thing every morning. And then identify one new concept to apply in your life and business.

Success thinking, combined with success activities and success vision, creates a "sweet" life.

Start today the "breakfast of champions" habit
of reading for inspiration and growth.

How *Real Estate Success in 5 Minutes a Day* Can Help You Achieve Your Sweet Spot of Success

The Sweet Spot of Success is the overlap of three strategies: success thinking, success activities, and success vision.

SUCCESS IN REAL ESTATE = SUCCESS SWEET SPOT

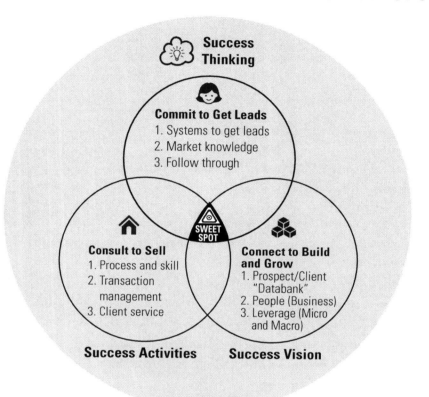

The Sweet Spot of Success is the intersection of all the best practices included in the *Real Estate Success in 5 Minutes a Day* model. The possibilities and abilities are there all the time. It is by applying the principles of the model on a consistent basis, one day at a time, that a real estate professional can best achieve the sweet spot of success.

Commit today to take the step every day to achieve the sweet spot of success in real estate.

How To Use This Book

STEP 1: Take 5 minutes every day for success—ideally, first thing each morning.

STEP 2: Read the daily entry in ***Real Estate Success in 5 Minutes a Day.***
Record the short takeaway in a journal or in the notes section.

STEP 3: Enjoy a reward, such as a cup of coffee or tea, for deciding to achieve success in 5 minutes a day!

Daily Topic Key

Special Note: There are graphic icons at the top of each daily selection of the *Real Estate Success in 5 Minutes a Day*. These symbols highlight the subject addressed for that day. They include:

 Success Thinking, Activities, and Vision: Motivational stories that increase growth mindset and are positive and future-oriented tools encompassing key components.

 Commit to Lead Generation: Develop effective prospecting habits, market knowledge, and follow-through systems.

 Consult to Sell: Strategies for process and transaction management, and customer service, encompassing everything from winning the business through settlement.

 Connect to Build and Grow: Take the practice of real estate to a business level by incorporating systems, developing relationships, and using leverage.

 Sweet Spot: Long-term success is achieved and sustained by the integration of all the secrets to success.

ARE YOU ALL IN?

In college I had a professor who had us visualize what our lives would be like once we graduated and entered the world of employment. The idea was that a student's full-time job in college was to learn, which meant that after accounting for classroom time, the remainder of the forty-plus hours of a typical work week should be allocated to preparation, learning, and studying. To be truly "all in" as a student meant giving everything one had to the educational experience.

To be "all in" as a real estate agent means to commit to complete consistently those activities that are known to lead to business. It is evident when an agent is working because there is production on the books, business in the pipeline, and an abundant source of leads. It is a lot like people who say they want to lose weight and get in better physical shape—their behavior is evident for all to see. They only cheat themselves. They are not fooling anyone; everyone is quite aware of what is really going on. The same holds true for real estate agents.

Being "all in" means giving the business everything you've got, even when things are difficult and even when the professional doesn't feel like it. During the Great Recession, many agents took on some challenging transactions in order to stay in business. Of those who survived the ordeal, almost all say that their business came out on the other side stronger and that as agents they are more competent and confident.

To be "all in" also means to close off all the exits. When one truly commits to the profession of real estate, there is a passion and singleness of purpose. It is like Homer's story of *Odysseus* and the seductive song of the Sirens. In order to protect the ship from the danger of the rocks, Odysseus had his men tie him to the mast so that the Siren song would not tempt him. There will always be shiny distractions that take away an agent's attention from the true activities that lead to success in the business. It is the true professional who is "all in" and stays focused.

Motivational expert Peter Lowe states: "The most common trait I have found in all successful people is that they have conquered the temptation to give up." That's another aspect of what it means to be "all in" to achieve and sustain success in real estate.

Commit to being "all in" and truly working on your business.

THE FOUR Ps OF MOTIVATION

There are primarily four forces that motivate people to make change, and conveniently they all happen to begin with the letter "P": push, pull, pain, and pleasure. Real estate agents are really change agents; we help people navigate the change of buying and selling a home and the process of moving. These four forces can occur in multiple combinations. For example, a "push" can occur at the same time as a circumstance that illicits "pain."

A "push" motivator is an event or factor that is "pushing" the person to move. Perhaps it is the loss of a job and the move is to economize. Another "push" example occurs when the next home has already been purchased and the seller does not want the expense of two mortgages.

The client feels the "pull" when there are circumstances that are pulling them to make a move. The "nesting" instinct when couples are expecting a child frequently creates a strong pull for purchasing a home. Another "pull" occurs at the other end of the real estate life cycle: that of the empty nester. People in this situation often feel pulled to a new life beyond that of raising children in a big house. Often this "pull" occurs around the same time as retirement, when moving to a warmer climate or somewhere with a lower cost of living is tugging at them.

"Pain" often occurs with a life event that is deemed negative at the time, such as divorce, death, loss of a job, or financial reversal. And "pleasure" in most cases is associated with joyful life events or circumstances, such as marriage, welcoming a child into the family, a new career, or financial abundance.

As mentioned, the driving forces almost always occur in some combination. A divorce pushes the family to sell the home, which is painful for everyone. And yet somewhere along the journey there is the pull of a new life and the pleasure of moving on.

Awareness is the first step I have found in understanding the four Ps. As a real estate agent, being cognizant of the factors motivating clients to make the move to buy or sell a home is how I can best meet their true needs. On the surface, it may seem as though it is just a financial and legal transaction, yet underneath there are multiple levels of emotion present.

Understand and use the four Ps of motivation
to help your clients navigate change.

SCRIPTS GET A BAD RAP

As a professional salesperson, I believe that scripts get a bad rap. People often think that because they are practiced or memorized, they come off as canned and unnatural. When used well, however, they can convey professionalism and free up the agent to be able to focus on the customer rather than trying to remember what to say next.

This really hit home to me when a friend was diagnosed with cancer. The couple sought the opinion of several specialists and found that they were really drawn to one particular doctor. He conveyed warmth while explaining in a clear manner the needed medical procedure, as well as the benefits and risks. At some point, the wife commented that his presentation was comforting because he covered everything so professionally and yet in a personal style. He explained that he followed a script and went on to share that he found most everyone had generally the same questions and concerns. By covering those up front in his presentation, he could then turn his attention to the individual's needs and situation.

This is to me the best essence of scripts: the focus is on the client. When the agent knows the material so well that she can convey it naturally, then she can direct her attention to the client's situation. As a practical matter, for my listing presentation I use a glossy marketing piece as my talking points. In this way, I am sure to cover what our team offers as a value proposition as well as share how our team works. This also assures a high standard of professional service for all our clients. It means that I do not go on an appointment and "wing it," hoping the right words come to me. Our clients deserve better than that, and so do yours.

Another profession that is well known for the use of scripts is the theatre. One always knows that the words of Shakespeare will be delivered as written when attending a performance of *Hamlet*. Just think what would happen if an actor decided not to memorize and rehearse his lines? Chaos would ensue, or at the very least a bad performance. It is in rehearsing that actors and agents gain the confidence to be natural when performing and presenting. Then their own essence truly comes through because they have the confidence of knowing their lines.

Use scripts in your presentations to increase standards of service and professionalism for customers and clients.

BUSINESS COACH AS PERSONAL TRAINER

Currently I enjoy good health for my fifty-plus age bracket and stay active by regular biking. My mother recently turned eighty and at her milestone birthday celebration it occurred to me that I am in much better physical shape and health than she was at my age. Thus, in all likelihood I will live as least as long as she has, which gives me about three more decades. As I want to live the fullest life possible in the time allotted, I realized that I should do something about it now. Even though biking is a healthy cardio activity, when it was my primary form of exercise I started to experience overuse injuries.

It is hard for me to commit to any form of exercise other than biking— I just don't find it enjoyable. I came to the conclusion that I would need to invest in a personal trainer for accountability. A personal trainer provides many of the same characteristics and benefits of a business or productivity coach.

The personal trainer pushes me to do exercises that are good for me that I just wouldn't do otherwise. Business and productivity coaches help their clients stay accountable for their activities. They explore new endeavors and systems for efficiencies and effectiveness.

My personal trainer makes certain that I perform the exercise correctly. At the very least, exercising incorrectly means it isn't as effective, yet on the other end of the spectrum, incorrect procedure can lead to injury. Business coaches help their clients see "blind spots" to be sure that injury to the company does not occur, as well as make certain that everyone performs at their highest capabilities.

Personal trainers and coaches both train on "best practices." It is their job to stay abreast of the industry standards and to make certain their clients perform at the highest levels possible.

The personal trainer can "spot" the athlete so that greater weights can be incorporated in the program. Without a "spotter," fitness typically won't progress to the highest level attainable, due to the possibility of injury. Business coaches and higher-level professionals in the industry have the knowledge and expertise that can help their clients break through ceilings of achievement to take them to the next level.

A personal trainer frequently "mixes up the program" so that different muscle groups rest while others are worked. This creates the highest potential performance possible. An overarching plan of development is a key aspect to business coaching as well. A coach helps the client see both the big picture and take action steps in the present to implement those goals.

Pursue coaching to take your business to the next level.

FEET ON THE STREET: KNOW THE INVENTORY

One of the primary responsibilities of salespeople is to know their product. Our son's first job during high school was at the local hardware store. One of his first tasks was to learn the location of all 40,000 items in the store. The store prided itself on customer service. When someone entered McLean Hardware and asked about an item, there was always a salesperson at the front to take him to the product. Once the product has been located, then the features and benefits were presented to the customer.

The same principle applies to other product sales. The shoe store salesperson must know what brands and styles of shoes are available in stock and by order. Professional software and financial service representatives stay knowledgeable of industry offerings to best meet their clients' situations. Office supply and food service vendors know the inventory available in order to serve their customers. Many companies offer "boot camps" and training programs to get new recruits up and running quickly on product knowledge. Professional salespeople and consultants upgrade their knowledge, skills, and abilities to stay abreast of new product lines and industry changes.

The real estate agent's products are homes and properties. With technology, one can view homes with a click of a button from the comfort of her office or on a smartphone or tablet. Yet nothing compares with actually going to see the property in person. It is feet-on-the-street observations gained from experience. The position of a home on the lot, what it backs up to, is across from, and the grade of the land are not always conveyed accurately in the Google Earth view and photos. Just doing a drive-by tells volumes about the nature of the neighborhood. Is it well-kept or experiencing decline, are there a lot of other homes for sale? Walking through a home conveys how well the home has been maintained: is there a good flow, and is the price in line with the market?

Another strong aspect of inventory knowledge involves prospecting for business. When viewing homes, a professional agent can use it as a time to think of people who might be in the market to buy the home. Further, if the agent happens to be conveniently in the neighborhood of people in her sphere or past clients, it is a great "warm" call or opportunity to pop by and touch base. Everyone wants to know what is going on in their neighborhoods and communities. In the call or visit, make the easy segue into inquiring if the neighbor happens to know of anyone in the market to buy or sell in the community.

The actual knowledge of inventory keeps the agent current on the market and comparables. This is particularly important when preparing the documentation that supports the contract value for the appraiser. It is the informed agent who best services her clients' real estate needs. There will always be business for real estate agents who are true neighborhood specialists and possess strong market expertise. Earn that distinction with "feet-on-the-street" knowledge of the inventory.

Preview houses to stay knowledgeable on inventory and for business development.

GO TO WHERE THE MARKET IS GOING

It is common knowledge that the stock market changes constantly. All one has to do is watch the tickertape for a short period of time to see the fluctuations. Many people are not aware that the real estate market is also very fluid. This occurs in fast-moving markets, as well as areas that experience a slow turnover cycle. Seasonal adjustments factor into market movements, too.

To strategically buy and sell real estate is best accomplished by getting ahead of the market, not where it was or even is at currently. The hockey player Wayne Gretzky similarly attributed his success on the ice: "I skate to where the puck is going to be, not where it has been." The key to success in pricing is to follow the same principle.

At any given point in time, sellers go active on the market, buyers write contracts, and transactions go to settlement. Depending on the absorption level, a market will be balanced between a seller's or buyer's market. Economists, appraisers, real estate professionals, and others knowledgeable in the industry consider a balanced market to be a six-month supply of inventory. More than that, and it is a buyer's market and less a seller's market.

When the market moves rapidly and homes go under contract quickly, that too is an indicator that it is or will soon be a seller's market. Very rapid absorption leads to price acceleration, which benefits sellers. For buyers to win contracts, it is important to look at the trajectory of price appreciation and write offers that reflect where the market is going.

On the other hand, when supply increases at a pace faster than related demand, those are conditions for a buyer's market. For sellers, it can be in their best interests to get ahead of the market by pricing aggressively. When sellers make smaller, more incremental price adjustments, they in effect follow the market down.

Appraisers typically establish real estate value by the use of comparables, which look at the market's history. The real estate professional takes her knowledge of comparables data and market absorption, as well as trends, and projects into the future.

"Go to where the market is going" is a key pricing strategy for the agent to achieve and sustain success with clients.

Institute the pricing strategy with clients to "go to where the market is going."

Top agents achieve and sustain success often with the influence and impact of a coach. Over the years, I too have worked with a number of coaches. One focused on lead-generation methods and productivity, another on sales techniques, and others on team and business building. In my work with executive coach Moira Lethbridge, a component of the "Take the Leap to Success" program is to journal five minutes a day. My initial reaction was, "I don't have five minutes a day to journal." Yet I came to the realization that if I was going to pay someone to coach me to success, the first thing I had to do was set aside my assumptions and limiting beliefs and embrace the change.

At this writing, I have journaled every day for at least five minutes for well over one year. There are others that tout the benefits of the practice. Hal Elrod refers to it as "scribing" in his book *The Miracle Morning for Real Estate Agents*. Elrod states: "By getting your thoughts out of your head and putting them in writing, you gain valuable insights."

Journaling dovetails well with the takeaways included at the end of each daily story in *Real Estate Success in Just 5 Minutes a Day*. Take a few minutes to reflect on how you can incorporate the technique in your business practice and life. In many cases, to get to the next level requires making adjustments along the way. Journaling can provide clarity in that pursuit.

A benefit of scribing that Elrod speaks to is that of the "gap-focus." The concept is that high-achieving individuals frequently focus on the gap between where they are and where they want to be. By looking back, one can often best see what needs to happen in order to propel forward. This is where *Real Estate Success* can be part of achieving your goals, as it provides real-time examples and techniques.

Getting started is often the hardest part. This is where habit can help to break the inertia. The beauty of a routine is that you don't have to think about it, you just do it.

In the coming-of-age movie with his name, Ferris Bueller shares this philosophy: "Life moves pretty fast. If you don't stop and look around once in a while, you could miss it." Consider what insights you might gain by taking the time to write down your thoughts.

Incorporate daily journaling as part of the real estate agent success journey.

FEEL, FELT, FOUND

The Feel, Felt, Found technique is an effective means of communicating with real estate customers and clients. The reason it is so powerful is that by empathizing with their situations, you convey that you truly care. Zig Ziglar eloquently put it this way: "People don't care how much you know until they know how much you care."

Once you have demonstrated that you truly understand their particular situation and how they feel about it, often they are open enough to hear about possible solutions.

First, repeat their concerns and state that you understand why they might feel that way. Next, tell them about somebody who has felt the same way. Close by sharing what other people have found worked for them.

Example when working with seller clients: *I understand you feel the feedback we have been hearing about your home seems negative. Many other sellers have felt the same way. And what other sellers have found is that by listening to and being responsive to the feedback by agents who are working with real buyers, then we can position the home correctly for the market and get it sold.*

Example when working with buyer clients: *I know you feel frustrated that there are no homes available to buy that meet your criteria. I've had other buyers who felt that way as well. What these other buyers have found is that by adjusting their criteria and expectations, we were able to find something that met their needs.*

The reason this style of communication works is that by empathizing with how clients feel, they believe you are on their side and are really hearing their concerns. This builds rapport and creates harmony. Next, when you share how someone else felt, you move the focus to a more objective place, so that they will be more open to consider learning how other people handled a similar situation. Also, they don't feel like they are the only ones who have ever been in this situation. At that point, most people are open to hearing and considering possible solutions.

Use the three Fs in empathizing with customers and clients to create an atmosphere for exploring possible solutions.

DATABASE IS YOUR DATABANK

Many people pass the real estate license requirements test and then are surprised to discover the world is not clamoring to hire them. In effect, the real estate agent has nothing to do until he has a lead.

Actually, this is true of other professions and businesses as well. Think of the doctor: there is no one to practice medicine "on" until the physician has a patient. In law, there are no means to practice the legal profession until one has a client. In a grocery store or a flower shop, until a customer arrives with a need to fill, there is no business to conduct. Lead generation is truly every person's job and opportunity.

One of the most common sources of business for a real estate agent is her sphere of influence (SOI). In the real estate profession, the SOI includes those people who would recognize the agent's name, known as a "strong" tie. There can actually be more social currency with someone who has a "weak tie." This phenomenon is documented by the Pew Research Center, according to executive and entrepreneur Kevin McKeown in "The Strength of Weak Ties in Social Networking: Seek to Be Worth Knowing."

The key to success is to engage with people, whether online or offline. Build a database of their contact information. This "databank" becomes the agent's source of current and future business.

There can be a lifecycle to a real estate business. At infancy, the agent is brand new to the profession. She toddles along the first few years, finally gaining a foothold and achieving success. Once past adolescence, she comes into her own and enters young adulthood with confidence. The databank is where the agent crosses over from being only as good as her last lead to that of a business owner. She continues to connect to build and grow the business through the middle-age years into maturity. As time passes, the agent plans for retirement. At this stage, many successful agents sell their past client and sphere list and earn a residual income. The databank has truly become an asset.

This is why one of the top priorities of professional agents is to treat the database as one would treat an investment account. It is a key to success to keep it current and to actively feed and grow this vital source of leads.

Take active steps to consistently build and grow your databank.

HOME INSPECTION STOPLIGHT ANALOGY

The home inspection contingency is a key juncture for purchasers. It is like being at a stoplight at a crossroads. Inspectors provide for buyers a clear understanding of the physical condition of the property. At this juncture, the informed client can then make "stoplight" decisions.

The first question the purchaser must answer upon completion of the home inspection is: "Do you still want to buy the property?" This is the "red light/green light" objective. On occasion, deal breakers have been uncovered. Or other factors are revealed that, had the buyer known, would have affected the offer made. If the client no longer wants to proceed and there is a provision provided in the contract to do so, then notice to void must be delivered in a timely fashion.

There are occasions when the home inspection results are not the root cause of the decision to void; in those situations a bad case of "buyer's remorse" may exist. Buyer's remorse is an emotional response that occurs in a sales transaction, which may involve feelings of regret, fear, depression, or anxiety. Experience shows that the best way to cope with buyer's remorse is to minimize its destructiveness and to be informed of available options.

In the majority of the cases, however, the purchaser does want to move forward with buying the property, often with the stipulation that the seller will take care of the issues addressed in the home inspection report. This is like being at a yellow light: proceed with caution.

The next step, as provided in most contracts, is to identify from the home inspector's report those items that the purchaser would like the seller to repair, replace and/or remedy. The verbiage may specify work that normally requires a licensed tradesperson to install or repair and should be corrected accordingly. Further, receipts for corrective actions should be provided to the purchaser prior to the presettlement walkthrough inspection, to allow time for verification. Sometimes a credit to the purchaser at settlement toward closing costs will be offered as a remedy. This can be problematic with some lenders, so be certain to verify that it is allowable before negotiating an agreement for a closing-cost credit or an adjustment to the sales price.

At this juncture, the purchaser and seller are back in negotiation mode. As so often is the case, the purchaser wants everything fixed and the seller wants to minimize costs and effort. It is the outcome of these negotiations that determines if the transaction moves into green light for "go" status or whether it becomes voided and thus is a red light and everything stops.

Utilize the "stop light" analogy to explain to clients the options available with a home inspection contingency.

LEAD DOMINO EFFECT

The domino effect occurs after one knocks over the first domino in a string. The chain reaction that happens can lead to an extraordinary outcome. In the words of author BJ Thornton: "Every great change starts like falling dominoes." In real estate, every lead has the ability to start a chain of business opportunity that can achieve geometric results.

A number of years ago, my business partner took a sign call lead off a listing I had in McLean. That particular home did not work for her buyers, yet Lizzy was able to sell them a home in nearby Great Falls. This also meant they needed to sell their home in Vienna, which Lizzy represented as the listing agent. An agent on our team held Sunday open houses at the home a number of times. Out of those opens, he made the acquaintance of two couples that each purchased an upper-bracket home in Great Falls. For one of the groups, he sold their home in Herndon as the listing agent. This led to two referrals on the street, which also resulted in sales. And another of the open house attendees actually bought the home in Vienna. Additionally, I sold the original listing in McLean. This one lead set up several chains of domino reactions, resulting in almost $10 million in transactions within a couple years.

The challenge is that the agent doesn't necessary know which one of the dominoes is going to set off the chain reaction. Gary Keller, in *The One Thing*, uses this as the barometer to decide which domino to focus on: "What is the *one* thing you can do, such that by doing it everything else would be easier or unnecessary?" Consistent, proactive prospecting is the one way guaranteed to create opportunity in real estate. It is the lead that starts the domino effect for the successful agent.

This may be hard to believe, yet I have heard agents actually say that they would be overwhelmed if they had too many prospects. This is a position of amazing power and opportunity. Yes, the agent must take on the challenge of learning to manage the workflow. This is where the agent goes from being only as good as her next lead to connecting to build and grow a business. Options at this juncture include referring the lead out for a fee, partnering with other agents, and employing staff to assist. These are all good challenges!

Scientists project that the chain reaction of one two-inch tall domino, doubled each time, would stretch from the Earth to the moon by the fifty-seventh time. The geometric power of domino progression is a secret to success, which can be yours as well if you embrace it as part of your business development plan.

Employ the power of the domino effect to achieve extraordinary results in your business and life.

ACT AS IF

The most common application of this phrase is to empower self-confidence. It is known most commonly as "fake it until you make it." The most practical way to "act as if" is to take the next logical step in the process. Amy Cuddy, a speaker, Harvard Business School faculty, and author of *Presence: Bringing Your Boldest Self to Your Biggest Challenges*, takes the concept one step further and states: "Fake it until you become it." Take on the persona and actions and you will become that person. She goes on to say: "Our bodies change our minds, and our minds can change our behavior, and our behavior can change our outcomes."

There are numerous applications for the real estate agent to change the outcome of scenarios by proactive thinking and preparation. For example, I always prepare for listing appointments as if I will win the business. In addition to the marketing material and comparative market analysis, I bring the listing contract paperwork as well. If the sellers are ready to move forward, then I am too! Let's say they want time to review or think about the decision; having the paperwork available sets the stage for the next appointment to occur.

When working with buyers, provide relevant comparables and information at the showings for homes on the short list. At the first sign of buying signals, prepare the offer for the clients' review and execution. It becomes the natural and easy next step for them.

Prior to presenting an offer to a listing agent or seller on behalf of a buyer client, "pencil" in the home inspection date. This demonstrates to the parties that the buyer is confident they are going to come to an agreement, and also that the buyer isn't going to waste time in removing contingencies. Along the same lines, upon review of the home inspection report, immediately set out to obtain estimates and proposals for the work identified. In this way, the parties can more quickly understand what is involved and arrive at an agreement.

When someone stops you in the grocery store and asks about the house down the street from where she lives, make plans to preview the home if you haven't already. Use that opportunity to follow up with information about it. Casual inquiries often are buying and selling signals. As it is on the customer's mind, "act as if it is" and often that will lead to the next step.

"Act as if" demonstrates that you as the agent have thought of the next logical step or steps in the progression and that you will make it easy for customers to navigate the process with you. It shows you are on top of things and that you intend to look out for their best interests. It shows eagerness and that you really want to work with them. It bridges the gap between where they are now and where they want to be. And as you take those steps, you will become it. Agents who achieve and sustain success "act as if" the opportunity and business is theirs for the taking. And then it is.

"Set the stage" in your business and life by "acting as if" until such time as you have become it.

WHY DO THE BEST HOUSES SELL SO FAST?

The best houses sell so fast for the simple reason that they are the best houses. At any given point in time, there is a pool of buyers ready, willing, and able to buy a home. Those buyers actively search the Internet, visit open houses, and tour homes with real estate agents. Those buyers know a good thing when they see it and tend to move quickly to snatch up the best on the market.

There is a trifecta achieved in real estate: the value of the location, price, and condition of the property relative to the market. It is frequently in flux, as the market is constantly changing. For example, if another home comes on the market in a neighborhood and it is a better price relative to the homes already on the market, it then will become the "best house."

Once the first pool of buyers views a home and it hasn't gone under contract, then that is in itself the market speaking. The message is silent and sometimes "hard to hear." What it is saying is that the home did not meet the criteria of those buyers. The market is the market study.

At that juncture, sellers can wait for the next pool of buyers to enter the market and/or do something to get the attention of the first pool of buyers. What experienced agents have found is that the next pool of buyers typically behaves in a similar fashion as preceding groups. There are effectively two ways of getting the attention of the market again. One is to change the condition of the home and the other is to change the price.

The best reason for the seller to make changes to the house is that there are issues that can be easily addressed. Or the items are of such a nature that all buyers will want them addressed, such as water intrusion in the basement. The critical condition issues become evident as the agent obtains feedback from buyer agents or from buyers directly at public open houses. The challenge for the agent is to get the word out to the marketplace about the upgrades. The most effective means I have found is to personally call all the agents who have shown and previewed the home and invite them back to see the fresh look. Another strategy is to host a broker's open house for agents to take another tour of the home. And, it almost goes without saying, be certain to upload fresh photos on the Internet if applicable.

Adjusting the price is the most effective means to grab the attention of the market. The reason is that price changes trigger Internet search criteria, which sends automatic notifications to those parties that have alerts set up. The same impact is not obtained with changes made to the home.

At some point, the price will become attractive enough that buyers will reconsider. At that juncture, the buyer decides that the home is now one of the best available and acts accordingly. Buyers, too, should be aware of "why the best houses sell so fast." As most people want to own "the best house," to do so often requires being able to move in an aggressive fashion.

Share "why the best houses sell so fast" with clients as they make pricing and buying decisions.

THE ROLLER COASTER OF REAL ESTATE BUSINESS

The business of real estate can be a lot like riding a roller coaster—with lots of peaks and valleys. The reason is that an agent has a client and is very busy with that buyer or seller, spending a great deal of time either finding a home for the buyer to purchase or marketing the home for sale for the seller. Once a home is under contract, then there are inspections and appraisals and financing contingencies to manage, and so forth. It seems there are a myriad of details to navigate and the agent is fully engaged and focused on the transactional aspects of the business.

After settlement occurs, then the agent has more time and gets busy finding another client to work with. The difficulty lies in that this can be a "feast or famine" way to do business. Many new agents find it challenging to manage several aspects of the business simultaneously. Thus, they tend to discontinue lead-generating activities when focused on contract details. What happens feels very much like riding a roller coaster, with huge up and down swings in activities.

Experienced agents know that lead generation must be an ongoing process. It never stops— even when busy dealing with other aspects of the business. It is like the roller coaster sending off a new train every five or ten minutes. That way there is always one train entering the station, which in this analogy would be settlement. There would be trains in every loop of the coaster at any given point in time. The illustration below shows what happens if this is done continuously; in effect, the top part of the curve "levels" off.

Roller Coaster of Real Estate

Thus, the best way to smooth out the rises and falls in the business is to constantly be generating leads so that clients are continuously being put in the pipeline. Some transactions will move quickly through the process, and others will take longer. The overall impact, though, is a business that can ride through market fluctuations.

Continuously put customers and clients in
your pipeline on a daily basis!

COMFORT THE DISTURBED AND DISTURB THE COMFORTABLE

It has been said that the mission in life for Martin Luther King, Jr. was to: "Comfort the disturbed and disturb the comfortable." King truly was a man who shaped our country and influenced the world. I find the words to be inspirational as well, as I serve out my mission to help buyers and sellers with their real estate needs.

The opportunities to demonstrate comfort to a client who is disturbed while in the process of buying and selling a home are countless. The logistics can be daunting, given that most people are only involved in a personal real estate transaction once every five to seven years on average. This, combined with the fact that most real estate transactions correspond with another stress-related life event, makes for an even greater need for empathy. These are but a few circumstances that often occur simultaneously with a home sale and are significant traumas in their own way: death, divorce, financial reversal, or the loss of job. Even for positive reasons—marriage, having a child, change of school, or a career move—moving is stressful for most people.

The scenarios to disturb the comfortable are often more difficult for a real estate agent to engage in. At least they are for me. This is when clients have their own ideas and choose not to listen to professional counsel. The most common situation is in regard to price, relative to the market. It is the responsibility of the professional agent to be honest with clients about the market and how it is responding. This is addressed in the National Association of Realtor® Standard of Practice 1.3: "In attempting to secure a listing, agents shall not deliberately mislead the owner as to market value." To be a true advisor means to engage in the difficult conversations, as well as the easy ones.

I have found it helpful to share with clients that I have their self-interests at heart. As the listing agent, it is my objective to sell the home for the top dollar the market will bear. To open up the discussion, I often pose the question: "Do you want me to be honest with you?" Be prepared, though, for potential backlash as you disturb the comfort that they have been living in.

Agents, too, on occasion need to be disturbed, as they have become too comfortable in their routine. Coaches, mentors, accountability partners, and mastermind groups all can provide the impetus for needed change. An outside perspective can be valuable, particularly when an agent is ready to take the business to the next level.

Use the sentiment of Martin Luther King, Jr.
to move clients through the buying and selling process.

THERE ARE NO PERFECT HOUSES

Just as there are no perfect spouses, there are no perfect houses. Actually, this applies to everything, in my opinion: there are no perfect children, no perfect jobs, no perfect churches, no perfect charities or schools, no perfect "you fill in the blank."

As a real estate agent, I most frequently share this line with buyers after a home inspection. It is the home inspector's job to evaluate the property and detail all the defects and issues discovered in a report. At this juncture, some buyers freak out and become unduly concerned that they are purchasing a money pit. But the reality is that no home is perfect.

Experienced agents know that even brand-new homes put through an inspection with a fine-tooth comb can come out with items to be rectified on the punch-out list. That is the purpose of handing purchasers a roll of blue tape to walk around the house with: they can put a small piece on every imperfection identified.

What is a purchaser to do with a list of deficiencies identified in a home inspection? First, realize that there are no perfect houses. Next, determine if the defects are of such a nature that they can be corrected. If that is the case, establish a monetary value. There is risk associated with any purchase; it is not possible to eliminate entirely. What is achievable is an informed assessment of the risk.

Counsel with experienced inspectors, contractors, systems technicians, engineers, and others as necessary about whether the issues are common for the age of home. Consult with your professional agent about the responsibility of the seller. In some cases, negotiation of repairs, replacement, and remedies can be obtained according to the market conditions.

It can be an uncomfortable and sometimes challenging experience for a seller to find out his home isn't perfect. It is the agent's opportunity to help him not take it personally! Prepare sellers for the probability that the inspector will uncover situations that they just weren't aware of and that it is the inspector's role to evaluate a home. Being proactive is a better course of action than waiting to deal with the after-burn of an upset client.

All of these are great strategies, yet it is best to start from the premise that there are no perfect houses.

Find opportunities to use the "there are no perfect houses" slogan to influence and counsel buyer clients through the decision-making process.

PURSUIT OF HAPPINESS

The "pursuit of happiness" is mentioned in the United States Declaration of Independence as a fundamental right. It is perhaps one of the most memorable phrases coined by President Thomas Jefferson.

Another famous president, Abraham Lincoln, stated: "Most folks are as happy as they make up their minds to be." That perspective rings true, having represented more than 1,000 clients and customers in the process of buying and selling real estate.

I recall the joy expressed by a first-time homebuyer at settlement. She was so excited that this one bedroom, one bath condo would be "her own place." On the other end of the continuum, I recall the dismay expressed when a multi-million-dollar estate purchaser was disappointed that the property was not her "dream home." There have been buyers whom, even though they purchased a home that met many of their needs, felt dissatisfied because there was another one that got away. Along the same line are buyers who want more than they can afford and anything less is a letdown.

Some sellers are delighted when paid a fair market price. Others are continuously frustrated and upset that the market does not respond the way they had hoped. There have been situations where sellers have done well for the existing market and yet are concerned that money was left on the table. Maybe they could have gotten more if they had waited. It is a case of "woulda, coulda, shoulda."

The *Pursuit of Happyness* is also the title of a movie starring Will Smith, based on the true story of Chris Gardner. In spite of numerous challenges, Gardner always looked for the positive and stayed focused on the objective—to improve his situation for his son and him. It was the pursuit that he found meaningful.

Real estate is a complicated business and there are sure to be challenges faced. The transaction involves people's personal lives, and the financial and legal ramifications are significant. There are times when it is good to pause and just be happy. There is always something good to be found and it is the agent's role to help the client find it.

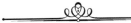

Find and focus on the good in the situation for the client and yourself.

"TALE OLD AS TIME"

The opening lyrics in the theme song of the movie *Beauty and the Beast*: "Tale old as time, true as it can be'" have applications in real estate. Consider the ugliest house in the neighborhood—the "beast," if you will. Everyone passes it by, just as many ladies did not consider the "Beast" as a promising beau.

And yet once Beauty gets to know the Beast, over time she finally sees his core character. It turns out that there is a handsome prince imprisoned inside. That can be the case for a home that has been neglected over time. Perhaps the landscape has become overgrown and the bushes and trees overshadow the home's potential.

A place to begin to look is at the "bones" of a home. If the structure still has good character, then there is something to work with. Once the old, undesirable aspects have been removed, then one can know what value is at the core. If there is value, then the task is to begin anew. The best value in real estate is often found in the lowest-priced property in a high-price neighborhood. This creates upside potential by virtue of sweat equity.

One option is to reconstruct from the studs what was originally there. Another is to strip away the old varnish and peeling paint and refinish to the original glory. Still another strategy is to keep the core and add on and adapt to make it better than before.

In the movie, the Beast at one time was a handsome prince. Through unfortunate circumstances rooted in selfish pride and arrogance, his true character was covered over. Yet beauty can be found again, even in what seems to not have value and is unlovable at first glance. The story is about those who choose to examine new possibilities

Love and attention can transform a house that has been neglected. Once renovation has taken place, then everyone can attest that, yes, the potential was there all along—they just couldn't see it. As the lyrics proclaim: "true as it can be."

Help clients find value in real estate that appears to be a "beast" yet can easily be turned into a "beauty."

WINN: WHEN IF NOT NOW?

WINN is an easy-to-remember acronym that stands for the question: When if not now? I have found it useful to pose when people are at a crossroads in making a decision. It helps them think through the process and can be a catalyst to create urgency.

To understand better a buyer's motivation, the question asks: If you don't buy now, when will you buy? Waiting comes with the possibility that prices and/or interest rates will go up. In a flat or declining market, that may not be the case. But what about the opportunity cost of waiting to move and thus putting off the time that one could enjoy being in the new home? For example, perhaps your buyer clients are waiting to save more money for a down payment. Provide recommendations from lenders to evaluate whether it would be beneficial to wait or to move forward with the next step. Probing with the question provides insight into what you can do to help your client explore the options. The question becomes: When will you buy, if you don't do it now?

With sellers, the question is similar, yet from their perspective. If sellers are waiting for the market to get better, then when will they sell? The market may or may not get better. Sometimes it takes decades for markets to recover. Thus, the time spent waiting may cause one to lose out on moving on with one's life—literally and figuratively. This happened with a number of clients who bought during the last market peak and have been renting out the home, waiting for the market to come back. Ten years later, the home is now that much older and the market is only marginally better. Just think of how much better off those owners would have been had they not put off making the decision to sell.

If the person is selling and buying in the same market area, there can be a positive effect by acting sooner rather than later. If the seller is buying up, then there is the possibility of the great arbitrage. If the seller is downsizing, then taxes, maintenance, and upkeep costs tend to be less, so why not take the savings benefit earlier rather than later? There are countless benefits to right-sizing of housing needs and costs. Further attempting to time the real estate market is like trying to time the stock market. So if your Mr. and Mrs. Seller aren't going to do it now, when will they?

The real estate agent can ask this question professionally, and personally as well. When will you contact that lead, that client, if you don't do it now? And the deeper question is: When are you going to live your best life, if you don't do it now? If it is helpful to have a tune to hum, the song by Incubus, "If Not Now, When?" is one you may want to listen to for inspiration.

Embrace the question, "When if not now?"
for your clients and yourself!

A BUSINESS OF ONE'S OWN

The famous essay, *A Room of One's Own*, by Virginia Woolf, is the inspiration behind the vision of a business of one's own. Although written with women in mind, I believe it can be applied to everyone. The premise of the idea is, in Woolf's words: "A woman must have money and a room of her own if she is to write fiction." To correlate, a person must have money and a business of one's own if she is to operate in the sweet spot of real estate success. This can be applied in numerous areas of the real estate success model.

In the "commit to get leads" portion, agents who are the lead generators truly have a business of their own over those agents who rely on others to provide leads. The lead-receiver position will always be dependent on others to be successful. In similar fashion, this occurs in the consult-to-sell aspect of the business. Those agents who have the ability and skill to get deals under contract and can handle the transaction management and customer service are the producers.

It is the next level that takes the agent into the territory of business owner. The successful agent who constantly and consistently connects these two aspects is the one who builds and grows an actual ongoing business enterprise. This involves the aspects of creating a continuous lead-generation machine—otherwise known as the databank. It also includes connecting and networking with people in and associated with the industry, colleagues, other agents and brokers near and far, mastermind groups, coaches and mentors, staff, and team members. And it involves leveraging on the micro, macro, and exponential levels.

The benefits of a business of one's own are as unique as each person's vision for her life. It is the freedom to live creatively and uniquely. To write one's own life story may begin as fiction—the actualization of the vision is when it transforms into reality.

*Create the vision that you want for your life
and business and take charge of it today.*

WHY THE FIRST OFFER IS STATISTICALLY THE BEST OFFER

The listing agent prepares an exhaustive comparative market analysis. The seller and agent evaluate the market conditions and set the list price accordingly. Perhaps a property has been on the market for a short time and an offer comes in. Sellers sometimes are reluctant to work with it because they think that if there is one buyer out there, that means that there may be more.

So often, it is the case that statistically the first offer is the best offer. There is a reason this phenomenon occurs and understanding the market dynamics that take place is helpful when advising seller clients. If the listing agent is confident that offers could come in quickly, it is best to prepare the seller in advance for the possibility and to establish a process to review any offers.

In any given market sector, at any given point in time, there is a pool of buyers ready, willing, and able to purchase real estate. Some have been waiting for the home of their dreams to come on the market. Others have just entered the market, due to either an internal or external urgency. The real estate market is not a static entity; it typically doesn't vacillate as much as the stock market, yet it does react to the existing market environment. There is an ongoing push-pull of market forces.

The particular buyer who writes an offer has more than likely seen everything available in the marketplace and is current on all the comparable sales data and what is under contract. When that buyer makes an offer, he has taken into consideration the present market conditions. If that pool of buyers doesn't purchase the property, or in effect "rejects the home," then that is in effect the "market study." Any number of statistical market studies can be prepared, but the true market study is actually *being* on the market.

Properties priced too high attract fewer buyers, showings, and offers. Properties priced at market value generate more open house activity and buyer interest. If properties are priced too high, then both buyers and agents lose interest. In fact, what they do is say to themselves that they will wait out the seller. Once the seller gets more realistic, then they may circle back. Often, though, when they do return, the home is at a much lower price.

Purchasers in these situations often want to write a deadline into the offer. The reasoning is concern that the listing agent will "shop" the offer. As representative for the seller, it is the listing agent's duty to obtain the best outcome for the client, so in fact that should be expected. Some jurisdictions require deadlines to be written into the contract. In most cases, a seller is in a position to respond within twenty-four to forty-eight hours. Anything longer can put the offer in jeopardy. Follow the protocol for your market area.

Well-priced properties generate immediate interest among buyers and agents. Experience—for better or worse—is often the best teacher. Unfortunately for the seller, to pass up on the first offer and eventually settling for a lower offer is a hard lesson to learn. "A bird in hand is worth two in the bush" has become a famous proverb for this very reason. Statistically the first offer is the best offer in most cases.

Advise seller clients about the phenomenon "statistically the first offer is the best offer."

ON BEING FAMOUS

While I was growing up in Columbia, Missouri, my father and uncle owned several restaurants. During the 1970s, they produced a series of TV commercials where the brothers would joke around about whether a "pi" was squared or whether it was round. The punch line was always my uncle throwing a pie in my father's face, proclaiming that it was messy. As a young girl, I was teased by classmates about the commercials. It is clear to me now, as a businesswoman, how brilliant the promotions were! Everyone knew who the Gebhardt brothers were and associated them with a restaurant they wanted to visit.

Fast-forward thirty years. There is a joke in the residential real estate field that an agent who doesn't tell people she is in the business is in effect a "secret agent." That tactic works well in the spy field, but not so much for the real estate professional. Thanks to what I learned from my father about promotion, I realized very quickly that one of the most important things is to be remembered. If people don't remember that you are a real estate agent, then it goes without saying that they won't call you about buying or selling a home or think of you if they have a referral.

The brain has an automatic mechanism function known as the Reticular Activating System (RAS). The RAS causes your brain to constantly bring forward relevant information to your conscious mind and filter out extraneous stimulus. It is an efficient operation, as otherwise we would be on overload! This is the phenomenon that happens when you are thinking about buying a car; you start to notice and pay attention to those cars. You have allowed that information to move forward into your conscious mind.

The purpose of marketing and advertising as a real estate agent is get the word out so that when people start thinking about buying or selling a home, they think of you. I have to confess that, in the beginning of my career, I struggled with the visible part of the profession and even considered not putting my photo on signs. Perhaps it brought back memories from my childhood— wanting to protect my kids from the embarrassment of having a well-known parent. It did come full circle when my son said at one point that he was glad I decided to wait and become "famous" after he left for college.

What I found, though, is that in most cases people know several real estate agents. Thus, being top of mind is one of the key secrets to long-term success. The people in my hometown had many restaurants to select from; yet there was often a line out the door at my family's restaurants because people wanted to see what those Gebhardt brothers were up to! Now it's my turn to be "famous" and have people seek me out when in the market for a professional real estate agent.

Promote yourself as a real estate agent!

FIRST, SECOND, OR THIRD POSITION

There is a saying in real estate circles among agents who have been in the business for some time: "You want to be the first born, the second wife, and the third agent." When a phrase has been passed around for years, it is often because there is a kernel of truth embedded in it. In this case, the benefit to the agent in terms of placement in the process has to do with the seller perspective.

The firstborn child position hardly requires explanation. New parents have all the time in the world to focus on that child. The second wife placement follows that at that juncture in life there are often more resources and attention available to offer her "the good life."

The advantage of being the third real estate agent takes some knowledge of the industry to understand the reasoning. In many ways, the first and second real estate agents do the "heavy lifting" communicating to the client the truth about the home and how condition and correct pricing is what gets homes sold.

In many situations, it could be the case that the home needs freshening up. For example, the seller should remove dated wallpaper or update the bathrooms. Often owners, particularly early on in the process, take comments about the condition and décor of the home personally. The seller most likely chose most of the furnishings. She has lived with the conditions for many years. Many do not understand why buyers do not feel the same way as they do. Frequently, by the time the third agent comes around and reiterates that message once again, the seller finally has ears to hear.

Another common scenario has to do with price. The hiring of the first agent often is based on the agreement to list the home at the seller's price. The agent may have made best efforts to provide comparable sales data and information about market conditions. Yet the agent succumbs to the pressure to please the seller in order to secure the listing. The second agent, in most cases, is able to obtain a price adjustment. Yet there is frequently still some resistance to the truth of market conditions.

In many cases, it is with the third agent that the seller finally faces the fact that the market conditions are what they are; that the forces of supply and demand are out of the agent's control. At that time, the seller is finally open to price the home correctly for the current market. The third agent represents a true "seller." Agents who achieve and sustain success over time understand these dynamics and are able to convey them to clients in an effective manner.

Understand the market dynamics of why sellers
go through multiple agents.

INVEST IN CLIENTS

One of the best investments that real estate agents can make is in their clients. Repeat business and referrals are the lifeblood of a professional's success. Just as one continues to invest in a financial portfolio every year, the investment into clients also pays long-term dividends.

A secret to my success early in my real estate career was creating a database of all the people in my community who would recognize my name. I realized there would be attrition to that list, so I committed to adding ten names each week. Just think: this one habit meant that my client list grew by 520 names every year!

Every time I met someone, whether on an official real estate appointment or just casually, I would update the database with the relevant information. It really makes people feel special when you remember their birthday and their kids' names. One of my earliest clients, whom I knew from church, called me when she wanted to purchase a home because she was so touched that I sent all the members of her family cards on special occasions.

On the real estate front, keeping detailed records of all conversations means that I can refer back to what was previously discussed, even if it occurred years ago. This reduces the chance of miscommunication. Further, it conveys that I care enough to keep track of what is going on with their situations.

Other agents ask if I put "everybody" in my database. My response is that I wouldn't purchase every stock on the stock market. So no, I don't. Consider your clients as your investment portfolio; your database should include those who will help you build and grow your business. The distinction is between being an advisor or just an order taker.

Financial counselors advise investing with a long-term perspective. Take that view with your client portfolio and I predict a long and successful career in real estate.

Invest in your clients today and every day for
a strong real estate business portfolio.

"EVERYBODY WANTS WHAT EVERYBODY WANTS"

"Everybody wants what everybody wants" is attributed to real estate superstar Barbara Corcoran. She tells the childhood story of going to pick out a puppy with her family and there not being enough puppies for the number of people who had come to adopt. The puppy owners timed the arrival of all of the potential puppy adopters so that everyone would see what they were up against in terms of competition for the limited supply. This is a classic case of scarcity, with more demand than supply. Everyone wanted to leave with one of the puppies.

The same scenario plays out in real estate all the time. When demand is high and supply is low, it can be a perfect storm for sellers. Barbara used this strategy to her clients' benefit in the difficult 1990s market in New York City. She utilized a bidding system on the fire sale of hundreds of co-ops for sale.

This is also the strategy agents have been known to employ when underpricing the competition. It is, in effect, a "mini-auction" because with multiple parties interested, it increases the likelihood of multiple offers. The good news is that it really only takes two interested parties to create an auction effect.

This can backfire, though, when buyers get wind of the competition; sometimes they back off, not wanting to "be played." Buyers don't always believe that there really is another offer at play. The oft-quoted saying rings true for sellers: "Be mindful of not losing the bird in hand over others that are in the bush."

Even when the price doesn't escalate, there can still be benefits to the seller for having multiple interests in a property. It isn't always about the money. Terms can be held firmer and stronger for the seller's position.

Putting a home on the market when there is a "lull" in inventory can create demand. Some agents employ "pre-marketing" activities to spur demand prior to listing a home for sale. Keep in mind, though, that perfect timing is very difficult to achieve. Further, some jurisdictions have guidelines on what pre-marketing is allowed.

Sellers sometimes wonder if it is beneficial to have two or more agents view a home at the same time, or if the buyers and their agents prefer to be there alone. In my experience, the more buyers the merrier! Just as the puppy owners did, this is a simple way to show there is interest, aka demand, from multiple people.

Another strategy agents have been known to employ is to leave all the business cards from agents out on the kitchen counter or table as showings occur, rather than picking them up right away. In this subtle way, agents and their buyer clients "see" with their own eyes how much interest there is in the property.

Professional agents implement these and other strategies to create an "everybody wants what everybody wants" scenario for seller clients. On the other side of the equation, when working with buyers, be mindful of how it can affect your client.

———— ❧ ————

Create "everybody wants" scenarios for seller clients.

COUNT YOUR LEADS AND
MAKE YOUR LEADS COUNT

The idea of "counting your leads and making your leads count" comes from the classic Bing Crosby song, "Count Your Blessings." The message of the song is: "When you're worried and you can't sleep, just count your blessings instead of sheep; and you'll fall asleep counting your blessings." In the real estate profession, being commission-based means the source of all income is a lead. And then the lead must be converted into a sale before any income is earned. It can be a long process and in the interim many agents become worried, wondering where the money is going to come from. If this leads to lack of sleep, it can become a vicious cycle.

This is where I came up with the practice, personally and in our business, to "count your leads and make your leads count." By tracking every lead, the agent gets a better understanding of the sources of business. This brings clarity on what areas of lead generation are more productive. So when I become worried about where money is going to come from, I can razor-focus on the areas that have the best potential for return on investment for time and resources.

All leads contain within them the seeds of opportunity. Many times it is a situation for a buyer or seller of "not now." These leads are put into the pipeline and account for future business. Many agents focus primarily on high quality leads and if the customer doesn't seem to have urgency, they lose attention. With this practice, the agent loses the gold-mine opportunity of creating future business. This is where making every lead count has great merit for building a long-term lead-generation machine and growing a business. A benefit to strong tracking is that when an agent on the team is low on leads, she can go back and "mine" the ones that have been sitting on the sidelines. Maybe now is the time!

Many agents consider working with rentals as low-level leads. Yet if the agent truly recognizes that every lead contains a seed of opportunity, she will stay in touch with those tenants and convert them into buyers at some juncture. Landlords, too, can be potential sellers, either selling straight out or "buying up" to a higher income-producing property. The highest conversion I've personally experienced was a four-star general who rented for one year and then purchased a $2.8 million home. My business partner secured a rental for a dual doctor couple for several years and eventually sold them a new construction, $4.2 million home. Both are situations where we made the lead count rather than "looking down" on the short-term rental leads generated as not worth our time.

Set up a system for tracking leads to make
every lead count today!

TALE OF TWO MARKETS

The famous opening line of *A Tale of Two Cities* by Charles Dickens is: "It was the best of times; it was the worst of times." The residential real estate market often follows the same theme, depending on the perspective.

One perspective is that of who is being affected, the purchaser or seller. If the market conditions are ones of high levels of inventory relative to demand, what exists is a buyer's market. In that situation, it would be "the best of times" for those clients. However, in those conditions it is typically also a time of flat or dropping prices, and those are not desirable conditions for sellers.

The reverse can be true. If the market conditions are such that there is very low supply and high demand, then that is by definition a seller's market. In that scenario, sellers can set the terms and it is "the best of times" for them. In these situations, the market often experiences rising prices, tough competition, and possible multiple offer situations. These scenarios all equate to "the worst of times" for buyers.

It is possible for the same market area to experience different conditions. It can behave much like a teeter-totter; it doesn't take much to get it off balance. The most common variables that cause that phenomenon are location and price point. Real estate closer to a city center, for example, tends to sell better and recover quicker than do outer suburbs, other factors remaining equal. Thus, it could be "the best of times" for sellers in one location and "the worst of times" for purchasers, and vice versa.

Price is a strong determinant for the potential quantity of purchasers and therefore demand. Thus, the number of potential buyers decreases as the price increases. This correlates to the principle that there is less demand for upper-bracket homes because there are fewer people capable of qualifying for financing or who have the cash available at that level. Generally homes priced at or below the conforming loan product levels sell better than homes that require jumbo financing products to purchase. In most cases it is "the best of times" to be a seller in the lower brackets, yet that would be "the worst of times" to be a purchaser. In the upper brackets, the opposite phenomenon takes place.

Understanding market dynamics is a key to success for the professional real estate agent. Study market trends to be in a strong position to make recommendations to clients about whether the conditions are "the best of times" or "the worst of times."

Determine "tale of two markets" scenarios for your area and find ways to use that knowledge to educate and influence clients.

"LEAN INTO THE SHARP POINTS"

There is a principle in yoga, which comes out of Eastern philosophies, to "lean into the sharp points." In her book, *Fail, Fail Again, Fail Better* by Pema Chodron, she writes that great learning can come from failure. Rather than running away or escaping, one should actually turn into or lean toward failure.

Those agents who practiced real estate during the roller-coaster years of the last couple of decades experienced failure over and over again. The market rose rapidly in 2001 through 2005, was flat for a couple of years, and then crashed with the financial markets in 2008. From there it continued to decline until 2010, when it began the slow process of recovery. When markets shift, professional agents respond and adapt accordingly. I began to feel the market change around Labor Day in 2005, when inventory first started to build up relative to demand. Also, deals that used to have been very easy to get together began to become more and more challenging. Every contingency had to be managed, and it required considerably more effort to get transactions to settlement.

Literally, I chose to "lean into the sharp points" by being proactive about every detail. The benefit to this experience was that I acquired valuable knowledge, skills, and abilities that are more difficult to obtain in good markets. Would I want to go through it again in order to learn? Probably not, yet it had to be dealt with head on. Those agents who couldn't or wouldn't adapt left the business, as evidenced by the vast decrease in the number of real estate agents during those years. Those who survived discovered that they could not only survive, but thrive in all market conditions. They became like chameleons and adapted to the market of the moment.

Another scenario that this concept applies to is being able to successfully engage in difficult conversations. It is human nature, I believe, to want to avoid delivering bad news. In real estate transactions, examples abound: advising the seller a price adjustment is necessary to be responsive to the market conditions; conveying to a purchaser that the home he wrote an offer on was not accepted; delivering a "low-ball" offer to a seller; conveying the information that there is a problem with the title because the house was built over the legal set-back requirements; or the lender just called to state there would be a delay in closing.

The possible "sharp points" in a real estate transaction are probably infinite, as the variables are so complex that it is truly rare for everything to go smoothly. It is the professional agent who leans into the situation by being up front and frank with all parties and seeks to work together efficiently and effectively to determine a solution and outcome.

Decide to "lean into the sharp points" in your profession and life.

CAN'T BUY THE FIRST HOUSE THEY SEE

As a real estate agent, you hit it out of the park by finding for your buyer clients the house that meets all of their criteria. They fall in love with it and yet someone tells them or they think to themselves, "We can't possibly buy the first house we see!" In many cases, by this time you as the real estate agent have invested considerable time with these buyers to find the right house for them.

This has happened to me on numerous occasions, and what I share is that yes, by all means one should probably not buy the first house seen. The paradigm shift is that people visit houses all the time that are not on the market for sale. People visit the homes of their family, friends, work associates, and neighbors. Thus, when they begin the buying process by looking at open houses and touring homes with a real estate agent, they have already been in or "seen" hundreds of homes.

With this knowledge, the buyers really have seen a lot of houses, albeit not on a conscious level or from a buyer's perspective. In the process, unconsciously they have come to know what they like and don't like. What floor plans and architectural styles work for their family? What location is best for their needs? What amenities, fixtures, features, and upgrades do they desire in a home?

On the other end of the spectrum is the seller scenario. What happens if one of the first buyers who visit the home writes an offer? There is a concern that if the sellers accept the first offer, they might leave money on the table. If in fact there is one buyer, then perhaps there are many more. Statistically, though, the first offer is most often the best offer.

There is a pool of buyers ready, willing, and able to purchase a home at any given point in time. When a house first comes on the market, those buyers quickly make arrangements to see the home. If it works for their situation, then they will make an offer. The pool of buyers may actually be just one buyer for the one home, and of course that is all the seller needs. The danger is that if sellers take the chance that there are more buyers out there and there aren't, then they have to wait for the next pool of buyers to enter the market or make a price adjustment to attract back the first group.

Whether working with a buyer or a seller, the effective real estate agent counsels her client on this phenomenon.

Counsel clients on the best strategy to utilize when helping them buy and sell homes.

KEEP THE LOVE TANK FULL

The relationship between client and real estate agent is much stronger if the "love tank" stays full. The idea of "love tank" was coined in the book for marriages by Gary D. Chapman, entitled *The 5 Love Languages*. The concept asserts that people have a preferred manner in which to receive appreciation.

There are five languages or means of demonstrating emotional support or encouragement: words of affirmation; acts of service; receiving gifts; quality time; and physical touch. People tend to have a primary and secondary language preference. However, all the methods serve to "fill the love tank."

Words of affirmation in a real estate environment include sharing feedback with seller clients; encouraging clients who are having a difficult time making a move; and keeping all parties positive and focused on the desired outcome when frustrations and stress rise. A handwritten note is always a wonderful opportunity for delivering words of affirmation to customers and clients.

Real estate agents perform numerous acts of service. Examples for those selling their home include meeting contractors at the property; installing the sign and lock box; taking photos and uploading them to the Internet; and creating marketing materials. For purchasers, some ways a real estate agent performs acts of service include coordinating inspections; providing recommendations for service providers; and negotiating the contract.

Gifts are common as a token of appreciation from real estate professionals to their clients at settlement and beyond. Ideas include sending flowers, offering a cleaning service, a magazine subscription, or a gift certificate to a local restaurant. Some agents stay in touch with their clients and referral partners by sending flowers on the first day of spring, planting flags for the Fourth of July, and delivering pies at Thanksgiving.

There is an abundance of opportunities for real estate agents to spend quality time with their clients. For sellers, there are broker's opens and public open houses. For purchasers, agents spend a lot of time showing homes and meeting inspectors. Other time-oriented activities include serving as the neighborhood specialist on community amenities and programs, schools, parks, transportation options, and more.

When a client's love tank is full, the relationship remains strong. Experience shows a strong client relationship can better weather the difficult aspects of buying and selling real estate as well.

Take action to keep your clients' love tanks full.

"THE SHOW MUST GO ON"

The real estate agent often has occasion to use the song title "The Show Must Go On" as a mantra. The British rock band Queen originally performed it in 1991. Houses must be shown when the buyer is available, even in all kinds of weather, whether the agent feels like going or not. And there is a performance element to a listing presentation.

One of the final steps I take before an appointment to meet with clients is to put on my lipstick. That act is a way of mental preparation for the "show." Other professionals have rituals that they perform to prepare themselves mentally for "going on stage."

The rest of the chorus further tells the story:

"The show must go on

Inside my heart is breaking

My makeup may be flaking

But my smile still stays on."

The smile still stays on such that the audience does not know what is going on inside the performer's life. The audience has paid to be entertained, not to hear tales of woe. Tales of accomplishment can be interpreted as bragging and "stage hogging."

Similar situations can occur within the real estate industry. It is important for agents to remain professional and not let their personal lives seep into the business of representing the client. Of course, even real estate agents are human and have life events. There are occasions where it is appropriate to share both unfortunate and positive aspects of one's personal life. Just keep in mind that the client is paying a fee for services rendered and that is the basis of the relationship.

There can be situations where the agent is working with a friend, relative, associate, or neighbor who already knows the personal situation. It is likely that they will be concerned that perhaps the agent cannot stay properly focused on their transaction. In this case, it is even more important for the agent to assure the client that they are a priority and that the "show must go on."

Establish rituals to prepare for when you "go on stage" as a professional agent.

TRAINING WITHOUT IMPLEMENTATION IS ENTERTAINMENT

The newly licensed real estate agent soon realizes that there is much to learn about the profession. It is eye-opening to many that there is much that they don't know and so they set about to acquire that knowledge. The National Association of Realtors® offers considerable continuing education opportunities. License renewal in each jurisdiction has requirements in order to maintain active status as well.

Ongoing training and educational opportunities abound in the industry through ancillary organizations and coaching entities. Brokerages offer training specifically for the agents in their company. Further, laws effecting real estate transactions frequently change and contracts are continuously modified to reflect the practices of the area, and new technologies are introduced. Government guidelines in lending and settlement practices affect the practice of real estate, which require the agent to continually expand her knowledge.

All of this information can at times feel like a fire hose. Opportunities abound, some required and some optional. Real estate agents could end up spending all of their working time on training and educational endeavors and not have ever gotten around to the business of actually helping clients buy and sell homes.

At what point does the benefit realized from the training cross over into the realm of being entertainment? That juncture is implementation. The sooner a new technology, practice, or strategy is implemented, the more likely it will "stick." That is why this book includes a "take-away" every day. The purpose of the "take-away" is to move the educational aspect of the idea to the implementation level.

Most would agree that some entertainment in training assures that the learning is more interesting and even fun. Training that is boring is not as effective. Yet, being a real estate agent is a business, and as a profession one must assure that time is being used both efficiently and effectively.

Implement training into your business practice for sustained success.

GROUNDHOG DAY PREDICTIONS AND THE SPRING REAL ESTATE MARKET

Groundhog Day is when Punxsutawney Phil predicts whether there will be early spring-like weather or another six weeks of winter weather. The celebration occurs on February 2 each year. Whether Phil sees his shadow or not often helps determine when the spring real estate market kicks off.

In those markets that experience winter months of snow and cold temperatures, people often exhibit cabin fever and are ready to get out and about and tour homes as soon as there is any sign of spring. Realtors® predict an early spring market by several indicators, the strongest of which is the attendance of prospective buyers at Sunday open houses. Thus, it is helpful to keep track of foot traffic—the actual number of people who attend open houses. If it is trending up, that is a good indicator.

There is often a significant increase in the number of sellers who prepare their homes for the market after waiting on the sidelines for springtime to appear. Thus, another indicator to watch is the rate that homes come onto the active market. If it is at a faster clip than demand is absorbing, that is a sign that supply is increasing.

Sellers may want to consider the potential advantage of getting their homes on the market early. In this way, they may beat out other significant competition. There is usually some pent-up demand from buyers during the winter months, and they are ready to move. They prefer not to wait until the spring season is in full swing, when buying may be possibly more competitive.

Spring always follows winter, thank goodness! Whether the groundhog predicts an early spring or six more weeks of winter, the spring market will come either way.

Discover the peak spring season for your market and prepare clients accordingly.

ACTIVITY BLOCKING

Many coaches and books on productivity recommend time blocking. This is where one sets aside a certain portion of time each day or week to generate leads or other key activities. Countless people find this means of accountability empowering. Others, though, "flitter away" the time and don't actually accomplish anything.

When our daughter was in elementary school, we discovered that she did not learn like other children. She had the great ability of appearing to be busy with homework and yet make no progress whatsoever in actually completing it. After paying numerous tutors to work with her, we still felt frustrated at the lack of progress. The sessions were set up for a specific time period, and when that time was up, she knew she could leave, even if the work wasn't completed. This is, to me, like time blocking.

Another tutor, who came highly recommended, held what she called "homework sessions." At these sessions, several students from different grade levels and skills met to complete their individual homework assignments. Everyone stayed until the work was completed, thus there was no incentive to use stalling tactics to put off doing the work.

Tutoring by several lead teachers was available during the homework sessions, as well as coaching by accomplished high school and college students. It provided an environment of group accountability as well—no one wanted to disappoint the other students in the program. On special occasions, if everyone was on target to complete their assignments, there would be a pizza party or other such event to look forward to.

Activity blocking is where a set number of completed activities are committed to for each day or week. Thus it is not time-bound, but rather completion-bound. One can "front load" the activities by working ahead if time off is scheduled. Also, "catching up" can occur if one falls behind. By tracking the activities, one can determine the results accordingly. Then an agent can project her goals and know what activities are necessary to reach those objectives.

---

*Commit to completing a set number of activities
each day and week for lead generation.*

THE BUYER IS JUST NOT
INTO YOUR HOME—EMOTIONS

FEBRUARY

4

The movie *He's Just Not that Into You* is based on the premise that if a guy doesn't pursue a lady, it is because he isn't really interested. The comedy rings true in the real estate realm as well. Agent and buyer feedback reveal reasons and fatal flaws that are polite ways of saying, "The buyer is just not into your home." No action means the buyer just didn't care about the home enough to pursue obtaining it.

Many home sellers could take some advice from the movie. The purchase of a home has at times been compared to falling in love.

A home is more than shelter; it is a place with many layers of meaning and so it is no wonder that deep emotion often goes into the selection. Sellers put their best foot forward, just like men and women in the courtship and dating phases of a relationship. A home seller emphasizes the best features of the property and makes an extra effort to be certain the home is presentable at all times.

When buyers do not select a home to see or doesn't return a second time, it can feel like rejection on a personal level. In many ways an owner's home is his castle, an extension of self. There are unspoken customs in American dating; for example, many believe that the guy should do the calling and pursuing. If a guy doesn't call and pursue, then the bottom line is, "he's just not that into" the girl. By deciding not to go after the girl, by default he is saying that there isn't even enough interest to come back a second time.

It is helpful as an agent to be empathetic as you share with seller clients this phenomenon. The feelings are very real. Keep in mind the words of author Maya Angelou: "People will forget what you said, people will forget what you did, but people will never forget how you made them feel." Use the "feel, felt, found" script to first acknowledge the feelings and move clients through the process.

Much can be learned about the emotional components of the home buying and selling process in other areas, such as media. Successful agents recognize these kernels of truth and use them to help their clients.

*Use scripts and dialogues to help seller clients understand
the emotional aspects of the home buying and selling process.*

BUSINESS STARTUP

There are startup costs associated with any business, and becoming a real estate agent is no exception. First, there are the coursework and licensure expenses associated with meeting state and jurisdictional requirements to practice real estate. Most brokerage firms require an agent to be a member of the National Association of Realtors®, as well as the local board. There are ongoing fees to access the multiple listing service and lock-box systems. All of these expenditures are prior to even one sale.

The most significant impact for a new agent is the lead time prior to receiving income. At the earliest, settlement occurs on a sale thirty days after ratification, and many closings can be delayed as much as sixty or ninety days. This assumes that an agent sells a home the first week in the business, which is rare.

Many people become real estate agents because of the potential income. And it is true that the earning levels that can be achieved are substantial relative to the upfront costs and entry educational and training requirements.

For these reasons, many people turn to real estate as a second career or as a secondary income that supplements that of the primary breadwinner. That was my case. I returned to employment after our children were in school full time. According to the National Association of Realtors® the average real estate agent is a fifty-seven-year-old woman with some college education and who is also a homeowner. This makes total sense, given the startup costs associated with the profession.

The next challenge of any business startup, real estate included, is, "Who are you going to sell to?" Most people already know several real estate agents, so how will you differentiate yourself? Even though this is a stumbling block for some, remember that everyone starts out in the same position. By virtue of being a licensed real estate agent, more than likely you know more than the majority of the customers that you will work with. There is a phrase that rings true in this setting: "Never be afraid to try something new. Remember, amateurs built the ark. Professionals built the Titanic."

If you are a longtime professional agent, keep in mind when recruiting agents to your team the startup costs associated with the profession.

Be aware of the startup costs and ongoing expenses related to being a licensed real estate agent and commit to lead generation for sustainable business cash flow.

PROPERTY TAX ASSESSMENTS AND FAIR MARKET VALUE

In the first quarter of the year, most jurisdictions send out property tax assessments for the coming year. This occasion frequently raises the question about whether the tax assessment value of the real estate is fair market value.

The definition of assessment according to the dictionary is: "An official valuation of property for the purpose of levying a tax; an assigned value." The true fair market value of any commodity (real estate included) is arrived at when a buyer and seller agree to a price with specific terms and consummate the transaction. Neither party is under duress, and the parties are unrelated and thus at "arm's length." The commodity has had adequate exposure to the open market and financing terms are typical. Thus, the technical answer is that the property tax assessment is not fair market value. However, as is so often the case, the answer is more complicated than a simple yes or no.

Owners of real estate typically want their property tax assessment to be low so that taxes remain low. Rarely do owners contact the tax assessor to request the assessment be increased, even if substantial improvements have been made. In fact, some have been known to not allow the tax assessor access to the home to decrease this likelihood.

Thus, homeowners almost always feel that their home is worth more than the tax assessment indicates. When homeowners believe the tax assessment is too high, typically they register a dispute of value. This creates a situation where tax assessment values are lower than market value. This is most frequently the case in a rising market.

Buyers often state that they do not want to pay more than the property tax assessment. Their justification is based on the fact that if the jurisdiction in which the real estate is located has determined a certain value, then they shouldn't pay more for a property than that amount.

Many government bodies mandate that real estate be assessed at fair market value. This is arrived at by the use of a mass estimating formula based on sales in the neighborhood with adjustments made according to the number of bedrooms and baths, finished square footage, lot size, number of garages, features, and improvements. The more homogeneous a neighborhood is and the more stable the market conditions, the closer the assessment is likely to be to fair market value.

If prices are rising, the assessment is usually below the market and if prices are falling, the assessment is typically above the market. This delayed reaction occurs with assessments because the process requires the assessor to look in the past and fair market value occurs in the present, in real time.

Stay informed about how tax assessments correlate to fair market value.

TOMORROW, TOMORROW

The song "Tomorrow" was written for the musical *Annie*. The chorus closes with the words: "You're always a day away!" It could be the theme song for the procrastinator. So how's the process been working for you? What do you think may be stopping you from achieving your vision?

Becoming a successful agent can be likened to a road trip to "tomorrow." I keep a basic checklist on my computer that I print out to use when packing for any trip. In this way, I easily remember all of the essentials and don't have to waste valuable energy on the basics. The destination is on my mind and yet I take time to enjoy the journey. There could be unplanned detours to which I will have to adapt. Then there are the spontaneous opportunities, as well. I might decide to do something that wasn't on the original itinerary and yet has piqued my interest. The same journey analogy applies to the agent as she connects to build and grow her business.

As the agent travels from "only as good as her next deal" to business owner, keep in mind the words of Arthur Ashe, an American tennis player once ranked number one in the world: "Start where you are. Use what you have. Do what you can." The operative word is "do." So many agents wait for perfect conditions before starting. The key is to not wait until "tomorrow" to begin. The best way to become a successful agent is to be one.

This means that today—not tomorrow—is the day that the successful agent generates leads, consults customers and clients to sales, and takes action steps in order to build and grow her business. Today—not tomorrow—is the day that the professional agent applies success thinking, activities, and vision to her business and life. It is these daily investments that lead to medium-sized gains. Incremental changes have great potential over time to lead to substantial progress. To read five minutes a day is not a daunting task, yet over time the results are longer lasting and self-reinforcing.

In the words of American author, entrepreneur, marketer, and public speaker Seth Godin: "The only way to become the writer who has written a book is to write one. The only way to become the runner who has just finished a run is to go running." And that is true of being a successful real estate agent: perform the actions of a successful agent on a daily basis to achieve the sweet spot of success. Don't wait until tomorrow—do it today!

Today is the day for success thinking, activities, and vision.

TRANSFORMERS CHANGE

Transformer toys were all the rage when our son was young. His favorites were the toys that changed from a robot to some sort of vehicle. What's not to love about mutation for a boy! The action-packed animated movie on the same theme, *Transformers*, tells the story of a teenage boy who combats alien life forces with everyday machines that disguised their true power.

Depending on the needs of clients, real estate agents can go through a transformation of roles as they work through the sales process. As an educator, the agent explains terminology and the process, as most people buy and sell real estate only several times in their lifetime. Markets, laws, and industry standards change rapidly, and the agent serves as the teacher and instructor in the process. At times, the agent takes on the positions of advisor, counselor, and trusted friend.

In other situations, the agent acts as the market economist by providing comparables and other relevant data and interpretation of information. The agent takes on the role of detective as she looks for buying signals and evidence that supports value.

The agent as an architect works with clients to visualize the end result to achieve the desired vision. On one end of the spectrum, it can involve the transformation of an existing home through remodeling and renovation projects, to the other end of the continuum of new construction. The process involves the skills of an event planner as the agent charts the course of the project and transaction for the client.

The agent serves as tour guide, navigator, marketer, and of course, as sales agent. All these transformations often occur before lunch!

The above examples fall under the category of exterior transformations, which have to do with the roles the agent assumes. There can also be the interior transformation that occurs as the agent gains experience and develops confidence and skill in the real estate industry. This is when the agent moves from salesperson to business owner.

Rather than being only as good as the next deal, the business owner takes on the responsibility to develop strategy and systems for an ongoing successful operation. By implementation of these steps, one creates a business that can carry on even after the agent retires or goes on to pursue other interests. There is power behind making this transformation. If I can do it, you can do it.

Take steps to transform your sales career to that of a successful business enterprise.

FEBRUARY

9

"REACH OUT AND TOUCH SOMEONE"

This advertising jingle, circa 1979, for AT&T is a great theme for real estate agents. The commercial series included mini movie-like vignettes about people reconnecting over a phone call. To achieve and sustain success as a real estate agent, a commitment to business development by "reaching out and touching someone" is an imperative.

In his book, *The Seven Levels of Communication*, Michael Maher illustrates the methods of communication in a pyramid. The base is advertising, next is direct mail, and above that is electronic communication. These three comprise the "informational zone"; that is, the sender delivers content that the recipient can choose to acknowledge or ignore fairly easily. Computers and hand-held devices offer e-mail for in-depth and potentially two-way communication. Social media and similar platforms provide ways to connect and stay in touch with clients, past clients, friends, and those in the agent's sphere of influence. Keep in mind that these methods often lack the personal touch and depth of emotion that a voice or personal touch can convey.

The next level of impact on the pyramid is handwritten notes. This is one of the key methods of communication I have used to great success. Many agents who work by referral also tout the effectiveness of this method to "reach out and touch someone" in a way that commands attention.

The top three levels of communication are: phone calls, events and seminars, and one-on-one meetings. These three make up the "influential zone" of impact, according to Maher.

Even with the advances in technology in the last decades, the telephone is still one of the best means of communication. With Skype and FaceTime, people can now view each other over a screen, just as depicted years ago in the *Jetson's* cartoons. For most people, a cell phone or smartphone is their primary number. It offers the option to text for quick and easy messages.

The top two levels of touching someone are literally in person, face-to-face, belly-to belly. Group opportunities include seminars, networking, and open houses. One-on-one connections in the real estate world can be scheduled appointments, showing homes, knocking on doors, or dropping by. There is something special about giving someone your time and personal attention. And it is important to truly be there and avoid distractions by turning off your phone!

No matter what the method, it is a high priority for real estate agents to reach out and connect with people on a daily basis. As American industrialist Henry Ford said: "You can't build a reputation on what you're going to do." The successful agent builds a reputation by "reaching out and touching someone."

Employ all levels of communication to "reach out and touch someone"
to connect, and build and grow your business.

THE HOUSE IS GONE!

"The house is gone!" my husband exclaimed as we were taking a walk in our neighborhood. Home builders in our community are often challenged to find available vacant land. We live inside the beltway of Washington, DC, and the location is highly desirable because of the commute and the schools. Thus, construction that is "in-fill" is predominantly the option for builders. It occurs in those markets where the land value is significantly higher than that of the existing home. In these situations, the older home is removed and a new one is built in its place.

Builders who concentrate their business on in-fill neighborhoods follow a formula based on the value that they are willing to pay for the land. Most seek to achieve the ratio of investment as follows: one-third spent on the lot or land, one-third on the construction costs to build the new home, and one-third on soft costs such as the planning and approval process, overhead, interest carry, commissions, and profit. Of course, these are rules of thumb, yet are a good baseline for a real estate agent to be cognizant of.

Neighborhoods tend to have ceilings on how much a buyer is willing to pay for a home. This is even more the case for new home in-fill construction. By way of example, let's assume the highest sold price ever paid for a new home in a particular neighborhood was $1.5 million. The builder then would be willing to pay $500,000 for the lot or land, assuming typical location and development costs.

As a neighborhood becomes more in demand and the land values rise, often the land portion of the formula becomes higher than the one-third portion. The reason for this is simple: good lots in preferred neighborhoods are frequently in limited supply when there is great demand.

This is a helpful guideline when as an agent you are working with buyers, too. They should be mindful of how much a builder would pay for the land and be careful to follow similar protocol to be in line with the future resale market value.

A challenge to builders is predicting how the market will behave in the future. The typical time frame from purchase of a lot or land to final completion of construction is often one year or longer. Home prices can fluctuate considerably during that amount of time. It is important for agents to keep builder clients apprised of the market conditions and for builders to have a strong relationship with an agent who understands the market trends for a particular neighborhood. Key metrics to track are the absorption of inventory of new homes, as well as what is projected to be coming on the market.

*Understand the market dynamics for new construction
to provide wise counsel to clients.*

HOME INSPECTION KEY OBJECTIVES

For a purchaser, there are three key objectives when having a home inspection on a property. The first is to have a clear understanding of the physical condition of the property so that the buyer knows what he is actually purchasing. The second is for the inspector(s) to educate the purchaser on recommended best practices for maintenance and replacements of the systems and the structural components of the home. And third is to create a list for the seller of those items that the purchaser would like repaired, replaced, or remedied.

A general professional home inspector will complete both exterior and interior visual inspections. In addition, the systems and mechanics of the home will be evaluated, which includes but is not limited to electrical, plumbing, and HVAC components. Foundation and structural areas, which include the attic, basement, and crawl spaces, will be examined to the extent that they are accessible and fall under the scope of the inspector's ability and experience. As identified, the purchaser may employ specialized professionals to inspect and evaluate for issues such as radon, mold, well, septic, structural, air quality, environmental, termites, and other pests.

It is preferable for the purchaser to attend all of the inspections. This is the ideal way that all three of the key objectives can be achieved. Some inspectors prefer to complete their evaluations and then will set aside time to review their findings with the buyer, agents, and relevant parties. Others allow for the client to participate more actively in the process. All welcome thoughtful questions and serve as a resource for determining the condition of the home. A thorough report, including photos and recommendations, will be available upon completion, frequently in digital format.

The home inspection period is a time set aside for the purchaser to get to know the home better. Suggest using the time to measure rooms and spaces to plot out furniture placement. The property insurance company, in most cases, provides a questionnaire to be completed. This is an ideal time to handle that detail. As the buyer gets to know the house he will soon call home, it is helpful for the agent to remind him of the key objectives and how the agent can help in the process. That's why you are there—to serve as a resource!

Understand the key objectives of a home inspection to achieve a successful outcome for the client.

MOTTO OF AN OLYMPIC-LEVEL AGENT

The motto for the Olympics is "Citius, Altius, Fortius" which means faster—higher—stronger. The objective of an Olympian is summed up in those three words and the scorecard is the medal: gold, silver, bronze.

The motto of the Olympic-level agent can be summed up with these three "P" words: professional—practice—perseverance.

First, Olympic athletes are professional. A professional Realtor® exhibits this quality by constantly improving her knowledge, skills, and abilities. One way to accomplish that is to pursue additional training and education. There are numerous designations that an agent can achieve, such as Accredited Buyer Representative (ABR), Certified Luxury Home Marketing Specialist (CLHMS), Graduate Realtor Institute (GRI), and Broker. An agent fulfills designation requirements by completing coursework, experience, testing, and in some case additional licensure.

Next, Olympic athletes practice. And they practice significantly beyond the average athlete's level. There is a reason why it is referred to as practice, as there is always room for improvement. Look at the fact that numerous athletic world records are broken and surpassed at every Olympics. This is because the athletes are all "on the road to perfection." No one ever arrives—it is the journey of constant practice and improvement that takes one to the next level of achievement and performance. A professional agent, too, continues to practice the profession, as the industry and market are constantly changing.

Olympic athletes persevere even through difficult challenges and obstacles. A professional agent also exhibits these qualities. Buying and selling real property is a complex, multifaceted process. Further, it is often the largest single investment most people enter into. It requires a high level of sophistication, knowledge, and skill to represent and navigate on behalf of clients and customers.

The potential hurdles for a real estate agent to overcome in a transaction are too numerous to mention. Just know that, like an Olympic athlete, the real estate agent professional does not stop until the finish line has been crossed at settlement.

Adopt the motto of an Olympic-level agent:
professional, practice, and perseverance.

YOU HAVE TO KISS A LOT OF FROGS . . .

One of the truths of the modern version of the fairy tale *The Frog Prince*, by the Brothers Grimm, is: "You have to kiss a lot of frogs before you find your handsome prince." The princess is encouraged to seek out true love, yet in the process she may have to endure some ugliness along the way. The tale carries a lesson for home buyers and sellers as well.

From the buyer's perspective, it may take viewing quite a few homes before "true love" is found. Each time buyers visit houses, inside their minds they put it through a "kiss test." Could they fall in love with this house, i.e., would it meet the needs of their family in terms of price, location, floor plan, condition, and schools? There are expectations, as there are with a romance. Could it be the home for them? Just as the princess evaluates consciously or unconsciously the attributes of a potential prince, buyers evaluate the benefits and drawbacks of a potential home.

From the seller's perspective, it is like being the gentleman in waiting. Numerous buyers view the home and conduct their own personal "kiss test." The gentleman may feel rejected if the princess kisses him and then moves on to the next guy who comes along. Unfortunately, the buyer may view the home like an unattractive frog, and for whatever personal reasons, has decided that home isn't the one for her. Just as in love, rejection can hurt in the home selling process.

It is the wise agent who recognizes the feelings that both buyers and sellers can experience throughout the process. Use stories to successfully help people understand and manage the circumstances.

Use this fairy tale as a script to help clients with the emotional aspects of buying and selling a home.

WHAT'S LOVE GOT TO DO WITH REAL ESTATE?

Valentine's Day in the United States focuses on people in love. Tina Turner belted the now-famous song, "What's Love Got To Do With It," and on this special day, think about how this theme applies to real estate. Is there any place for love in the purchase and sale of real property? Often there is. There is an old saying that most people buy on emotion and justify the decision with logic.

An alert agent will notice the glimmer of love in the eye of a buyer when looking at homes. There is usually something about the home that triggers a positive memory or hopeful future. One couple with two young daughters paid particular attention to the photos of the owners' two daughters. This knowledge created a bond to the home for the buyers, as they could visualize what it would be like to raise their girls in that setting.

Another example is a couple with two boys looking for more space for them to play sports. The mother didn't want a cookie-cutter home typical for the area, but rather was looking for something charming. The only thing I could come up with that would be "charming" was a farm house with a porch that expanded across the front—and truly for her it was "love at first sight." When we talked later, she recalled that the home was very much like the one she grew up in, complete with the front porch where family and friends sat to relax and visit, rocking in a swing or sitting in chairs. She could imagine herself there reading a book and enjoying a cup of coffee as she waited for her boys to get off the bus after school.

What's love "got to do with it" for sellers? Honestly, have you ever had a pet owner that didn't just think his dog is adorable? Every pet owner I know believes that his pet is special. This is the same emotion sellers often feel about their homes. Logic just seems to go out the window! A professional agent seeks first to understand what the sellers love about their home. When that emotion is tapped into, it can be used to influence and nurture the same love in a purchaser.

Research supports that people buy on emotion, and that most of those feelings are hidden from us. Harvard Business School professor Gerald Zaltman states that 95 percent of purchase decisions happen in the subconscious. It is an alert real estate agent who picks up on these love signals and then assists buyers and sellers in understanding the logic that supports the purchase or sale.

Be alert to the signals of "love" to help clients
with the purchase and sale of their home.

FILL THE PIPELINE

In sales jargon, to "fill the pipeline" and "keep the pipeline full" means to have business somewhere in the process that will lead to earned income. It goes without saying that a prospect or customer must be converted to a client in order to be able to move it along in the queue. Thus, the first order of business for all salespeople is to generate leads.

There are many methods and styles of prospecting. To keep a steady input, an agent should systematically, with no variance in schedule, actively solicit leads. Those agents who develop daily habits are the most likely to sustain long-term success. James Clear, author of *Transform Your Habits*, states: "The quickest way to build a new habit into your life is to stack it on top of a current habit." My prospecting habit is to "touch" five people each day. Early in my career, I attached that process with the new habit of tracking the touches in a spiral-bound notebook. This act creates a self-accountability loop, as well as gives me the satisfaction of knowing when I have done my five for the day.

The successful agent determines the amount of prospecting necessary in order to sustain current production. This is best achieved by creating and following a tracking system. To succeed to the next level requires stepping up activities known to lead to new business.

Invariably life happens along the way, as it should. For real estate professionals, in addition to the core responsibility of keeping the pipeline full of leads, most also handle other key functions: marketing, listing and buyer consultations, showing homes, contract negotiations including managing inspections and other contingencies, as well as the actual settlement process. All of these are part of the process of moving clients along through the pipeline so that at the other end there is an output of earnings for the agent.

In addition, there are cycles to the business and seasonal fluctuations to manage. So how does an agent do it all? One strategy is to "front load" prospecting. In anticipation of a busy time of the year, a vacation, or being out of the office for training for an extended period of time, an agent will "front load." This means conducting work ahead of schedule such that more lead generation occurs than is in the business plan.

Another strategy is to "back fill." In construction that term literally means to fill back in the material that was taken out. In this context, it means to fill the hole in the lead-generation plan that the agent has not yet completed. Runners use this concept when training for a marathon. If they miss a day running, they make it up on the weekend or go for a longer run a few days in a row.

True professionals follow good habits to do the work and are committed to lead generation.

Establish daily habits to keep the pipeline full.
Track, back fill, and front load as necessary.

UPSTREAM IS PREFERRED TO DOWNSTREAM

In real estate, upstream is preferred over downstream for a geographical and fundamental reason. As water is a basic human need, most communities began and were developed near a water source. Waterways were and still are a primary means of transportation. When there is waste and storm "run off," the water and thus associated smells will naturally run downhill.

It is thus highly desirable to be "up wind" of those smells, sights, and sounds that are less attractive to the senses. The more financially capable and savvy people select their home sites on the upstream end of a community and frequently at the top of a hill. Those who do not have the means are left with the lower lands and dredges, such as land near a low-flowing river on the "other side of the tracks," or near where waste is disposed of and sewage facilities are located.

There is a further correlation to north being preferred to south. In a study conducted by Brian Meier, associate professor of psychology at Gettysburg College in Gettysburg, Pennsylvania, he wrote about this phenomenon: "When all else is equal, people have this bias to think that northerly areas are better or more affluent." It is because in most areas they are better and more affluent.

As often happens, people have a preference and may not even understand why. If the affluent over time tend to settle in the northern end of an area that becomes a town, eventually a city, and ultimately a metro area, then the higher-quality homes would have been built in those locations. The schools with the best facilities and parental support attract the best teachers and administrators, which leads to better academic performance and ranking. City services are superior, as the tax base would be strong in those locations.

Upscale shopping follows the income level of residents. Higher-end retail establishments, restaurants, grocers, and other services focus the majority of capital and advertising toward this clientele. Employers want to be conveniently located in close proximity to where the affluent reside, as often they represent the knowledge workers of industry and top level professions.

In an analysis of many of the metro areas in North America, the best and most expensive real estate tends to concentrate in the northern sections. There are a few notable exceptions, as there are to any rule. For example, in Fort Worth, Texas the stockyards are located on the north side of the city. Thus, much of the upscale market housing has been built south of Fort Worth. Inside metro areas, too, there are segments that both follow and are exceptions to these phenomenon. The successful agent is knowledgeable about the factors that determine value in order to represent her clients well.

---

*Understand the preferences in the market area
to be the real estate expert of choice.*

"THAT WAS EASY™"

The Staples™ "Easy" button is a must-have for all real estate professionals. There are days and situations when an agent needs inspiration and motivation to carry on. On those occasions, having an "Easy" button to push can create the stimulus to keep on keeping on.

By their very nature, real estate transactions are complex. Bringing together a buyer and seller that instinctively differ in their objectives for the outcome is just one part of the puzzle. The energy necessary to continue to prospect in the face of frequent rejection can be a mojo downer. Thus, it is a rare occasion in the real estate business that something is truly "easy." The variety of the day-to-day operations and tasks involved is what draws many agents to the profession. So if it was truly too "easy," that would imply that anyone could do it. To be successful in real estate is a challenge that appeals to many people because it isn't easy.

That is a good day to have an "Easy" button as a reminder and top-of-mind method of inspiration. In the commercial launch for the Staples™ "Easy" button, the company stated that the goal of the product was to "tap into the empathetic humor that consumers have come to expect from Staples™, while reinforcing how the company makes buying office products easy," said Joyce King Thomas, chief creative officer of Staples™ advertising agency, McCann Erickson in New York.

You too can tap into that empathetic humor, as it is helpful to remember that not everything has to be complex. Parties can choose to create win-win scenarios. Referrals from past clients arrive in the "in-box" when an agent is discouraged. On occasion, everything goes as it should and all is well. Take those occasions to press your "Easy" button as a mini-celebration of accomplishment.

A third reason for having an "Easy" button is for the purpose of setting intentions. Sometimes people unconsciously make situations difficult. Take the proactive approach to find the "easy" solution in the circumstance, as it can be one of intent. If one projects that the situation and everything is "hard," then perhaps that is what is being attracted. If the agent projects that the resolution will be "easy," then that too can be what is attracted.

Get your "Easy" button today as a reminder to think and act as if it is easy!

Use the "Easy" button as a tool for success in your business and life.

"BROKEN PROMISES"

The lyrics of the song "Broken Promises," by Element Eighty, communicates what can happen in the relationship between lovers when promises have not been kept. The same can hold true in real estate transactions between clients and agents, as well as other concerned parties.

People have expectations whether verbalized, written, or communicated by actions and mannerisms. When those expectations are not met, it is like a broken promise. A little bit of the love light can go out. Sometimes, as in the song, feelings associated with the disappointment are not shown or communicated. These "broken promises" can burn inside the client, which can cause irreparable harm to the relationship.

One of the best ways to establish a strong relationship with customers and clients is to set expectations ahead of time. With a seller this should occur at the listing appointment and with the buyer at the first consultation. Further, the agent, as the professional, should set the standard by maintaining good communication throughout the process.

It is best to mirror the communication style preferred by the client in order to be most effective. Follow up on all conversations with a written summary in order to maintain proper protocol on contractual items, deadlines, and key issues. Updates and progress reports keep everyone on the same page. That way if something is unclear, it can be identified and addressed before the situation has time to fester into a negative one.

Real estate agents are human, too, and even with one's best efforts, problems and issues can and do arise. Requesting and embracing feedback on an ongoing basis, I have found, shows clients that their comments and concerns are valued. Even better, seek to exceed client expectations. Conduct business in this way and the parties involved will not be "left with broken promises" as in the song.

Keep promises with customers and clients to achieve and sustain success.

HEART VERSUS HEAD DECISION-MAKING

In the purchase and sale of real estate, in most cases both the heart and the head are involved in decision-making. Many people are not consciously aware that that is what is taking place. The heart represents where feelings and emotion originate. The head is known as the base of intellectual thought and objective reasoning. The transactions in which the heart may not be as involved are with investors.

The home is one of the most personal aspects of people's lives. It is where one keeps and enjoys personal possessions, creates and eats meals, spends time with family and friends, and at the end of the day where one rests his head. It is where special memories are made, as well as everyday routines. From the location, architectural style, and décor, a home is a reflection of one's identity and thus is very personal.

Being in a home is an emotional experience. As an agent, when I recognize the buying signals of someone "falling in love" with a home, it almost always is a "done deal." There is a saying that people buy on emotion and sell themselves on facts. This is often very true in a home purchase.

On the sale side, it can at times be very emotional, although there is the numbers side as well. After the kids have left the nest, intense feelings can arise when selling the family home. It is the place where so many childhood memories reside. People who design and build a home or have had it specially remodeled for their unique tastes often take it very personally when buyers don't appreciate the special features. Even normally rational sellers, such as commercial real estate agents, have been known to be emotional when it comes time to sell their personal residence.

A home is, in many cases, the most expensive asset most people own. Thus, financial and legal considerations are a significant component of making the buying decision. The first hurdle is being capable of affording the purchase. Once that bridge is crossed, buyers then become concerned with obtaining a fair price and that the home is in good condition relative to the market. Some buyers focus solely on getting "a good deal" and can be very numbers-driven in the process. After making the heart decision, many have a strong need to be able to validate the decision rationally as well.

Sellers, in most cases, are quite knowledgeable about what the homes in their neighborhoods have sold for and how their home compares. The challenge is that typically sellers focus on the highest sales in their area and rarely consider those that went for "low-ball" prices in their opinion. In almost all cases, sellers want to be certain they obtain top dollar. In some cases, the rational side of the brain isn't as strong as the emotions generated from the heart that their home is worth top dollar.

Keep in mind both the heart and the head when
helping clients make real estate decisions.

ROCKET LAUNCH VERSUS ORBIT

The rocket launch is where the space industry focuses the majority of its energy, time, and resources. Once the rocket is in orbit, to keep it there is a matter of sustainability. To get it there, an incredible amount of energy is expended just to overcome the force of gravity. This analogy applies well to the real estate profession.

Obtaining a real estate license is just the first step in becoming an agent. Next, it takes time and resources to launch a successful business. Examples in marketing include concept development, business cards, presentation materials, and a website. Many brokerage firms offer baseline programs for newly licensed agents. For anything beyond the basics, the agent creates her own brand at personal expense.

Next, there are the myriad advertising choices to consider: print, social media, pay-per click, collaterals such as pens and door hangers, flyers, brochures, and postcards. Once an agent decides on her advertising platform, then there are the design considerations, as well as advertising frequency and what markets to target to build a personal brand to attract potential clients.

Target marketing is the most efficient means of reaching potential customers. This includes establishing a database and some sort of contact engagement system. There are digital media options, as well as print media. Many longtime successful professional agents recommend a hybrid of both.

All of this can be overwhelming! When does an agent actually have time to prospect and consult with customers and turn them into clients? In comparison to other fields, real estate has an easy point of entry into the industry relative to the income potential. That is why many people enter the profession, yet it has a high attrition rate. Further, there is little or no return on investment in the up-front costs. Coupled with the time from actual client transaction to settlement being at around thirty to ninety days, this leads to a challenging launch environment.

The good news is that after the business is off the ground, just like the rocket, staying in orbit is much easier. Once the agent has determined the combination and "secret sauce" of what works for her, then it is just a matter of making adjustments and tweaking as the market and industry changes. If your business is in lift-off mode, take heart—success is possible with commitment and hard work. Consider, too, that if your business is successfully in orbit, perhaps it is time to "launch" another endeavor.

Invest the energy, time, and resources for a successful launch and sustainable orbit of your real estate business.

SHOPWORN

Those who are familiar with the retail trade are well aware of this concept. During high school, our son worked at the local hardware store. He quickly discovered that merchandise that sat on the shelf for some time and not purchased became shopworn. In many situations, particularly with seasonal and trendy items, the merchandise had to be marked down in price in order to get it sold.

The broader dictionary definition of shopworn is "not interesting because of being used too often." Thus, shopworn can occur in real estate, as well. If the original pool of buyers to visit a home has made a decision to pass, they have in fact rejected the property. To get them to return, it is more than likely the price that has to change to get them to reconsider. The other option is for the seller to wait for the next pool of buyers to enter the market. Just as in retail, though, the next group typically feels the same way as the first.

In order to make the most impact on the market and to get more buyers' attention, changes to list price in real estate should be in the range of 5 percent to 10 percent or more. Some sellers prefer to stagger the price adjustments to be sure that they aren't leaving any money on the table. This can work, just as the merchant can continue to slash the price until buyers respond. However, this strategy can take on the effect of "death by a thousand cuts."

The seller and merchant both should be mindful that they don't end up "following the market down." In such a scenario, it can be better to get "ahead of the market" by making more significant adjustments to find buyers quicker.

Demonstrate the concept of being "shopworn" on the real estate market to clients and how best to counteract the effect.

ON BUYING AND SELLING

The financial guru and billionaire Warren Buffett is quoted as saying: "Be fearful when others are greedy and greedy when others are fearful." In other words, sell high and buy low. To follow Buffett's mantra, one would be a contrarian and watch what the crowds are doing and behave in a counter manner.

No one can accurately time the market, whether real estate, commodities, or stocks. Only in retrospect does one truly know for certain the trough and the pinnacle. To buy "low," one has the option to buy on the way down or on the way back up. To sell "high," one can sell during a rising market or after the crest has been reached.

It seems intuitive, yet is much more difficult to apply when in the heat of the situation. When everyone is buying, that's when one should sell. And when everyone is waiting to see "how low can it go," that is exactly when one should buy. This is where the professional agent takes on the role of consultant, advising clients about the market conditions.

There can be submarkets and strata within any market. For example, in many areas of the United States, upper-bracket home prices took considerably longer to recover to peak levels, although lower ranges in the same community had and were experiencing appreciation.

The Oracle of Omaha goes on to share this wisdom: "Fear is instant, pervasive, and intense. Greed is slower. Fear hits." The financial crisis of 2008 and the Great Recession from 2007 to 2009 hit the market broadside with uncertainty. It took considerably longer for recovery and consumer confidence to return to the market. During the crash, as well as the ongoing market slowdown, Buffett remained calm and continued to conduct business: "The lower things go, the more I buy." Most did not exhibit that level of market confidence.

The best way to overcome a bad case of market fear and greed is to counsel with wise advisers, those who possess experience and have operated through a number of market cycles. Much like a roller coaster, there are patterns that become evident with astute analysis.

Counsel clients on buying and selling real estate from
those with market wisdom and experience.

"I WILL SURVIVE"

Real estate markets fluctuate. There are cycles of months, quarters, and even years that are up and then there are those that are down. There are changes that have both major and minor impacts on the industry. It is helpful to determine if what is occurring is situational or systemic.

Situational indicates that "this too shall pass." An example was the Great Recession of 2007 to 2009 in the United States, which was a period of dropping prices. During this time, in order to sell many homeowners had to do so for substantially less than they would have in the previous period of a strong, rising market. In that time frame, many real estate agents dealt with clients who lost their homes to foreclosure or had to manage the arduous process of a short sale. Even if the sale was not distressed, it still was a challenge to help people manage financial loss. In a time of falling prices, it may appear that the sky is falling.

In a time of rising markets, buyers are in a situation in which it can be a struggle to find good houses at affordable prices. Agents in those scenarios write numerous offers that lose out in bidding wars. It can be very disheartening to buyers to not be able to find the house of their dreams, or in some cases just not be able to find a house they can afford.

Systemic is something that affects an entire industry or market. The proliferation of information on the Internet is systemic. To think that the way real estate agents conduct business will return to pre-Internet modes of operation is highly unlikely. In order to survive and thrive in the industry means the agent has to embrace technology. Even in times of relative market stability, there is still the challenge of managing multiple demands on resources and time.

In all of these situations, the lyrics to "I Will Survive" by Gloria Gaynor offer inspiration to the professional real estate agent. The first line sets the stage for the fear that can develop when circumstances appear out of control or are rapidly changing: "At first I was afraid, I was petrified." Yet she goes on to realize that she grew strong in the adversity and "learned how to get along."

The secret to sustained success as a real estate agent is to tell fear to "walk out the door" because it is "not welcome anymore." That is how to thrive—not just survive—in any type of market, situation, or new system that one faces.

Survive and thrive both situational and systematic changes in the real estate business.

WHY DO BUYERS HAVE GOOD MANNERS?

Agents often hear from seller clients after a home has been on the market for a while: "Just tell the buyer to make an offer." It seems so simple, so why don't buyers do that? I believe it is because buyers have good manners. In most cases, buyers do not want to offend or hurt the feelings of a seller by making an offer that could be considered "low ball" or "bottom feeding." Instead, experience shows that buyers wait until the price is within the range of what the market has determined to be the value of the property.

In a rising market, sellers can overcome overpricing as the market moves toward them. When demand is great, buyers have less choice. Basic supply and demand fundamentals indicate that it is a time of rising prices. When supply is great and buyers have lots of choices, then there is usually downward price pressure.

The market is a very efficient mechanism, as it is the collective wisdom of countless independent parties constantly evaluating conditions. When sellers make statements such as, "This time is different" or "My home is special," an agent should proceed with caution. Those sentiments are likely originating from a subjective frame of reference. The seller's perspective often justifies his own point of view rather than listening to the market and counsel from real estate professionals.

The market is totally objective. This is the same reason that attorneys do not represent themselves and medical professionals do not practice on family members: it is difficult to remain objective when one is too close to the situation.

What is a good indicator of whether a home is priced at market value? A rule of thumb knowledgeable agents employ is if a purchaser has not made an offer or come back to visit the home a second time within thirty days, then the market is speaking to the seller. In some markets, it takes sixty to ninety days to allow ample time for exposure.

Statistics demonstrate that buyers, in most cases, will make an offer if the differential is within 10 percent of what the market perceives the value to be. In order to make an impact on the market, a seller should adjust the list price by 10 percent preferably or at least by 5 percent. Follow the procedure to adjust the price every thirty to sixty days until the market is found.

To expedite the process, either increase the price adjustment amount or decrease the time between changes. At some point, the market will recognize the inherent value and respond accordingly.

*Demonstrate market dynamics to sellers with the
"buyers have good manners" illustration.*

"INSIDE OUT"—THE SILVER LINING OF MOVING

The Disney Pixar movie *Inside Out* is the story of a girl named Riley. At the age of eleven, her family moves cross-country because of her father's job. The movie illustrates the five emotions that all people possess: joy, sadness, disgust, fear, and anger. Riley and her parents go through all of the emotions during the process of the move and after arriving at their new home.

Riley experiences sadness about leaving behind her good friends, both at school and on her hockey team. Disgust enters the picture when the new home does not live up to her expectations. Riley is filled with fear that she won't be able to make new friends and that she may not make the hockey team in the new town. At one point, anger rears its ugly head as she thinks about the move. She thinks it is her parents' fault for uprooting her at a pivotal age and making her have to experience change that she doesn't want to have to go through. It feels to her that they didn't even consider her feelings when making the decision to relocate.

Over time, Riley realizes some positives about the move: she gets to travel to and learn about other parts of the country; she is able to decorate her new room; she gets involved in some new clubs and activities, as well as experience one of her favorites, hockey; and she makes new friends while keeping in touch with her old ones.

Riley grows up through the process by learning how to handle all her emotions. And by working together with her parents, who are experiencing emotions of their own, she gets through the difficult times. Together they discover the "silver lining" of the move and that there can be joy in change.

The movie *Inside Out* and related books and materials are great resources to share with clients who are moving with children. It is a healthy way to illustrate that moving can be difficult, yet also can have a positive outcome for the whole family. There is always a silver lining!

Help families who are moving with children find the silver lining by using the movie Inside Out.

LEARNING TO WALK MEANS GETTING BACK UP

Our daughter is an equestrian and one thing she learned early on is that when a rider falls off a horse, it is important to get right back on. This caused me to reflect on how my experiences as a mother prepared me for being a successful real estate agent. When children are young, everything they do is new to them. A child will most likely take on new challenges with a sense of adventure and fearlessness.

Just consider the process a child goes through to learn to walk. Toddlers fall down countless times before they figure it out. Bruises and bumps with lots of kisses and Band-Aids are part of the process. Parents and older siblings cheer her on with positive and enthusiastic words of encouragement. A child may hold another's hand or fingers to steady himself. Tools such as a pushcart for balance lends confidence—just watch him take off!

This is a great process to follow as a new agent learns the real estate business or even tackles learning a new process or computer program. You will fall down countless times, perhaps even make a few mistakes, but you will figure it out. The learning and growth occurs in the doing. Seek out more experienced agents and peers to cheer you on as you develop your skills. Perhaps you can "lean on them" and obtain a bit of wise counsel to steady yourself. Consider using tools to increase your confidence. Soon we will all be saying, "Watch her take off!"

The teaching and transfer of knowledge is often the next new frontier for those who have mastered a field. That is where I am in my journey. I visit with and coach new agents and see them fall down. This is, in its essence, a book of wisdom. The mother instinct in me tells them to get back up on that horse.

I urge you to constantly take on new challenges. That is where the growth occurs and "the gold is," as my business coach Moira Lethbridge reminds me! A favorite fortune cookie of mine states: "What would you attempt to do if you knew you could not fail?"

Falling down in the profession of real estate is inevitable, as it is a challenging and demanding industry to be sure. Recently I was visiting with a relatively new agent in our office, and she was lamenting to me how hard it is. She was so surprised. Metaphorically she had fallen down. Her challenge and opportunity were to get back up again. I counseled her that other agents have felt this way before and that the important thing is that she gets back up, brushes herself off, and does it again. That's where the growth happens.

Attempt the next thing, and if you fall down, get back up and try again.

FOLLOW-THROUGH

The expression to "follow up" is common in the language of sales, as when a salesperson says she will follow up on a lead. However, I have found that "follow-through" is what gets the job done. Follow-through is a principle in sports, particularly golf, in which the athlete continues the stroke or swing through to completion and in the direction of the desired outcome. The golfer lines up the stroke to the hole, beginning above the ball. The backswing that occurs prior to contact gives the club the momentum required to propel the ball into the air. If the athlete were to "pull up" or stop the swing short in some fashion, then the success of hitting the ball in the desired direction is unlikely.

Follow-through in real estate sales has similar principles. The sales agent often begins the effort prior to making contact with the customer. An example is that many agents use open houses as a means of prospecting. Just showing up at the designated time and putting signs out does not fully leverage the opportunity. The preparation that an agent performs prior to the event increases the likelihood of meaningful conversations and connections to occur at the open house. This is analogous to the "backswing," the effort that propels the ball forward. These activities can include viewing comparable homes on the market in the neighborhood and surrounding communities; preparing market studies and information to have available for open-house visitors; inviting the neighbors to visit; and previewing the home and becoming familiar with the attributes, features, and upgrades.

After the open house and contacts have been made, then the agent has countless opportunities to connect with the leads. Meaningful follow-through includes thanking all attendees by e-mail, a phone call, or handwritten note; providing answers to inquiries made; sending further market studies as relevant; and doing research on neighboring communities that might be a better fit for the customer.

Follow-through activities for lead conversion have taken place once the customer has become a client. The next follow-through process includes the listing agreement through to contract to settlement for sellers and buyer agreement through contract to closing for buyers. The professional athlete and real estate agent truly never stop following through! This is because another correlation to sports is that both require practice in order to perfect the craft and skill. Professional golfers spend about three to four hours every day concentrating on their full swing and an equal amount of time on their short game. Successful real agents follow a similar schedule for prospecting and conversion to sell after winning the business.

Conduct follow-through activities for both prospecting
and selling conversion.

AGENT AS MATCHMAKER

The objective of a matchmaker in romantic love is to bring compatible individuals together as a couple. First, the matchmaker seeks to understand the personalities of each individual and the needs and desires each is looking for in a mate. When I think of a matchmaker, I invariably hum the tune to the song "Matchmaker" from the *Fiddler on the Roof* musical:

Matchmaker, matchmaker

Make me a match

Find me a find

Catch me a catch

Matchmaker, matchmaker

Look through your book

And make me a perfect match

The ideal match is one in which the couple is compatible and there is a spark, that something special that can be difficult to quantify and qualify.

The agent is like the matchmaker when buyers come with a list of needs and desires they want in a home. If it is a couple, and particularly if there are children involved, the agent must seek first to understand the personalities of each of the parties. Each comes to the purchasing decision differently. Then the agent, as in the song, "looks through her book." The dedicated agent possesses intimate knowledge of the area, what's currently on the market, and even those homes that could be a "match" yet are not currently on the active market. It is often more "art" than science. It is like putting together the pieces of a puzzle without having the virtue of the box to know what the final outcome will look like!

There is a young man from our church for whom friends have been trying to find a "match." We asked him what he was looking for in a lady, and he said that he would like someone with these three "S" qualities: sexy, smart, and sweet. Sexy, as there has to be a physical attraction; smart, as he wants a partner that is an intellectual equal; and sweet, in that he would enjoy her company.

The same qualities have correlations in real estate "matchmaking." To be sexy means the home has a "wow" factor to the buyer, and a spark ignites when the buyer enters the property. To be smart means that the home is a good investment, that comparables support the value, and the condition of the property is evaluated and appropriate remedies are negotiated. And to be sweet, the house isn't just a building, but feels like home.

The best agents see the twinkle in the buyer's eyes upon entering a home. In the years I have been "matching" buyers with homes, finding the right home is truly much like falling in love.

Be a real estate "matchmaker"!

TAKE THE LEAP TO SUCCESS

If you are reading today's entry, that must mean that this is a leap year. Just think—you've been given the most precious of gifts, twenty-four extra hours! What are your plans for the day? I propose that you spend some time focusing on the vision of your future. That way, you can begin now to put into place the mindset, habits, and actions that will help you take the leap to success.

Think back to four years ago. Where were you on the last leap day compared to today? Now think who you want to be, where you want to be, and what you want to do in the time span of four years. That's the leap of faith. Actually, whether you do anything different today or not in four years that time will have passed.

A powerful visualization technique is to create a storyboard. It is a compelling tool to bring future success to the present moment. Over time, by virtue of the law of attraction, your brain and the universe conspire together to make the vision a reality.

The storyboard I created for my "leap to success" was based on writing this book. My vision was for *Success* magazine to publish a feature article with me as the cover story. In addition to my photo on the cover, it would include quotes from respected people in the industry who endorse the book. There would be images and illustrations about *Real Estate Success in 5 Minutes a Day*, as well as sidebars with take-aways from the book.

What does your future hold?

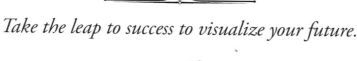

Take the leap to success to visualize your future.

LEAP OF FAITH

MAKE THE JUMP

WHERE I AM

WHAT I WANT TO BE

DON'T BREAK THE CHAIN

Story has it that Jerry Seinfeld designed a self-motivating technique for writing his comedy show routines that became known as "Don't break the chain." A key to success for him was to consistently create new material. He found that just the act of writing improved his writing. For Seinfeld, time on task was the key to creating better jokes. The challenge was accountability. So he used a physical calendar and would literally mark off the day with a big red "X" when the task was accomplished. The long-term objective was to not break the chain, which became another level of motivation for him. Very simply, Jerry's process was to repeat an activity every day and by doing so achieve success.

This idea has numerous applications to life. Some examples that come to mind are exercise, reading something inspirational or newsworthy, calling or touching base with a loved one or friend, and eating for good health. There are apps available that one can use to track these activities, or one can do it the old-fashioned way and use a paper calendar like Jerry is purported to do.

For a real estate agent, some daily habits that lead to success are touching base with five past clients or those in one's sphere each day, previewing or showing three houses each day, and entering ten people into a database each day.

Reading the book *Real Estate Success in 5 Minutes a Day* also follows this basic principle. A key to success is to perform productive habits every day. One way to do so is to keep true to Jerry Seinfeld's mantra: "Don't break the chain."

Use the "don't break the chain" motivational technique to hold yourself accountable.

OH, THE PLACES YOU'LL GO

Today, as we celebrate Dr. Seuss' birthday, think about the title of this classic book. The story encourages the character to take off on his personal journey of discovery. In classic Seuss rhythmic form, she is carried through the opportunities and perils of following her passion in life. It serves as brilliant inspiration for the real estate professional to achieve success.

An agent new to the profession is at a juncture similar to that of a high school or college graduate—it is a new beginning. In the words of Seuss, "You'll be on your way." Seuss would likely characterize a real estate agent as being "brainy" and "footsy." Both are key attributes for making things happen. There will be great days, when after a tough negotiation the parties come to an agreement or you help someone find his dream home. Those are times when you will "soar to high heights."

And yet there will be those times when, after a lot of work, a contract voids on a technicality or a customer decides to work with another agent even though you have spent many weekends showing him homes. Seuss eloquently illustrates those times of disappointment, too: "I'm sorry to say so but, sadly, it's true that bang-ups and hang-ups can happen to you."

And then there is that dreaded slump, a phase in most every agent's business that we all want to speed through. Yet Seuss reminds us that we too will somehow push through "the waiting place"—"somehow you'll escape." Once you've made it to the other side, watch out because "Whether you like it or not, alone will be something you'll be quite a lot." The practice of real estate for most agents is an entrepreneurial solo pursuit.

The closing lines by Seuss are an inspiration to persevere through the good times and the bad: "Today is your day! So . . . get on your way!"

Think of the applications from Oh, the Places You'll Go
that motivate you to achieve success.

HOME INSPECTORS ARE LIKE
GENERAL MEDICAL PRACTITIONERS

A ratified contract is when all of the terms have been agreed to in writing and delivered back to the parties. In the case of a home purchase, if there are any contingencies in the contract, in most cases the number of days to satisfy that contingency begins at that point. It is like pressing the start button on a stopwatch.

One of the first items typically to be addressed is an inspection of the home. The role of the home inspector can be compared to that of a general medical practitioner. According to the Merriam-Webster dictionary, a general practitioner is a physician or veterinarian whose practice is not limited to a specialty. In a medical practice, the general practitioner examines a patient and with that information identifies if there are areas of concern. If there are, she will recommend further tests or evaluation by someone with more specified knowledge and training. On these occasions, she will refer the patient to a specialist.

The inspector assumes a similar role in the home purchase process. He examines the different components of the exterior and interior of the home and property. Just as a medical practitioner updates records, the inspector prepares a report identifying the items that do not meet industry standards and codes. She may recommend further tests and evaluation by experts with more specified knowledge and training.

Let's say, for example, that by visual examination the inspector identifies some areas of concern on the roof, such as missing and loose shingles and inadequate flashing. The next best step is to contact a professional roofing company to complete a more thorough examination. The home inspection report often includes the projected age of the roof as well as recommendations on repairs, remedies to extend the life of the roof and systems, as well as full replacement options.

There are instances when the medical specialist determines that there is little or no cause for concern. For example, if the general practitioner hears something unusual in a patient's heart and a respected cardiologist examines the person and does not find anything of concern, the patient has several options. One is to trust the professional's evaluation. Another is to seek additional advice and counsel, particularly if there is a compelling reason to do so. And third, the parties can "watch" the progression of the condition at periodic intervals to determine if future action should be taken.

These counsels apply to the condition of a home, as well. Experience tells us that if identified issues have been examined by a specialist in the field, that evaluation overrides the observations of the generalist professional. Achieve and sustain success in real estate by having great analogies such as this one to explain the process to both buyer and seller clients.

*Use this analogy to explain the home inspection
process to buyer and seller clients.*

EAT WELL, SLEEP WELL

The adage "eat well, sleep well" in the investment world refers to the trade-off made between risk and return. The more risk one is able to stomach, the higher the potential return and thus the possibility of eating well. However, with risk there often exists great uncertainty and volatility, and thus the possibility of sleepless nights. Conversely, one can invest conservatively, which means sleeping well, but the return will likely be lower, which translates into not eating as well.

This subject will address the investment component of the sale of an owner-occupied property. The real estate investor scenario is for another discussion. What is the trade-off between risk and return in pricing strategy as it relates to selling a personal home on the market? A common desire agents frequently hear from sellers is that they want to sell for top dollar. In the pursuit of that objective, there exists the risk of pricing too high. And yet to price a personal home too low seems counterintuitive. Pride of home ownership is human nature. How could one logically and emotionally underprice one's own home?

The greatest risk in pricing too high is that the market will not respond, buyers will not come to see the home, and agents will not want to show the home. Then the property racks up days on the market and people start to wonder if there is something wrong with it. When the price does come down, the best buyers have probably already purchased, so what is often left are the second-tier buyers. Another option is to wait for market conditions to change or new buyers to enter the market, all of which takes time. And time is money.

The greatest risk in pricing too low is the possibility of leaving money on the table. Experience shows that the force of supply and demand is extremely strong. If a property is truly underpriced, the market responds. In those scenarios, there can be multiple offers and bidding wars.

The most typical process owners choose to follow in the sale of a personal residence is to start the list price at the high end of the range. The strategy is to invite buyers to "make an offer." At that juncture, parties negotiate price to obtain the market value at that point in time. This is the tightrope theory of pricing. It attempts to balance both "eat well" and "sleep well." The best method of successfully walking a tightrope is to continuously move forward—don't look down and don't panic.

Use "eat well, sleep well" to explain to clients the balance between risk and reward in the real estate market.

CAN WE FIX IT? YES, WE CAN!

Real estate transactions are complex, as they require numerous parties to work together to get a deal to settlement. It starts with an agreement between buyer and seller on price and terms, which occurs in most cases by the negotiation strategy of a real estate agent. The agent then serves as general contractor of the transaction. Each deal is a unique design, which is constructed by bringing together parties from a variety of trades and services to complete the plan.

Inspectors, contractors, technicians, and surveyors verify the condition of the property. The lender, along with the underwriter and appraiser, coordinate and validate the financial aspects of the purchase. Even a cash deal requires fund disbursement. Preparation, execution, and timely delivery of documents require the services of an attorney and settlement facilitator. It is a rare transaction that proceeds smoothly from consummation to settlement. In most cases, issues occur that require solutions in order to proceed.

In the British children's TV show, "Bob the Builder," the characters are presented with challenges that require fixing. When posed with the question: "Can we fix it?" the response is always emphatically: "Yes, we can!" That is a success-oriented posture and attitude. Resolution is achieved by working through, rather than avoiding or denying, problems that develop.

With creative thought and proactive implementation, almost every situation can be resolved. On occasion it is to the betterment of both parties, but sometimes one or the other has to give a little in order to keep the deal together. A comradery centered on the purpose of the transaction often focuses on a solution. At the very minimum, an effective approach is to keep everyone mindful of the fact that the seller wants to sell a home and the buyer wants to buy a home.

Just like Bob the Builder, the agent serves as both general contractor of the transaction and can-do attitude cheerleader. Success thinking, activities, and vision means to believe the situation can be "fixed"—and it can!

Build a "yes, we can" motto into your business practice and life!

LETTING GO OF THE "MENTAL MONEY" ON A HOME

At any point in time, sellers seem to have a value in mind of what they think their home is worth. The value most often reflects peak market prices. The challenge is when the market shifts. For example, if the current market indicates that the value of a home is around $750,000 and at the peak the home would have sold for $825,000, the seller clings to the hope of obtaining the higher price. This differential is "mental money." It isn't actually money in the bank until a buyer is willing to pay it. To let go of that "lost" mental money on a home can be difficult. No one ever seems to complain if the reverse scenario occurs, where market value is greater.

Letting go of anything can be painful, whether the loss is perceived or real. However, it seems that in financial terms, there is more trauma associated with one's home. One of the primary reasons this is true is that homeowners tend to focus on the best-case scenario. This is related to the old adage, "A man's home is his castle." The owners love their home with all its unique characteristics and quirky issues. The investment is considerably more than just financial; it is the location of many emotional ones, as well.

It is interesting that homeowners tend to focus on the "gain" and yet don't ever want to see the "loss." Perhaps it is a case of eternal optimism, yet it may even be more deeply rooted than that. It is similar to how people feel about their pets. Have you ever met an ugly dog or cat? Other people may not see the beauty in the animal, yet the owner sure does!

As homeowners, having purchased the home, lived in it, and made it their own, they love their home in a way that is no longer objective. The market doesn't look at the purchase of a property in the same light. The market looks at the house as a commodity.

It is the value that causes a purchaser to pay for something—not what it costs the owner and not what the value "might have been" sometime in the past or someday in the future. It is effectively the same premise as in the stock market. If the owner of a stock doesn't sell at that moment in time, then the differential becomes an unrealized loss or gain, whichever the case may be.

This unrealized loss or gain—the "mental money"—is what people need to let go of in order to be able to become a true seller and move on. Successful agents are able to explain and help people make the adjustment to the market conditions, while at the same time remaining sensitive to the client's unique circumstances.

Use scripts and dialogues to help seller clients let go of "mental money."

HABITS AND 66 DAYS

Today marks day sixty-six in your journey of reading *Real Estate Success in 5 Minutes a Day*. Sing the song "(Get Your Kicks on) Route 66" in celebration of the significance of the date. Studies have shown that it takes, on average, sixty-six days for a person to form a new habit. Congratulations! As of tomorrow you will be above average!

People who achieve success in beginning a new habit or stopping an undesirable one go through a "habit loop." This is a three-part process, according to Charles Duhigg, author of *The Power of Habit*.

Days one to twenty-two mark the period when it is helpful to be an evangelist about your habit. Get out and tell people and solicit support. This creates the desire to complete the goal or risk embarrassment with friends and family. This process alerts your brain to focus on the behavior you want to make happen. During days twenty-two to forty-four, many people pause in self-reflection. Often people seek to understand the motivation and desire for wanting to create a positive habit or to stop a negative one.

The next period of days forty-four to sixty-six is when people start to experience burnout and might have difficulty sustaining the habit. Routine begins to kick in. Focus on the "light at the end of the tunnel" or at least catch glimpses of success and push through. During this stage, some people begin to experience the benefits of the new habit and the attributes of being in a "virtuous" cycle.

Day sixty-six is a milestone, one to celebrate. Get your kicks today on day sixty-six! Take a moment to circle back to those folks who supported you in the beginning and share the accomplishment. And if there were naysayers, call them, too—now they will be believers. The reward is key to putting the habit loop firmly in place.

Keep on keeping on. According to science writer David DiSalvo, it can take eighty days for a habit to become automatic: "Psychology research tells us that the average amount of time necessary to reach 'maximum automacity' (a habit) is sixty-six days. But when you are trying to develop a healthy habit, it's likely it will take eighty days for it to become automatic. The more complex the habit, the longer it takes to form."

Put the power of getting your kicks at day sixty-six with the 66 Day Challenge Calendar available on the "One Thing" website (www.the1thing.com/resources). Good habits, such as reading *Real Estate Success in 5 Minutes a Day*, are key to achieving and sustaining long-term success.

Celebrate today by getting your kicks at day sixty-six!

WHY 50 PERCENT OF SOMETHING IS BETTER THAN 100 PERCENT OF NOTHING

This famous quote, "50 percent of something is better than 100 percent of nothing," by the financial guru Suze Orman has numerous applications in real estate. Orman shares that she passes on this sage advice that came to her from her father.

Consider an example that applies to sellers. The client determines that his ideal list price is $500,000. If he does not receive an offer at that price and thus does not sell the home, then he "loses" the entire $500,000. If the market price is actually $450,000 and the seller recognizes that dynamic, then he achieves his objective of selling. In fact, he achieves, in effect, 90 percent of his goal. This is significantly more than if he did not accept a market price and continued to sit on the asset. That is what is meant by "100 percent of nothing."

A home—or actually any commodity—is only worth what a buyer is willing to pay and a seller is willing to accept. If, in fact, a buyer would not pay an amount, then the seller really never had anything.

Another scenario applies to rental property. In this case, the landlord establishes the rent to be $2,250 per month, or $27,000 per year. If the property does not rent in one month, then the landlord stands to lose $2,250 in cash flow. Every month that the property is vacant, the owner experiences the loss in cash flow of another $2,250.

Consider if the landlord follows Orman's counsel and offers the property for rent at a bit under market, say at $2,150. The property is more likely to rent quickly and there is no vacancy for the month. The landlord receives $100 less in rent per month for that year, or a total of $1,200. Remember, though, that because the landlord did not lose one month's rent in vacancy, the landlord gained 100 percent of the $2,150. Bottom line: the landlord is ahead by $950 for the year.

Orman also shares this wisdom, which is relevant in these examples: "Calculating the price you 'could have had' is a dream." The most common mistake sellers and landlords make is being greedy. Even in a rising market, sellers often have expectations that are unrealistic. It is better to have 50 percent, 60 percent, 70 percent, 80 percent, or 90 percent of something than 100 percent of nothing.

Find applications for the wisdom of "50 percent of something is better than 100 percent of nothing" with clients.

THERE IS NO "TRY"

Sellers often will say that they want to try and sell their home. Another version of this sentiment is to test the market. The implication is that they will only sell if they can achieve the price that they want. This is truly a situation of not being a "real seller."

The wisdom of Yoda in the *Star Wars* movies comes to mind: "Do or do not: there is no try!" Something happens when a person makes a decision to *do*. At that crossroads, she believes that it will happen and takes the steps necessary to make it occur. For a true seller, this includes preparing the home for show condition and pricing it such that it is "in the market" with comparable properties.

The trouble with just "trying" is that it implies one foot is in the "do it" camp and one foot is on the "don't do it" side. I have found that this, in effect, sends mixed messages to the market. Buyers pick up quickly the behavior of a real seller, and vice versa. The seller may be "on the market" but not "in the market," which is best defined as the range that sends the message that she is ready, willing, and able to sell.

The same principle can hold true with real estate agents. Those who "try" real estate often have a backup plan: if real estate doesn't work out, she will just go back to teaching or pharmaceutical sales or whatever was the agent's previous profession. Another scenario that often occurs if a person isn't successful as a real estate agent is that she will look to related fields, such as with a lender, property management firm, or settlement company.

Lead generation is an activity I have found that agents often "try" more than they "do." They will "try" knocking on doors, yet when nothing happens after the first ten houses, they give up. Or they will "try" open houses and yet not follow through completely with the visitors. Or they will "try" sending out postcards, yet only do it one or two times and then discontinue because it didn't work.

The challenge with all of these scenarios is that full effort was not expended. It takes considerably more than "trying" to be successful as a real estate agent. It takes a lot of "doing."

Take Yoda's words to heart and just "do."

REAL ESTATE AGENTS ARE LIKE WEATHER FORECASTERS

The role of a weather forecaster or meteorologist is to scientifically study the weather conditions and make predictions about what it is likely to be in the future. The forecaster does not make the weather, obviously. Nor can the meteorologist change the weather. Their job is to report the current conditions and provide their best conjecture on what the weather in the near and distant future will be, given experience gleaned from scientific analysis. The further out the prediction, the less accurate the forecast will be.

The correlation to real estate is the preparation of a comparative market analysis. The agent studies comparables to make predictions about what the real estate market is likely to be in the future. The agent doesn't make the market, obviously. Nor can the agent change the market. The agent's job is to report the current market conditions and to provide her best counsel on what the market is likely to do in the near and distant future.

The accuracy of weather predictions increases based on the level of information that is available and the shorter the time frame. The forecaster is there to inform the public on what the external environment is experiencing. It is up to the individual to decide whether or not to stay home or to go on a picnic. A short-range prediction of a few days is likely to be more accurate than long-range conjectures. There are numerous instances when the weather forecast is correct only 50 percent of the time.

The same holds true for a real estate comparative market analysis. It is by using predictive analytics that an agent projects how the market will respond. The challenge is that the market is constantly changing. Homes are coming active on the market daily, closing to settlement, and going under contract. The closer to "real time" the analysis, the more likely predictions are to hold true.

Who gets blamed when the weather is bad? The meteorologist! Who sustains the brunt of the frustration of a seller when a home doesn't sell for what a seller wants or the buyer can't find a home that works for her needs? Often it is the real estate professional. In many cases, the person who bears the "bad news" is the one who is associated with the negative situation.

The weather forecaster and the real estate agent convey the message of preparation. If storms are on the horizon or a market correction is imminent, the professional advises accordingly. It is up to the people to heed the warning and take appropriate action for the situation.

How can an agent best handle these instances when the client strikes out and "shoots the messenger"? One can use the weather forecaster analogy to explain that the meteorologist doesn't make the weather any more than the agent makes the market.

Find applications to use the weather forecaster analogy to explain the market to clients.

PROSECTING FROM A TO Z

There are occasions when agents literally get stuck and don't know where to begin to prospect. Who should they call first and how often? This paralysis actually can happen to me too, as I have countless people to follow up with, including past clients and sphere of influence, as well as warm and cold leads. This is a wonderful position to be in. The challenge becomes whom should I contact first? In order to make progress, I came up with a system to easily and quickly decide which lead to pay attention to first.

Every time someone makes a real estate inquiry or visits with me about listing their home, I prepare a file folder. My business partner, Lizzy Conroy, keeps her leads in a spreadsheet. Notes and information related to the real estate and the people involved are logged in both the file and in a database. This data dump clears my head so I am able to focus on the task that is in front of me without fear that I may forget something important.

The monthly calendar lines up fairly closely to the same number of letters in the alphabet. Voilá! A built-in system to prospect the leads, literally from A to Z. On the first day of the month I contact those people whose last name begins with "A." The second day of the month I call "B" prospects, and so forth. It works even when calling warm or cold leads.

True, there is not an exact match; some of the letters, such as "X," may not have many surnames associated with it. In those cases, I just do a bit of combining, similar to how a phone pad has WXYZ on the number 9 button. Another minor tweak is the reverse concept. Some of the letters, such as "M" and "T," are the first letter for many surnames. Since in all cases there are more days in the month than there are letters in the alphabet, I use those days to circle back and enjoy the opportunity to pick who to call at random.

What about the agent whose program to generate leads is based on business days? This just requires a bit of a work-around. For example, in 2016 the first day of the month fell during the workweek ten times and only twice on the weekends. Following this program, the agent will progress through the alphabet of contacts three or four times per year. An agent can still touch base with past key customers and her sphere several times per year by working only business days. The idea is to use the program as a tool for success.

The technique is a simple application to improve the consistency of an agent's business development. Everyone has contacts in their phones, databases, and e-mail lists. Use the A-to-Z lead-generation method to connect with people on a regular basis to achieve long-term success.

Incorporate prospecting from A to Z to achieve success
in your real estate business.

"IT'S NOT PERSONAL, IT'S BUSINESS"

The process people go through to buy and sell a home is often very personal. As agents, we are aware of intimate details about our clients' financial situations, if working on the purchase side, and how orderly their closets are kept on the sales end. Often sellers feel self-conscious and exposed the first time a real estate agent visits their home. Even though they set up the appointment to talk with the agent about the marketing and sale of the property, just the act of having someone other than close friends and family walk through their home can make them feel uncomfortable.

Whenever people are going through change and it doesn't work out the way they want it to, it is common for them to feel anxious, angry, numb, frustrated, and irritable. Even when the change is positive and things are going well, it can still be overwhelming and disconcerting. I believe that because people know intuitively that buying and selling a home can bring out these emotions, they select their real estate agent accordingly.

There are some people who want to work with a friend who knows them well and whom they inherently trust because of that relationship. It provides a level of comfort for them to know that they have a friend on their side. There are those on the other end of the spectrum who would prefer not to work with a friend. The reasoning often is that they are worried if something goes wrong it could damage the friendship. Also, there is the underlying concern about having a friend intimately aware of so much personal information.

What happens to you as the real estate professional when a friend, relative, associate, or neighbor does not select you as their agent? Or when something does not work in your client's favor in the negotiations and he blames you or becomes angry. Do you take it personally?

I admit that I'm human and it does bother me on occasion. When I need to renew my confidence, I watch the movie *You've Got Mail*. In the movie, the corner bookstore owner, played by Meg Ryan, is losing business to the big-chain bookstore. She doesn't realize that she is actually chatting online with the owner of the competition when she asks him for advice. That character, played by Tom Hanks, offers this counsel: "It's not personal, it's business. It's not personal, it's business." Recite that to yourself every time you feel you're losing your nerve.

That's the mantra I've adopted and I recommend you do as well: "It's not personal, it's business." Clients are more likely to have confidence that they made the right decision when the professional real estate agent treats the situation as a business relationship. By not taking things personally, you are more likely to preserve the friendship and win the business.

Adopt the mantra, "It's not personal, it's business"
in your customer and client relationships.

LEVERAGE IS LIKE COMPOUND INTEREST

Compound interest is paid on both the principal and the accrued interest. The interest is poured back into the original investment, and ongoing interest is calculated on the new amount. It is constantly building and becomes exponential over time. In the beginning, it can appear to have a minimal effect and so some people consider it inconsequential. It is the continued application over time that has the greatest impact.

Albert Einstein once declared compound interest to be "the most powerful force in the universe." Along the same lines, properly utilized leverage can be a very powerful force in business and in life. With the strategic use of leverage, one is constantly earning benefits on both the original investment as well as the new creation. It allows for exponential growth of one's time, energy, resources, capital, intellect, ability, people, and business, to name just a few.

In financial terms, compound interest is one dimensional. It provides the growth on a fiscal asset. Leverage offers much broader possibilities, as it can be incorporated on practically anything. There are small, incremental opportunities for leverage, thus at the micro level. In real estate, the most common are related to technology and systems.

Macro opportunities for leverage are limited only by the agent's ability to visualize possibilities. For example, a common expression is that already having a job is the best way to secure the next opportunity. In the same way, having business is the best way to secure future business. That is a form of leverage. Leads beget leads. Listings beget listings. Listings also generate buyer leads, as well as corresponding marketing and promotional opportunities. Thus, the business itself is a form of leverage. Agents who connect the dots to build and grow find ways to leverage in all things.

In leverage, it is important to aim for progress, not perfection. Success is obtained as the agent connects to build and grow the business over time.

Find ways to benefit from the compound effects of leverage in your business and life.

IF YOU GIVE A MOUSE A COOKIE AND HOME RENOVATION PROJECTS

Real estate agents are frequently asked for advice from homeowners about whether they should renovate and add on to their existing home or sell and buy "up." In the process, it is uncovered what they would need to do to make their existing home what they want. Usually it entails either bumping up or out, due to a need for more space.

After consultations with architects and contractors, the homeowner discovers that while he is going to considerable trouble and expense, he should look at what else he needs and wants to do. The one simple decision progresses into a domino effect, which turns into a major project. The popular children's book, *If You Give a Mouse a Cookie*, by Laura Joffee Numeroff, illustrates well the progression of what often happens with home renovation and remodeling projects.

In the book, the youngster opens his home to a hungry mouse and, as a good host often does, offers him refreshment, in this case a cookie. The boy finds that the cookie isn't enough; the mouse then wants a glass of milk to go with the cookie. Once the mouse finishes his cookie and milk, he happens to glance in the mirror to be certain he doesn't have a milk mustache. The rest of the book tells the tale of all of the consequences of being a good host and giving the mouse a cookie.

The "moral of the story," as it applies to the homeowner contemplating renovation projects, is: where does it all end? Investing in the ongoing maintenance and improvement of a home is almost always a good practice. However, what often happens is that while busy renovating a home, the question arises: "Why not just do the next thing on the list while the contractor is here and the house is under construction?" This is when the counsel of an informed real estate agent is a smart decision prior to proceeding.

The agent can counsel the homeowner about the trends for the neighborhood. Return on investment on home improvements is always important to take into consideration. If the property is over-improved, then it may be difficult to obtain the value at resale. It also depends on how long the homeowner anticipates residing in the property. A longer duration justifies a higher level of improvements. That is the case for remodeling and renovating early on so that the homeowner can enjoy the updates, rather than waiting to make changes right before going on the market for sale.

The professional real estate agent can discuss these considerations for the homeowner prior to embarking on significant renovation projects. Perhaps money would be better spent in making a move "up."

Assist clients in determining the improvement value of home renovation projects.

GOLF SWING PERFECTION

The quest of most golfers is to perfect their golf swing. Even pros consistently train and practice to achieve this ideal. The challenge is to take the steps necessary to improve one's game while at the same time not losing the momentum of current success.

Every small adjustment and tweak has a consequence. Sometimes the swing gets worse before it gets better. Further, by attempting to master several skills at once, a golfer can lose focus. This can potentially damage the techniques that had been working well.

These can be challenges for the real estate professional too. What worked well in the past may require adjustments in order to improve one's business and take it to the next level. Yet making too many changes to one's business practice has the potential of losing focus of the main thing . . . helping people buy and sell houses.

What is the main thing? In golf, most professionals would say to keep your eye on the ball. For the real estate agent, it is prospecting. If a golfer doesn't focus on the ball, it doesn't really matter how great the swing is because the golfer is likely to miss the ball entirely.

The same thing can happen with the real estate agent. The agent cannot take her focus off of consistent lead-generation activities. If she does, even for a short time to attend to other pressing business issues, the agent can potentially lose the momentum necessary to sustain the business into the future. For without a lead to work with, there is not a house to help a customer buy or one to list to sell.

This is the paradox of the golfer and the real estate agent. Continue to perfect the game and the business, and at the same time stay focused on the one thing key to a successful outcome.

Keep the focus on the main thing in real estate—prospecting.

MAKE IT THEIR IDEA

There is a scene in the movie *My Big Fat Greek Wedding* in which the main character, Toula, her mother, and aunt have a conversation about persuading Toula's father to let her work for her aunt at the travel agency. The mother states emphatically, "We must let Kosta think this was his idea." The reasoning follows that if they could make the father think he came up with the idea, then he wouldn't have any reason to object with what effectively was their plan.

This strategy works well in real estate negotiations too. The more clients and parties are involved with the solution, the more buy-in there is and thus support for the idea. The process effectively lights up the parts of the brain that cause the other party to come up with solutions.

In the movie, the strategy the ladies employ is to persuade the father to "talk, talk, talk, all the time!" In working with buyers and sellers, I propose that the best way to influence is to "listen, listen, listen, all the time!"

It is in listening that an agent best finds out the true crux of the issue for the client. It is also in listening that the agent can help find the solution and outcome that works best for the parties involved. The desired outcome may not always be achievable, yet handling it in this manner means that at the very least everyone will feel heard. Dean Rusk, former US Secretary of State, eloquently stated: "One of the best ways to persuade others is with your ears."

Think about what you as an agent are really trying to achieve. Is it to win a listing or to get agreement? Would you rather have the deal or be right? Behave and take actions that will most likely end up with that result. Keep the goal at the forefront and make sure it is about the client and not about you as the agent. The strategy to "make it their idea" is one that professional agents have employed to great success and you can too.

Seek to make it "their idea" so that the parties buy into the solution.

WHAT'S LUCK GOT TO DO WITH IT?

On Saint Patrick's Day, one thinks of green, lucky charms, and four-leaf clovers. It is a common expression to wish someone "good luck" for a positive outcome. This occurs in the real estate setting when agents are on their way to a listing appointment with potential sellers or to show homes to a buyer. Another occasion is during contract negotiations; it is common to hear agents casually asking for "good luck" to get the deal done.

Luck implies a game of chance, that "winning" is achieved by some random occurrence of variables over which one does not have any control. In the book *The Luck Factor*, author Richard Wiseman states: "People are not born lucky. Instead, lucky people are, without realizing it, using four basic principles to create good fortune in their lives." These four principles are: "1) Lucky people constantly encounter chance opportunities; 2) Lucky people also make good decisions without knowing why; 3) Lucky people's dreams, ambitions, and goals have an uncanny knack of coming true; and 4) Lucky people also have an ability to turn bad luck into good fortune."

As a practical application, agents prepare a listing presentation and comparative market analysis prior to meeting with a seller regarding the marketing and sale of the home. The agent meets with a purchaser to ascertain her needs and wants. Next, she screens available properties to determine which meet the criteria. This may involve previewing the home(s) prior to showing them to the buyer clients. All of these efforts require preparation, knowledge, skills, and ability. No luck is involved.

Contract negotiations involve skill in understanding comparables, market trends, and psychology of people. It often requires tact, diplomacy, and the ability to get people who are far apart in perspective to come together. Experience, strategy, and technique are paramount. Once again, luck does not come into play.

Actors and actresses do not wish each other "good luck" prior to a performance. It is because they too believe that all of the rehearsals, memorization, and practice learning lines are work, not luck. What performers express to each other prior to going on stage is to "break a leg."

That's the expression we share around our office when agents are on their way to an appointment, whether with a potential seller or buyer customer: "break a leg." There is a performance aspect to the practice of real estate. Agents who achieve and sustain success do not rely on luck. Thus I wish for you to "break a leg."

Make the shift today from "good luck" to "break a leg"!

BUYING A NEW HOME IS LIKE DRIVING A NEW CAR OFF THE LOT A TALE OF A CUSTOM/LUXURY HOME PURCHASE

Building or purchasing a new custom home can be compared to driving a luxury vehicle off the lot. Statistics show that value can drop initially as much as 10 percent to 20 percent once a new car has left the dealership. Custom and luxury homes often experience a similar phenomenon. There are several situations in which this is likely to occur.

One scenario is the client who designs and builds his "dream home." This scenario typically involves an architect, selection and purchase of a home site, and interviewing and contracting with a custom builder. The "dream home" is unique from design to end product. Because of these qualities, it can be so individualized that finding another buyer with the exact same tastes can be like finding a needle in a haystack. Also, keep in mind that top-of-the-line features are constantly advancing. In five or ten years, there will be new "bells and whistles" in home design.

Another scenario is the luxury home builder who builds speculatively and the purchaser buys the builder's design. On occasion, there is the opportunity to make adjustments in the plans and feature selections along the way. Often the home has been completed or is so far along in the process that the new home buyer doesn't have as much voice in the final product.

In cities where there is little land left to develop into residential neighborhoods, new home builders frequently rely on in-fill construction. This is when a builder tears down an older home to build new. There are some buyers who think an inconsistent neighborhood decreases the value and will only purchase a luxury home in a developed community with homes built at approximately the same time.

Time does not stand still, however, and other custom and luxury builders continue to construct new homes. That is how builders make money, and if they stop then they effectively shut down their business. New custom and luxury homes, in most cases, will experience a loss of value in the first five years, as is the case for new tract or production-built homes. As long as other new homes are available to buy, purchasers instinctively prefer new.

It is like the "new car smell"; many people prefer the "new home smell." For some, it is important to live in a home where the kitchen and bathrooms have never been used by other people. As a professional agent, it is important to understand why this phenomenon occurs and to advise clients accordingly. Of course, by all means sell the client the home. Just be sure to counsel the client that the market impact is similar to that of purchasing a new luxury car.

Advise clients about the possibility of the "new home" phenomenon in a custom and luxury home purchase.

Literally and figuratively, the best strategy is to be on the same side of the table as customers and clients. Orchestrate the seating such that you are seated next to your clients, whether at a listing appointment or buyer consultation. When people sit across the table from each other, the posture is not as effective. What often happens is that you will be stretching to present the materials prepared on the marketing plan and comparative market analysis for the home. Another challenging logistical situation is when a client couple sits one on each side of you. In that scenario, your head and body will be bobbing back and forth, as well as the sliding of the materials in order to keep all the parties engaged in the conversation.

One of the first steps all professional agents take at a listing appointment is to view the home with the owners. The time spent during the tour allows the agent to connect and bond with the client. It is a great time to obtain information on the attributes of the home that will be discussed during the presentation, as well. While walking through the home, identify either the kitchen or dining room table as the best place to sit for the presentation and ask the owner if you can put your materials down there. That way, once the tour of the home concludes, all parties know that everyone will convene at the table.

On occasion, owners will suggest sitting in the living or family room. That can present a challenge about how to best show written materials. In many cases, when seated in chairs the people are on the sofa and are positioned too far apart. These logistics often do not convey the same message as being at the table together does.

The act of literally being on the same side of the table as the potential client has the benefit of transmitting unconsciously that the agent is on the same side of the situation. It conveys that everyone is in it together, working hard as a team to get the home sold for the highest dollar the market will bear. That is a good frame of mind to maintain throughout the process of the marketing and sale of the home. There are countless ways to "sit on the same side of the table" with clients to achieve success.

---

*Show by actions that you are on the same side of the table
as customers and clients.*

FIRST DAY OF SPRING AND "HOPE SPRINGS ETERNAL"

The first day of spring is usually in mid-March and is known as the Spring Equinox. On the equinox, the length of the day and night is nearly equal, as the sun shines directly on the equator. As the daylight becomes longer, people begin to feel hope in the air! The quote "Hope springs eternal" comes from the classic poem by Alexander Pope and it speaks to the common human trait of optimism.

In climates where there are seasons, the coming of spring is welcomed with fanfare and celebrations. Daylight savings time provides more hours of sunshine during the evening. Outdoor activities and entertainment benefit from setting clocks forward one hour. It provides for more hours of daylight to enjoy the sunlight. Flowers are blooming and birds chirp morning greetings.

Springtime is traditionally the peak selling season for residential real estate. One reason for this is that many people plan to move over the summer months to minimize disruption in schedules. People with children rely heavily on the school calendar to time moving decisions. Others with more vacation time available in the summer months use the time off to navigate the logistics of a move.

People who live in climates that experience winter weather have been cooped up inside over a long winter. Thus, they are usually ready to get outside and do things. A third reason is that everything just looks fresher and better in the springtime. New life is visible all around.

This idea of hope in a new life is central to making a move. Often people need to be able to visualize where they are going before they can leave behind where they have been. Hope in this new life is what creates the impetus for people to pursue the home buying and selling process. This is but one reason professional real estate agents will always be in demand. It is their role to help people make their dreams come true, as that hope springs eternal.

Find ways to instill hope with clients that are in the process of moving.

START AT THE VERY BEGINNING

"Let's start at the very beginning, it's a very good place to start" are lyrics of the song "Do-Re-Mi" that Maria and the children sing in the movie *The Sound of Music*. Maria begins to sing and the children chime in. She teaches the fundamentals of music and once they know those, then all they have to do is mix them up to sing a "million different tunes."

Often real estate agents just don't know where to start. And so I say the same as Maria: "Let's start at the very beginning," which is lead generation. The fundamentals of prospecting are like the notes Do-Re-Mi-Fa-So and so on.

Consider "Do" as a customer lead. It's interesting to note that "do" has another meaning when used in a different context. To take action means to "do" something. Once a real estate agent has a customer or client lead, then the agent has something to "do."

"Re" could be the houses that are in the same neighborhood of the lead, which the agent could preview and find out more about. This leads to "Mi," which could be to delve deeper to find out more about the customer's situation. "Fa" could be the agent finding ways to be of service to clients to meet the needs of their particular circumstances. "So" is the follow-through involved. This includes developing a strategy on how to stay in touch and adding the lead to a database for follow up. "So"—what are you going to do as an agent to take this business opportunity to the next level?

Just as in the song, these steps in the process are the tools an agent can use to build a business. Once you know them well, creatively mix them up to find a million different ways to build a business through lead generation.

"Do" the activities today to generate leads and build a business.

THE PRICE IS RIGHT!

The Price Is Right game show is an American classic. The Range Finder game illustrates the combined value of the merchandise showcased. The objective for the contestant is to accurately determine the total price of the products. The red bar moves down the barometer and the player hits a button to stop it at that point in which she believes the price falls. The winner bell rings if the contestant selects correctly; if not, a buzzer sounds.

In some ways, this is similar to what an agent does when preparing a comparative market analysis. The best strategy is for the agent to provide the client with a pricing range. The reason is that the market is constantly changing, and no one really knows what the true market value is for a property until a buyer has made an offer that a seller accepts.

Just as in the game show, the listing agent almost always knows quickly whether the home has been priced correctly or not. One of the first clues is that the agent's phone rings with inquiries by agents and buyers. The first question being, "Is the home still available?" Open houses are well attended. There are a high number of showings for the market and price point. And buyers write offers. That is when the winner bell rings for both the agent and the seller.

When the phone doesn't ring, silence is, in effect, an answer by the market as well. If there have been no showings, or a low amount relative to the market, that is a strong indicator too. When there hasn't been an offer, that is truly the market's ultimate answer—that the home was not priced correctly.

In order to increase interest by the market at this juncture, it is advisable to adjust the price into the next "range." As with the barometer on the *The Price is Right* game show, the price needs to move into the market range in order to get the desired response.

Use The Price Is Right *principles to advise clients to price a home correctly for the market.*

"NEW YORK, NEW YORK"—VERSE 1

A great theme for real estate agents can be found in the final lines of the Frank Sinatra song "New York, New York": "If I can make it there, I'll make it anywhere." If an agent has attained success in other professions or markets, it follows that the agent will find acclaim in real estate sales as well. Many people enter the ranks of real estate professionals after having been in another career field. The most common is that of an outside sales representative for products and services. It seems logical that sales in one field would translate to sales in real estate. Frank Sinatra said it is so.

Often a person will become licensed as a real estate agent and think that the world will be knocking down her door to hire her. What becomes apparent is that first the world must know you are an agent. In this case, the real estate agent shouldn't be a "secret agent." The first task of agents is business development, to get the word out that they are ready, willing, and able to assist with people's real estate needs. Without a lead, a sales agent does not have anything to do.

Education is also a field from which many agents enter real estate. There is plethora of information to learn and then share in a compelling way to customers and clients. Thus, there can be a great advantage to have a teaching background. Sue Huckaby, my deceased business partner, became an agent after being a teacher for many years and rose to high ranks in the industry. She attributed her success to being a storyteller.

Experience and knowledge in law and the financial industries have significant correlations to the practice of real estate. There are advantages to customers and clients from an agent possessing expertise in these professions. One must follow jurisdictional guidelines for disclosure to whether one is offering legal advice or a professional opinion. The building and construction fields offer knowledge in that arena that can be beneficial backgrounds for the real estate profession.

The other theme to the song is the transfer of market knowledge. To expand the business and create streams of income, often agents will pursue similar endeavors. One is that of purchasing and holding investment property. Another is the flipping of homes by fixing up and selling quickly. Other agents expand into commercial real estate or markets in other locations. At some juncture, once an agent has proven success in one area, there is the desire to take the business to the next level. If the agent can "make it there, she can make it anywhere" is the motto.

As Sinatra belted out, success leaves clues. Success in one profession and market are strong indicators of the future probability of success in others. To succeed, discover and apply your past experience and unique selling proposition to your real estate business.

Find ways to offer value from previous professions and experience to your real estate endeavors.

MIND THE GAP—NEGOTIATE THE SPACE IN BETWEEN

"Mind the gap" originates from the United Kingdom's mass transit warning system. It is a visual or audible warning to train passengers to take care when crossing the space between the station platform and the railway car door.

In real estate negotiations, "mind the gap" is the space between the parties. The seller strives to achieve the highest price the market will bear. The buyer's objective is to pay the least amount possible. The "gap" is what the real estate agent is paid "to mind" in the interests of the client.

The top classic strategy for negotiations is to "meet in the middle." The seller kicks the process off by listing the home for sale. The buyer makes an initial offer. In theory, the buyer would offer an amount whereby if the parties "split the difference," they would end up at the buyer's desired final number. The gap is the play between the parties. By the initial offer, the seller has a clue about what number the buyer will accept by determining the middle figure.

America's negotiating coach and author Jim Thomas, in *Negotiate to Win: 21 Rules for Successful Negotiating*, recommends that negotiators make the most dramatic concession at the beginning, and then all following concessions diminish significantly. In other words, go close but not quite to the middle. Each counter should be smaller so that the other party obtains less each time he comes back to the table.

This strategy works brilliantly. Parties are more likely to believe everyone is going to come together if there is significant movement toward reaching consensus. Once people realize that it can become a win-win if they "meet in the middle," more often than not agreement is reached.

As an example, my business partner, Lizzy Conroy, represented a purchaser for an upper-bracket property. After numerous times back and forth, the parties were $200,000 apart. When she shared that with me, I immediately saw the solution and suggested that she go back to the listing agent and offer to "split the difference." It was so apparent to me, and yet it slipped past everyone else. Once the parties saw the win-win situation they were in, it was quickly ratified.

The real estate agent's role is to offer clients visual and audible warning phrases so that they "mind the gap" safely. The objective is to reach agreement between the parties. The agent that achieves and sustains success applies this negotiating strategy as appropriate for the circumstance.

Apply the "mind the gap" strategy in negotiations with clients.

URGENCY INTERIOR OR EXTERIOR

It is helpful for agents to understand the source of urgency for buyers and sellers when entering into a real estate transaction. The urgency is internal if the client's personal life or situation to move has an internal motivation. The reverse is true when there is an external force driving the move. In order to best be able to help the client, it is important for a real estate agent to be knowledgeable on what is precipitating the move.

The majority of interior motivations have to do with a client's life stage. In the beginning of the real estate lifecycle, we see buyers move outside of the family home or educational environment and set up their own place. The motivation to move relates to this new stage in life. Other examples are when couples marry or set up housekeeping together.

Typically the next phase is when children come along. This stage can actually occur in multiple steps as the family expands, thus requiring more space. At the end of the housing lifecycle are the empty nesters who find there is now too much space and maintenance issues, which cause them to consider other housing options. The seller's motivation is in effect complimentary or the reverse of the buyer's in the above situations. They are moving on to the next housing stage.

Internal motivators that do not relate to lifecycle can be a job change, divorce, death, and financial reversal or windfall. In some ways, there is more of a sense of urgency in these circumstances, as it is more of a necessity than just merely a desire to improve the housing situation (except in the case of a windfall).

Exterior motivations are broader and tend to be more global. Interest rates rising or falling can be a major factor in a purchaser's buying power. This actually affects both buyers and sellers. If a buyer can't pay more for a home because of financing costs, then prices are impacted accordingly.

Government policies both domestic and abroad affect economic conditions and political stability, which can either enhance or suppress the real estate housing market. The media affects consumer opinions on whether buyers or sellers consider the market to be good or bad. Companies relocating to the area can be a strong external market motivator, as it is when employers close down or move out of the area. Unfortunately, catastrophic events such as the effect Hurricane Katrina had on the New Orleans market and 9/11, which impacted the entire United States, especially New York City and Washington DC, are also external motivators.

Professional agents are knowledgeable about both interior and exterior urgency factors. It is a key to real estate sales success.

Discover whether clients have an interior or exterior urgency factor to move and use that information to influence and motivate your clients to take action.

VELCRO® IS STICKY

The inspiration for the fastening device Velcro® occurred when the inventor was hiking in the woods. He became frustrated by burrs that stuck to his clothing with a tenacity that made them difficult to remove. The secret to the product is that one piece has multiple tiny hooks that attach to the other piece of material that has "mating" loops. This design creates such a strong force that the two pieces can be pulled apart, yet retain their original form. The first applications were in clothing and since have gone on to be used by NASA and other industries. Think about the ways that the Velcro® concept applies to the real estate business.

What first comes to mind is lead generation. The more touches the agent has with a potential buyer or seller customer via marketing and prospecting activities, the more likely that person will convert to a client relationship. This is based on the sales principle that 80 percent of sales are made after the fifth to twelfth contact, according to the National Sales Executive Association. Thus, multiple hooks increase the connection with prospects. The process creates stickiness, so that the agent is top of mind when the buyer or seller is ready to make the decision to move or to make a referral.

The next example applies to the process of a client actually buying or selling a home. Although it is possible for buyers to purchase the first home they see, typically it is a more involved process. In most cases, the agent conducts a thorough buyer needs-and-wants analysis. Then the agent shows the client multiple homes before a decision is made.

On the seller side, very rarely does the first buyer who views a home write and present an offer. More common is that the agent engages in extensive marketing efforts to generate multiple potential purchasers to view the home. These processes contain countless steps to fasten the parties together. The more connections made between the parties, the securer the engagement is and the greater the commitment.

To build and grow a business, the agent who achieves and sustains success does so with multiple clients and numerous transactions over time and in the pipeline. This process has a greater potential for success than the agent who is only as good as her next deal. In these and other ways, applying the Velcro® effect is a more sustainable business model.

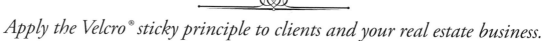

Apply the Velcro® sticky principle to clients and your real estate business.

"WAIT FOR IT"

The line "Wait for it," coined by Barney on the popular American sitcom *How I Met your Mother*, became so epic that it is now included in the Urban Dictionary. It is a device used by the character to emphasize what he says next, much like a long pause. There are several applications for the concept "wait for it" in real estate strategy and negotiations.

After presenting a comparative market analysis to the sellers at a listing appointment, it is helpful for the agent to know what the customer feels the value of the home is. Frequently the seller will turn the tables and want to know what the agent believes the home is worth. Once the agent says a number, the opportunity is often lost to find out what the seller really thinks.

Experience shows that it is helpful to know the sales price the seller has in mind in order to better manage expectations. In many cases, sellers will say that is why they are consulting with a professional real estate agent—to find out the agent's view of the value. This is when the use of the "wait for it" pregnant pause is most effective. Allow the silence and perhaps discomfort of the moment to emphasize that it is important to hear what the sellers have to say.

If pressed, the agent can reiterate that one of the objectives of the process is to achieve the client's goals. In order to be able to do that, the agent needs to know the seller's perspective of value. At this juncture, if the agent has provided enough of a pause, the seller will almost always share his thoughts. If not, refer back to the comparative market analysis data and ask about which homes the owner feels are most like his own. In this way, the agent can often "tease" out the information.

The other opportunity for the "wait for it" pause is in contract negotiations. The time period between delivery of an offer or counter and the return can be uncomfortable. People like to know if they have a deal or not. It can be tempting to push the other side to move more quickly. However, that approach implies anxiousness, which conveys the message to the other party that your client wants the deal very much. Share with the client that to "wait for it" is in his best interests.

It may seem that there is a sense of "drama" in using "wait for it." As long as the intent is to understand and benefit the client, the purpose seems worthy.

Apply the "wait for it" strategy when appropriate with clients.

BROKER AS REFEREE

Real estate terminology can be confusing to the general public. Brokerage relationships in particular can be challenging to explain, including those that real estate agents have with their clients and with the broker for the office.

An analogy that is helpful is a sports game. One scenario is two teams playing against each other. Team A is the buyer or tenant side, and the B team is the seller or landlord side. The referee is present to make certain the players and coaches follow the rules of the game, which are established beforehand. The real estate broker in this scenario acts as the referee in the transaction, applying the laws of the jurisdiction and the Realtors® Code of Ethics.

The individual real estate agent serves as a "coach" for her team—whether it is buyer/seller or tenant/landlord. If each real estate agent works for different companies, then in effect each team has a referee, too. This can be compared to high school and collegiate athletics, in which teams play against different schools.

In the case in which both agents are in the same real estate office, there is one broker who serves as referee. The agent the broker "assigns" for the purchaser/tenant will be known as a "designated agent" for that client and the one "assigned" by the broker for the seller/landlord likewise will be designated accordingly. Each "team" has its own agent as "coach," with one broker to serve as referee. This is similar to playing sports in house leagues, in which all the players attend the same school.

If the same real estate agent represents the buyer/tenant and the seller/landlord, that is known as dual agency. The agent performs two roles, in effect dual capacity. In this case, there is one real estate agent as coach and one broker as referee. There are situations in a small office in which the agent is also the broker.

People ask whether true representation can actually occur in the case of dual agency. That is a valid consideration. There are instances when one agent, by being familiar with the entire transaction, can handle the process smoothly and fairly. There are others in which people rightly want their own "coach."

The professional agent is able to explain agency relationships so that customers and clients are well informed about their rights and the responsibilities of the parties.

Use the "broker as referee" analogy to explain agency relationship terminology.

IF SHE CAN DO IT—I CAN TOO!

The "We Can Do It!" poster depicts a strong iconic woman with her fist raised in fighting mode. During World War II, men were "over there" fighting the battle. It became necessary to look for other labor sources to fill the void. Thus, women were called to assume positions traditionally held by men.

The poster reminds me that if others can do it, that means I can too. For inspiration, this poster hangs in our office as a reminder that success is achievable.

"If she can do it, I can too" is a theme that resonates in my life and real estate business. I became partners with a top agent and when she passed away, I took over her business. There was so much that I learned from Sue Huckaby and in her memory want to pass that knowledge on to others. Being partners with Sue inspired me to seek out someone to mentor. I am honored that Lizzy Conroy joined me in 2009, and now we run the business together.

Imitation of others is known as the sincerest form of flattery. It is also a means of leverage. That is why you are reading this book. You observed our success and want to achieve that as well in your professional life. Following and emulating the strong habits of success that others practice is a proven means to achieve one's own goals.

Establish success principles in your life and business based on others who have reached high levels of achievement.

CHANGE AND THE "FIVE STAGES OF GRIEF"

Change has the potential for people to feel a sense of loss, which can trigger grief-like emotions. It is helpful for real estate professionals to understand the stages, as the process of buying or selling a home is a time of significant life changes. Moving often occurs alongside other life events that can exacerbate and provoke increased feelings of loss. The five stages of grief model was developed by Elisabeth Kübler-Ross. It affirms that people progress through stages of grief, which are denial, anger, bargaining, depression, and acceptance.

In the case of sellers, the home may be on the market for sale due to the death of a family member or the couple is going through a divorce. Even if the sale is positive—for example, children leaving home for college—it can still provoke mixed feelings about leaving behind many family memories. If the home doesn't sell quickly, then sellers often feel rejected by the market and go through the five stages before they are ready to actually be "real" sellers.

Buyers sometimes "feel" when owners continue to hold on to memories and haven't truly "let go" of the home and moved on. At the very least, there can be the loss of what was hoped for that didn't occur. Or there is the loss of what was, even if the future has positive aspects to it.

Buyers also can go through the five stages of grief. Perhaps they are in a major life change as well, such as a recent marriage or new job that precipitates relocation. Even if the change is desired and positive to the people involved, it still has an impact. For example, consider a couple having a child. In almost all cases, this is a joyous occasion. The couple and others involved will go through substantial changes in their relationships and lifestyle. The amount of time available to pursue interests and financial considerations also are going through an adjustment. Purchasers can experience what is known as "buyer's remorse," when in fact what may be occurring is that they are progressing through the five stages of grief.

Clearly it goes without saying that if the real estate professional is not a licensed mental health profession, then she should not provide any counseling, grief support or otherwise. However, it is still appropriate to be human and sensitive to what the client is experiencing so you can be mindful of her feelings. Provide assistance and professional advice as appropriate when you detect that the client may be progressing through the five stages of grief.

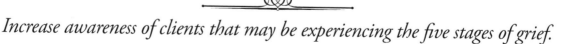

Increase awareness of clients that may be experiencing the five stages of grief.

THE TENNIS GAME OF NEGOTIATIONS

Contract negotiations for the sale or purchase of a home can be compared to playing a tennis match. As long as the ball is in "play," then there is still a game to be played, just as in negotiations. In tennis, there is either a winner or loser. In negotiations, the outcome can be win-win, win–lose, lose-win, or lose-lose. Seek to achieve a win-win, as it represents the best-case scenario for all parties. In the sport of tennis, as well as in negotiations, one improves her game by playing against a worthy opponent.

A key to playing tennis well, as in many sports, is to keep your eye on the ball. As long as you have the ball on your side of the court, you are the player in charge. As soon as it is hit over the net, then it is in the opponent's side of the court. All of these parameters apply to contract negotiations as well. One can lose a point in tennis and in negotiations and still win the match or deal; the cumulative effect is what determines the outcome.

In the real estate scenario, the serve is most often delivered by the seller, who lists the property for sale. The first return is then the volley by the purchaser's offer. When the "ball is in their court," each side has the opportunity to return or to allow the ball to drop. In the majority of negotiations, offers usually have only one more set of volleys. If agreement isn't reached by that time, it is rare for the parties to come to an agreement. When illustrating the negotiation process with clients, use the tennis game analogy. It demonstrates the process of what will occur and creates a visual with which most people are familiar.

Sportsmanship in tennis, as in other sports, increases the enjoyment of the game for the players. In negotiations, sportsmanship-like behavior occurs when parties act in good faith. One honors the real estate profession by abiding by the Realtors® Code of Ethics to treat all parties fairly and honestly. Apply the tennis game of negotiations to achieve success in your real estate business.

Use good sportsmanship and the tennis game of negotiations as strategies for success in real estate.

REJECTION IS NO JOKING MATTER

April Fool's Day is traditionally a day to play practical jokes and pranks on people. In the real estate profession, there is a lot of rejection involved, but it is no joking matter. Early on in my career, I would take it personally when people did not use me to help them to buy or sell a home. My husband encouraged me to put on my imaginary bulletproof vest. He said that way I would develop a thick skin, yet keep my tender heart.

David Letterman's career spanned over three decades, first as the host for *Late Night* and then the *Late Show*. He delivered thousands of jokes during that long tenure as America's twilight comedian. Of those jokes, many fell flat and on those occasions, in his trademark fashion, he would flick the card off stage and proclaim, "Next!"

Prior to a joke even making the cut, it first had to win David's approval. Over the years, more than ninety writers churned out countless monologues, bits, and jokes. For every one piece that made it to the show, more than one hundred were cut. Thank goodness those writers kept a sense of humor under their thick skin so that we could enjoy the comedy that could only be delivered by Letterman.

It took a team of writers to polish Letterman's monologues to perfection. In the words of the Persian poet Rumi: "If you are irritated by every rub, how will you be polished?" So even though being rejected is no joking matter, it is possible to recognize the value. Take it in stride or even in a light-hearted manner. Try the "next" response that Letterman used. Or use the bullet-proof vest visualization, which has served me well for many years.

Develop your own personal technique to move quickly past rejection!

THE CLASSIC CHICKEN-AND-EGG DILEMMA

Professional real estate agents are often presented with the classic chicken-and-egg dilemma with clients. The questions go something like: "Do we buy the new house first and then sell our home?" or "Do we sell the house we live in first, not knowing where we will go after it sells?"

I begin the dialogue with people in this situation by inquiring, "Can you qualify and afford to own two homes at the same time?" If the client is not capable of that financially, then the question has already been answered. He will have to sell first and then figure out where to go. That may entail living in temporary housing or renting while determining the next move.

If one can qualify and afford to own two homes at the same time, then the next question is, "Do they want to?" Many people cannot tolerate the risk associated with that scenario. So once again, the question has already been answered: put the home on the market and get it under contract, then go out and purchase a home, requesting coinciding settlements in the offer.

Coinciding settlements is when the money that is coming from the sale of the current residence is applied to the purchase of the next residence. It is important to be mindful of the jurisdictional and legal requirements that come into play with the use of this type of clause. Lending guidelines may make coordinating simultaneous settlements challenging. This scenario once played out with seller clients who were moving out of state. First, they put their home under contract locally and then went to their new location and quickly identified a home and put it under contract, timing the settlements accordingly.

The question on the other side of the coin is, "Can you tolerate not knowing where you will move if your current home sells first?" Often when buyers have very specific requirements for their next home and satisfying those are the priority, that determines the order. This was the case for another client's family. There were only a couple of town-home communities where they wanted to live. At the same time, we were confident that their single-family home would sell if priced correctly for the market. The client shared that the family would be living in the town house for some time to come and thus that was their priority, which easily answered the dilemma.

*Help clients determine their priority of selling or buying first
by asking probing questions and exploring options.*

50 FIRST DATES

The romantic comedy *50 First Dates* is a movie about a woman who suffers from short-term memory loss. The gentlemen character is attracted to her and begins to court her. The challenge is that she can't remember anything that happened before, so every day is like a starting all over again. The solution he comes up with is to create a video that explains "the story." This gets her quickly to the current day so they can then enjoy it together. In real estate, it can be a lot like *50 First Dates*. No matter what the agent has done on behalf of the client previously, the question is, "What are you going to do for me today?"

For sellers, the past marketing efforts are in the past; they want to know what is happening now and what future efforts are planned. Therein lies the subtle question: "If what was done before worked, my home should have sold." In these situations, the clients are often looking for answers and solutions that include the agent stepping up her marketing efforts.

Some examples of demonstrating value to sellers that our team has incorporated to success are: delivering a "your home is now live" e-mail with a list of all completed efforts and those scheduled for marketing the home; sending the "tear sheet" from any print advertisement to the client along with a letter; delivering feedback on a consistent manner from agent showings and open houses; preparing and sending market studies on a monthly basis or more frequently if the situation warrants; and scheduling periodic phone or in-person meetings to discuss the status of the efforts. The more proactive the agent, the more likely the seller clients will feel that the agent is representing their best interests and that all efforts are being made on their behalf.

The Internet provides access to properties on the market, as well as a phenomenal level of information—so much so that many buyers question what value the agent can bring to the transaction, particularly in the cases in which the buyer "finds" the home. The agent's value proposition includes services such as access to lenders, inspectors, contractors, vendors, negotiating strategy, market knowledge, and transaction management.

Some clients are direct in their delivery. Others suffer in silence. The agent may be alerted to something not being quite right in the relationship when the client reacts irritably or no longer responds to the agent's communications. The best course of action I have found is similar to what the character did in the movie: create and build a system to consistently remind the client of your efforts. It is a secret of success to demonstrate value on an ongoing basis to the client.

Establish systems to show the agent's value to clients
as well as efforts taken on their behalf.

CAREER BASEBALL PLAYERS' AT-BAT STATS

In professional baseball, the top career batting average is held by Ty Cobb at .366. In order to be considered in the rankings, a player has to have been at bat in at least 1,000 games. The top 178 baseball players rank between .300 to .366. The remaining 822 players' batting averages fall between .264 and .299. These statistics show what it takes to be a top baseball player. Ted Williams, ranked #6, once commented that those players who fail "only" seven times out of ten attempts will be the greatest in the game.

The same statistic holds true with top professional real estate agents. For every three listing appointments, one seller will become a client and the home will sell. One seller will select another real estate agent and the home will sell. The final seller will decide not to do anything at the time. So with this "at-bat" experience, the best agents "win" one listing out of every three opportunities.

There are a couple of strategies that are known to yield a higher "at-bat" ratio; both include the agent staying in touch with the customer. Thus, when ready to make the move, the customer remembers you.

These scenarios have played out over and over in my business. One such example is a seller that I met with more than ten years ago about listing his home for sale. As is typical for our market area, the seller interviewed three top agents. It wasn't the right time for him then, yet I continued to touch base faithfully a couple times every year over the course of the following decade. When finally ready to sell, this customer shared with me that he didn't even consider another agent this time around. I was the only professional that by perseverance showed I really wanted his business. That is the kind of diligence that he wanted in the sale of his home.

Another example is one in which I interviewed for a listing and wasn't selected. The other agent made promises about market value that I didn't feel would be achievable. When after nine months the home didn't sell, I touched base with the customer after receiving the alert that the listing had been withdrawn. The customer was impressed that I was aware of her situation and was ready to listen to the guidance I provided about the current state of the market. This time around she was ready to price correctly for the market and the home sold in a reasonable period of time.

It is important for baseball players to know their statistics. It is just as important for the real estate professional to track hers. If you are batting .333, then be happy—you are among the best in the industry!

Track your annual statistics for success—listings taken and sold versus appointments.

"I WILL SELL THIS HOUSE TODAY"

The mantra "I will sell this house today" is a line from the movie *American Beauty*. It has become a classic refrain of many professional real estate agents. The character, played by Annette Bening, gets a home spruced up for the market. At the same time, she repeats the affirmation, "I will sell this house today," which influences her outlook and mindset.

Affirmations with action gain traction; there is something to hold onto. The actions that the agent in the movie takes while preparing the home for a public open house are squeegeeing clean the windows; scrubbing the counters in the kitchen; vacuuming the carpet; and, don't forget, putting on her lipstick. These external activities cement the affirmation that she repeats: "I will sell this house today."

Energy is released by taking positive action. It is, in a way, setting the intention that you are willing to do whatever it takes. In the words of Nobel Prize winner Albert Camus: "Real generosity toward the future lies in giving all to the present." Listing agents continuously live in the future. Marketing and advertising expenses are assumed, as well as time and effort expended in the present in the hope that the home will sell. And only then will the agent be paid a commission.

Is it possible the house would sell with streaks on the windows, dirty countertops, and no lipstick on the agent? Yes, that is possible. Is it possible the house will not sell even with sparkling windows and vacuumed carpet? Yes, that has happened too. The most significant paradigm shift was in the attitude of the agent, with her intent for a positive outcome. She believed she could sell it, conceived of a way to do so, and so achievement was ultimately hers.

***

*Along with a positive mindset, take action
to help clients buy and sell houses.*

ALL ABOUT THE BASICS

The chorus of the song "All about that Bass," by Meghan Trainor, reminds me that real estate is "all about the basics." Rather than being "no treble," as in the song, the agent who sticks to the basics is more likely to have "no trouble."

The beat of the song drums in the message of the lyrics. In real estate, the agent who uses the basics as a framework for the way she conducts her business will find a rhythm that creates consistency. In music, the beat sets the tempo and cadence of the song. In business, the basics set the standard of daily, weekly, monthly, and annual activities.

Being all about the basics is about systems leverage. In the words of management guru and author Peter Drucker: "What gets measured gets improved." The agent who achieves and sustains success follows the SMART principle: specific, measurable, attainable, relevant, and time-related. The real estate profession is a knowledge management business of all the details, from marketing the property through settlement of the transaction.

Checklists are a fantastic tool to establish and follow process protocol. For example, an agent could have a checklist for these procedures: preparing a home to go active on the market; contract to settlement; changing the price; preparing for open house; conducting a buyer consultation; walk-through details; and home inspection negotiations. Systems allow others to step in and handle as well as manage any and all parts of a process. This additional leverage is beneficial for the agent as she goes from sole producer to business owner.

When the basics are played well—as when the bass is played well—then the rest tends to follow along. Put the foundational work in place and then the creativity has a framework on which to hang. Remember to keep it "all about the basics."

Implement processes that form a basic structure to the business.

BRIGHT-LINE RULE

Applying a bright-line rule can be a helpful tool for success. It is a principle used in law that, according to Wikipedia: "is a clearly defined rule or standard, composed of objective factors, which leaves little or no room for varying interpretation." The purpose of a bright-line rule is to produce predictable and consistent results in its application. As a new real estate agent, there are so many options for lead generation, marketing ideas, and training opportunities that it can become difficult to decide what to do first.

One such bright-line rule is to not spend any money until income has been earned. Print advertising costs money, so an agent who follows this bright-line rule and has not sold any homes yet would not engage in print advertising. This is one reason why new agents frequently employ open houses as a lead-generating opportunity. There is time involved, yet little or no monetary expense. To extend the concept further, this means an agent would engage in active prospecting activities that involve her time, rather than marketing opportunities that cost money.

As a new agent, one of the bright-line rules I followed was to view three homes each "working day." This is a standard that I continue today, well over a dozen years later. This predictable and consistent practice has reaped countless benefits. I quickly became knowledgeable about the market, which truly made me a neighborhood expert, not just a marketing tagline. It is a powerful lead-generating opportunity as I think of people who might be interested in the home or neighborhood. In addition, I touch base in a meaningful way with people who live nearby to find out if they know anyone who might want to live in the community.

The benefits to applying bright-line rules in an agent's real estate business are countless. When one wakes up in the morning, one can immediately get into productive activities rather than thinking, "What will I do today?" It is a form of leverage, as the agent uses the standard to create space. The habits themselves free the agent up so that there is energy and time to focus on higher-level thinking and opportunities.

Apply bright-line rules to your business as a tool for success!

SEASONS OF REAL ESTATE

There are many variables to the seasonal nature of real estate. Four seasons are represented in nature. Tourist season impacts those market areas that have a high concentration of people during certain times of the year, weather, and events. Tax season can affect buying and selling decisions. The commencement and ending of the school year are seasonal aspects that impact many in the marketplace. And then the end of the year influences investors and people whose urgency is tied to that part of the calendar.

The most obvious are the four seasons. For many markets, the spring selling season is the strongest, which can run from March through June. Those areas that experience the true natural seasons—the end of winter and the budding of new life—cause many people to consider making a home change. There is something about coming out of hibernation and one's cocoon for the winter that makes people want to go look at houses. Perhaps being cooped up during a snowstorm caused the family to realize that they have outgrown their home. Or maybe it is the shoveling of the snow that makes a widow realize that the home she raised her family in is just too much for her to maintain.

Families with children wanting to time their move during the summer months create urgency for many people to start the process in springtime. The peak moving season of the year is statistically from Memorial Day to Labor Day, according to industry data. This is for those people who want to make the transition while the kids are out of school. Many start the home search process as early as Super Bowl Sunday or Groundhog Day and put their own homes on the market soon after.

Throughout the tax season in the US, from the end of January through April 15, my CPA firm has "all hands on deck." A similar thing occurs in the real estate industry. It is like a farmer planting seeds in spring that will be harvested months later.

The next busiest time of the year for many markets is the fall through the end of the year for those people who aren't tied to the school calendar. Often after summer vacations are over and schedules have gotten back into a routine, people are ready to make a change.

The end of the year has a strong market presence as well. In fact, one of the busiest days of the year for home searches on the Internet is December 28! Truly, those people are ready for a new home for the New Year!

Determine the seasonal fluctuations of your market and leverage accordingly.

"WHERE EVERYBODY KNOWS YOUR NAME"

"Where Everybody Knows Your Name" is the memorable theme song to the 1980's hit television comedy series *Cheers*. This is a great theme song for real estate agents too. Remembering a person's name is one of the greatest compliments you can subtly give. There are numerous mnemonic devices for committing a person's name to memory.

One is the use of a physical location as a way to "tag" the person with that location. This provides a much "richer" memory source surrounding the person, which aids in recall. Usually recommended is to use a familiar location, such as one's kitchen or living room. What has worked for me is to use the customer's actual home. When introduced, ask the person where he lives. As a real estate agent with familiarity of the community, this is a quick way to associate the person's name with a neighborhood. The conversation can be richer if you know people who live in the neighborhood and make immediate connections. This also works as a great conversation starter. It enables you to introduce your profession as a real estate agent in a soft-sell manner.

Another way is to do a quick Internet search on the person as soon as you can. Numerous search resources abound: Google, Facebook, and LinkedIn are the primary ones I use. This enables me to see if we know any of the same people. Also, I can sometimes find a little bit more about them, their profession, where they are from, and where they currently live. Hobbies and interests often are displayed, which can make for excellent connecting conversations.

At a public real estate open house, agents often ask visitors to sign in on a guest register. Many times, attendees do not use the most legible handwriting. This is an opportunity to request gently that they spell their name for you. Some agents have found that digital sign-in programs make it more likely that people will "spell" their names correctly. Use this as an opportunity to find out something about people that can help you remember their names.

These words in the song are helpful to remember when hosting an open house: "There's one place in the world, where everybody knows your name, and they're always glad you came."

Establish the habit of knowing everybody's name.

ACTS OF OMISSION OR COMMISSION

My first real career job out of college was with a real estate development company in Dallas, Texas, an affiliate with Trammel Crow at the time. As a young woman, the interview process was a bit intimidating and yet decades later I still vividly recall a few key points that were made. One that stands out is something the senior vice president said to me: "Our best work as professionals is to do everything we can to not engage in any acts or errors by omission or commission." It turns out this principle is a core basic to business ethics.

Wow, you can see why this has stuck with me for more than three decades. It is truly one of those overarching principles on which one can build and grow a business. If one were to follow this guideline her entire life, it would be an amazing achievement.

As applied to real estate, an omission involves those acts that an agent should have done and did not. It could arise from the failure to recognize the need, the urgency, or the duty. As real estate agents are human, almost every broker in the United States requires agents to carry "errors and omissions" insurance. The insurance is to provide a safeguard for those situations in which an agent either makes a mistake or fails to act correctly. However, it does not cover acts of fraud or those situations in which the agent actually commits an act that is not professional. Those are acts of commission.

The legal and medical professions, as well as many religious traditions, all follow these standards. It has stood the test of time as a great barometer to use in making decisions, as well as determining a course of action.

Set as a standard to not engage in any acts or errors of omission or commission in your business dealings.

GO UP SWINGING

Calico Joe is a novel by John Grisham about baseball. In the book, when one of the ballplayers is heading to the batter's box to hit, he is told to "go up there swinging." In baseball jargon, this encouragement means to not just stand there and watch pitches fly by. It means to be the kind of player who makes something out of every pitch thrown—even if the pitches are not very good or are hard to swing at. The player goes up to the plate and makes something happen.

Baseball is as American as mom, apple pie, and home ownership. As a top real estate agent, I see the relationship between being a Realtor® who is proactive and the baseball player in Grisham's book. There is passion there; the agent is playing to win, not lose. Some agents and ballplayers just sit back and wait for the business or ball to come to them. An agent who "goes up there swinging" actively pursues all leads, even if it requires a great deal of work or research.

An example of "going up swinging" was a short-term rental need that was referred to our team from a preferred vendor. My business partner, Lizzy Conroy, took care of those people in such a professional manner that they in turn had her list a property owned by the family. That listing led to two neighbors also hiring Lizzy to represent them. One of the buyers purchased the lot to build a new home and was so impressed with her professionalism that he hired Lizzy for that transaction as well. Often the most important thing in baseball is to get on base, which can lead to more opportunity that eventually results in a score.

When representing a seller, the agent who "goes up there swinging" does more than just put a sign in the yard and the listing into the system. This professional is proactive and doesn't expect the house to sell on its own. The agent takes action to make something happen. Even when the market is difficult, even when the offers presented are low-balls, the agent "goes up there swinging" to make the best of what is presented.

Take the "go up there swinging" stance in your business!

TAKING A PAY CUT

Imagine the boss comes to you and says that the company needs you to take a 10 percent pay cut for the company to stay in business. How would that make you feel?

Now imagine you are a listing agent with a seller client. The feedback from buyers and agents indicates that the home is priced 10 percent above market. You believe that it is necessary to make a reduction in the list price in order to sell the home. A similar scenario occurs when a buyer presents what the seller feels is a low-ball offer, but which falls within the 10 percent range of the list price. In all likelihood, the reactions of the seller in both situations will be similar to the "pay cut."

The reason for this is that our brains quickly do the mental math and base what we are now getting on what we though we "had." When it is less than what we thought we had, we think loss and that the situation is spiraling negatively. When it is more than we expected, our brains quickly become accustomed to the new standard.

In many cases, this reaction occurs even when the outcome would be the same. Many times sellers want to price the home above market to leave "room for negotiation." An expectation has been created. Thus when offers are received at even what was originally anticipated, it still can have the feeling of being "less than."

The other side of the coin is sellers who price at or less than market value. If the home sells quickly for top dollar and possibly even escalates over the list price, often sellers wonder if they could have gotten more, that perhaps the home was underpriced.

There are three Ps that impact how fast and well a home sells for on the market: product, place, and price. The product is the architectural features and improvements of the home, which all go toward condition. Place is the location, which cannot be changed. Price is the easiest of the three to adjust and has the most immediate impact on the market.

It is the professional agent who informs sellers about the market and how it is likely to respond. In this way, they are prepared to "take a pay cut" on the price of the home if necessary.

Take the steps to prepare sellers with market data to price correctly.

GROUP BICYCLING BENEFITS

One of the most significant benefits of bicycling with a group is the opportunity to take advantage of drafting. Riding a bicycle appears to be a lone sport, as does being a real estate practitioner because most agents are independent contractors. The same principle of drafting can occur when agents work together with colleagues and other professionals. A few scenarios in which this phenomenon can apply are with a team, partnerships, office environment, or coaching/training and mastermind groups.

First, there is the camaraderie. When times are good, there are celebrations. When times are tough, there are friends and associates who will encourage as well as commiserate. In many ways, there is power in support and numbers.

When bicycling as a group, one of the major benefits is the ability to draft. Essentially this occurs when the riders take turns being the lead cyclist, who in effect breaks the wind. Every pedal stroke is much more effective. Real estate can become a 24/7 industry and agent burnout is common. Thus, being a part of a team or partnership in which agents take turns allows for a healthy balance of business as well as other responsibilities, along with recreation and leisure for recharging.

There are strategies in bicycling as a group, depending on the direction of the wind: headwind, crosswind, and tailwind. These have applications in real estate as well.

Riding during a headwind is one of the most difficult conditions, as the wind is in effect pushing against all forward motion. In real estate, this is when the market is very difficult and it is a constant struggle to get any deal done. Being a part of a group, an agent can strategize on how to survive down market cycles.

When bicycling during a crosswind, it is important to notice which direction the wind is blowing and to lean slightly into the wind. "Lean in" can be an effective strategy when the real estate market is behaving erratically. One technique is for members of the group to fan out and take turns moving to the front and then being behind. In real estate, it can be effective to have agents focus on different market segments to diversify.

"Enjoy the ride" is the mantra when cycling downhill and with tailwinds. Some riders use the opportunity to sprint and push beyond what they normally can achieve. It is important to remember to ride in control, as speed can lead to overconfidence and careless errors. This is true in the real estate industry. When the market is strong, some agents act as if it will last forever, particularly those who are new to the industry. Connecting with experienced colleagues provides the perspective to sustain real estate success.

---

*Incorporate the technique of drafting to achieve
success in your real estate practice.*

HIGHEST AND BEST USE

The concept of "highest and best use" originates from economics and is the principle under which a commodity or person must operate in order to achieve maximum productivity. Taxing authorities apply the concept to real estate to determine assessment values. It has also been incorporated into the appraisal process. The Appraisal Institute's definition is: "The reasonably probable and legal use of property that is physically possible, appropriately supported, and financially feasible, and that results in the highest value."

Thus, one must consider first the potential uses of a property, which represent the utility function of the real estate. The principle of substitution means examining what options are available. By way of example, almost all vacant land can be used as a dump or a park. To apply the definition, we have determined a possible use as a dump. Then one would consider if it is legal to operate a dump in that location, which includes whether it is appropriately supported. The financial feasibility of it would involve the preparation of a cost-benefit analysis.

There are multiple levels of real estate use, beginning with vacant land, residential, and all the way up to heavy commercial. Residential has subsets on the spectrum, from single-family homes on acreage to town homes and apartment or condominium buildings. Usually uses are mixed. One often finds in predominately residential communities different types of housing options. Additionally, frequently in residential areas there is retail shopping, schools, and public facilities such as libraries, police and fire stations, as well as green space and parks. There are grades of commercial uses as well. Office buildings are considered light commercial, and heavy commercial includes manufacturing and industrial, airports, shipping centers, and so forth.

Think about how areas are developed and if the property is truly at its "highest and best use." Are you at your "highest and best use"? When people apply this principle to their businesses and lives, it can be very powerful. Personally, I have found my calling in residential real estate sales. The reason is that in "mixed use" fashion it combines many of my strengths. Truly I am at my "highest and best use."

Determine applications for the principle of
"highest and best use" today in real estate and life.

MORTGAGE INTEREST DEDUCTION, CIRCA 1913

Mortgage interest deduction has been a part of American income tax system since 1913 — more than one hundred years of benefiting the American Dream of home ownership. It is one of the tax deductions frequently placed on the chopping block. What would happen to the average homeowner if this deduction was eliminated from the tax code? Many believe that it would have an immediate and significant impact on home values. It would definitely make home ownership less attractive.

The mortgage interest tax deduction matters! In 2016, the mortgage interest deduction is allowable for up to $1 million for a primary loan and $100,000 for a HELOC (Home Equity Line of Credit). The interest deduction gives owners the ability to "leverage" the funds attributed to the mortgage. This leverage then increases the affordability for the owner (of course, advise clients to consult a tax advisor about the requirements and to verify qualification).

This is particularly the case in market areas in which the cost of housing is expensive relative to the majority of the United States. It is not surprising to learn that in these high-cost market areas, the size of the mortgage interest deduction utilized by taxpayers is the highest. By correlation, this means that the areas of the United States that have high housing expenses will be disproportionately impacted by any changes to the tax code related to the mortgage interest tax deduction.

The National Association of Realtors® states its support of the deduction as follows: "Housing is the engine that drives the economy, and to even mention reducing the tax benefits of home ownership could endanger property values. Home prices, particularly in high-cost areas, could decline 15 percent if recommendations to convert the mortgage interest deduction to a tax credit are implemented."

Without the mortgage interest tax deduction, it will make home ownership more expensive. Any decrease of the allowable amount will have a substantial impact on the US economy. There is a saying: "So goes housing, so goes the economy." Owner-occupied homes are key to the strength of the housing market in the United States.

Understand how the mortgage interest deduction benefits your clients.

PLANT THE SEEDS

In a lot of ways, a real estate agent is like a farmer. In fact, the process of business development in a geographic location is commonly known as "farming." The business tends to have a seasonal nature to it, as well.

The springtime is when a number of homes go on the market, which for the real estate agent is a time to plant the seeds of business. The fall often can be a time of harvest—the sale and settlement of the business. In the summertime, the agent focuses on the watering and nurturing of clients, including proactive weeding by providing service. Tending to clients includes fending off pests to make sure the seeds have a chance to come to fruition. The hot summer months require labor that isn't for the faint of heart. In the winter months, the agent prepares the soil, her sphere of influence and past clients. It is then ripe for spring planting right around the corner.

The illustration is meant to be figurative, as every season for the professional agent requires her to plant, tend, nurture, harvest, and prepare for the cycle to occur again. Every season has a lesson to be learned in order to achieve a more bountiful harvest. An area of focus is to increase the quality and quantity of the seeds that are planted.

In Ecclesiastes 11:4, it is written: "Farmers who wait for perfect weather never plant. If they watch every cloud, they never harvest." This means that the agent should not wait for a perfect market. It means he should not be discouraged by every difficulty that comes along. He should do the work regardless of the outcome. It is those agents who take action who are successful in spite of the market and the difficulties.

The amazing thing about planting real estate seeds is that one seed can lead to a bountiful harvest or multiple opportunities. An example was a Sunday afternoon when I was out viewing homes at public opens. It is part of my weekly soil-tending to keep current on the market. Little did I realize that I had walked into what effectively was a FSBO (for sale by owner). As a commercial broker, he decided because of his license to sell his own home. We chatted for a few minutes and I casually said that if he decided he was tired of doing it himself and wanted a professional, full-time agent to do the work for him, to give me a call.

The seed I planted in his mind took hold and a couple weeks later he did call me. I sold that $1 million home. Yet that's not all! He referred me to his neighbor; I sold his $1.7 million home and an $800,000 investment property. The original client called me a few years later and I sold his $2.4 million home when he decided to downsize. The buyers of the original home contacted me too, as they were impressed with the way I represented the seller side and hired me as their agent. I sold that home again for $1.1 million and sold them a $1.6 million home. That one seed led to a harvest of around $8.6 million worth of business. All of that bounty came from one seed.

Plant the seeds. Tend, nurture, harvest, and prepare
to build and grow your business.

CROSS-TRAINING

At one time, being able to claim one multitasked well was considered a desirable skill. Recent research has determined that what really occurs is task *switching*, that the brain really can only pay attention to one thing at a time. Yet there are occasions when one has to be able to manage more than one important thing equally well.

An example that comes to mind is a mother who has more than one child. The mother loves and cares for her children, and she meets their needs as required. In real estate, the scenario is when the agent has more than one client. It seems obvious, but in order for a business to grow the agent has to take on more clients. And in some ways, the second and subsequent clients may wonder if they will receive the undivided attention that they want and need if the agent's time and energy is spread too thin.

Being able to perform two separate functions at the same time is a key aspect to core physical training. For example, my personal trainer will have me stand on one foot while also doing bicep curls. This type of training strengths the core, the standing leg, and the arm muscles all at the same time. It is efficient, but more than that, it expands my capabilities. I truly did not know the breadth of my ability until I went beyond my comfort zone. It took a coach to push me to do the work necessary to go to the next level.

The long-distance swimmer and motivational speaker Diana Nyad, in her book, *Find a Way*, states: "It looks like a solitary sport, but it's a team." As most agents are independent contractors, it appears to be a lone profession. Yet at some point in business development, she determines she has more business than she can handle on her own.

Implementation of systems is one of the first strategies successful agents employ to become effective and efficient in providing superior customer service to multiple clients. Not wanting to turn away opportunity, she turns to leveraging people as the next key to success. Some choices available are to hire staff members, connect with a partner, or team up with other agents to have more people available to serve the client needs. Cross-training is beneficial for all team members so that standards of service are upheld.

As we have built the team and it has grown into a real estate business, we have employed all of these strategies. On occasion, a customer will ask about the number of listings we currently have. The question behind the question is: "Will you be able to take care of me?" The assurance is in selling the cross-training principle, that in fact a team can be able to better meet customer-service needs.

Establish cross-training principles to provide quality standards of service for clients.

STARTING POINT MATTERS—THE RULE OF THREE

APRIL 18

The "rule of three" negotiating strategy maintains that there are extreme ways to proceed that are at the opposite end of the spectrum, and then there is a middle ground. This holds true in the manner in which sellers and buyers come to an agreement on a market price, as well: auction, price high and make cuts, or price with "room to negotiate," in which parties banter back and forth until a final price is arrived at.

The greatest risk in pricing too low is the possibility of leaving money on the table. That is why at some auctions a reserve number is established. To truly have an auction, there has to be more than one interested party. The price starts low and goes higher, as there are parties willing to increase the bids until the transaction is consummated.

In an open market, the forces of supply and demand are extremely strong, similar to that of gravity. Thus, if a property is truly underpriced, the market will respond, as it finds value. This situation can lead to bidding wars and multiple offers.

The other side of the spectrum is the seller who prices high for the market. Then if there are no "takers," he makes adjustments to the price until the market is arrived at. Many times with relocation companies, shorts sales, and bank-owned properties, price adjustments are scheduled to occur on a regular, frequent basis until an offer is received. In these instances, the owner is a real "seller" and not in the business to hold onto real estate at a price unrealistic for the current market. Quick divestiture of the property is the priority.

The starting point matters because if the parties are too far apart, they often tire and give up. Also, people have an aversion against countering themselves, as they should. If the seller starts too high and the buyer comes in too low, the negotiations can stalemate. To move forward, one of the parties may find the only option is to counter himself.

The strategy that is in the middle ground is more typical in the sale of a personal residence. This is where the seller starts the list price at the high end of the range, which invites the buyer to "make an offer." At that juncture, the parties negotiate the value to obtain a market price. The challenge is compelling buyers to make an offer if they perceive the price is too high. That is where pricing correctly is the most beneficial strategy to the seller in the final picture.

There is a psychological effect that occurs when little or no negotiation occurs. That is, one or both of the parties have in the back of their mind that they could have achieved a better outcome if they had been more aggressive. Always remember "quid pro quo," that is, "something for something" to assure the best negotiation results.

*Use a strong negotiation strategy to help buyer
and seller clients achieve the best results.*

HOBBY OR BUSINESS?

Newly licensed real estate agents enter the industry every year on a part-time basis or as a second career. Many have been encouraged to "try" real estate because they have always loved people and looking at houses. I too fell into that category in the beginning. My husband was the primary breadwinner for the family as a trade association executive. As my main responsibility to the family was raising our children, my income was supplementary.

It is interesting to note that the IRS distinguishes between an enterprise that is a hobby and one that is a business. There are a number of criteria for operating as a business, the most significant being that the operation earns a profit. The IRS provides for the possibility that there may be some lean years. Thus it presumes that a profit will be made in at least three out of the last five years. Those efforts that do not meet the criteria are considered a hobby.

Our daughter graduated from Dickinson College in Pennsylvania. In the fall, during family weekend, we enjoyed attending the community farmers' market and craft show on the town's main street. The merchandise varied from food to arts and crafts and everything in between. The booths that operated for profit were readily apparent; clearly those proprietors engaged in a business enterprise.

This seems to be a viable model for real estate agents, as well. One should earn a profit at a minimum three out of five years; otherwise the agent is really engaging in a hobby. What often happens is that an agent falls into the loop of generating a lead and then consults to sell the lead. Then she repeats the two-step process. To go beyond this requires creating a sustainable business. This is where successful agents implement the connect to build and grow part of success in real estate. The sweet spot of success model offers the systems and tools to transform an agent's efforts into a real estate business. If I can do it, you can too!

Implement the connect to build and grow
success tips to create a sustainable business.

DID YOU ASK FOR THE BUSINESS?

This is a question I remind myself of continuously. My natural inclination is that I do not want to be perceived as pushy, particularly around friends, relatives, neighbors, and associates. It is a fear of mine that when people see me, they will quickly want to turn and go in the other direction. This concern was compounded by a mortgage broker at a church our family previously attended. She was so aggressive that literally I could see the reaction on people's faces as she approached.

And yet, I am in sales, and it is my obligation to ask for the business. If I fail to do so, then perhaps customers may think that I am too busy or do not want to work with them. An example of this scenario is that my husband and I met with a CPA firm for an evaluation of our financial situation. The CPA firm provided wise counsel and offered several excellent suggestions on what we could and should be doing to improve our financial situation. And yet, the CPA never followed up. So I was left wondering, "Did he really want my business?" Perhaps he was too busy and didn't need me as a client.

In the James Bond movie, *License to Kill*, the leading lady pleads to her lover in the ballad, "If you asked me to." The words are:

If you asked me to

I just might change my mind

And let you in my life forever.

These words remind me to ask for the business. The customer just might change her mind and let me in her life. Perhaps she is waiting for me, too.

Not too long ago I was previewing homes on a Sunday afternoon when I saw a longtime friend who lives across the street. It was lovely to briefly visit and catch up. Afterward I sent a handwritten note to offer my services should she ever be in the market to buy or sell a home or know someone who is. Shortly after, she contacted me and expressed her thanks for my note and reaching out. She thought that I would be too busy to deal with homes in her price range and did in fact have a real estate need to both sell and buy. This reinforced the concept that it is important to personally ask for the business.

Another practical application is to bring listing paperwork to all appointments with sellers in the event that they are ready to sign. It means also bringing a contract packet on all buyer consultations as preparation in the event the client is ready to write an offer. And it means reminding myself as I generate leads on a daily basis: "Did I ask for the business?"

Make it a practice to ask for the business!

IF IT WAS EASY . . .

If they were to admit it, there are moments in almost all professional real estate agents' careers when they want to quit. It just gets too hard. A deal has just fallen through. A client has just gotten very upset over something that was out of the agent's control. A customer who the agent had been working with for some time decides to "try" another agent. Or it is something bigger—the market has crashed, interest rates are high and rising, inventory is low, or inventory is high. And the agent has just grown weary of the effort.

At times like these, I find it helpful to remember the scene in *A League of their Own*, in which one of the lady ballplayers has decided to quit and go home. She doesn't need the headache of baseball and playing doesn't provide the rewards it once did. The coach in the movie, played by Tom Hanks, is surprised because he thought she had the makings of a really good ballplayer. He states: "It's supposed to be hard. If it were easy, everyone would do it."

And that can be the case with really good agents, too. At times they hit a slump. That is when it is helpful to have a mentor, partner, a respected team member, or a broker remind you that, like baseball, real estate can get inside you. That person helps you remember the successes when you lit up after getting that tough deal done with the relocation company. The time a family was able to buy a home with a yard where the kids could play because of your strategic negotiations. The widower whom you helped move on after the loss of his wife. And the young professional who now enjoys the benefits of home ownership because of your hard work.

And if that doesn't help you reconsider, then remember the lines in the movie: That you are not like everyone. You are a professional, with the good and the difficult clients, through the easy and hard market cycles.

Develop relationships with people who will cheer you on through market slumps and challenging situations.

HOUSE VERSUS HOME

A house is a physical place, even to the level of being a commodity. Some residences are more easily interchangeable than others. "Home," on the other hand, is a word that is so much richer with meaning. A house becomes a home when people live there and feelings are associated with the place and memories are created. Thus a home can be both a physical place and an emotional place.

There are hundreds of songs written with the theme of "home." In the song by Edward Sharpe and the Magnetic Zeros, the chorus speaks of these feelings: "Ah, home, let me go home; home is wherever I'm with you." This illustrates that the idea of home as being wherever the people we care about are. Thus when there is change, it is often felt at a deep level. This occurs whether the situation is commonly viewed as positive or negative.

The Holmes-Rahe Stress Inventory provides a list of situations that are known to cause stress. In the top ranks are many scenarios that coincide with the buying and selling of a home: death of a spouse, divorce, marital separation, death of a close family member, marriage, gaining a new family member (birth, adoption, older adult moving in), taking on a mortgage, change in residence, and change in school. In many cases, there is a combination of several stress-inducing situations. For example, someone who has lost a loved one often changes his residence around the same time, which will increase the likelihood of high stress levels.

This is what makes the relationship between agents and their clients in residential real estate transactions so vital. Professional agents are mindful of the underlying emotions associated with the process. It is not just the physical nature of being a house—it is a home in so many ways.

*Be mindful of clients' feelings associated with
buying and selling a home.*

THE "WIMPY" STRATEGY

In the classic cartoon *Popeye*, one of the main characters is affectionately known as Wimpy. Wimpy is a robust and jolly man who loves food and is particularly fond of hamburgers. As he is very frugal, one of the classic scenes is of Wimpy getting others at the diner to pay for his food. The line "I'll gladly pay you Tuesday for a hamburger today" has appeared as a punch line in several modern American sitcoms. Some consider Wimpy to be financially irresponsible. Another way to look at it is that he is a skilled negotiator.

In a way, real estate sales that are paid on commission are based on the Wimpy scenario of payment. Real estate agents and brokers expend untold time and resources with the assurance that payment will occur by the seller if a buyer is secured and settlement occurs. There are situations, to be sure, in which the agent puts in considerable effort and for myriad reasons a sale is not made and thus no commission is paid. Just like Wimpy, the hamburger was eaten, but no money exchanged hands on Tuesday.

Another way the Wimpy strategy is employed is that of the promise for future opportunity and compensation. Business partnerships are often entered into with the promise of payment later in time if the enterprise is successful. In those situations, there are a lot of hamburgers eaten today in the hopes of payment on Tuesday.

One other scenario is that of repeat clients. Many agents offer to reduce their commission on multiple transactions. For example, on the purchase transaction a full commission will be earned, with the promise that on the sale of the client's home there will be a discount applied. Sometimes clients change their minds and decide to rent the home or just not sell it, particularly in an off-market. It behooves the agent to employ Wimpy's strategy and make any reduction to commission apply to future transactions. In that way, you are sure to receive a hamburger today.

Find ways to utilize the Wimpy strategy to your benefit in negotiations.

"YOU'VE GOT TO GET UP EVERY MORNING"

Success thinking begins every morning. If you are blessed to be alive, you have to get up anyway, so why not with a song on your lips? Success thoughts that resonate with me are those in "Beautiful" by Carole King:

You've got to get up every morning with a smile on your face
And show the world all the love in your heart

The truly beautiful thing about this attitude is that most people you come into contact with will mirror your disposition. The words in the song express the truth of this outcome:

Then people gonna treat you better
You're gonna find, yes, you will

Then it becomes a self-fulfilling prophecy:

That you're beautiful as you feel

The real estate profession has its share of stress and frustration. Sellers can be difficult and unrealistic about how to price their homes. Buyers have been known to run agents all over the place to see homes and end up either not buying or using an agent they just met at an open house. Industry, lending, and contractual requirements are continually being adapted and modified, which makes the process of buying and selling a home more challenging for the parties. The Internet exponentially increases competition and changes at such a rapid pace that it becomes a full-time effort to stay current.

Yet in all of the frustration, there is also abundant opportunity and the potential for great accomplishment. You must do the things you think you cannot do. Make it a part of your daily habit to not only overcome the negative influences, but to actively pursue the positive. Leadership author and coach John Maxwell proclaims: "If you want to see where someone develops into a champion, look at their daily routine." Success thinking and a growth mindset are habits that can be learned and developed.

You do have a choice. If I can do it, you can too. If you need encouragement today, I suggest you do as I do and break into song. It will raise your spirits to carry on your success thinking, activities, and vision.

Choose to start every day with a growth mindset
and intend to take positive action toward the future.

PEDAL TO THE METAL

Job one for the professional real estate agent is to prospect for clients. Until there is a lead, the agent truly has nothing to do. This situation applies to other professions and industries as well. Lawyers and CPAs call their leads clients, doctors and dentists refer to them as patients, churches refer to them as parishioners, and the hospitality industry knows them as guests or visitors.

Once an agent has either a buyer or seller client to work with, then all too typically the agent pulls his foot off of the accelerator or stops lead generating all together. The reason often is that he gets busy selling the client and the processing of the transaction to settlement, which are no doubt important tasks as well. Yet the distinction between those agents who sustain success year after year and those who experience great variance in their business cycles is the consistency of prospecting.

The reason is that once the momentum is achieved in anything, then it is much easier to sustain. Letting up on the gas can slow down the engine to a point that it requires maximum effort to regain the speed once had. Gary Keller, founder of Keller Williams, in his book, *The Millionaire Real Estate Agent,* states: "Nothing is more important to your sales career than prospective buyers and sellers."

It is also tempting to put the process on cruise control. Cruise control on a car still requires a thinking person, even though some features are available that are precursors to self-driving cars. The danger of cruise control is complacency. The engine maintains speed, yet still requires someone in control behind the wheel in order to navigate a detour up ahead. Another scenario is when the car is dangerously close to veering off the road or into traffic. The corollaries to a real estate agent's business are if the market shifts and one should "step on the gas" to get ahead or take the business in another direction. Or if the lead-generation method on cruise control is being derailed because that market niche has changed significantly, such as before and after the era of short sales and bank foreclosures.

There are some agents who take their foot off the accelerator in fear that there will be too many leads. Should that occur, it is an opportunity to leverage, delegate, and apply management skills. When there is more business than the agent can handle, options include referring out the business and other top-grade opportunities.

Putting the "pedal to the metal" is action that has urgency; it is a verb. Lead generation will always be top priority in the professional real estate agent's business.

Keep the "pedal to the metal" in your lead-generation activities!

SUPPLY AND DEMAND ARE LIKE GRAVITY

Supply and demand are like gravity because they are both extremely strong forces. By definition, gravity is the natural force that tends to cause physical things to move toward each other. Overcoming gravity is possible, but to do so requires a significantly stronger counterforce. Supply and demand is an economic model, whereby the buyer's desire for a commodity, product, or service owned by a seller determines the price in a competitive market. The force is competition, and it is, in my view, as strong if not stronger than the force of gravity.

It never ceases to amaze me the phenomenon that occurs when more than one buyer wants to purchase a house. As soon as there is competition, the desirability of the home increases, and the competitive force is magnetic. That is one benefit to having public open houses that perhaps sellers do not always consider—if there is more than one buyer group present, and they see that there are other buyers interested, it often increases the desirability of the house. A seller client of mine asked if he should allow two agents to schedule to see his home at the same time. I said, "Absolutely." It showed that there was interest in the home by other people.

The market story is that action creates reaction. Projections and comparative market analysis provide only so much insight. It is actually being on the market that truly determines whether there is demand. That is why when people inquire about pocket listings, I share that being on the open market is the best determiner of value. It becomes apparent very quickly whether the calculations made are in line with the market and thus the pricing is correct.

An area with high demand for homes is always coupled with low supply of inventory. Economists and other experts consider a balanced market in real estate to be when there is about a six-month supply available. More than a six-month supply is considered a buyer's market, and less than that is considered a seller's market. So it is no surprise that a market segment with low supply and high demand experiences quick sales with multiple offers, escalation clauses, and limited if no contract contingencies.

In the market segments in which purchasers have a lot of choice, there is usually downward pressure on price. It is common in those scenarios to find that homes are on the market considerably longer, waiting for more buyers to enter the market. Price will solve this situation; at some price point there is always a buyer.

Use "supply and demand are like gravity" to explain to clients about the strength of the market forces.

SPINNING PLATES

In variety and acrobatic shows, often there is the spinning plate act. You have a visual already in your mind—of the performer using the gyroscopic effect and setting one plate spinning on a long pole. Then off to the next one and so on until the first spinning plate starts to wobble and requires attention.

This is a feat that many real estate agents attempt. It is that last spinning plate, though, that can cause all of them to come crashing down. The challenge is that there are so many opportunities, and some of them are good. The important consideration is if the activity is effective and if it is sustainable by the agent.

In the world of prospecting, options abound: hosting open houses; door knocking in a target neighborhood; connecting via social media, which has myriad choices; phone calls to both cold and warm leads; blogging; events; seminars; client parties; digital marketing; newsletters; handwritten notes; working with investors or flippers; purchasing leads from Internet sites; developing relationships with relocation companies; mass letter-writing campaigns; and pursuing expired or withdrawn seller listings. There are countless other options available—this list is not complete by any means.

Agents who build and grow a business focus on a few key strategies that go deep rather than wide. To keep with the analogy, it would look like successfully setting two plates in motion and sustaining the effort for at least one year. The benefit to this practice is that the agent can hold the activity accountable and determine whether it is actually an effective means of lead generation.

It is easy to find examples of agents who are successful at deep prospecting. An agent in our office focuses on the first-time homebuyer market by conducting seminars for people who currently live in apartment buildings. One agent works primarily with investors who buy and flip, and others who buy to hold and rent. Another agent has long-term relationships with relocation companies and has become an expert in that niche.

Now, each of these agents can confidently start another activity in motion. Only a very experienced, high-level performer would attempt to set two new plates spinning simultaneously. Agents would be wise to consider only one strategy at a time. Once it is set in motion and determined to be successful, then commence another one.

Set one new lead-generation activity successfully
in motion prior to starting another one.

WHO IS THE AVERAGE REAL ESTATE AGENT?

According to the National Association of Realtors®, the average real estate agent is a fifty-seven-year old woman with some college education who is a homeowner herself. It's interesting to note that in 2016, I turned fifty-seven on April 28, and I am a homeowner. Thus, per the data compiled by the NAR, I fit the profile of the average real estate agent.

Many women turn to real estate as a profession once children reach school age and they have more time to devote to work. The benefit of a flexible schedule and the potential of earning significant money make this an attractive profession for this demographic. This is my story, as well.

Others find themselves as a primary breadwinner. A number of agents enter the field of real estate as a second or later career. There tends to be not as many young adults, as it is challenging to build a business based only on commission income unless there is another source of income.

Whether you fit the profile of an average real estate agent or not, discover what you can learn from your fellow colleagues. There is much knowledge to be gained from both those who are above and below you in the industry.

Real estate professionals with more experience offer knowledge, skills, and abilities that have been acquired by time on task. They provide perspective and wise counsel. The lessons I have learned at the feet of the masters have been invaluable. Often these agents have stories to tell and are happy to share their wisdom whenever asked.

Those new in the industry, and thus perhaps younger in age, offer a fountain of inspirational ideas. New agents are often more innovative and pioneer new practices. One of the millennial-age agents in our office was instrumental in implementing the digital signature application. That one tool has saved me countless hours in not having to fax contracts, in addition to providing better-quality documents. Agents new to the business often possess enthusiasm and drive that sometimes those who have been around a while have lost.

There is much to gain from having colleagues on both ends of the spectrum. Embrace the benefits of the bookend effect of learning from those before and after you in the business.

*Seek to learn from those with more experience
and agents newer to the industry.*

GLASS CEILINGS AND PEAK PRICES

The most common usage of "glass ceiling" is in employment terminology. It typically refers to women and minorities. The phenomenon occurs most often in the corporate world and describes the situation in which an employee has hit the top of the income-earning and advancement potential. It is an invisible barrier, and yet very real to the parties affected. It is a rare occurrence to break through the glass ceiling.

In real estate, streets, neighborhoods, and communities have "glass ceilings" as well. There is a saying that one doesn't want to own the most expensive house in the neighborhood. Of course, there is always a most expensive house. Buyers by nature do not want to overpay. In order for prices to rise, someone has to pay more than the last most expensive home. And yet buyers resist being the first one to break the peak price.

Further, appraisers establish value based on comparable properties that have sold. Evaluation methods then tend to keep prices from rising above the most recent data available.

The scenario when the peak price barrier is most easily breached is during a rapidly rising market. This occurs during a seller's market when inventory is really low relative to demand. Most typically, there are multiple offers and escalation clauses. These types of markets push prices up as buyers offer more money in order to be able to compete. Further, buyers are more likely to forego contingencies such as financing and appraisals.

In a comparative market analysis, it is helpful to determine when the street, type of home, neighborhood, or area last was at peak prices. Next, look to see the history of pricing to determine where the pricing is relative to peak. This is the best indicator of whether it is possible to break through the next glass ceiling.

The professional agent follows the market trends and watches for the cycles. In this way, she can best counsel her clients on pricing matters.

Follow market trends to be aware of glass ceilings and times of peak prices.

AN EMPTY ROOM
IS AN OPPORTUNITY

Inside Out is a Disney Pixar movie about emotions and how they affect behavior. The main character, Riley, moves across the country with her parents. When the family arrives at what will be their new home in San Francisco, she runs upstairs full of excitement to see her new room. The emotion "sadness" projects what a disappointment the room is because there is nothing there. The emotion "joy" kicks in full of energy and exclaims that she once heard that an "empty room is an opportunity." And so it can be if one makes that paradigm shift.

The home staging industry has influenced American real estate sales by its marketing message that a professionally staged home sells at a higher price and often more quickly. And that can be true in many situations. Most owners benefit from professional staging services, and our team offers them to our clients. Yet there are those people who prefer the vacant space, the open room to visualize their own life in that home. In the words of Shakespeare in *Hamlet*: "For there is nothing either good or bad that thinking makes it so." It is how the situation is framed as to whether someone views it as a benefit or a detriment.

There is no statistical evidence that provides what portion of the home-buying population falls into each category. Experience would say it is about fifty-fifty. About one-half of people benefit from having a home staged so that they can visualize placement of furniture and accessories. People are most often persuaded by the lifestyle presented if it fits with their own needs and dreams. One thing is for certain—space overflowing with furniture and stuff appears cluttered and prevents a buyer from being able to see the possibilities. The other one-half benefits from having an empty room to create and envision their own lives there. Thus, my recommendation to clients is that we do what works best for their situation and needs.

There is also the broader interpretation of "an empty room is an opportunity." When a person has space to think and dream, then there exists the opportunity to create something better than before. Thus, it is important to keep some space available so that there is room for growth and creativity. Make that paradigm shift in your business to connect to build and grow your success vision.

Embrace the view that an empty room is an
opportunity for clients and your business.

ONE-HIT WONDER OR PROFESSIONAL?

The concept of "one-hit wonder" comes from the music industry. It is those artists, songs, or both that only made it to the top forty once. And there are "double one-hit wonders" too—those who could do it for a second time. Yet it is a true professional who achieves the repetition of success. This same scenario plays out in the real estate industry.

There are agents who can successfully sell one or even a couple of homes. There are those who can have one or two good years. The people who repeat the actions and achieve the outcomes of success—those are the ones we recognize as professionals. This is particularly evident during shifting markets. In rising markets, there is increased competition. In downward markets, there is often less business to go around and keeping transactions together can be a challenge. Even in "normal" markets, it takes commitment to do the work, day in and day out, delivering excellence to customers and clients.

There are clues to success, which are most often found in those who have achieved the level of a professional. In most cases, those agents can point to repeatable habits, systems, strategies, and behaviors that led to their success. Reading this book is but one hallmark of a professional. True professionals are life-long learners and consistently and frequently take part in personal and business development.

Take the steps today to be a professional rather than a one-hit wonder.

CATCH BUYERS AND SELLERS WHEN YOU CAN!

The movie *Catch Me If You Can* is an American crime drama based on a true story. The title reminds me that real estate agents should seek to catch buyers and sellers when they can! In order to be selected, an agent needs to be easily found and top of mind.

Houses are, in most cases, the most expensive asset people acquire and sell. Due to that reason, many customers choose to work with a trusted advisor to assist in the process. A common source is a referral from someone who has had personal experience with the agent.

Sources of recommendations can be from friends, relatives, associates, and neighbors (FRAN). This is an easy acronym to remember. The objective for the agent is to be front of mind so when someone expresses a real estate need, a referral will take place.

Another strategy many customers employ is to determine which real estate agents have been successful in the area. Past performance is no guarantee of future results, yet it is the best likelihood. An agent who has worked in the community knows the value of the location, the model of the home, and the neighborhood attributes. Along the same lines, real estate agents who live in a community often have a vested interest to provide top-notch customer service and keep prices strong. Many agents meet customers by being involved in the community through chambers, faith-based organizations, children's schools, arts and theatre programs, and volunteer organizations.

There are numerous marketing efforts that an agent can pursue to be well known in a community. She can host public and neighborhood open houses. She can knock on doors in order to meet the homeowners and sometimes renters who may be in the market to buy soon. Postcards that announce "just listed" and "just sold," newsletters, and market studies are all marketing pieces that capture attention and demonstrate that the agent is a producer.

Then there are the customers who start their search online. One of the agents on our team secured a listing because the sellers saw a blog about the neighborhood on our website. The sellers searched for agents who were familiar with that community and found the blog. Working with an agent with a hyper-local focus was important to them. The key to success in real estate is to commit to lead generation to catch buyers and sellers when you can.

Seek to catch buyers and sellers when you can!

NEGOTIATIONS 101

Truly everyone negotiates all the time; they may just not be aware of it. This hit home for me when our son was three years old and I was pregnant with our daughter. At the time, I was completing my Master's degree at Southern Methodist University in Dallas at night. By day I was a mother at home.

One of the required courses in the Cox School of Business was on negotiation. Teams were graded on mock-negotiation presentations on the outcome achieved for the client. I was up against people who were negotiating full time in business, government, and professional environments. Who was I to know anything . . . I stayed home all day with a strong-minded, red-headed little boy. Turns out my son had honed my techniques after all, as I earned our team the top points. The experiences in my life that occurred organically were the basics of a key negotiation strategy.

First, I discovered how to determine the BATNA (Best Alternative to Negotiated Agreement) for all parties. This occurs with open dialogue to create advantageous and productive courses of action. Know that people intuitively move toward gain and pleasure and away from pain and loss. Most people's BATNA falls along their gain-pain continuum. Create "win-win" solutions. A common negotiation technique is to "meet in the middle." It includes protecting one's interests while still working to achieve objectives that are acceptable to the other party.

In crucial conversations, recognize that there are three essential options: accept, counter, or walk away. To keep cool in the face of pressure, remember who is the professional and, in my case, the adult. This turns out to be a key strategy—it gives the brain space to consider options. Just because the other party has "bad manners" does not mean you need to succumb to that level. Retain a calm demeanor throughout for the most effective outcome. Strong and passionate emotions can lead to great things if the energy is channeled appropriately.

Judy Garland said: "Always be a first-rate version of yourself, instead of a second-rate version of somebody else." The "rest of the story" is that our son Drew is now a rock-star commercial real estate broker. Our family affectionately calls him "Karen on steroids." So not only did I learn how to negotiate with him, he honed some amazing skills negotiating with me. Today, on his birthday, this is a proud mom doing a "shout out" to honor his achievements.

Hone the skills you have to achieve the best negotiation outcome for your clients.

WINNER WINNER CHICKEN DINNER

The exclamation "winner winner chicken dinner" is one that can be heard in casinos when a player has met with success. The origins are from Las Vegas back in the day when a three-piece chicken dinner with vegetable cost $2, the same amount of the standard bet. Thus, winning the bet meant that you could buy yourself a chicken dinner.

Successful real estate agents incorporate celebrations with their clients, in the office and beyond. This can be done with words of affirmation, gifts, celebratory meals, parties, events, and traditions. A spirit of positive mojo boosts morale for team members and other agents, and creates self-motivation. This type of environment is known to take people to even greater levels of achievement.

Words of affirmation always create positive energy. For example, when I deliver an offer to a seller client, the first words of the e-mail or in the conversation are "Congratulations!" Even if the offer isn't everything the seller wanted, all offers are good offers if managed properly by the agent, as they are a "bird in the hand." With buyers, when their offer has been accepted or the parties have come to an agreement on repairs on a home inspection, be sure to take time to recognize the accomplishment. All people thrive on affirmative acknowledgement of efforts and achievements.

Gifts show appreciation in a tangible way. Settlement is an opportune time to present a gift to maintain a positive client-agent relationship. End-of-year gifts, too, are a means to touch base and thank a client for the business or referral. Cupcakes or treats to celebrate birthdays for allied resources, other agents, and colleagues are always welcome! Meals, parties, and events are ways to spend quality time with customers and clients. Many agents host special client-appreciation events; ideas include sporting events, golf tournaments, spa days, private theater movie showings, hosting a breakfast with Santa, charity fundraisers, and concerts. Ideas abound on how to celebrate and thank past clients.

Small traditions to increase motivation around the office include doing a "happy dance" or "high five" when a referral is received; ringing a gong when a contract has been ratified; and having a silly slogan like "winner winner chicken dinner" when someone has hit a jackpot, such as monthly prospecting goals. Progress is often made in lots of small steps, as well as leaps. Celebrations take every-day business from a world of black & white to Technicolor™.

Incorporate traditions of celebration with clients and business partners.

IT'S NOT ABOUT YOU

As a professional real estate agent, it is important to remember that it's not about you. The Carly Simon song, "You're So Vain," laments that the partner is so vain that he probably thinks the song is about him. In the real estate transaction, the "song" is not about the agent. It is about the buyers' desire to purchase a home that meets their needs. It is about the sellers' objective to be able to settle and move on to their next residence in a timely fashion.

Real estate agents often become an integral part of clients' lives as they go through the process of the transaction. And in that journey together, sometimes agents share what is going on in their personal lives. Relationship-building is a key part of earning the confidence of customers and clients. Just keep in mind that the professional and business aspects to the transaction are to take precedence.

An application is a story that sellers shared with me on a listing appointment when I queried whether they planned to contact the agent who sold them the home. Apparently, at the time they were buying their home the agent was building a new home of her own. It felt to them that her focus was on the construction and the selections for her home. The clients felt as if their transaction took second fiddle and that left a bad impression.

Clients care about what's in it for them. That means sell the benefits. For example, our team hires a professional photography company to shoot the photos for our listings. According to statistics from the National Association of Realtors®, nine out of ten buyers start their search on the Internet. Thus, the benefit to the seller client of an agent who employs a professional photographer with high-quality photos is increased exposure to the greatest number of potential buyers. Keep in mind the customer has in the back of his mind, "So what does this mean to me?"

Remember, it is important to be conscientious when you are in someone's home viewing a property with clients or previewing on your own. A little courtesy goes a long way. If you are running late or the client decides not to see the home, be sure and contact the sellers and let them know. Perhaps they have young children who need to be fed and put to bed. Or maybe they are circling the block with the dog in the car. Having a home on the market active for sale has enough inconvenience without adding inconsideration by the agent.

The buying and selling of residential real estate often involves becoming intimately involved in people's lives. This is not Monopoly money we are playing with. Put the client's interests first by remembering, "The song is not about you."

Be certain the focus is on the clients' needs and situations.

SECRETS OF LEAD GENERATION

My secret to success in lead generation can be summed up with these words: "The power of persistent, positive, professional, polite phoning and follow-through pays off!" This mantra is key for success as a real estate agent. Let's unpack these words by considering them in definition form.

Power is the ability to do something or to act in a particular way. Persistence is to firmly continue in a course of action in spite of difficulty or opposition. Positive is affirmative, or of constructive quality or attribute. Professional means a paid occupation rather than a hobby or pastime. Polite is to have or show behavior that is respectful and considerate of other people. Phoning is to give someone a call. Follow-through is the act of continuing a plan, project, scheme, or the like to its completion. Payoff is to receive money for services rendered.

The idea is to just do the "Ps" and not be tied to the outcome. The results, I have found, come from the consistency. It is like the "Energizer Bunny"—it keeps going and going and going. As inspiration, I keep one of the pink icons, complete with a drum, on my desk.

Agents ask me under what conditions I would consider not contacting someone. First, if the party is under a representation agreement with another broker, then it would be unethical to do so. And second, if they truly have asked me to stop. To quote the movie, *The Wolf of Wall Street*, I stay in touch until the customer "buys or dies."

---

*Commit to follow the "Ps" lead-generation practice
today and the next day and so on.*

"NEW YORK, NEW YORK"—VERSE 2

The chorus of the Frank Sinatra song, "New York, New York"—"If I can make it there, I'm gonna make it anywhere" has an application in real estate investment. If a market has been successful and proven strong in value, it follows that properties in similar markets should perform as well.

For example, one residential neighborhood may present strong fundamentals in terms of superior schools and access to the city center. It should follow that an adjoining neighborhood with similar attributes would be a good investment.

A community in a metro area offers quality restaurants and shopping, walkability, and nightlife. A region with similar amenities should "make it as well," following the words of Sinatra.

This is how developers determine the area that is to be the next "in" community. By watching what works in one location, one can determine the core factors that make for success in another neighborhood. In *The New Rules of Real Estate*, the founders of Zillow, CEO Spencer Rascoff and chief economist Stan Humphries, address the correlation between the location of Starbucks and home values. This "Frappuccino Effect™" is the fuel for appreciation. In an updated version of the book, it was noted that homes near Trader Joe's and Whole Foods tend to experience the same halo phenomenon.

Builders look for these fundamentals as well, particularly when considering neighborhoods prime for in-fill development. An investor considers what has worked before in similar communities and finds other neighborhoods that present those same fundamentals.

In the chorus of "New York, New York," Sinatra sings that success leaves clues. Success in one real estate investment is a strong indicator of the future probability of success in a similar real estate investment.

Discover the fundamentals of value for "up-and-coming" areas in your market to determine those that represent a strong investment.

24/7 PROFESSIONS

In honor of Mother's Day, consider the correlations between that calling and being a real estate agent. Our son came home from the hospital on Mother's Day, so it has a special meaning for me. Even those who don't have children have a mother or people who have been like a mother to them. Many women are drawn to become real estate agents because they often naturally possess the attributes of caretaking and encouragement.

In the stand-up routine by comedian John Mulaney, he affectionately tells the story about how their real estate agent was like a mother to them. She nurtured them through the process of finding and buying a home. His conclusion is that real estate agents are basically heroes because they never give up on finding the possible in the impossible.

Then there is the 24/7 nature of both the real estate business and being a mother, especially during a child's infancy and early years. One of the characters in Jodi Picoult's book, *My Sister's Keeper*, poignantly says, "(24/7) once you sign on to be a mother, that's the only shift they offer."

One of the techniques from real estate that worked well in raising our children was to inspire them to "achieve their highest and best use." A basic premise to real estate development is that land has the potential to be a dump or a park. It can be a single-family home, a school, or a shopping center with a grocery store that meets the community's needs. What is important is that it be utilized at its peak performance.

This was the encouragement I used with our children. When one was not selected for the team or not invited to a party or merely fell down, that was an occasion to pick them up. Then help them catch the vision that just maybe there was something better out there—to not take it personally, but rather strive to achieve all that they are capable of.

Mothers instinctively want what is best for their children. I have found that real estate agents, too, strive to obtain the best outcome for their clients. To persevere with buyer clients until they find the home that meets both their needs and wants. To work with a seller client to complete the laundry list of items to prepare the home for the market so that it presents at its best. The ability to work toward solutions while serving as encourager is a valuable skill for both a mother and a real estate agent.

Apply the skills you have to achieve the best for your clients.

AGENT AS FORWARD HORSE

Secretariat is the famous American thoroughbred racehorse that, as the ninth winner of the US Triple Crown in 1973, set new records in two of three of the events. Secretariat was a "forward horse," bold and impatient to run his race. Secretariat's owner, Penny Chenery Tweedy, also was aggressive to run her race. In the 2010 movie, *Secretariat*, there is a scene in which Lucien Laurin asks Penny Chenery why she wanted him to train her horse. Penny responds, "I was hungry and so were you." This is another version of being forward and bold—that "fire in the belly," the desire to want something so badly you will do whatever it takes to achieve it.

Are you, as a real estate agent, a forward horse? Or are you the type that needs to have a rider with a crop at the ready? Who do you think sellers or buyers prefer to have as their representative in what is likely their largest financial transaction? One who frequently needs a prod, only half focused on the business? Do you think customers would prefer an agent who thinks she knows it all and isn't open to new ideas? Or would they rather have one who is hungry, bold, and always pursuing new opportunities? Do you think it is better that an agent is always pushing herself to perform at her best by being learning-based and staying abreast of industry trends and practices? And who will be aggressive in marketing and contract negotiations? In most instances, clients would select the forward horse, the agent who is proactive on their behalf.

Another scene in the movie that is poignant is when Penny Chenery Tweedy confronts her brother and husband. They were pushing her to sell Secretariat early on because of the need to raise money to pay estate taxes. Both asked her why she was so driven to keep going, even with the possibility of losing everything should the horse not turn out to be a winner. Penny's answer: "This isn't about going back, this is about life being ahead of you and you run at it because you never know how far you can go unless you run!"

The appraiser, in performing due diligence, looks back at values of homes recently sold to best determine the current market value of a home. The real estate agent looks forward into the future marketplace. It is by listing a home on the market for sale that he can run the race that is set out before him. It is when working with buyer clients, showing houses, and writing contracts that he is successful.

Motivational and leadership author John Maxwell states: "Champions don't become champions in the ring—they are merely recognized there." And so it is with real estate: the forward agent is the one who gets her client across the finish line!

Adopt the aggressive and proactive attributes
of the forward horse for clients.

UPPER LIMIT

The first full year that I was a residential real estate agent, I sold twelve homes, effectively one per month. Not having anything to compare it against, I thought it was a respectable number and my capacity. So when my broker shared with me his vision—that I was capable of selling one house per week—at the time the idea just blew my mind. What I experienced was that my belief system and my mental status had an upper limit.

As we are constrained by time and space, it goes without saying that people have limits. Space is becoming less of an issue as the Internet expands the world as we know it. Real estate is unique in that it truly is about the location, which cannot be moved. And time is of defined quantity; everyone gets an equal amount per day. The number of days one is given is unknown in most cases, yet always finite.

The mind, though, has infinite possibilities and is only limited by one's belief system. In my case, that broker crashed through my belief system that selling one house per week was beyond my conception. It is rare that one's ability grows past a person's belief in herself. Thinking and acting in one's comfort zone seems safe, and yet even that presents challenges. The world is constantly changing and evolving. Just since the turn of the millennium, the use of the Internet has exploded the way properties are marketed and sold. Social media has added another level of communication and connection. Who truly knows what's next or what the future holds?

One way to push past limiting beliefs is to get into a more progressive and larger environment, likened to swimming in a bigger pond. Some agents do this by switching real estate companies or brokerages. Others push through by getting smaller and becoming a big fish in a small pond. There can be the combination of both extremes, for example, creating a niche, boutique-type company inside a very large brokerage house. These are all physical manifestations of limits.

Truly, though, the real change occurs in the mind. In this analogy, rather than jumping from one fish bowl or pond to another, it would be like leaping into the ocean and learning to swim there. The breadth and depth of the ocean effectively removes the upper limit and opens one up to an expansive way of thinking beyond the horizon.

For success, push through the upper-limit boundaries and limiting beliefs of how you think about your business and life.

"DON'T CONFUSE BRAINS WITH A BULL MARKET"

One really only knows the outcome of market dynamics after it has actually taken place. Past performance is still the best indicator of future results in the purchase and sale of real estate, just as in the stock market and commodities trading. Real estate agents prepare a comparative market analysis and broker price opinions, and financial advisors generate a prospectus or offer documents. These are all based on future projections.

The quote, "Don't confuse brains with a bull market" is attributed to Humphrey B. Neill, financier and author of *The Contrary Thinking*. It is interesting to note that both ends of the market spectrum are characterized by a large animal—a bull for robust and vibrant markets and a bear for slow and declining conditions. A herd mentality occurs more often in a bull market. Yet in the case of a bear market, people are known to follow the prevailing trend and actually cause the market to crash. What takes brains is seeing the market shift. It requires courage to act differently,

The best way to feel the winds of change in the real estate market is to track supply and demand. As long as the market is balanced, then typically the conditions remain stable. The bull market shift occurs when there is consistently over time more demand than supply. The bear market shift happens when inventory continues to build over time, surpassing balanced market conditions into considerable oversupply.

The book by Michael Lewis that became a movie, *The Big Short*, chronicles the housing buildup and credit bust during the 2000s. There were people who recognized the bubble for what it was, unsustainable. It was not growth, but rather irrational exuberance. It was a time when many people were confusing brains for a bull market. Thinking people recognized that a crash was inevitable.

Neill was known for his "contrary opinion." He isn't the first financial advisor, nor will he be the last, to encourage people to be contrarian and "buy low and sell high." The market forces are very strong and sentiments run deep. When the market is rising, people feel they can't possibly go wrong. And when it is falling, no one knows how low it can or will go, and fear abounds. The astute agent pays close attention to the market dynamics and advises clients accordingly.

Recognize the signs of a market shift by paying close attention to supply and demand trends.

ON GETTING FIRED AND STILL SELLING THE HOUSE: A SELLER'S TALE

The stories I tell that seem to intrigue new agents the most are the ones in which I've been fired and yet I still sell the house. First off, they seem to find it surprising that I would be fired in the first place. And then they want to know how I turned such a negative situation around. This is a true seller tale.

The client's home was for sale when the broader market was going through a major correction. In our area, it was taking longer than normal to sell this higher-price range of home. Even though she was a past client, she was becoming quite frustrated with the low level of showings. At some point, she felt that the problem wasn't the market or the pricing, but rather the agent—me. And this led to her decision that she would be better off making a change in real estate agents.

I remember the call vividly, as I was on vacation in Europe celebrating a milestone birthday with my husband. It is my business practice to work only with people who want to work with me. So as I promised in our listing appointment, I allowed her to cancel our agreement at no cost to her. Yet I was careful to leave the door open by telling her that if for any reason she wanted to come back, I would be there for her. The reason for my saying this is that oftentimes people find out the grass isn't actually greener with a different agent, and I want them to know that I will welcome them back with open arms. Needless to say, any new agent would not able to change the challenging market conditions.

In a very short period of time, she was back and ready to listen to me about what I thought it would take to sell her home. She finally made the price change that I had indicated earlier in the process and soon after a buyer appeared. The buyer wasn't working with an agent, and so I was able to represent both sides of the transaction. I went on to sell this client her next home, as well, since she still needed somewhere to move after the sale.

Agents often want to know how I handled this situation emotionally. One technique I use is what my personal trainer calls the "power boost," like in the Mario Kart video game. In the game, the player taps into a burst of energy to go to the next level. This is what my trainer encourages me to do physically when I need a push to complete an exercise. I use this power boost mentally as a creative way to take my emotions out of the situation. In this way, I take myself and business to the next level of professionalism.

Create a "power boost" for situations in your business in which you want to rise to the next level to achieve success in real estate.

DRAW A LINE IN THE SAND

A challenging situation for real estate negotiations is when one party takes the posture of "drawing a line in the sand." This stance creates a barrier between the parties that states, in effect, "Either you are with me or you are against me." In the Zox song "Line in the Sand," the lyrics ring true: "Everybody has a moment when they wake up; everybody has a morning when they've had enough."

In difficult situations, many times people feel that to find out where others stand, their only alternative is to "draw a line in the sand." It can backfire, though, as what can happen is like in the song—it can push the other party's "back up against the wall." Not a preferred position to be in.

The least-expensive concession a party can make is to listen to the other side. That doesn't mean that one agrees with the other party. Active listening opens up the possibility of coming to an understanding and often an agreement. "Drawing a line in the sand" is rejecting the other side, which can cause even more of a reactionary response. That can create an adversary rather than an ally.

A real estate scenario that occurs frequently is when sellers say, "Well, for that price, tell the buyers I'm not doing anything on the home inspection." This puts the buyer in a "take-it-or-leave-it" situation. If the seller would consider addressing some of the items, the buyer would probably move forward with the deal. Given the "line in the sand" position that the seller won't do anything, the buyer is backed into the corner, with the only option being voiding the contract.

Another common situation is when negotiating price. Buyers or sellers often request the agent to state to the other party, "That's my best and final offer." That is a "draw-a–line-in-the-sand" mentality. If the party who says this actually comes back and is willing to do more, it places him in a less favorable position, as his word has now been compromised.

Better strategies to "drawing a line in the sand" are: "That's all we can do right now"; Let's cross that bridge when we get to it"; "I can do x if you can find a way to do y." Use "and" language more often than "but." These language and negotiation postures keep the door open to an agreement and successful deal.

Strategize with clients on the use of open-door negotiating positions rather than closed "draw-a-line-in-the-sand" postures.

"KEEP CALM AND CARRY ON"

"Keep calm and carry on" is a popular phrase that has its roots in the United Kingdom right before World War II. The theme was printed as a motivational poster designed to raise the morale of the British public soon to be at war again.

Recently, it has been commercialized and appears on coffee mugs, t-shirts, posters, and other paraphernalia. Further, it has been featured in innumerable media references and popular culture. As a real estate agent, it makes an inspiring business motto. What follows are but a couple of real-life examples.

April is known for rain showers in many areas, which does lead to beautiful May flowers. However, it can also lead to significant flooding and water damage. It is particularly important to keep water from penetrating a home with a basement. In this example, the day prior to the final walkthrough of a home, there was significant rain in the area. It was a primary concern to the purchaser to verify that no water had entered the basement. Upon inspection, the bad news was that there had been water in the basement. The gutter system appeared to be the culprit, as in one area it was not sufficient to handle the water flow that came off the roofline at that juncture.

This is when the motto, "keep calm and carry on," is critical. It is the professional agent who can stay "cool under pressure" until all parties come to a resolution. In this situation, it meant taking and sending some photos to the listing agent to document the scope of the damage. A contractor was located and a remedy took place in time for settlement.

Another situation was a potential delay in settlement because a purchaser's permanent mortgage loan was not completely approved and the lender needed a few more days to finalize everything. A delay in settlement on the one sale caused a domino effect. The sellers of that home needed to close on that date so that they could purchase their next home.

This scenario required this agent to "keep calm and carry on." In this situation, the creative solution was that the purchaser placed in escrow the entire down payment with the settlement company. Further, the lender prepared and delivered bridge-loan documents to the settlement company so that all parties would have the added assurance that the purchaser could close on a loan. By keeping calm and carrying on with creative thinking, it enabled everyone to achieve their objectives.

Apply the motto, "keep calm and carry on" with your clients in challenging situations to raise morale.

TAKE YOUR PART IN THE APPRAISAL PROCESS

As a professional full-time real estate agent, it is my experience that we can make a vital contribution to the appraisal process! The agent has the unique advantage of being able to go inside and view comparable properties and provide distinctions that may not be readily evident. She can point out and provide a list of the features and improvements of the property, as well as other vital information that demonstrates value. Further, she best knows the micro-market where the home is located. It is difficult for an appraiser to know every nuance of every market niche.

First, it is important to understand what an appraisal is and is not. The definition of an appraisal is: a valuation of property (e.g., real estate, a business, an antique) by the estimate of an authorized person. True fair market value of any commodity is arrived at, real estate included, when a buyer and seller agree to a price with specific terms and consummate the transaction; neither party is under duress, the parties are unrelated, and thus at an "arms length," the commodity has had adequate exposure to the open market, and financing terms are typical.

Many people assume that an appraisal determines fair market value. The short answer is "no," an appraisal does not determine fair market value. But as is so often the case, the answer is more complicated than a simple yes or no can provide.

The most common approach for an appraisal is the sales comparison method in obtaining a purchase-money mortgage or refinancing of a home. It is based on the principle of substitution. That is, an intelligent purchaser will pay no more for a property than it would cost to purchase a comparable substitute property. The more homogeneous a property is and the more stable the market conditions, the easier it is to obtain comparables and thus the closer the appraisal will be to fair market value. For example, town-homes tend to be more homogeneous than single-family homes. The reason being, it is more difficult to add space and change exterior elements, as most town-home communities require association approval to do so.

There is a delayed reaction that occurs with an appraisal, as the process requires the appraiser to look at past settled transactions and those that are already under contract. Fair market value, on the other hand, occurs in the present, in real time. Further, since the most unique factor of real estate is its location, which fundamentally cannot be changed, true substitution can never really occur. So what takes place is an estimation of value based on many factors, which are put into a formula.

It is in the best interests of all the parties for the real estate agent to take an active role in the process. One way I do that is to meet the appraiser at the property and provide relevant information.

Take steps to participate in the appraisal process.

ACRES OF LEADS

The classic story, *Acres of Diamonds*, is an ancient tale told by Russell Conwell that has been shared in countless motivational speeches. The story is of an African farmer who, not believing his own land was worth anything, sold it to travel the world in search of wealth. The farmer who acquired the land took the time to work with what he had. Although in a rough state at the time of purchase, he discovered through effort it held countless riches. Truly acres of diamonds were there the entire time.

In real estate, experience shows that successful agents work the market that they know best—most likely their neighborhood and surrounding community. To work with the people they know, their "sphere" in sales language. The market in which I live and practice real estate is high income and thus sales are at a higher dollar average than the surrounding communities. There are countless agents with offices in this market area, in order to capitalize on the potential. In effect, they drive past perfectly good opportunities in their own communities that they know well to search other marketplaces for wealth.

There is a real estate proverb that states an agent should list where he lives and sell to a buyer wherever he is licensed. The reason being is that listing a home for sale requires a deep knowledge of comparable properties, time is used more effectively servicing and showing a home that is close by, and owners have more confidence in an agent who has a vested interest in the sale. Selling a home to a buyer requires being able to, by license, open the door, negotiate the offer, and manage the logistics to settlement. This is also why most real estate agents new in the business begin by working with buyers.

The beauty of a tale such as this one is that it is timeless, in effect evergreen. The application stays true regardless of the market conditions.

The same is the case for many of the stories in this book. The stories are designed to stimulate and inspire you to take action. You have within you tremendous potential; start with what you have now. Connect to build and grow and you will discover the sweet spot of success in real estate.

Take action on the acres of leads that are around
you and work them to their potential.

MY BLACKBERRY FELL IN THE SEWER, CIRCA 2011

In the blink of an eye, a million thoughts ran through my head about what was lost and how to recover. First a bit of self-incrimination; how could I have been so careless! Immediately my mind went to solution-based strategies. It isn't what happens to you, I've found, but the response. This incident occurred in 2011, and yes, I now have the latest and greatest iPhone.

Saga part 1: Attempt to retrieve the Blackberry. Fortunately it slid into the sewer right at a manhole cover. My husband, Andy, stores some basic tools in his vehicle, so he was able to use them to lift off the lid. A quick look into the sewer showed empty bottles, trash, debris, and my Blackberry sticking in the mud at an angle. Yuck! Someone had to go in, and since I was the careless person who allowed the device to slip from my hands and the smaller of us, I was nominated.

One idea was to take off my shoes and socks, roll up my pants, and jump in feet first. That would have meant stepping into "who knows what!" Andy suggested I go in head first while he held my legs. Have you got the picture?

Saga part 2: Resuscitate the Blackberry. After taking it apart, we used the pieces of a soft towel to dry the components. Still it would not cycle back on. Next we held it in front of the car vents, with the fan blowing full blast. Even after several attempts of resuscitation, it was evident the Blackberry was gone. Cause of death: drowning.

Saga part 3: Data recovery. Off to the local phone carrier store to acquire an updated model. Even though I had not been quite as consistent as I should have been about backing up the device, it was not a total loss. I had become a loyal "cloud" account user, so many of the functions had been synchronizing on a regular basis. All other key data was stored on "cloud" sites as well, so most recovery was doable.

One of the lessons I learned from this incident was to be humble. This story is here to assure you that even top professionals make mistakes. Also, it is the favorite story of Jennifer, an agent on my team. She encouraged me to share it to show that I too am human. In the words of Arnold Schwarzenegger: "The greatest mistake you can make in life is to be continually fearing you will make one."

The other lesson is that when "stuff happens," you choose how you will respond. In this case, it was to come up with solutions and perseverance of purpose. If I will go to that level of effort and commitment for a Blackberry, what will I do when working with customers and clients on the purchase or sale of their home? Those assets are far more precious than my Blackberry.

Choose to respond to adversity by not succumbing to fear and being solution-based.

"MOMMY, MOMMY, MOMMY"

A client and friend shared with me that everything about life changed once the couple had their first child. They moved frequently for her husband's career and when she would go house hunting, she used the "Mommy, Mommy, Mommy" factor to determine whether a house would work for their family's needs.

Curious, I asked what that meant for her. She shared that when a child wakes up in the night, how many "Mommies" does it take before the child finds the parent? When her children were small, three "Mommies" was the most she would accept. As the children grew older, the parameters adjusted accordingly.

A home that has the master suite on a different level from other bedrooms can be considered by prospective purchasers with small children to be an unacceptable floor plan. Even with technology for both sound and video monitors readily available, parents often do not feel comfortable sleeping on a different floor than the children. One reason is that if an emergency occurs during the night, such as a fire, the parents would not be nearby to be of assistance. Another reason I've been told is to minimize the loss of sleep by both parents and child. The closer the child is in proximity to the parents, the less disruption there is in calming the child and getting him back to bed after a bad dream or something that awakens him during the night.

Homes with a master suite on another level can work well for a family with older children. In that situation, the concern I've heard expressed isn't always how many "Mommies" it takes for the child to reach the parent. In those circumstances, it often is more of an ability to monitor whereabouts and whether a young person has met curfew.

As a professional agent, it is a critical to understand the needs of people in different life stages and how best to meet their expectations.

Help clients determine their buying parameters.

TANDEM BIKE RIDING

Bike riding is something that my husband and I enjoy frequently for both fitness and fun. On a recent beach getaway, he thought it would be a treat for us to try something new—riding a tandem bicycle. While we were being fitted for the special cycle, the shop proprietor gave us a quick tutorial on how to operate a tandem. The counsel she provided was that it was very important to be in constant communication with each other before taking any action.

Soon we discovered how absolutely right that advice was. In order to be able to move and stop safely, we had to be on the same page. To turn and even to balance, it was critical to follow the same cadence. The heaviest person navigates best when in front, so my husband was the lead rider, and my role was one of support. Soon we developed a rhythm and enjoyed the ride. The experience remains vivid in both of our memories.

Real estate transactions are a lot like being on a tandem bike. The agent as the professional and the "heavy" in the transaction is in front to navigate the way. Yet it is critical that the client is aware of all movements prior to them being made. It is important to keep in mind that most people only buy or sell a home every seven years. Thus, the client comes into the transaction with a low skill level in the process compared to the professional real estate agent.

Just as in the tandem experience, it is teamwork that leads to smooth transactions with both buyer and seller clients. Buyer participation includes the timely meeting of all lender guidelines and instructions, as well as completion of inspections as outlined in the contract. For the seller client, cooperative activities involve maintaining the home in show condition, leaving the house for buyer showings, and completing all work to be performed per the contract on the home. All parties are to meet deadlines and contractual obligations.

Strong, consistent verbal and written communication is one of the most important aspects of the real estate process. It becomes even more critical if there are roadblocks, detours, potholes, or other unforeseen challenges. Professional agents foster and maintain good communication among all parties. It keeps everyone in balance to arrive safely and on time to the destination of settlement.

Establish and maintain strong communication between clients and parties in the transaction.

"WE'VE GOT TO GO THROUGH IT!"

The reason why children's books become classics is that there is a timeless element to the simplicity of the story. In the case of the book *We're Going on a Bear Hunt*, by Michael Rosen and Helen Oxenbury, the lesson learned is: "We've got to go through it." On the journey, the protagonists encounter numerous obstacles: mountains; long, wavy grass; a deep, cold river; thick, oozy mud; a big, dark forest; a swirling, whirling snowstorm; and a narrow, gloomy cave. In all of the situations, the mantra is that they are not afraid and that they've "got to go through it."

In real estate transactions, agents will encounter all sorts of obstacles. To name a few: finance issues with the buyer's loan; numerous inspection items; difficulty obtaining an appraisal to contract value; challenges with timing the move; problems scheduling and coordinating with the parties involved; and clients going through a divorce, medical concern, distressed sale, or job change. The possibilities are endless. The objective for the agent is to get the transaction to settlement by going through it with the client.

One example that comes to mind is with clients who were selling due to divorce. As often is the case in these situations, it seemed more negotiations were occurring between the separated couple than with the other side. I am a middle child in my family, and that position in life means that I can see both perspectives. In effect, I was equal distance between my older and younger siblings, just as what was happening with this couple. And like a family, there is good and bad. First, I reminded the parties that everyone's objective was to get through the transaction so that they could move on. Further, that my responsibility was to them both and that I was not a divorce attorney. Once we had something all the parties could agree to, then I was able to break down who would be responsible for what to make settlement happen.

Similar scenarios often play out in distressed sales or when people are losing a considerable amount of money. There is something to be said for employing the "Band-Aid'" strategy: that is, just pull it off. Often the pain is less than having it drag out.

When encountering obstacles, it is helpful to keep the focus on the purpose of the transaction—to buy or sell the home. It is much like in the book, the characters kept their focus on the "bear hunt" and that overarching purpose carried them through.

Navigate clients through obstacles encountered
in a real estate transaction to get them through it.

FIGHT, FLIGHT, TEND, AND BEFRIEND

People respond to stress and change in different ways. The home, in almost every situation, is the most expensive asset people own, coupled with the emotional attachments. It is no surprise, then, that the act of buying and selling a home has the potential for high levels of stress.

The most well-known responses to stress and change are fight or flight. In those situations, the person responds to the situation by fighting back or fleeing, which can be physical or emotional. An example of fleeing is when customers or clients "go dark" by no longer responding to e-mails and requests to speak by phone or in person.

There are two other more positive responses to stress, and those are to tend and befriend. To tend means to take care of. The clients will feel taken care of by the agent when actions and communication show that she is on top of the details. Having the assurance that there is someone with experience navigating the process increases the confidence of the one going through the change and stress. The clients recognize that they don't have to fight for their rights because the agent is tending to them. And it isn't necessary to flee the situation, because the agent has a positive intention for the client.

To befriend is to say the words and take the actions that help the clients see that you are on their side, that you are both on the same team, and that you "have their back." Even though the situation may be difficult, together you will help them get through it. One effective communication tool is the "feel, felt, found" method. It conveys empathy while at the same time moves to a solution.

There are those who say that fight and flight are male responses, and tend and befriend are female responses. Truly, these are all human responses. It is the responsibility of the agent as the professional to recognize the situation. Once the situation has been identified, help the client through the process in a positive manner to best achieve their objectives and meet their needs.

Incorporate "tend and befriend" to help clients through stressful situations during the real estate transaction process.

THERE ARE NO UGLY BABIES—OR HOUSES

There are no ugly babies . . . to those who love them. The rest of the world may call a "spade a spade," yet the cherished one will be viewed through a lens of love. One is hesitant to be "brutally honest" to parents about their child's true beauty, talent, intellect, or lack thereof.

The same phenomenon occurs with home sellers. Many times, the home can become like a child to owners. There are considerable financial and time investments for the care and maintenance of both. A home takes on the personality of the owner via décor, design, furnishings, and even landscaping. With children, people frequently comment on familial resemblance and traits. People invest so much of themselves into a home, when buyers or agents like it or even go so far as to "fall in love," then sellers are happy. Those messages are very validating. It feels like when someone recognizes a parent's baby as being beautiful, talented, and smart.

However, when the design, selections, and even furnishings of the home are not the taste of most people in the market, there is a form of rejection that takes place. In fact, by not buying the home, buyers are in effect saying that the home is not beautiful to them. This reflects back to the sellers many times as if someone were to say the same about their child. The listing agent should take care when delivering agent and buyer feedback to the owner so as not to offend.

This phenomenon is not as common in investors, as typically their focus is on the financials of the deal. However, even for people in the industry, when their home is on the market, "all bets are off." Being rational about one's own home is difficult, even for real estate and related professionals.

"For sale by owner" is another scenario in which this phenomenon occurs. This is why it is best to have a real estate professional who is not directly invested in the property represent the transaction. In this way, true objectivity can be provided.

Tact and diplomacy is the best way to comment on a baby . . . and an owner's home!

Remember, "there are no ugly babies" or houses when sharing feedback about the market with seller clients.

QUANTITY VERSUS QUALITY

Quantity versus quality is an age-old question. The debate is often heard in the platform regarding raising children. Which matters more, the amount of time spent with the child or the depth of interaction? Truly, I believe both are important. And it applies to the real estate profession as well, on several fronts.

In regard to experience, there is a school of thought that the number of years in the business is a good barometer to determine the quality of the agent. The best in real estate achieve that distinction by quantity of time. Other frequent standards of calculating success are based on number of transactions and the amount of dollar volume sold annually. And then, how many years the agent, team, and company have sustained those levels of achievement. The logic follows that whoever has the most business is the one who is the most qualified. Past performance is the best indicator of future success.

On the other side of the equation is the agent new in the business who does not have the quantity of experience in the industry to bring to the table. Yet many new agents succeed through their drive, hard work, and creativity. Unlike those who have been around a while, these agents often see new solutions and bring forth ideas that disturb the status quo in a positive way.

In lead generation, the quantity of activity can lead to quality. When a professional has an abundance of opportunity, the agent has more choices. Options include prioritizing the leads, referring out the business for a fee, and leveraging with other agents, team members, and staff. It often becomes a self-fulfilling prophecy that the more leads one has, the more leads one gets. The quality frequently increases with the quantity.

The client, too, has needs—both for quantity and quality time. Frequently customers ask how many listings an agent currently carries or how many buyers the agent is working with. The reason, I have discovered, for those questions is they feel deep down that at a certain number the agent won't have time to devote attention to them. And yet you have surely heard the Ben Franklin adage: "If you want something done, ask a busy person." With systems and standards of service, quality can be achieved with quantity.

Thus, we come full circle to the original statement. Both quantity and quality are necessary for a successful real estate agent.

---

*Apply both quantity and quality principles
to your clients, business, and life.*

INSIDE- AND OUTSIDE-THE-BOX THINKING

Inside-the-box thinking starts with a framework of what one already knows. The concept of "outside-the-box" thinking is where one thinks creatively and is the space in which innovation occurs. The best thinking happens when there is a combination of the two. It is "and/both" rather than "either/or."

Twyla Tharp, the famous dancer, choreographer, and author of the book, *The Creative Habit: Learn It and Use It for Life*, writes: "Before you can think out of the box, you have to start with a box." Once the "box" is mastered, then by all means discover and innovate all the different variations, uses, and applications of that box.

The comparative market analysis is a real estate application in which it is helpful for the agent to understand the "inside-the-box" data first. It is important to identify the homes that the subject property best compares to. Then the agent can think creatively about what makes the particular home "unique." There are instances in which the market might behave differently and taking that into consideration is beneficial as well. Market indicators such as supply and demand, as well as trends, may be predicting that the market is moving in a particular direction. In this way, the agent combines the attributes of all factors that determine value.

Many new agents enter the profession with a multitude of creative ideas for their business plans. Yet, without the basics, that is a weak foundation for the business to connect to build and grow. Often the agent has so many ideas that she becomes paralyzed with choices. This leads to nothing of substance being accomplished.

In *The Millionaire Real Estate Agent*, author Gary Keller illustrates that a business built on creativity first is like a pyramid balancing on its tip. Applying models to creativity actually makes the structure top-heavy. The stable business is one that has a solid foundation based on models. Then creativity is applied at the top of the pyramid structure. By using creativity first, it is harder to develop repeatable systems for an ongoing business to survive and thrive in market fluctuations. This is an example of when thinking "outside the box" before thinking "inside the box" can be detrimental to the health of the business.

The astute real estate agent employs both inside- and outside-the-box thinking to benefit clients, and applies the principles to build and grow a business.

Master inside- and outside-the-box thinking to
success for clients, your business, and life.

PRACTICE MAKES PERFECT, WHICH LEADS TO PERFORMANCE

It is interesting the number of professions that are considered a "practice." The most commonly known are the practice of law, the practice of medicine, and the practice of real estate. In order to practice any of these professions, a license is required in the jurisdiction in which the person wants to work. The level of entry for law and medicine is considerably higher in terms of educational requirements than is the case for real estate, which is the most significant differential. All involve significant aspects to other people's lives, however.

In all of the fields, once one has met the requirements and achieved the license, then that is when the practice begins. Frequently I share with new agents that what they need to know to pass the real estate exam is not necessarily what they need to know in order to be successful as an agent. That is when the true practice of being a real estate agent begins.

As in anything that requires practice, it is in the repetition that one obtains success, whether an instrument, a sport, or a profession. It seems that people want to achieve performance and the associated rewards without putting in the practice time and effort.

Science has discovered that the human brain actually modifies throughout life based on the experiences a person has. This "learning-dependent plasticity" is the difference between the amateur and the professional. The professional puts in the time on task that the amateur or hobbyist isn't willing or able to do. And that practice leads to performance and success.

Remember, too, that one must practice correctly in order to perfect the skills that lead to quality performance. This is when having a coach, mentor, broker, or an agent with more experience can help one take the agent's skill to the next level. Continuing to do the same activities over and over again without achieving results is at the very least ineffective and at the worst can be harmful.

The concept of a profession as a practice intuits a career of continuous learning. Aspects of the real estate industry are constantly changing: the market, the laws, the technology, and the required documents. It takes an ongoing commitment to practice to provide the best quality service to customers and clients.

Commit today to practice the profession of real estate.

UNREALIZED GAIN OR LOSS

The concept of "unrealized gain or loss" is most commonly associated with the investment sector. It truly is "paper money," not actual profit or loss. It is upon sale that the investor has a true determination of value, as that is when it is a known quantity. Until that time, it is considered unrealized. The most common usage of these terms is in the stock market.

Every month, I receive a statement for my investment account, and it shows the gains and losses over the previous period. Let's say I own stock in Apple. If I were to "cash out" and sell at that point in time, then I would realize my true gain or loss. If the stock drops, then I have an unrealized loss until such time as I sell it. If it rises and I decide to sell, then I can realize those profits. Should I decide to hold, then it all becomes speculation!

The same terminology applies to real estate. The statements that most homeowners receive to determine value are tax assessments, appraisals, and online evaluation models, such as Zillow. Truly, if the homeowner doesn't sell and the tax assessment, appraisal, or Zillow evaluation goes up, it is an unrealized gain. And if the evaluation goes down, it is an unrealized loss.

The interesting phenomenon is that homeowners focus on the unrealized gain and want to know why they didn't receive it when their home was on the market for sale. I have yet to meet a homeowner who readily recognizes the loss potential.

The best way I have found to explain it to a homeowner is to suggest that they call the county assessor and ask him to pay the amount of money listed on the assessment statement. If he will, then it has now become a realized gain. The same holds true with the appraiser and Zillow. Until that happens, it is unrealized because a ready, willing, and able buyer has not come forward.

An evaluation is only truly a realized gain if someone will pay the homeowner that amount of money to purchase the property.

Understand the premise behind "unrealized gain or loss" terminology so you can use the concepts to explain market value to clients and customers.

I'M JUST THE MOTHER

The humorous response, "I'm just the mother," is well known in our family. The origins are from when our kids were young and would seek counsel and wisdom from others, yet not listen to me effectively saying the same thing. This is particularly funny when the query is something that I may actually know something about. There are other versions of the saying, as in, "I'm just the dad."

This has found its way into the real estate environment. The most common usage is when sellers or buyers seem to think that they actually know more than the professional. In this situation, the agent, perhaps with a tint of humor, says, "What do I know, I'm just the real estate agent." Or for example, in my case, "I've been part of 1,000 home sales and you've sold five in your lifetime. I'm just the real estate agent, what could I possible know?" This is, of course, just back-office real estate humor, not to be used on the front lines with the client.

The other version is, "I may be wrong." It implies that I probably am right, but am willing to consider that I may be wrong if someone can offer evidence otherwise. A real-life application of "I may be wrong" occurred in the sale of our own personal home. My husband and I had a difference of opinion on price. He felt that I was underpricing it a bit and that we could get more money. I, on the other hand, knew first-hand that it was a tough market. It was important to me to get a quick sale because I didn't want to own two houses at that point in our lives. Thus, I wanted to be sure we priced it competitively to get the market's attention.

In the spirit of "I may be wrong," I allowed my husband to set the list price, provided that we adjust it down every week until it went under contract. The good news is that we only had to make one adjustment before receiving an offer that we came to an agreement on. The question remains: would we have obtained the same price or less if we had gone with my strategy of a lower list price to begin with? Of course, we will never know. But the "I may be wrong" strategy was successful.

Sometimes you may be right and sometimes you may be wrong; just be mindful of what is appropriate for the situation or what the market may be indicating.

APP TRIES

It seems that new applications for my smartphone are available daily. How many times do you think the average user tries to use an application before deciding to stop? A survey of smartphone users has determined that it is 4.5.

The statistics for prospecting are similar. Salespeople stop trying to make contact after the fourth call in 90 percent of the cases. And yet 80 percent of sales are made after the fifth touch. The biggest impact you will make in your career as a real estate agent will be made after the majority of people have quit trying. That is powerful knowledge.

Think about how to apply smartphone strategies to real estate lead generation. First, you might reach out to others who have gone before to obtain recommendations on what to try to stay inspired. Next, reboot to get a "fresh screen," which could include going for a walk or meditating. Try another application and then return to the task, most likely with a fresh perspective. Do some research and then circle back; this time you might connect in a new way. And for the fifth try, just do it.

Just when you think you have your device or application figured out, something changes. There is an update to the software, which requires learning and adapting to the upgrade or perhaps even a completely new program. In prospecting, many agents give up too soon because of the fear of rejection. In either case, one direction is to fear the change and rejection and to either directly or passively resist taking any action.

The other, better way is to embrace the change and opportunity to connect as exciting and progressive. This perspective takes on the challenge to learn something new as forward-thinking and proactive. The same view applies to prospecting, as you consider how you can take the customer to the next level. No one really knows what the future holds. In a yogurt shop in Austin, there is a tip jar on the counter. It made me chuckle at the profound statement: "Fear change? Leave it here." Leave the fear behind and go enjoy your yogurt, learn a new app, or connect with a customer!

Dr. Orrison Swett Marden, inspirational author and founder of *Success* magazine, states: "There are two essential requirements for success. The first is "go-at-it-iveness" and the second is "stick-to-it-iveness." The professional real estate agent exhibits both!

---

*Commit as much effort to lead generation as you would
in learning a new smartphone application.*

GOING STANDBY—A HOME-BUYING STRATEGY

Hot real estate markets occur in those areas and price points that over a period of time experience low supply and high demand. In order to be competitive in those situations, it takes strong strategy and negotiating skills. In one such case, I was working with a purchaser client who had already lost out on five contracts. Shortly before working with this client, my husband and I had been traveling by air and thus the "going standby" strategy was conceived.

Our flight was canceled from Dallas/Fort Worth to Washington Reagan due to weather. The good news was that out of DFW there were numerous flights that depart daily to DCA, our desired final destination. The bad news was that there were a couple hundred people from our cancelled flight also trying to get onto the first available flight. After unsuccessfully going standby on three flights in a row, my husband suggested that rather continue to compete with the same people, we skip a couple of flights to be first in line for a later flight. That's what we did and were successful in getting on the later flight. It is always a good feeling to be home in one's own bed!

As my purchaser client was also a seasoned traveler, he immediately related to the "going standby" story. We discussed how it would work to compete in a real estate purchase for him. The next time a couple of town-homes came on the market in the communities he had identified as wanting to live in, we were prepared with the strategy.

Out of those properties, the preferred town-home was clearly evident—it had more upgrades and was in a more private section of the community. The purchaser and I felt that everyone else would make offers on that home. There was another town-home that was priced a bit lower, had fewer upgrades, and backed up to a busier road. All of those constraints were not of concern to my client, as his primary objective was to purchase at a good price value.

Just as in the "airline standby" strategy, we skipped the town-home that ended up having eight offers and wrote a strong offer on the least-desirable home, "the wallflower." This idea proved successful and my client happily settled on the property.

Strategize on how you can incorporate the
"going standby" concept in negotiations with clients.

LEVERAGE OF LEARNING

One way successful people over the millennia have achieved the exponential benefits of leverage is through learning from other people. Knowledge can be acquired from books, in- person and off-site seminars, audio and video formats, webinars, and coaching on both an individual and group level. We can learn from ancient scribes and modern-day authors, business people and experts. The challenge almost becomes one of discernment, what to read, subscribe to, and apply.

Clearly there are principles that have stood the test of time for a reason. Advancements in thought and experience, even in the last few decades, have improved business and opportunities at the "speed of thought," to quote Bill Gates. Someone is always at the forefront, ahead of the crowd, and in effect pulling people into the next great breakthrough.

Learning from others is a means of leveraging their knowledge and experience. It is an exponential way of acquiring knowledge by building on what is already known and has been previously achieved. It isn't humanly possible to know everything, do everything, and participate in every experience. Where will you achieve the greatest return on investment?

As a real estate agent, a great place to start is by learning from the top agent in your office, company, community, and association. What are they reading? Are they offering training? Who are their coaches and mentors? There are professional designations available to the real estate professional through the association, which lend credibility and acknowledgement of expertise in a particular field. Awards and distinctions recognize accomplishments.

A person who is a lifelong learner is motivated intrinsically by curiosity and the desire to develop new skills and expand existing abilities. This agent achieves by gaining knowledge and seeking out challenges. She views making mistakes and learning from them as part of the process.

Often it is beneficial to look outside one's immediate profession to achieve a broader perspective. There are numerous industries that are knowledge centers beneficial to the real estate profession. These include lending institutions, settlement companies, and economic development organizations such as the chamber of commerce.

There will always be a maverick out there breaking ground. Observe closely the territory that is being charted; it could in fact be the new expansion and indicator of things to come. This is how people, companies, and industries go to the next level. By leveraging knowledge and experience, you can achieve more than possible as an individual.

Leverage the knowledge available from successful people in the real estate industry and beyond.

BUYING A NEW HOME IS LIKE DRIVING A NEW CAR OFF THE LOT A TALE OF A BUILDER/DEVELOPER PURCHASE

It is common knowledge that once a new car has been driven off the lot, the value drops significantly. According to insurance companies and vehicle evaluation resources, the minute after leaving the dealership, a new car decreases in value between 10 percent and 20 percent. At the end of the first year of ownership, the car will have decreased a total of around 25 percent to 35 percent, which is in line with the typical annual depreciation rates of used cars. After five years, the value has decreased by at least 65 percent of the original cost paid to the dealership. Used cars also decrease in value. Logically, the first owner takes the biggest "hit" on the depreciation, so subsequent owners only experience the deterioration in value based on usage and on annual wear and tear.

A similar phenomenon occurs when building and purchasing a new home. It may seem counterintuitive, as over time real estate tends to increase in value. The National Association of Realtors® statistics show that the price of existing homes in the United States increased by 5.4 percent annually from 1968 to 2009, on average. The general inflation rate during the same time period was 4.5 percent, so housing appreciates at just about 1 percent more than inflation.

One scenario to purchase a new home is by a tract homebuilder or developer. The buyer is often captivated by the gorgeous model homes with all the top-of-the-line features and décor that are as enticing as a new car. In this case, there are numerous homes being built simultaneously and the builder/developer experiences the benefits of scale. Typically these homes are of a "builder grade," which is adequate quality with lots of "bling" and attractive design for the current market. Over time, though, the "bling" loses its luster and the core structure and systems can sometimes require considerable unexpected maintenance costs.

The base price seems reasonable at first glance, but just as with a new car, it is the upgrades and extra features that tag onto the original value and jack up the price. As long as the builder/ developer continues construction in the community, any resales for about five to seven years tend to not recover the amount the seller paid. The reason is that as long as a buyer can purchase new for a similar price, they will almost always prefer new. It is usually after the five-year mark that resales begin to recover the "new home" pricing and can be competitive again in the marketplace without a loss. The return to the original value paid to the builder is prior to accounting for commissions and other costs of sale.

*Apply the "new car" analogy to help buyer
and seller clients understand value.*

"YOU'VE GOT MAIL"

In the early years of the Internet, AOL was one of the primary providers of personal e-mail. The ding "You've got mail" as a notification became a trademark in American culture of the time. The romantic movie, *You've Got Mail*, capitalized on the times and the expectation of someone special wanting to connect.

In the ensuing years, e-mail has become one the most prevalent means of communication. Real estate agents at one time conducted business only in person or by document delivery services such as US mail and then FedEx. When fax machines became readily available, that mode of delivery increased the speed of communication. Now the majority of the transactional process of buying and selling a home is conducted by e-mail or some form of digital delivery. Due to the volume of e-mail most people receive, it has lost the personal element for many.

The proactive, customer-service-oriented agent provides consistent professional communication to clients. Sellers love to hear feedback about their homes. Buyers want to know about what houses are available that meet their criteria. There exists for the professional real estate agent the happy expectation of someone wanting to connect. Rather than using an auto-delivery feedback service for sellers, share tidbits and more personal antidotes from open house and agent feedback. With buyers, instead of using auto-alert services for new listings, take the time to personally view the homes. Then deliver the information that is above and beyond what the buyer will learn off the Internet listing. These are e-mails that customers and clients are sure to read and connect with.

All agents prefer that there only be positive communication to share with clients. Sadly there are occasions when people void the contract, the home inspection indicates serious issues with the property, and agents share negative feedback about an owner's home. In these instances, experience shows that it is best to share the information via phone or in person. A follow-up e-mail that provides an overview of the conversation and options and action items is appropriate, though. In that way, the agent maintains a high level of professionalism in communication, while at the same time recognizes that certain situations and client personal preferences warrant different styles.

There are some clients who prefer other means of communication, such as texting. Again, keep in mind that the transaction and relationship is professional and that strong written documentation of all communication is part of an agent's best practices protocol.

Utilize the positive expectation of "you've got mail"
to communicate with customers and clients.

HOW DOES HEAVY TRAFFIC = A DAY AT THE BEACH?

One of the most valuable attributes of real estate is location on or near water—be it a river, lake, or ocean. The obvious benefit is that water typically occurs naturally and thus there is a limited supply of locations that are in close proximity. Man-made lakes and water features also can be valuable locations. The sound of water rushing, splashing, and even crashing are desirable, as they can be calming to the senses.

A few years ago, I represented a client who wanted to purchase an upper-bracket home in McLean, Virginia with a view of the Potomac River. That narrowed down the selection to what is known as the "gold coast." The downside to that location is that it is adjacent to the George Washington Parkway, a major transportation artery for the Washington, DC metro area. The primary negative to being near a major thoroughfare is road noise.

A University of Sheffield study in Britain shows that the brain hears the sound of heavy traffic and that of crashing waves as fundamentally the same. Michael Hunter from the university found that people weren't able to make the distinction from auditory clues alone. The visual element was necessary to aid them in determining the true source of the sound. When the visual element was provided, then the subjects had an emotional response. Beach scenes, not surprisingly, induced the emotional response of tranquility. When the view was of speeding cars, on the other hand, the subjects experienced tension. The researchers surmised that the disconnect was in response to the sound being thought of as calming when combined with the visual element, which was thought of as stressful.

The study enabled me to sell the client the house on the Potomac River. The paradigm shift to think of all of the sounds as though he was at the beach was all that it took. When our team represents sellers who have homes with significant road noise, we include this information in the marketing materials.

An oft-used strategy by landscapers is to incorporate fountains or waterfall features in hardscape in order to orient the setting toward one of tranquility. This reframes the sound of heavy traffic to equal a day at the beach. Just close your eyes and imagine that you are there.

Change the perspective on road noise with how it can be viewed as a day at the beach.

BECOMING REAL

The children's book, *The Velveteen Rabbit*, by Margery Williams, is the story of transformation that occurs through love and attention. The stuffed rabbit goes through both good times and bad times with the boy. Through the metamorphous of the boy's love, the rabbit goes from being inanimate to becoming a real animal. One of the characters explains the process like this: "It doesn't happen all at once," said the Skin Horse. "You become. It takes a long time. That's why it doesn't happen often to people who break easily, or have sharp edges, or who have to be carefully kept."

The process of becoming a professional real estate agent is a similar transformation. For most people, it takes three years to have completed enough transactions to be ranked as a successful professional. Many of the state jurisdictions require that level of experience before an agent can become a broker and in a position to manage others. Thus, time on task is a key characteristic of "becoming real" in the real estate industry.

The concept of resiliency is a factor in real estate, as well as in the story. People who succeed have an inner strength and are capable of rising above rejection, challenges, and setbacks. In the words of the Skin Horse, they do not "break easily." The majority of real estate agents are independent contractors and thus are self-motivated and initiators. They do not rely on others to be sure they are "carefully kept."

Being an agent is first and foremost a people business, and those who achieve are well respected and liked by their customers, clients, other agents, and associates in the industry. Thus, they usually don't have "sharp edges" or have taken the necessary steps to smooth them out. Leadership author and expert John Maxwell says: "I think you can only be transformational to people if you've been transformed yourself. Most people are informational—all they have is knowledge. But you become transformational when you've had a change in your own life, an experience that has changed you."

Consider how you have been transformed to become a real estate professional.

AUCTION AS MEANS OF ARRIVING AT PRICE

An auction is where goods or services are purchased by people bidding on an item that is sold to the highest bidder. My father is a licensed auctioneer, and I have attended many auctions throughout the years. A true absolute auction is when there is no reserve, or bottom-line number that has to be reached in order to sell. Sometimes there is a "plant" in the audience who raises the bid to achieve a higher sale price. Perhaps you have attended a charity auction and are familiar with the process. Real estate can be sold at an actual auction, most frequently in estate, foreclosure, or distressed situations.

One strategy the auctioneer may use is to set the price high going in and then come down until he finds someone willing to step up and bid. This is known as a Dutch auction, or open descending-price auction. When a seller lists a property for a price that they want to "try," this is in effect a Dutch auction. The seller then makes price adjustments or cuts until the market responds, the same as the auctioneer. Thus, price is determined by what a buyer is willing to pay and a seller is willing to accept by starting high and descending until the market is found.

It also can work in the other direction. The auctioneer can set the price quite low for the market. This is known as an English auction, or open ascending-price auction. When sellers list their homes on the low end of the market, they do so in the hopes that it will drive up demand. With more buyers and thus bidders, the price will then ascend over the list price. Price, though, is still determined based on what a buyer will pay that a seller will accept; this time it is achieved by starting low and rising until the market is found. The danger with this method is it may backfire on the seller. There could end up being only one party truly interested, and thus with no one to bid against, the price does not go up. Or there may be multiple bidders who decide they do not like being "played" against each other and all back out. To truly be an auction, it requires more than one interested party.

In my experience, standard sellers do not want to risk leaving money on the table. Therefore, most follow the process of a Dutch auction. The price starts high for the market, which "leaves room to negotiate." If the market does not respond, then they adjust the price accordingly until the market is arrived at. My father, as an auctioneer, counsels that it is important to move very quickly off a price if there are no takers. That is what I have found to be the best strategy for the home seller, as well. Once the market has had ample time to react, then it is in the best interests of the seller to correct the price in a timely fashion.

Understand pricing strategies so that you can best help clients obtain the top dollar the market will bear.

"I DO, I DO, I DO, I DO, I DO"

The constancy of customer service in the real estate industry reminds me of the ABBA song, "I Do, I Do, I Do, I Do, I Do." There are so many opportunities to provide service to clients. Experienced professional real estate agents have checklists and proven systems that they follow to keep clients happy and bulletproof the transaction. The challenge is that the industry is constantly changing and evolving. What was once standard can quickly become obsolete.

What makes it meaningful, yet also challenging, is that each client and corresponding situation is unique. Even with all the things that can be standardized, real estate is first and foremost about people and thus is a customer-service business. I have been personally involved in 1,000-plus transactions, and each has been unique in its own way. The ones that are the most memorable are the occasions when I've had to sincerely apologize to clients for difficult situations, even when I wasn't the one who caused the problem.

One such example stands out in my mind. An agent on our team was scheduled to hold a vacant home open. He ran late, so brought his lunch into the house, thinking he would finish eating there. When some visitors entered the home, he stuffed the leftover food into a kitchen cabinet. He subsequently forgot about it being there, as he was busy with customers the rest of the afternoon.

The sellers lived out of state, but decided to make a surprise visit a few days later to check on the home. They discovered not just an unpleasant odor, but critters and bugs in pursuit of the abandoned food. Of course I apologized profusely, took all steps to rectify the situation, and humbly requested the opportunity to have another chance to do over and do better. The clients stayed with our team, and we sold their home for a strong price for the market. A bad situation became better as they referred two of their neighbors to me. The reason, I believe, is that they were impressed that I accepted responsibility and did everything I could to turn the situation around.

So that is the principle of "I Do, I Do, I Do, I Do, I Do" customer service. It is one of a spirit of constantly doing over and doing better—doing whatever it takes to get the job done, to get it done correctly, and to the customer's satisfaction. Do everything you can to exceed the client's expectations. The added benefit of having the principle tied to a song tune is one can hum along as well!

Establish systems to assure top-level customer service for your clients.

HAPPY WIFE, HAPPY LIFE

Today is my wedding anniversary. In 1987, my husband Andy and I married. Over the years, he has loved and inspired me in so many ways. The one mantra that he holds fast to is: "Happy wife, happy life." It turns out it can be a good sentiment to share at the appropriate moment when working with homebuyers.

The home may be the man's castle, yet in many cases it is the wife's domain. The husband typically focuses on capital improvements and the financial aspects of the property. The wife most often is concerned with the livability of the home, and how the move will impact the family. Because of this dynamic, the choice of the home often weighs more as her decision. In many cases, she is the one who spends the most time there. If she is pregnant or there are children involved, then the nesting instinct can be very strong.

It takes sensitivity on the part of the real estate agent to know when and how to share this sentiment. I have found it usually happens when everyone is gathered in the kitchen. In one situation, the kids had already "picked their rooms" and were outside playing in the yard. All the buying signals were there that this was the home for the family. The husband was unsure, yet I could tell the wife was convinced; she just needed something to tip him over the edge. That is when I casually shared that my husband has this saying, "Happy wife, happy life." The husband smiled and laughed, saying that he had heard it too. The wife then cuddled up to him, and I knew that was the time to bring out the contract for everyone to sign.

The other version, of course, has happened to me as well. Those scenarios involve a bickering couple that cannot seem to come to an agreement. When those conversations happen in front of me and the tension feels as though one could cut it with a knife, that's when I share that "I don't do relationship counseling." Most times the couple laughs, which breaks the tension. Then someone suggests that perhaps they should continue the conversation privately and get back with me.

The purchase of a home is personal; it takes a great deal of empathy and understanding of psychology to help people navigate the process. Some say that people buy on emotion and justify with logic. These are just a few ways to help clients through the process.

Share appropriate scripts and dialogues, such as "happy wife, happy life" that help people make purchase decisions.

"SLIDING DOORS"

There are points in one's life when making one choice takes you on a different journey than if you had stayed on the current path. This reminds me of the movie *Sliding Doors*, about the alternative lives the character leads, depending on which train she catches. The plot splits at a blink of an eye, with one small act, such as dropping an earring, taking the character on a different trajectory.

Everyone has "sliding doors" moments, such as meeting a spouse or significant other; just missing an accident; or hearing a speaker or song that changes one's perspective. For me, it was the decision to become partners with the very successful real estate agent Sue Huckaby. At the time, Sue was number ten in the United States in residential home sales production, truly rock-star status. I was a successful agent on her team and doing respectfully well enough. One of Sue's comments I recall clearly was, "Karen, you have the capability to do much greater things, yet you may be happy with what you have." She invited me to consider that the assumption of a business of her magnitude would be like boarding a train to a completely different destination.

The decision reminded of the poem by Marianne Williamson:

Our Greatest Fear
It is our light, not our darkness, that most frightens us.
Our deepest fear is not that we are inadequate.
Our deepest fear is that we are powerful beyond measure.
It is our light not our darkness that most frightens us.
We ask ourselves, who am I to be brilliant, gorgeous, talented and fabulous?

Actually, who are you not to be?
You are a child of God.
Your playing small does not serve the world.
There's nothing enlightened about shrinking so that other
people won't feel insecure around you.

Being encouraged by a mentor I respected was empowering. Yet the question remained: did I believe in me? Playing small, I realized, would not benefit as many people. So I decided at that juncture to get on the train and take the journey that would require everything that I have. By doing so, it has been a grand adventure to discover all that I am capable of being. If I can do it, you can too.

Reflect on the "sliding doors" experiences that have changed your life.

GREAT ARBITRAGE IN REAL ESTATE

There are times in the real estate market when a great arbitrage can occur. The most frequent scenario in the residential sector is when homeowners sell their home for a strong price relative to the market conditions and buy up at a price that is still low relative to the market potential. Arbitrage is the practice of taking advantage of a price difference between two or more markets. This involves a combination of matching deals that capitalize upon the imbalance, the gain being the difference between the market prices.

This is best illustrated by an example. A buyer wants to purchase a home in the $750,000 range, where values have experienced increases in the area at a steady appreciation rate of 10 percent per year. In most cases in this situation, there will often be multiple offers on similar homes and frequently prices escalate well over list price. If the current appreciation rate continues, that means similar homes will be selling for another 10 percent the next year, or $825,000. If the buyer waits until the next year to purchase, it is likely that he could be priced out of the community.

On the other side of the great arbitrage scenario is the sale of a condo. In this situation, the owners bought at the peak of the market, for $450,000. To wait for the market to completely recover, the majority of their investment and cost of sale expenses might not benefit them in the long term. This part of the market recently returned to peak prices from the correction that occurred during the Great Recession. It appreciates year over year at a rate of about 5 percent on average. At that rate, the property would increase in value at best to around $472,500. Even if the market achieved a rate of 10 percent, the client would still lose ground on the buy side.

The higher-priced home, appreciating at a rate of 10 percent per year, meant a $75,000 potential increase in value; even if the lower-priced property achieved 10 percent per year, that only meant a potential $45,000 increase in value. As you can see, by waiting, this family would have lost ground of $30,000 in one year alone.

Clearly this was an instance of great arbitrage. There was some risk involved. To know where they were going to move meant getting the higher-priced house under contract prior to selling the condo. Further, the clients had to qualify with a lender to carry the debt on both properties and be willing to possibly pay two mortgages for a period of time. At one point, the clients asked if we could sell their condo and I said absolutely yes it would sell, it would just depend on whether the price would be acceptable to them. The client listened to our recommendations, priced the condo correctly for the market, and it went under contract quickly. The couple became one of our raving fans for negotiating a successful arbitrage scenario for their family.

Find great arbitrage scenarios for your market.

THROW SPAGHETTI AGAINST THE WALL TO SEE WHAT STICKS

Experienced pasta cooks have a saying: "Throw the spaghetti against the wall and see what sticks." The reason being, if the pasta sticks, then you know it is cooked. Another interpretation is that it isn't possible to know what will stick, in most cases, until we actually do it. Trying to figure that out by sitting back and waiting to see what sticks doesn't provide any more information.

This saying is one my deceased business partner, Sue Huckaby, would frequently proclaim with her charming southern accent. Listing agents prepare a comparative market analysis (CMA) for seller clients. The CMA is the industry standard to understand the current market conditions and to assist the seller in establishing a market list price. Until the home actually goes on the active market, though, there is no way to truly know the outcome. Once the property is on the market, in effect the market is the market study. The level of activity and feedback are strong indicators of whether the list price was "cooked" thoroughly enough, to use the pasta analogy.

Author Amy Wilkinson, in the book *The Creator's Code: 6 Essential Skills of Extraordinary Entrepreneurs*, references a study performed with two groups of people with the objective to create a project. One group of participants was provided with as many supplies as they needed and were encouraged to try multiple times to create the project. The other group was only given the supplies for one project and told that they were to think and plan before they built the "perfect" project. The successful group was the one that had the opportunity to try and fail, because they learned so much each time they tried it. It was in the actual doing that the best outcome was achieved.

Real estate is an active pursuit. It is in the engagement with the market and clients in real time that determines what pricing strategy works—and thus sticks. This phenomenon applies to lead generation, as well. The agent who proactively prospects consistently on a daily basis is like the experimental group that was encouraged to try multiple times. Real estate is not a "one-and-done" endeavor.

Throwing spaghetti against the wall is the best way to know whether it is fully cooked; putting a home on the market is the best way to know how the market will respond. And consistent business development is the best way to achieve and sustain success as a real estate agent.

Take action to achieve best results in market knowledge and business development.

WHO IS YOUR SUPERHERO?

During the month of June, Americans honor fathers with a special day. The two fathers closest to me are my own father and my husband. Fathers are often a child's first superhero, and to them possess x-ray vision, super strength, speed and agility, invulnerability, and are capable of leaping tall buildings in a single bound. Everyone can benefit from having role models and mentors to look up to and emulate. Let's consider how real estate agents can tap into these superhero capabilities.

X-ray vision for a father is being able to see what's really going on, often referred to as having eyes in the back of his head. A real estate agent can hone his x-ray vision by being in tune with the market and being alert for trends and shifts. The physical strength of a superhero correlates to the agent's ability to power through difficult situations—even break through walls of indecision and challenging situations.

Speed and agility are achieved by the superhero and agent alike by being on the top of their game. One can move quickly when focused and in shape both figuratively and literally. These are skills that can be learned and perfected with practice. The real estate market changes quickly. An example that comes to mind is that the best houses almost always sell really fast. The agent must be alert to when one hits the market so that the client can move quickly.

True superheroes always have some vulnerability—that's where the villain attacks. This is when the hero engages his powers to overcome challenges with super strength. The hero knows his shortcomings and takes action to rise above them. Professional agents, being human of course, have weaknesses, as well. What are yours and what steps can you take to overcome them? One strategy that has been successful for me is to seek counsel from a trusted mentor or coach. And like many superheroes, I am in business with a partner who encourages me and pushes me back out into the marketplace to do the best for our team.

The superhero effortlessly leaps tall buildings in a single bound. This happens for my clients when I cut a deal that beats the market. Achieving the highest sale ever for a neighborhood or type of home is a super feat to be celebrated. So is getting a complicated transaction to settlement—truly a superhero feat.

Emulate superheroes in your life and business by tapping into their strengths to propel you to new heights and success for your clients.

A HOME INSPECTION CONTINGENCY IS LIKE BEING ENGAGED TO BE MARRIED

JUNE
11

Just as there are no perfect spouses, there are no perfect houses. If one were to pick apart her partner of choice with a fine-tooth comb, many flaws would probably be revealed. This is why premarital counseling is advised by many faith traditions and wedding officiants. The engagement period is a time to get to know each other and to affirm the decision to go forward into marriage, for better or for worse. Or it can also be the time that one or both determine they are not compatible and call the wedding off.

The same holds true for the purchase of a home. The inspection contingency period is designed for buyers to determine the condition of the home. This can include conducting their own assessments and/or bringing in specialists and others to provide professional evaluations. Home inspectors, by the very nature of their job, are charged to go through a home and evaluate in detail the components and the whole. Very few properties, even brand-new homes, come through a home inspection with a completely clean bill of health. This can sometimes lead to "buyer's remorse."

This is when it can be helpful to seek outside counsel. In the case of marriage, it is a good idea to visit with people who have been married a while to determine if the perceived flaws are reasonable and common—or if there should be concern about the intended partner. In the case of home buying, there is great wisdom in listening to the counsel of a professional real estate agent and other advisors. They should be able to provide perspective about the issues identified. Sometimes additional discovery is advised, perhaps by having a specialist in the field conduct further evaluation.

An example in which this application occurred in my business was a case when I represented both the seller and the purchaser in the transaction. The home inspector found evidence of moisture in the basement. The seller hired a licensed contractor to remedy the situation by correcting the drainage and extending downspouts as advised by the inspector. The purchaser hired the same inspector to conduct the walkthrough, at which time the moisture meter reading indicated the situation was improved, yet not fully resolved. The purchaser consulted with a specialist in the area who determined that the ground likely had springs flowing underneath. In that situation, some things could be done, but perfection would not be achievable. The purchaser, with this counsel, agreed to move forward with the settlement for better or worse. The good news is they have lived in the home "happily ever after" for the past decade.

The home inspection contingency process is one that can cause buyer's remorse. It is the professional agent who uses strategies of success to help clients make good decisions for their situation.

Prepare buyer clients for the home inspection contingency period to make the best decision for their situation.

TAKE THE NEXT STEP

Inquiring agents often want to know how often to contact prospects. On the continuum of doing nothing to being considered a pushy salesperson, there are a lot of choices in between. One of the secrets to my success is that I had the attitude of being helpful to people. And so I would just take the next natural step.

An example of a situation that happens frequently is someone stops me in the grocery store, at church, or at book club and asks me about the home down the street that is on the market or recently sold. We chat briefly and then I tell them I will do some research and get back to them. This enables me to get their contact information if I don't have it already. If it is about a particular home and I haven't seen it yet, then I will go see the home. Afterwards I call or send a follow-up e-mail with the requested information. My goal is to do so within twenty-four hours, no later than forty-eight hours. On occasion, I also send a handwritten note thanking them for reaching out to me and to let them know I am always available to assist with any of their real estate needs or questions.

Many agents naturally do this. What happens next is what I believe makes the difference, and that is to keep the conversation going. Enter the person's contact information in your database. This step helps you build your database to grow your business. Then put a "watch" on the house they inquired about or set up an alert to follow up with them. With some gentle probing, I ask if they are in the market to buy or sell a home. At this juncture, people are typically forthcoming and I have a better sense of next steps. Then I just "put them in the pipeline" to stay in touch.

How often I contact them from that point forward depends on several factors. Of course, I will contact them when they ask me to, usually just a bit ahead of schedule. If they get in touch with me in the meantime, I mirror their step, again usually just one step ahead but not pushy. It is like dancing the tango: move with confidence and try not to step on anyone's feet. If there is new or relevant information, I send that. Typically I reach out a minimum of one or two times per year just to stay in touch, to see if anything has changed, and to offer my assistance. This contact is a gentle reminder that I am an active real estate agent and want to earn their business.

What I see that challenges agents is just taking the next step. The words of Antoine de Saint-Exupery are my inspiration: "What saves a man is to take a step. Then another step. It is always the same step, but you have to take it." Really, the step I have found doesn't matter nearly as much as the action of actually taking it.

The quote applies equally well to building and growing a business. To paraphrase: "What builds and grows a business is to take a step. Then another step. It is always the same step, but you have to take it."

Take the next step today!

FLIPPING BURGERS

Flipping burgers is a well-known phrase in the real estate industry that refers to the transactional nature of the business. I put myself through college working in my family's restaurant business, so I have ample experience in flipping actual burgers. The transaction in the food service industry is typically short, relatively speaking. The patron orders, is served, and leaves within minutes if it is fast food or maybe a few hours in the case of fine dining. The transaction in the real estate business is typically several months and sometimes years in duration. There are, to be sure, some very short real estate transactions, in the case of an auction and occasionally with a cash sale. Yet even those are known to take a few weeks.

The challenge presented to many business owners is that as their business grows, they in effect have two jobs. One is to conduct the actual transactions of the business—to cook the burgers or to deliver the product or service. In the case of real estate, these include showing and listing properties, negotiating contracts, handling inspections, managing finance and appraisal contingencies, and finalizing details to settlement. This is sometimes referred to as working "in" the business.

In the words of musician and actor Snoop Dogg, being good at your job is important: "If it's flipping hamburgers at McDonald's, be the best hamburger flipper in the world. Whatever it is you do, you have to master your craft."

The other responsibility of the business owner involves continuous development of plans to build and expand the client base and grow to stay on top of the industry, trends, and future customer demands. This is often known as working "on" the business. Michael Gerber, in the *E-Myth* series, states that many entrepreneurs are challenged by this dichotomy and that the business owners who break through are those who run successful operations. This often becomes apparent to real estate agents when they realize that to go to the next level in production, they are going to have to operate it like a business. Many agents hire staff, others partner with another agent, and still others build a team.

It truly is a both/and situation. The agent must continue to provide top-notch customer service in order to keep clients happy so that they will be repeat clientele and raving fans. Yet the agent must also continuously seek out new customers and opportunities, as well as plan for the future in order to stay competitive in the marketplace.

Master your craft to be known as a top-notch professional.

MAINTAIN THE PACE OF PLAY

On the golf course, it is apparent how important it is to maintain the pace of play. The principle is that players are responsible to assure that they do not hold up the other players by their actions. This includes staying up with the group in front, as well as not holding up the group behind. There are techniques professionals use for staying on schedule that amateurs are well advised to heed. Failure to play the course in a timely fashion can result in a warning from the course marshall, penalties, not being able to finish the round, and sometimes not being invited to play the course again.

In real estate transactions, "time is of the essence" is the principle most similar to "maintain the pace of play." The agents are responsible to assure that their clients meet deadlines and deliver documents as per the contract. This includes staying on track as well as not holding up other parties by their actions.

By way of example, recently I represented a seller on the negotiations related to the home inspection. The agent for the purchaser delivered the report and addendum as per the contract. I assured him that the seller responded in a timely fashion. The agent for the purchaser and I had visited, and I was told verbally that we were in agreement. However, she seemed to be "sitting" on the ratified addendum. When I asked about the reason for the delay, she shared that she had another day. When I recommended that she read the contract and recalculate her days, she realized her error. If she had failed to deliver the addendum, her client would have lost her rights under the home inspection contingency. This is clearly more significant than being asked to leave a golf course!

Real estate professionals have techniques for maintaining the pace of play in transactions, just as pros do on the golf course. One of the key processes our team uses is a whiteboard with contract deadlines. This way, the staff and agents are all aware of the timelines. Second, upon contract ratification, a team member provides a schedule of deadlines to all the parties involved in the transaction. Third, read the contract, several times if necessary, to make certain that all the terms are being met. And finally, checklists are an invaluable method to keep track of details. A timely and successful closing is the professional real estate agent's goal.

Take steps to be sure that you
"maintain the pace of play" in your transactions.

"THERE'S NO PLACE LIKE HOME"

In the movie *The Wizard of Oz*, Dorothy discovered that the red shoes from the Good Witch of the North contain a special magic. That magic would return her to Kansas if Dorothy closed her eyes, spun around as she clicked her heels, and said over and over: "There's no place like home." By Dorothy believing in the magic, her dreams did come true, and she was transported back to her home in Kansas to her family and friends.

Home ownership is still a significant part of the American dream as is the movie's message. When Dorothy clicked her heels in *The Wizard of Oz*, she didn't say, "There is no place like renting someone else's property." She said, "There is no place like home." Owning your own home is a fundamental human desire. Sometimes people have to be reminded, just as Dorothy did.

Dorothy had her red shoes on the entire time she was going through the perils of the winged monkeys, the castle guards, the Wicked Witch of the West, and standing up to the mighty wizard. Even though she was not aware of the power they possessed, it was present. That is the power of knowing one has a "home" to go to.

A home is so embedded in the American fabric of life that there are numerous clichés attached to it, such as: "Be it ever so humble, there's no place like home"; "A man's home is his castle"; "Bring home the bacon"; "Nothing to write home about"; "Until the cows come home"; "Home is where you hang your hat"; and "Home sweet Home."

The heart of being a Realtor® means helping people pursue the satisfaction of realizing that ultimate dream—a home of their own. And for those who own a home and are selling, it is working with them through the process of not just the logistics and financial aspects, but the emotional ones as well.

Take the time to share with your clients the message:
"There's no place like home."

SELLER COLD FEET AND JILTED AT THE ALTAR

The seller has a perspective on what the analogy, "Being under contract is like being engaged" means for them. On occasion, a seller can experience "remorse," even though it is not as common as it is for buyers. One end of the spectrum is when the seller has a loss of nerves and confidence about the decision, which is more commonly known as "cold feet." The other extreme is that of being jilted at the altar, a rejection that is unexpected and without warning.

In almost all real estate transactions, the seller opens up the sales process by listing the home on the open market. The real estate agent actively markets the property for sale on the Internet, with print media, signage, brochures, hosting open houses, and so forth. The seller, through the agent, is proactively soliciting buyers.

It should not really be a surprise, then, when a buyer makes an offer. If it happens quickly, though, that is when we more often experience instances of cold feet on the part of the seller. In one particular situation, the sellers expressed a desire to move in order for their children to attend a different public school. As the neighborhood was transitional, in which older homes were being torn down in order to construct new, the most likely buyer would be a builder. We presented the property to the top builders in the community, and one wrote an offer. The agent negotiated a very strong contract in favor of our client, the seller. Further, it provided ample time after settlement for them to remain in the property while they found their next home. Even though they got everything they wanted and more, they literally froze and couldn't move. This is the ultimate example of "cold feet."

There can be situations in which it might not be in the sellers' best interest to enter into a contract with a buyer. Or it may be that it appears to be beneficial and then once the process has begun, the seller realizes that it would be best to not go forward. Another scenario is when the buyer places too many demands on the sellers that they are not willing to entertain.

The other end of the extreme is when the seller ratifies a contract and later does not want to go forward. Contractually, in most cases, there are not as many options for a seller to void a contract for sale as there are for purchasers. Many times, the contract provides the buyer recourse of "enforcing specific performance" on the seller. Thus, as in an engagement, sellers should not enter into a contract without careful consideration of the intended.

The professional agent is aware of and understands the options available to her clients and advises accordingly. All parties should seek legal counsel in the appropriate jurisdiction in order to best protect their rights.

Use commonly known terms such as "cold feet" and "jilted at the altar" as ways of explaining seller contractual obligations.

CINDERELLA STORY
REAL ESTATE AGENT REMAKE

The classic folk tale *Cinderella* tells the story of a young woman whose attributes were unrecognized and unappreciated. Through twists of fate, she becomes the favored one.

The most common remake for real estate agents is also my story. Though not oppressed, I put my career on hold to stay home and raise a family. As the children grew older, at the encouragement of others I decided to "try" selling residential real estate. Similar to many women in this situation, I have always loved working with people and looking at homes.

The fairy godmother is played by a broker or mentor who encourages the agent new in the business and equips her with a transformed pumpkin as an office. Perhaps there is some magic waved about and promises made of transformation.

The character in the story is the "belle of the ball." She meets and dances with the handsome prince. The agent quickly learns the steps to the dance of the real estate transaction, charming both buyers and sellers with her grace and skill. She is swept away with a bit of success, just as the handsome prince sweeps Cinderella off her feet. Her glass slipper is her confidence and belief in herself now that she has a career of her own.

Then midnight strikes, and all the magic the fairy godmother created with the sweep of her wand vanishes. Cinderella, in her haste to not be discovered as the ash girl she once was, runs in haste and loses her glass slipper.

The midnight strike for the agent is when the magic of the business disappears. This is the point when the agent discovers that lead generation is not a one-shot process. It is an activity that has to occur daily and consistently. The agent learns quickly that she is only as good as her last deal. All the time invested in getting a client's transaction to settlement took away from her energies and focus on obtaining the next client. She discovers that everyone knows many real estate agents and experiences rejection when her friends, neighbors, and husband's business associates don't choose her to work with. And the magic stops, too, when the first deal voids through no fault of hers. Or a client gets really angry over the market or a home inspection report, or anything in which truly the agent has no control over.

This is when the agent needs to remember that the glass slipper still fits. She is both worthy and capable; she has shown that she can dance. Her attributes, once unrecognized, have been demonstrated at the ball to the world. There will always be those who don't believe and perhaps even competition that will seek to undermine, like the evil stepmother and stepsisters. Yet she will persevere through it all and show her true value and grace by becoming a leader in the industry.

Demonstrate to the world that you are the
"belle of the ball" of real estate.

REALTORS® ARE LIKE JOURNALISTS

The role of a journalist is to seek the truth and report it. The journalist does not make the truth, nor does he "make" the news. Rather, the reporter is on the cutting edge of where the news is happening. According to the Society of Professional Journalists, there are several key standards to the profession. It states: "The duty of the journalist is to further those ends by seeking truth and providing a fair and comprehensive account of events and issues. Conscientious journalists from all media and specialties strive to serve the public with thoroughness and honesty."

The role of the agent, like the journalist, is to know the market in great depth and to report that information to all parties in a professional manner. The agent does not make the market; rather, he is on the cutting edge of where it is happening. By having intimate knowledge, he often is capable of understanding the nuances in ways that someone not actively involved could possibly be aware of.

Buyers and sellers sometimes believe that an agent can and should influence the market, in effect steer the outcome to their advantage. These activities often include putting the best spin on the condition of the home, market statistics, and even not sharing all the details of a property. The slant could be positive or negative, depending on who the target audience is and the party the real estate agent is representing.

However, there is a point when one may cross the line into "puffery." The dictionary definition of this term is: "Advertising or sales presentation relying on exaggerations, opinions, and superlatives, with little or no credible evidence to support its vague claims." Puffery may be tolerated, to an extent, so long as it does not amount to misrepresentation (false claim of possessing certain positive attributes or of not possessing certain negative attributes).

A key aspect to ethical journalism is to minimize harm to the public it serves. In many cases, this means telling people the truth, rather than only what they want to hear. The same applies to the professional agent. It is imperative that she is honest and forthright in dealing with all parties, even when it might jeopardize an outcome that would benefit her.

Information and data is readily available on the Internet, which once had as its source the real estate agent. So much so that some predict the demise of the Realtor®. Just as I believe in the professional journalist, I believe there will always be demand for the conscientious Realtor®. This professional seeks the truth by providing a fair and comprehensive account of the market condition and contract negotiations. Further, this agent strives to serve the public with thoroughness and honesty.

Seek ways as a real estate agent to report the market in a professional manner.

PAINT NITE

JUNE
19

"Paint Nite" is an opportunity to be social and creative at the same time. The event is typically held in a local restaurant, and so food and refreshments are available for enjoyment. Supplies and guidance are provided, and no experience is necessary. By following the sample painting and the step-by-step instructions, each person creates their own masterpiece.

I have enjoyed attending a number of these "paint and sip" sessions. The most interesting aspect to the experience to me is that each person's artwork is unique. The same materials are available to all of the participants, the same painting is provided as a guide, and all follow the same instructions, yet every creation is truly one-of-a-kind.

A similar phenomenon occurs in the real estate industry. Almost every agent has access to the same or similar materials, such as multiple listing service, contract forms, digital signature, and marketing platforms. And yet each person has her own style. As long as agents follow the legal requirements set out by the licensing bureau, the code of ethics set up by the National Association of Realtors® and the brokerage standards, then truly the rest is up to them.

This flexibility is why a lot of people enter real estate. As independent contractors, they are their "own boss." This can be both freeing and actually overwhelming when there are so many choices available.

The question is, where to start? In *The Millionaire Real Estate Agent*, Gary Keller maintains that those agents who build a base on the fundamentals are found to achieve success quicker and sustain it longer. Once the foundation is established, then the agent can add her own flair. In a way, it is a lot like "Paint Nite." The basics are provided and taught, and then the artist adds her own personal touch.

Establish the fundamentals before incorporating the creative element to the business.

VIRTUOUS CYCLE

The concept of a virtuous cycle has applications in economics and management theory. It is based on the idea that success leads to more success via the feedback loop. The reverse concept is that of the vicious cycle, when circumstances spiral in a negative and undesirable direction.

An example that comes to mind is that of weight training. In the beginning, the results of the exercise are not obvious. The athlete completes the movements based on the knowledge of the future benefit promised. At some point, the exerciser feels stronger and has more energy, sees the toning of the muscles, and recognizes the health benefits of increased metabolism. As results become more apparent, the virtuous cycle causes the exerciser to commit and remain consistent in the program.

In real estate, those new to the profession have to trust in the process, as it takes time to build the virtuous cycle. The sales cycle in real estate is much longer than in many industries. One simple way to create a virtuous cycle is by staying in touch with and cultivating past client relationships. Homeowners move, on average, once every seven years, which in many cases can mean both a buy and a sell transaction. Further, many salespeople build their business on referrals, which are frequently obtained from happy past clients. Providing quality service to referrals is also a positive self-fulfilling prophecy. People want to refer business to people who provide top-notch professional service.

Listings are another opportunity to create positive momentum in a real estate business. With a listing, an agent has the opportunity to conduct marketing that goes beyond the sale of just the one home. Agents, in many cases, meet other sellers while hosting public open houses and neighbor receptions, by door knocking, or calling those living in the neighborhood. Those sellers may be in the market soon to sell their home. Buyers often contact listing agents directly for information about the home for sale, which opens up a dialogue that can potentially turn into a client relationship. Mailing just-listed and just-sold postcards to homes surrounding the listing or buyer-represented sale are also known to generate additional opportunities. Statistically, for every listing sold, professional agents on average generate one additional buyer or seller lead.

There is also the mental virtuous cycle. When one is on a positive roll, the chain of events feed themselves in a favorable direction. In the words of Warren Buffett: "Time is the friend of the wonderful habits, the enemy of the mediocre ones."

Professional agents consistently take those actions that continue this success-oriented momentum.

Establish and sustain activities that project your business and life into a virtuous cycle.

THE BUYER IS JUST NOT INTO THE HOME—SIGNALS

JUNE 21

The basic premise of the movie, *He's Just Not That Into You*, is that if the guy hasn't pursued the lady, it is because he isn't really interested. Women rationalize and create any number of excuses, but when all is said and done, he just didn't care enough to contact her again. The story is humorous because there is an element of truth to it. The ladies in the movie learn how to read the signs whether a guy is interested or "just is not that into them." As a professional real estate agent, I have found it helpful for sellers to be able to recognize buying signals, as well.

There are a number of rules of thumb that agents use to determine when a home has been "rejected" by the marketplace. It depends on the price point and the current market conditions. Some parameters to consider: fifteen showings or fifteen days on market, whichever comes first. If after thirty days no offers have been presented, that is a strong indication that buyers aren't interested. Just the fact that a buyer doesn't come back a second time in effect means that the home was not right for him.

In the upper brackets where there are a smaller number of potential buyers who qualify, there could very well be as few as six viable purchasers. The number of available buyers in a marketplace is determined by how many sales there have been in a certain price range in the previous six months to one year. When there are so few available purchasers, some properties require more days on the open market. For certain, if no offers have been presented in normal conditions and exposure, there is no doubt that the "market has spoken." All of these indicators point to the same bottom line: "The buyer is just not that into the home."

In the movie, a woman gets a man interested by allowing him to pursue, by not appearing needy and desperate, and moving on when she realizes that he just isn't that into her. How do I know if buyer is into the home? My phone rings! The buyer attends all public open houses and wants to view the home multiple times. She asks buying-signal questions, like "When does the seller want to move"; "What local swim club does the family belong to"; and "Do you know when the roof was last replaced?"

So how does a seller increase a buyer's interest? There are a few fundamental points of value in real estate: location, home condition, and price relative to the market. It is impossible to change the location of a property; that's what makes it so unique. That leaves only two things that a seller can affect to increase interest by buyers: home condition and price relative to the market. In the book and movie, the light bulb went on as soon as the characters realized where they really stood in relation to the intended other—and were willing to adjust their actions accordingly! Sellers are well advised to pay attention to the signals as well.

Share with seller clients the buying signals or absence thereof and how their home is being perceived in the marketplace by potential buyers.

THE PICTURE ON THE SIDE OF THE ROAD

It is much easier to remember a face than a name. That is why a photo of a person is often incorporated in marketing a service or product. The reason why it is easier to remember a face compared to a name is because it "is really a much richer stimulus," according to Richard Russell, an assistant professor of psychology at Gettysburg College who has studied facial recognition. Names are a collection of letters, sometimes in an unusual and difficult-to-remember combination and spelling. Photos tell the story of gender, age, ethnicity, personality, attractiveness, and much more. It truly is a case of "a picture is worth a thousand words."

When I meet people in the community, many times they will recognize me but cannot recall how we know each other. In many situations, we actually don't know each other personally. So I respond with something to the effect of: "Oh, I know what it probably is. I'm a real estate agent in the area. You've probably seen my picture on the side of the road!" Then we all have a laugh because they put "two and two" together and realize they know me from the real estate marketing signs with the photo of myself and business partner.

On one occasion, a client called our office in a panic. She was quite embarrassed to tell us that she needed to have a new sign installed. Through inquiry, I discovered that her sons had used the photos on our real estate sign for target practice with their paint-ball guns. I thought it was hilarious and of course assured her that it was not a problem at all, we would get a new sign installed. It was truly humbling, as well. Now when I meet people, I have another story to tell.

The professional agent connects to build and grow a business that is well known and respected in the community. Throughout the process, remember the words of author Anna Quindlen: "If your success is not on your own terms, if it looks good to the world, but does not feel good in your heart, it is not success at all."

Marketing is a key to success to build and grow a business.

ALL REAL ESTATE IS LOCAL

"All real estate is local" is one of those sayings that has become part of common knowledge because it is true. The primary factor that determines value for real estate is location, as the unique nature of property is such that it cannot be moved. Typically, a home closer to a city center will be valued differently than the same exact home built in a suburb farther out. Both homes may have similar square footage, lot size, and comparable school systems, but the location is what makes the value different.

Location in real estate can even be so specific as to mean where the home is located in a neighborhood. For example, a home that backs up to a busy road is going to be valued differently than one at the end of a quiet cul-de-sac. In a condominium, the floor and unit views are location-driven; the higher up, the greater the value.

Location determines proximity to employment, access to public transportation, which public schools the students in the neighborhood attend, as well as private education availability. Location goes so far as to establish what sun exposure the home will receive. The distance, quality and quantity of shopping, cultural and community opportunities, and parks and governmental services all are based on location. Location controls myriad factors—some may even be unique to the location!

A real estate tycoon in Britain, the late Lord Harold Samuel, coined the expression: "There are three things that matter in property: location, location, location."

So when people ask, "How's the real estate market?" The answer has to be: "It depends." It depends on the location, first and foremost. The professional real estate agent understands market conditions are multifaceted and pursues a deep understanding and knowledge of the factors that contribute to value—the greatest of which is location.

Seek knowledge on how location influences
market value to proactively inform clients.

MINISTRY OF A REAL ESTATE AGENT

One of the secrets of successful real estate agents is that they seek to meet people's needs. The business aspects in the real estate transaction are "head" oriented and the personal and emotional concerns are related to the "heart." The professional agent meets both levels of client needs.

The definition of "minister," as applied to the process of helping someone buy or sell real estate, means to give service, care, or aid; attend, as to wants or necessities; and to contribute, as to comfort or happiness. In this way, the profession of real estate agent can be viewed as a ministry.

The real estate industry distinguishes "ministerial acts" as those routine duties that a licensee can perform for a person. In most jurisdictions, licensed agents may perform these "ministerial duties" for customers, as well as clients who are under a brokerage agreement.

In almost all situations, when people are in the process of buying or selling a home, another life event has occurred to precipitate the move or some change is anticipated. These include positive life events such as marriage; having children and/or children reaching an age when more space is required; transfer of job; increased income justifying purchase of a larger and/or more expensive home; empty nest; receiving a financial windfall; retirement; pursuit of additional education or training; or desiring better schools for children.

Moving in many situations is predicated on life events that can be stressful and not viewed typically as positive, such as the loss of spouse or loved one; illness of self, spouse or loved one; divorce; marital separation; job loss or demotion; financial setback; or tax planning.

The Homes and Rahe stress scale ranks these and other life events that often lead to stress. "Change in residence" is one of those life events and, combined with one or more other stressful situations, increases one's need for "ministerial acts." The reward is the knowledge that you have helped and served people in need. I personally have found great meaning as a professional real estate agent in being of service to people. It is a noble calling!

Develop a heart for service as you care for clients and customers.

THE DANCE OF NEGOTIATIONS

Real estate negotiations can take on the cadence of a dance, as both have two partners. The seller asks the buyer to dance by listing the home on the market. The buyer accepts the invitation with an offer. When a buyer presents an offer, it means the seller is a wallflower no more! She has finally been asked to dance. If there are a lot of buyers available, then the seller has options and can fill up her dance card with any number of partners.

Once asked to dance, the seller can match the buyer, step back, or can decide to take off in another direction. Experienced negotiators are familiar with the steps, just as with any dance partner.

Early in my real estate career, I went on a listing appointment at the home of a past client of my business partner. After my presentation, the couple said that they were going to go into another room to talk and would be back with their decision. In the meantime, if I was interested I could look over the book, *Negotiate to Win: How to Get the Best Deal Every Time*, by Jim Thomas. It turns out the author of the book was one of the people I was meeting with.

The listing presentation must have been persuasive, as I was hired as their agent. And I went on to successfully sell their home. In the process, I learned a number of new negotiation strategies. Further, I have taken to heart the section in the book, "The Practice of Negotiating." What I have found is that the more I practice both negotiating and dancing, the better I become. It helps, of course, to have an experienced partner on the other side.

Even if the partner isn't strong, the leader can set the pace and carry the other. My husband is a Texan and a natural at the two-step country-western dance. It is a pleasure having him propel me around the dance floor. That is the way good negotiations led by a professional real estate agent can progress as well—like a well-choreographed dance.

*Learn and practice the steps to negotiate
the best outcome for your clients.*

A CONTRACT ON A HOME IS LIKE BEING ENGAGED TO BE MARRIED: MORE ON BUYER'S REMORSE

June is traditionally known as "wedding month." My husband and I have now celebrated three decades of marriage. Still, after all this time, I vividly remember a conversation with one of his sisters shortly after we became engaged. She said to me, "Now that you are engaged to marry my brother, please stop looking at other guys." It seemed an overly protective sentiment to me, as he was about to turn thirty-five. Over time, though, I have come to realize she just did not want to see her brother hurt.

This conversation comes to mind as the phenomenon in real estate known as "buyer's remorse." During that period of time after an offer for a home has been written and accepted by the sellers, often there is reconsideration by the buyers. The buyer wonders things like, "Did they get all the terms they could?" "Did they overpay?" Or "Is there another better home out there?" Often they visit with other parties, such as family member or coworkers, who plant seeds of doubt or concern about the contract and home. In many cases, there are contingencies written into the offer that provide for the purchaser to void the contract if a "deal-breaking" issue arises.

What my sister-in-law was saying, I believe, was that even when an engaged couple is in love, if either person continues to look to see if the "grass is greener on the other side of the fence," then unhappiness and a "buyer's remorse" of the soon-to-be marriage partner can occur. Professional real estate agents see this when buyers continue to look at Internet sites and make requests to see every house that comes on the market. This can be problematic, as the buyer is in a contractual arrangement with a seller. The seller has, in effect, taken the home off the market, has become engaged to that buyer, and is expecting a respectable level of commitment. On the other hand, it can be beneficial to show these other homes, as perhaps the buyer could do better. The agent is obligated to represent the client, while at the same time be fair to all parties and assure the contract terms are adhered to.

In most cases, though, a wandering eye does not benefit any of the parties. Thus, I most often recommend to buyer clients to "turn off the automatic notifications on their device for new listings." There will always be more homes that come on the market. Further, I advise that when parties are contractually bound in real estate, it is similar to being engaged to be married; they should be fully committed to that house!

Be proactive with buyer clients to prevent buyer's remorse.

AUTOPILOT

The takeoff and landing of a plane are key moments that require a pilot's full attention. Once in the air at cruising altitude, though, the autopilot performs a vital function. With autopilot, the plane will fly on course, thereby reducing the pilot's workload and fatigue. The autopilot takes care of the basic functions of speed, maintaining altitude, and staying on course so that the pilot can focus his attention on those situations that require a thinking person. Systems are to a real estate agent what autopilot is for a pilot.

First, agents should establish a system for prospecting. This can be set up as activity blocking, which means to contact a set number of people each working day, or time blocking, which is a set amount of time per day allocated to that task. Once this process is set up in place and functions smoothly, the professional agent can put it on autopilot.

The next system to establish is one that tracks leads and sets up a plan for follow-through. This often occurs simultaneously with lead-generation activities. Some agents use a database such as Wise Agent, Top Producer, or Contractually. Keep in mind that some of these tasks can be performed by a staff person, which is both an autopilot and leverage strategy. Once the systems are in place, then everyone knows their responsibilities and can be held accountable to metrics daily.

Advertising, distribution of postcards or mailers, social media, and other content-related marketing activities, once in place, can be put on autopilot with monitoring. Our team has staff members who oversee all of these functions under agent direction. In the beginning, as is typical of a new real estate agent, I did all of this. As the business grew, staff took on more and more of these types of responsibilities.

My husband is a private pilot and reminds me that it is during takeoff and landing when the pilot needs to pay the most attention. So it is with a real estate practice, as well; when getting the systems off the ground, the agent should plan to put in the most effort and time.

There can be a danger to autopilot that I must warn you about. Flying a plane is still a hands-on operation; it requires a thinking person. Sometimes putting a system on autopilot causes one to become complacent, and then fail to check in and verify that everything is operating properly and as intended. Autopilot can be your ally when everything is running smoothly, and your enemy if it gets off course or isn't sufficiently monitored. The key to this success strategy is to remain always vigilant.

Determine what systems can be put on autopilot so that you can focus on the more demanding opportunities of the business.

HONEYMOON PERIOD

The honeymoon period is most commonly known as a short time period after a couple has married. The broader definition according to the dictionary is: "Any new relationship characterized by an initial period of harmony and goodwill."

Professional real estate agents recognize that there often exists a honeymoon period during which it is important that the parties come to an agreement. The phenomenon, I have found, is very much like a new romance. Buyers have the most goodwill toward the home and sellers early on in the process. If negotiations become sticky or mired down too much in the details, then they start to feel that it will be difficult to "harmonize" with the other party. In many cases, the home buying and selling decision is emotional for the clients. At some point, the rational part of the brain kicks in, and people often start to question whether it was "meant to be."

This positive aurora seems to last about twenty-four to forty-eight hours. Some purchasers and agents write a deadline into contract offers. The reason frequently shared is that they don't want the seller and the listing agent to shop the offer around. I believe the motivation can be deeper than that. What I have found is that, after that time period passes, they are not sure they will still "feel the love." And they want to be free to explore their options. Once the home is under contract, it is a lot like "being engaged." The parties become connected to each other and feel a greater commitment than just during the offer stage.

It is beneficial for the agent to help her clients recognize this emotional component. Whenever possible, I recommend that we respond within the "honeymoon period." Should meeting that time frame present a challenge, it is best to provide an explanation and when a response could be anticipated. Say, for example, it is an estate sale and there are four family members involved. Explain that the parties want to have time to visit with the financial advisor and when a response can be expected.

A generally acceptable rule of thumb is that people want to "sleep on it." Continuous procrastination, though, can cause bad will. Thus, it is important to be aware of what a delay message sends to the other party. At listing and buyer consultation appointments and in subsequent conversations, the agent should alert clients to the "time is of the essence" nature of real estate negotiations. I have found that when people are prepared in advance for the likelihood of an occurrence, it speeds up the process.

In the one-thousand-plus real estate transactions I have been a part of through the years, at least 80 percent ratified within forty-eight hours. Experience speaks for itself—understanding the honeymoon period is a key to success.

Take steps to prepare clients for the honeymoon period of negotiations.

"MAY THE FORCE BE WITH YOU"

"May the force be with you" is a mantra proclaimed by several of the characters in the *Star Wars* series. The statement achieved cult-like status in 2005 after being named to the top one hundred movie quotes of all times by the American Film Institute.

For real estate agents, the "force" is the energy drawn from one's mental and psychological strength. The positive intentions combat the negative energy that can arise from fear, anger, and frustration from challenges. It is, in a way, both a mindset and a muse. The force is the inspiration for the journey, to be strong in adversity, and to succeed in the mission.

When an agent is heading out of the office to meet with sellers for a listing appointment or to show houses to a buyer, the natural inclination is for people to wish the agent "good luck."

Truly, luck does not have anything to do with the work of influencing clients to buy and sell houses. It takes a unique blend of knowledge of the market, negotiating strategy, hard work, a positive mindset, intelligence, an understanding of human nature, plus many more attributes. None of those rely on luck. Instead, our team members encourage each other with: "May the force be with you." Positive and proactive thinking is yet another way professional agents sustain long-term success.

Develop mindset mantras such as "May the force be with you"
for success in your business practice and life.

FREE CAN BE EXPENSIVE

The idea of obtaining something for nothing is very enticing. The psychology behind offering or receiving something for free is complicated. In effect, it can create a reciprocity cycle whereby the receiving party feels obligated to do something in return for the giver. That is one of the principles for agents to provide a free comparative market analysis to sellers. Or a free home-buying guide for purchasers. Once the party has accepted the "free" service or item, then it is assumed that they will use the services of the person who provided the benefit.

There is a Japanese proverb along this line: "There is nothing that is more expensive than that which comes for free." It means that if there truly is value, then there will be an associated cost. Something that is free may have strings attached that later could be more costly.

For example, a seller who sells his home without the benefit of a licensed agent may find that even though there was no commission, the home sells for less. So in actuality, the cost of sale was higher overall. According to the National Association of Realtors®, in 2014, 8 percent of home sales in the United States were For Sale by Owner (FSBO). The typical FSBO home sold for 18.6 percent less than those in which an agent was involved in the transaction ($210,000 versus $249,000).

Free offerings can actually be so readily available and commonplace that at times people do not place any value on them. If all agents provide similar resources, then what is the uniqueness that causes one to stand apart from another? Providing professional advice, counsel and services without any fee associated with those services can be very expensive in the long run. Consider the opportunity cost of your time. Rather, take the time to demonstrate the value-add associated with your services and remind clients that "free can be expensive."

Apply the concept that "free can be expensive" by demonstrating the value of your services.

TWO GOOD SHOTS IN A ROW

My first professional job out of college in the early 1980s was with the residential lot development division of Trammell Crow Companies. Quickly, it became clear that many of the commercial deals were transacted by men while on the golf course. So a lady colleague and I decided that to be competitive we needed to learn to play golf. Still good friends, we have fond memories of early-Saturday mornings playing the back nine on a local public course where we took lessons. We both play golf today and attribute our interest in the sport from our salad days in the real estate business.

At one point, our pro imparted some wisdom that has stuck with me for more than thirty years and goes something like this: "The key to getting better in golf is to have two good shots in a row. And then do it again, and again, and again." Yes, if there comes a day that I ever play golf that well, I would quit my day job and go out on the professional golf circuit. Truly that is a joke; it wasn't meant to be one for me then and still isn't today.

The wisdom applies to the real estate business, as well. Just think, if you were to have two good transactions in a row. And then do it again, and again, and again. The agents who generate leads two days in a row, and then do it again, and again, and again. It is those agents who have set up systems for success and are consistent in the implementation of them who are the true professionals.

The key to sustained success is in the continuity of performance. And that begins with skill development, which is created by strong habits and practice. Otherwise it involves being stuck in the loop of being only as good as the most recent transaction.

For my golf game, it meant evenings taking lessons and hitting balls on the driving range, as well as playing the course early on Saturday mornings rather than sleeping in. For real estate, it means consistently prospecting, tracking for productivity, and conversion to sales. Two good transactions in a row—that's a goal any agent can strive to achieve.

Take the steps to achieve two good transactions in a row.

WHEN YOU HEAR HOOFBEATS . . . A BUYER'S TALE

The origin of the counsel "When you hear hoofbeats, think of horses, not zebras" is from the medical field. Dr. Theodore Woodward gave this instruction to medical interns in the 1940s. In that setting, it means to think first of the most logical and common diagnosis before considering the exotic.

The real estate application concerns the diagnosis of a home's condition. Experience shows that it depends on how one views the situation as to the response. There are those buyer clients who take the perspective of the house just as it is and don't read anything more into the circumstances. And then there are those buyers who have an active imagination and allow it to spiral into the worst possible scenarios.

The buyer, when presented with the inspection reports, can take several directions. At one end of the spectrum is to accept the home in "as-is condition." Options that are in the middle range include request the seller to repair, replace or remedy the situation, or negotiate for either money toward closing costs or a reduction in sales price. The most extreme scenario is to void the contract.

The buyer on the lighter end of the spectrum who reads the report may say something along the lines of: "We realize it isn't a new home and there are some things we were going to do anyway when we move in. Let's just ask for the things that we really need."

At the other end of the continuum is the buyer who proclaims: "This house is falling apart and we've paid too much for it. I want everything on the list done. Also, the seller should increase the closing-cost credit by $10,000. And because of that one leak in the pipe in the basement, I want the seller to conduct a full range of mold testing and remediation."

It is the agent's duty to fully represent their clients' interests. If, in fact, there are problems with the property, then by all means the agent should pursue every measure to have them addressed. It is even more important for the real estate professional to be a voice of reason should the buyer be emotional and not thinking logically.

To apply "when you hear hoofbeats," an agent should counsel the buyer to consider the actual evidence rather than to take the extreme position. Recommend obtaining evaluations and estimates from licensed contractors to determine the true extent of the issues identified. In this matter-of-fact manner, buyers tend to be more reasonable and willing to listen to and accept wise counsel.

Use the "when you hear hoofbeats" strategy to influence clients to follow wise counsel.

WRITE YOUR OWN
STORY OF YOUR DESTINY

What is the story you tell yourself about you? Do you like it?

Gandhi said:

> *Your beliefs become your thoughts,*
> *Your thoughts become your words,*
> *Your words become your actions,*
> *Your actions become your habits,*
> *Your habits become your values,*
> *Your values become your destiny.*

It all starts with your beliefs. Do you believe that you are capable and worthy of becoming and being a successful real estate agent? If you do believe it, then are your thoughts of being a top producer? If you think like a top producer, then are your words those that a successful person would use? If your words are of a successful person, then are your actions that of a professional? If your actions are that of a professional, then are your habits of a high-achieving Realtor®? If your habits are those of a high-achieving Realtor®, then are your values evident to the world? If your values are evident, then your destiny is your unique calling to achieve.

As a mother at home when our children were young, I immersed myself in that role. It was my calling at that time in my life, and I am grateful to have been given the opportunity. As they grew older, I decided to "try" selling residential real estate. The difference is that I did more than "try." I actually "did." So much so that people who knew me when the kids were young were amazed at my transformation from "mom at home" to "businesswoman."

A few years later, one of my friends was conducting research for a media publication on people who had gone through transformations. She interviewed me because she felt I was a different person from whom I was before. Her explanation was that a lot of women become real estate agents, but not all of them become businesswomen at my level.

Statistics affirm her opinion. The majority of Realtors® are women, yet only 1 percent arrive at top levels of success. And from my research, less than 20 percent run the top real estate teams and groups in the United States. I rewrote my story from "mom at home" to "successful businesswoman" by believing that I could, and then followed Gandhi's words and did it. If I can do it, you can too!

Write your own story of your destiny.

FOURTH OF JULY IN AMERICA: FREEDOM ISN'T FREE—HOME OWNERSHIP ISN'T EITHER

Today, as the United States celebrates the Fourth of July, I am reminded of a sign our son Drew had in his room growing up that stated boldly: "Freedom." Drew bought the sign because he found it incredibly ironic that he could purchase something that says "freedom," but that it wasn't "free." In order to acquire it, there was a cost expended.

As we celebrate the Fourth, let us remember the benefits associated with living in a democracy. Those rights come with a cost. There are many who have given their lives and sacrificed deeply so that America could become a democracy. Many fight daily so that our freedom is maintained. And there are those who will fight in the future so that our children and grandchildren have the opportunity to know the meaning of freedom.

It may seem obvious, but home ownership isn't free, either. Homeowners plan for the monthly payment, which typically consists of principal, interest, taxes, and insurance. But there are many more costs, as well. Bottom line: the purchase of a home is just the beginning. As a rule of thumb, homeowners should budget between 1 percent and 3 percent of the value of the property annually for maintenance costs, as well as ongoing updating and renovation of a property.

Diligent agents know that homes that have been consistently refreshed over time sustain value better than those "stuck" in another era. There is an exception, in which sometimes a look becomes "retro," but that's not the rule. Thus, a homeowner should plan to update kitchens and bathrooms, as well as other design features, on an ongoing basis.

If the property is within a planned development or a condominium, there will be association dues. In addition, those entities can and often do charge fees and can levy special assessments to pay for repairs, replacements, and improvements of shared components to the association. Well-run associations maintain reserve funds for major projects.

Just as freedom is not really "free," yet still worth the cost to sustain and maintain it, the costs to home ownership are certainly worthy of the investment, as well.

Take the time to inform homeowners of the costs and benefits of real estate ownership.

PASSING THE BATON

In athletic relay races, games are most often won and lost on how successfully the baton is transferred. There are numerous applications to the real estate industry, from the single producing agent to large teams and the ultimate transfer of selling one's business.

The most common scenario is that of a referral. A referral to another agent means that the passing agent trusts and relies on the receiving agent to take care of the client. For a successful pass, the receiving agent must be both capable and willing to provide quality service. What happens if the receiving agent "drops the baton"? This reflects badly on the passing agent and leads to both agents losing the race and the client.

The same holds true for referrals to vendors, lenders, title companies, and other recommendations provided to customers. When allied resources take care of clients at a high level, then you want to refer them more business. However, when substandard services are provided, if you are like me, those people are removed from my referral list. It is similar to Yelp. A glowing review from a client is a positive baton transfer. If not, then an opportunity is provided to repair the situation and do better. The objective is to win the race for all the parties. Providing high-caliber service can be a win-win for all referral partners.

One technique to assure a successful baton transfer in a relay race is for the next runner to begin moving so that the pass occurs while both are in motion. The application I observe in real estate is when the receiving agent is an active participant in the process. This agent does his homework by proactively taking care of the customer's needs. The passing agent does her part by letting go of the baton while running alongside him during the critical portion of the race.

This is a key aspect to a successful transfer. When I refer a client to an agent on our team, I come alongside them for a while, provide encouragement and guidance, as well as some details about the clients and their situation. At some point, it is best that I let go, thereby empowering the agent. It is helpful at this juncture to tell the clients that they are in great hands with the receiving agent.

The same strategy of empowerment works with staff members. At the listing appointment, I present the team and sell the benefits of having a staff of people skilled at their professions working on the client's behalf. And then it is important to let those people do their jobs and not micromanage. In this way, everyone on the team is part of winning the race for a successful outcome for the client.

The ultimate baton transfer is that of selling one's business. Just remember, at some point everyone either passes their baton or it drops when they pass away.

Perfect your baton passes to referral partners,
team, staff members, and beyond.

THANK YOU FOR SHARING

"Thank you for sharing" is the response that I learned from Dick Dillingham while attending a training at Keller Williams' headquarters. The format was for each candidate to present, and then the other participants would provide their feedback. Think of it like *American Idol*, when the judges tell the singers why they were or weren't selected. The difference is that at KW, it was colleagues doing the judging.

The instruction from Dick was very clear; all feedback was to receive the same response: "Thank you for sharing." There were to be no excuses, no "but only," no "if only," no "the dog ate my homework." The idea was that the feedback was to be received and accepted as a gift. The gift of feedback is that when it is truly accepted, one has the opportunity to learn and grow.

The other lesson I learned was one of humility. When up against the best and the brightest KW colleagues, only a few would pass. And I was not one of them. Just know that completing the program remains on my bucket list.

This was a turning point in my business and life, a true paradigm shift. Until that time, I thought it was important to explain my position and to make my point—that being heard was the objective. Afterward, I considered that listening to what was being said and even validating others' opinions with a "thank you for sharing" actually could have more of an impact.

The value of this lesson now resonates throughout my business and life. One application is when clients share their feedback. Typically it isn't positive. Sometimes it is true and right and my team and I need to do it over and better. Oftentimes it is out of frustration over the market or things that we have little or no control over.

In all cases, the best response I have found is, "Thank you for sharing." This conveys that their concerns have been heard and are valid for them. I am careful to not argue, make excuses, lament about my own problems, or try and cover up. The best approach is to say, "Thank you for sharing" and then take action steps to address head-on what and how we can do better.

Say "Thank you for sharing" the next time someone
gives you the gift of feedback.

"DANCE LIKE NOBODY'S WATCHING"

Agents new to the real estate profession often feel that customers may not want to work with them because they are newly licensed and thus don't have experience. Established agents can get stuck in ineffective processes and find that change needs to happen in order to take their business to the next level. It is true for both that the only way that one obtains experience is by actually getting out there and doing it. It is a catch-22. At the beginning of any endeavor, everyone starts out at the same place, with no experience.

In the popular song by Austin & Ally, "Dance Like Nobody's Watching," these lines resonate: "What will they think, you're so afraid to make a move; you're second-guessing every, every step." The answer in the song is to dance anyway. The answer to the new real estate agent is to take a chance anyway. Contact friends, relatives, associates, and neighbors anyway. The answer to the seasoned agent is to make the changes anyway, even though you don't have firm assurance it will work.

Yes, some may be "naysayers." Yet some new ideas may work. The only way to show the world that you can do it is by doing it. Sing the words for inspiration if you need to: "Forget about what everyone else says, show 'em what you got and that you're ready to rock it."

It may seem safe to only work with people who don't know you are a new agent, and to stay in the comfort zone of hosting open houses and prospecting among people whom you don't know well. Those are proven methods of getting a new agent's business off the ground, to be sure. At some point, though, you have to stop second-guessing every step.

For the experienced agent, to build and grow a business frequently requires advancing to a new level or market. That means operating outside one's comfort zone, into the growth zone. New and longtime agents both benefit from dancing anyway. At first it may appear no one is watching. Once you achieve and sustain success in real estate, though, you will show them what you've got.

Dance from your comfort zone into an arena of growth.

THE ROLLER COASTER OF THE MARKET

In the summer months, many people enjoy visiting theme parks for recreation. Riding the roller coasters was one of our kids' favorite amusement park activities. The highs and lows and twists and turns make for an adventurous ride. The real estate market also has highs and lows and twists and turns. No matter how long you have been riding it, there are some parts that you can anticipate and others that can take you by surprise.

When the market is in an upward trajectory, the climb is filled with great expectation. Sellers may be seeing price appreciations they never experienced before. Many wonder when the crest will be reached and try to time when to jump on for the ride.

For buyers, rising prices create urgency; they want to get in the market prior to being priced out of it. Also, they want to take advantage of future price appreciation. Buyers, too, can be filled with excitement of the potential of gains. At the same time, many express concern of not wanting to be left behind, paying top dollar when the market turns.

The crest and downward cycles almost always happen much faster than the uphill ride. At this juncture, both sellers and buyers can feel their stomachs drop. Sellers often beat themselves up for not moving fast enough to catch the air present at the top. The challenge of trying to time the top is that, in most markets, the peak exists only for a very brief time. All of a sudden, the course is reversed and turns downward.

Once a market reaches the top and begins descending, buyers then wonder, "How low can it go?" In this market cycle, buyers hesitate to purchase and can be worried that if they do, the home may be worth less tomorrow or the next day.

The level of inventory for any given segment determines what type of market it is: seller's, buyer's, or balanced market. A seller's market is one in which there is high demand and low inventory for the segment. A buyer's market is the opposite: low demand and high inventory. Balanced markets, as discussed above, typically do not stay that way for long. When balanced, in any given segment the number of homes sold and under contract is the same as what is on the active market to buy and those coming soon.

Markets are constantly changing, and thus the ride can be both exhilarating and nerve-wracking for agents and their clients.

Understand the market dynamics in your area
so you can best advise your clients.

THAT'S WHY IT'S CALLED WORK

The rewards that come with real estate success have different meanings for people. Many enter the industry for the potential of achieving financial independence. Others pursue it for the freedom to set one's own schedule and to be their own boss. There is also the recognition of peers, industry, and community. Those who have a heart for helping others derive pleasure from the satisfaction of helping buyers achieve their dream of home ownership and assisting sellers through the details of marketing and selling a home.

It is surprising, to me, how many new agents whom I train and coach exclaim how difficult the real estate business is. Perhaps professional agents make it look easy. It could also be that reality television shows have sensationalized the process, thereby removing all the obvious elements of effort.

What I have found to be helpful for these agents is to first listen to their situation. Then I offer my counsel on steps to take. Next, I assure them that what they are going through is both normal and typical. To procure a client, negotiate the terms of agreement between the buyer and seller, and then to navigate that transaction through to settlement takes work. In fact, I remind them at this time, "That's why it's called work," and add, "That's why agents get paid." Truly, if it was easy, then, as my husband would say, "Anyone could do it."

I always try to leave them with a bit of encouragement, that they aren't just anyone. That if I can do it, they can too. At this point, some ask me why I take my valuable time to coach and train agents. Just as some of them entered the business to help others buy and sell homes, there is another level of reward in leading others to achieve success.

After accomplishing a high level of personal and professional success, paying forward is what inspires me. I remember my first years in the business and truly appreciated those who took the time to teach and encourage me. It is now my gift to current and future agents.

Treat the profession of real estate as your job.

SHORT-TERM PAIN—LONG-TERM GAIN

When something is challenging, especially in the beginning, it is tempting to quit before the results can be felt. An example of this, for me, is weight training. At the start of my program, all I felt was sore! Yet, it is after sustained effort that one starts to reap the benefits. Seth Godin, in *The Dip*, has a great litmus test to use when in doubt: "Never quit something with great long-term potential just because you can't deal with the stress of the moment."

For success as a real estate agent, the sustained effort of effective business development has the greatest long-term potential. Even when top agents don't feel like it, the professionals generate leads day after day.

How does one power through the pain or stress of the moment? There are many proven success strategies. One is to set an appointment on the calendar to prospect, just like I do for my personal training sessions. Another is to work with an accountability partner. If someone is expecting you to be there, you will more likely keep the commitment. Track your progress; being able to see how far you have come is empowering. Create consequences for unmet expectations. For example, work an additional four hours on the weekend if lead-generation goals have not been achieved during the workweek. On the positive side, establish rewards, big and small, for reached milestones.

As way of example, this is personal story of how consequence and reward led to completion of a very important goal. In high school, our son was very close to achieving the rank of Eagle Scout. All that was left was his project. Becoming an Eagle Scout is an accomplishment that his father and I knew, later in life, he would be very glad that he completed. At the time, all he could see was that he had other things he wanted to pursue.

The Boy Scouts call it the siren call of "grades, gas, and girls" that lures young men away. At the time, Drew was very close to being of age to obtain his driver's license. So his father and I created the combined consequence-reward scenario that we would take him to obtain his license "once the Eagle had landed." Until it was done, our assistance was not available. You never did see such a motivated young man; it was truly amazing the speed at which the project was completed.

Remember, no one is making you be a real estate agent. You chose this as a profession, so you can choose to be successful at it.

The short-term pain of prospecting may be difficult,
yet it is worth the long-term gain of a successful business.

ON GETTING FIRED AND STILL SELLING THE HOUSE: A BUYER'S TALE

JULY 11

The occasions that turn out to be the biggest lessons are those in which I have been fired and yet still find a way to win the clients back and sell them a home. Yes, I get fired by clients, too. The better story is how I turn the situation around from a negative into a positive. What follows is a true buyer's tale.

A past client engaged my services to help him purchase a larger and more expensive home. Over many months, I showed him every home that met the criteria he provided. While accompanying my husband on an out-of-town business trip, he stumbled on a home he liked at an open house. Interesting to note that the home he found on his own didn't really meet the stipulations he had set out with me in the buyer consultation. This was due to the fact that he changed some of the wants and needs on the list and expanded his financial parameter, but hadn't thought to share this information with me.

I prepared and sent a comprehensive market analysis to the client; however, he arrived at his own offer amount, which was very low. My business partner wrote the contract for him, since I was out of town. The negotiations didn't go anywhere, and the offer was withdrawn. The client contacted me soon after and shared that he felt I wasn't fully representing his interests because he was the one who found the house, and I wasn't successful in negotiating the deal. One of my business practices is to work only with people who want to work with me, so I requested the broker release him from the buyer agreement.

In the meantime, I put a "watch" on the house he was interested in. About thirty days later, the price was reduced substantially, so I sent him a link to the listing with a brief message that if he hadn't contracted to work with another agent, I would be delighted to have another opportunity. He agreed, and this time around he followed the negotiating strategy I recommended. We came to an agreement and went to settlement. Since that time, he has referred me more business, saying it was my tenacity and persistence that enabled him to purchase the home of his family's dreams.

New agents often wonder how I could go back to a client who has fired me. I view it like riding a bike, which I do frequently for pleasure and exercise. If I fell, it would never occur to me to not get back up and ride again. Sure, I might have some bumps or bruises from the fall, yet the pleasure of riding is considerably more powerful.

Get back up and persevere when you fall down, as there is a great sense of accomplishment in overcoming adversity.

Real Estate Success in 5 Minutes a Day | **219**

LEVERAGE WITH MEDIA

Agents can become known experts on their local markets by writing blogs and articles for publications and social media outlets. Barbara Corcoran, star of ABC's *Shark Tank*, made her fortune selling residential real estate. She put her name on the map in New York City, though, by writing a market report she named *The Corcoran Report*.

I incorporated Barbara's idea and expanded it into my marketplace a number of years ago by writing a quarterly market report. In addition, agents on our team write and submit "Where we live," personal-interest stories about neighborhoods and community events. The local media is delighted to have great content to publish, and in almost all cases the article is printed word-for-word. Agents become known as true "local neighborhood experts" via social media, as well. Everyone loves to read about what is going on in their community and what makes it special.

This is effectively free public relations and influences the public significantly more than paid advertising. Some experts place the value of a third-party endorsement at twenty times that of traditional branding efforts and advertising. The media publication can also become a tool for lead generation. Agents use their neighborhood interest story to door knock and meet the community face-to-face. It makes for a "warm call" to have the story as the introductory piece.

The market report is a valuable tool at listing appointments, as well. Sellers are quite impressed when they see that the local paper considers the report relevant for publication. A case in point is friends from church, who called me in November to set up a time to visit about listing their home. They were going to wait until the spring, yet after reading my market report in the paper, decided that it was a good time to sell.

Social media offers multiple platforms available to the agent for connection and promotion. The most popular portals are in a state of constant change and evolution. Keys to success include staying abreast of current trends and being relevant. Synergy with other media is a great approach for a comprehensive media plan. To be effective, the best in the business find a niche and are in constant dialogue with their constituencies. Author and mega agent Tony Giordano in "the social agent" states the opportunity best: "We have been given the ability to network in ways never dreamed of - and anywhere in the world."

Leveraging media is a powerful force, as there is the potential for exponential exposure. It is one of the foundational strategies of success for the professional real estate agent. In the words of PT Barnum: "Without promotion, something terrible happens . . . nothing!" Make sure something happens in your real estate business!

Leverage media to promote awareness of your brand.

"YOU CAN'T ALWAYS GET WHAT YOU WANT"

The Rolling Stones' hit song lyrics ring true in real estate applications: "You can't always get what you want; but if you try sometime, you find you get what you need." It has been said that a good outcome in negotiations is when both parties feel as though they got some of the things they needed and they gave up some of the things they wanted. Almost all sellers are under the impression that they just "gave their house away." Almost all buyers are concerned about overpaying.

Thus, when a seller truly finds that he gets what he needs and realizes that he can't get everything he wants, in most cases that is the best-case scenario. When buyers honestly evaluate their wants versus needs and makes the decision to focus on needs, at that point a compromise usually is reached. Many decisions fall into the "good enough" category. People become more open to the paradigm shift from idealism to realism and from subjective to objective when the focus is on needs rather than wants.

One of the benefits of agent representation to clients and customers is that of another perspective. On occasion, I am tempted to break into song when these lyrics ring true for the situation. Once everyone realizes the poor level of my singing capabilities, laughter erupts. It is then that people are ready to focus on their needs, which in most cases, as the song proclaims, they are likely to get.

The lyrics also have a message for the real estate agent who wants to be a rock star in her field. You may want to achieve success by possessing a love of houses and people. To be a superstar, though, the agent needs to have a strong commitment to prospecting, consulting expertise, the ability to connect to build and grow a business, as well as success thinking, activities, and vision.

In negotiations, business, and life, remember the words of the song to achieve success.

Focus clients on needs versus wants in real estate decisions.

MEET CUTE

A "meet cute" occurs when a couple meets for the first time. Most common in romantic comedies in movies or on television, it sets the stage for a future relationship. The scene unfolds with them meeting in either an embarrassing circumstance or a humorous clash of personalities or situation.

As a real estate agent, I have experienced "meet cute" situations with future clients. One such occasion was on a flight to Texas to visit family for the Christmas holiday. As many people do, I struck up a conversation with the gentleman sitting next to me. I asked if he was going home, or if he lived in the DC metro area. He explained that he was heading to San Diego to visit family and that he lived in Falls Church, Virginia. As we had just purchased an investment town home in Falls Church, I delved deeper into the closest intersection. It turned out that he lived on the next street over from our property and went on to share that he was renting.

A "meet cute" opportunity just landed in my lap. After explaining that I was a real estate agent, he indicated that he wanted to purchase a home after the New Year. Contact information was exchanged and future plans were made to see houses when he returned from the holiday.

Other people can have a "meet cute" and when they think of you as a real estate agent it can turn into an opportunity. An occasion that comes to mind involves my husband. He sits on the board of an organization and during a coffee break conversation with a fellow board member, it came up that I was a real estate agent. Turned out that his daughter was pregnant with her second child and the couple was looking to move into a single-family so that they could have a yard. Andy put me in touch and that led to both selling the young couple a home, and also listing and selling their town home.

The secret, I believe, for "meet cute" opportunities is to be open to the possibility. Truly, any situation has the potential. And share with those you know that you are open to their "meet cute" scenarios as well!

Look for "meet cute" lead-generation opportunities in your life!

"YOU DON'T BRING ME FLOWERS"

The duet by Barbra Streisand and Neil Diamond, "You Don't Bring Me Flowers," is a love song about a romance that has lost its spark. The lovers no longer do the special things for each other that they did early in their relationship, like bringing flowers and singing love songs.

This can happen between a real estate agent and her clients too. Early on, it is easy to be eager at having a new prospect. Most agents practically jump at the opportunity to take a new buyer to see homes. Then, after months of showing what seems like dozens of homes, it is tempting to just go through the motions. Or just send the client out on Sunday afternoons to view open houses. It is a challenge to stay as eager as early on in the relationship.

The same loss of luster can happen with seller clients too. At the initial appointment, when perhaps competing for the business, the agent really pulls out all the stops to win over the client. Then, after countless open houses, follow-through on feedback, and investment in marketing, it is easy to get discouraged. Seller clients often can become needy and require even more attention the longer the home is on the market.

Romantic relationships that thrive long-term require love and attention. Current clients benefit from frequent communication and nurturing, as well. Do not wait until the relationship begins to drift apart. The words of the song share some wonderful ideas on how to rekindle a romantic spark: bring gifts, sing songs of praise, and take the time to talk. Those are great strategies to employ, equally as well with clients as with a romantic partner.

There are real estate coaching and training companies that advocate by-referral-only systems of lead generation and nurture that follow the tenants of the theme song. Ongoing customer- and client-for-life appreciation programs lead to referrals and more business. It is reciprocity at work.

It is the agent who is the professional in the business relationship; thus, it is her job to keep the client relationship happy and healthy.

Take steps today to nurture the relationship with clients and customers.

UNIQUE VALUE PROPOSITION

Since the millennium, access to listings and data via the Internet has changed the role of the real estate agent. There was a day in the United States when the listing agent retained control of all of the information. When governments began digitizing public records, that data was readily available. The benefit to consumers is the explosion of information that is now easily accessible to them.

There are some who believe that the functions of the real estate agent will diminish as consumers are able to find homes on their own via the web. This concern follows the demise of much of the travel agent industry that occurred as people were given the ability to book their own travel arrangements online. The key to sustained success for real estate agents is to focus on their unique value proposition as they navigate industry changes.

The ability to search for homes and properties on the Internet is just one step. If one were to chart the beginning to end of the real estate purchase process, the finding of the home involves less than 10 percent of the whole. First, there is the necessity of access to show the property. The majority of owners want to know who is entering their home. It is one of the key factors in why for-sale-by-owner transactions account for only 12 percent of sales, according to the National Association of Realtors®.

The availability of information to consumers can quickly feel overwhelming to them. This is when the wise counsel of a diligent agent is truly a valuable skill. Being able to interpret the data in a meaningful way is actually more important than being just a source of information. Further, agents can provide expertise related to comparables, pricing, and negotiation. Then there is the facilitation of all the steps from contract to settlement, which often accounts for more than 75 percent of the process.

One way to establish your unique value proposition is by being a true market expert.

Another is to add value to clients by providing concierge-type customer service.

Look outside of the real estate arena to industries that have navigated change and have come out on the other side. Those perspectives often provide insight. For example, with the advent of software programs, many people now prepare their own income taxes. And yet there is still a demand for professional CPAs, as there are those who recognize the value provided. In the same way, there are clients who recognize the complexity of the real estate transaction and embrace hiring a knowledgeable professional to oversee and manage it.

*Establish your unique value proposition and use
it to market and sell your services.*

TRAFFIC MANAGEMENT DEVICES

Transportation authorities have a cadre of management techniques that they employ to both speed up and calm traffic. On one end of the spectrum, to speed up the flow are signal synchronization, high occupancy times, and turn lanes to take cars out of the main flow. On the calming end of the continuum, there are speed humps, lane narrowing, roundabouts, and the use of detours and signage.

Government policy is known to affect the real estate market traffic flow. On the local level is the restrictive nature of the development and permit process. The more developer and builder friendly, then typically the more projects and homes are built. The more restrictive the regulations and the longer the process takes, then typically that slows down the construction process.

On the federal level, the obvious example is interest rates. The Federal Reserve sets the rate at which funds are loaned to depository institutions. This mechanism affects the amount the borrowing bank will pay the lending bank, which in turn affects the interest rate that purchasers pay for a mortgage. The Fed adjusts the rate in order to speed up or slow down the market, as housing is a huge segment of the economy. Economists have a saying: "As housing goes, so goes the economy."

Another example is legislation. Dodd Frank was implemented in response to the financial market crash of September 2008. This led to the creation of the Consumer Financial Protection Bureau, which was put into place in October 2015. The lending and settlement procedures were designed to help the consumer better understand the mortgage process. In effect, it narrowed the point of entry. Thus, this policy turned out to be a calming device for the housing market.

My husband commuted to Washington, DC daily for more than a decade. He has many stories to tell about the traffic in the nation's capital. All that is necessary for chaos to ensue is a detour or road closure. This creates a traffic jam, and the normal route is now no longer an available option. This, of course, meant finding alternative routes. He listened to traffic reports to learn of other options, followed GPS, and somehow managed to persevere through the snarl, as he always made it home.

The professional real estate agent can use these techniques and strategies also. On an individual level, we may not be able to influence government policy, yet we can learn to adapt and develop workarounds or alternative routes. The buying and selling of real estate flow will continue on, maybe at a different pace.

Understand how government policy affects the real estate industry and develop strategies and techniques to manage the traffic flow in your business.

THE MARKET IS THE MARKET STUDY

The market is the true market study. A comparative market analysis (CMA) looks forward in the market by considering relevant recent past sales and those homes under contract, as well as what is currently active or coming soon. Past results are really the only indicator that a professional can use to project future outcomes. Yet, just like with the stock market, there is no guarantee. Clearly there are many different factors that determine value—being objective and experienced become even more critical. It is like true north in that it determines direction.

Having a home on the market for sale is a little like sailing. What makes sailing tricky is the wind, as conditions are constantly changing. And yet it is the wind that makes sailing possible and challenging. The worst condition is when there is no wind. A sailor can operate the boat with gauges and barometers that predict weather conditions, use skill and experience, or a combination of both. Yet, it is when actually out on the water that the true measure of a sailor's competence is realized.

In the real estate market, the activity is the wind. If it is dead, then the market is going nowhere. The real estate professional uses the available comparable data to analyze the market, incorporates her own knowledge and expertise, or a combination of both. She is aware that conditions are constantly in flux, as homes are coming on the market for sale, going under contract, and to settlement. Further, there is the possibility of shadow inventory and new buyers who will enter the marketplace. There is intuition involved because no one really knows what the future holds. It requires living in the unknown.

People are uncomfortable with not knowing. Sellers want the agent to tell them what their home is worth. Keep in mind that the agent has an ethical obligation to be honest. The National Association of Realtors® Standard of Practice states: "Realtors®, in attempting to secure a listing, shall not deliberately mislead the owner as to market value." It is not possible to know for certain what the true value is until a buyer comes forward.

Buyers also want to know what they can buy a home for, and push the agent to tell them how they think the seller will respond. There exists less negotiating room the closer an offer is to market value. No one really knows what a seller will take until an offer is made and rejected, countered, or accepted.

The best way to sail is to listen to the wind. The best way to be successful in real estate is to listen to the activity and the market. Either one can listen, or one can learn from what happens and be responsive.

Use "the market is the market study" to influence clients to respond to the conditions of the market of the moment.

LUXURY HOME CHARACTERISTICS

What makes a home a luxury property? According to the Institute for Luxury Home Marketing (ILHM), it is those properties in the upper 10 percent of value for their metro area. The institute awards the prestigious Certified Luxury Home Marketing Specialist (CLHMS) designation to agents who have sold a certain number of luxury homes, as well as having completed additional related coursework.

The book *Rich Buyer, Rich Seller*, by Laurie Moore-Moore, the founder and CEO of ILHM, is insightful into this unique market niche. Properties in the upper brackets are often highly customized. Determining value when there are not many comparables available requires the knowledge, skills, and abilities of a professional. It is even more critical for an upper-bracket real estate agent to know all of the relevant properties and what makes each unique.

As is true in all real estate, yet perhaps magnified due to price, location is the first key. In most cases, proximity to a city center is the primary criteria. The second factor is typically neighborhood and schools. Next in priority are lot size, typography of the land, and proximity to desirable locations. Final considerations are usually square footage, layout, and features of the home. The progression of priority logically follows the degree to which the owner can institute change. A purchaser, for example, can easily upgrade kitchen and baths, while relocating a home to a more desirable location is unlikely.

It is critical that the agent be intimately knowledgeable about luxury properties in order to best serve the client. The purpose of the ILHM is two-fold. The institute provides training, information, and cutting-edge tips for the current market, specifically geared for the upper-bracket home market. Further, the institute creates connectivity among others in the industry across the United States and abroad, which further expands the marketing capabilities of its members.

The Certified Luxury Home Marketing Specialist (CLHMS) designation assures affluent buyers and sellers that the real estate agents who have earned it have the knowledge, expertise, competence, and confidence they require. It is recognized as the mark of accomplishment in luxury markets around the world. The certification requirements assure that members are currently active in the luxury home marketplace.

Understand the key factors to value for upper-bracket homes in your marketplace.

LICENSED TO VIEW HOUSES

In the James Bond *007* movie, the secret agent is authorized per the title: "Licensed to kill." Real estate agents are "licensed to view houses" and should be anything but secret agents if they want to be successful.

In order to sell houses in the US, real estate agents must be licensed by the jurisdiction in which they want to conduct business. The purpose for issuing and governing the licensure is to protect the consumer. This is a worthy objective, given that the transaction of buying and selling a home is most people's largest financial purchase, ongoing obligation, and sale. Further, the licensure assures for the seller the security and safety of the property as a responsibility of those who are allowed access.

Real estate agents frequently take for granted that this is an additional benefit of licensure—having the right of access to people's homes that are on the market for sale. There are some occasions when the public is permitted to view, but in most cases that is at open-house events. The agent, though, is presented with substantially more ingress. Sometimes access is granted via lock box, either secure or combination. Sometimes that access is granted at special Realtors® events, such as broker open houses. Sometimes access is granted via the listing agent with appointment-only homes and properties.

Knowledge of the inventory is one of the best ways for real estate agents to become experts in their markets. Being permitted to view houses is one of the benefits of being licensed that differentiates a real estate agent from the general public. All professional agents should take full advantage of this right!

Keeping current on the inventory is the best way to generate leads and be a true neighborhood expert.

WHO WANTS TO BE A MILLIONAIRE?

The TV game show, *Who Wants to Be a Millionaire?*, offers contestants the opportunity to win cash based on chance. There is a more certain way—create your own millions. Owning income-producing real estate as an asset class is a proven means of wealth creation.

To net $1 million after taxes actually requires an investor in the US to earn between $1.25 to $1.5 million. Let's assume that an investor can expect to earn an average 6 percent annual rate of return on stocks, mutual funds, and other such investments before fees and taxes. That is an annual income of $60,000, which translates into $5,000 monthly cash flow. Thus, if one owns an asset that provides a cash flow of $5,000 per month, then it correlates that that investor is in possession of a $1 million asset.

A residential real estate investor typically can purchase a single-family home with 20 percent down. That means the investor owns 100 percent of the asset with only 20 percent actual cash outlay. This leverage is unique in that to own 100 percent of a stock or mutual fund portfolio requires 100 percent funds. One can buy equity investments on margin, but that just allows for the future purchase, not ownership. Real estate investment property leveraged has the tenant paying the mortgage—the 80 percent balance borrowed.

As the tenant pays down the mortgage, the positive cash flow increases. At the juncture that the cash flow is $5,000 a month, then the investor owns a million-dollar asset. There are some rules of thumb that are best to follow, and the values will vary depending on the market area. The best returns typically peak at a $500,000 asset, which earns rental income of $2,500 plus or minus monthly. The rental income earned ratio to the asset tends to go down as the price of the property increases, the reason being that there exists a larger tenant pool in the lower monthly rental amount.

It was truly an epiphany moment the day I realized that there are many ways to become a millionaire. One is to earn $1 million after taxes, which then could be invested for cash flow. Another is to own assets that earn annual cash flow equivalent to $1 million. Once you become a millionaire, seek out clients and customers, who want to be a millionaire, too.

There may be additional tax benefits unique to owning investment real estate that real estate professionals can take advantage of. Please be certain to consult your tax advisor.

Consider how the real estate investment as an asset can be part of your long-term success vision for your life and business, as well as for clients and customers.

STANDARDS OF SERVICE

As an agent's business grows and expands beyond what she can handle alone, many consider leveraging the time and talents of others. This can include hiring administrative staff or agents. The challenge, which is also the opportunity at this juncture, is that an agent has become accustomed to doing everything. One of the difficulties I experienced during the transition is that staff or other agents won't do it like I would. As in many cases, I have turned this challenge into an associated opportunity and call that process Standards of Service (SOS).

The Standards of Service establishes the protocol and process for our team up front rather than waiting until there is a crisis. That way there is dialogue about the expectations for working with customers and clients. And as situations present themselves, it is constantly being updated and expanded.

The idea came to me on a Sunday afternoon like an epiphany when yet another unhappy seller client called me about something that had happened. It always seemed to concern the open house agent who was assigned to hold the open house. It occurred to me that our team held open houses practically every Sunday, so surely there was a way that many of these issues could be addressed up front prior to Sunday afternoon.

Thus was born the Preferred Open House Agent Agreement. It includes all of the "war stories" of things that have happened that tend to upset seller clients. For example: be early, keep the home clean, confirm all the doors are locked, know the features and upgrades of the home, be informed about the comparables, and accentuate the positives to the home. The beauty of the agreement is that now my phone hardly ever rings on Sunday afternoons, unless it is for an offer or a true emergency.

At listing appointments, I sell the benefits of the team. I emphasize that we have both staff and agents who are talented people and very good at their jobs. One of the key aspects of people leverage is to believe in those who work for and with you and empower them to be able to do their jobs at the highest level. I am good at what I do, also, which is negotiating and staying current on the market. Leverage allows me to focus on my skill set and achieve success at a high level. The Standards of Service protocol assures that everyone who works with our clients are top-notch as well.

Develop your own Standards of Service to provide top quality customer experience to your clients.

ARE YOU MY PRIORITY?

To be a successful, real estate agents require the ability to prioritize. This is when many people get stumped: "What is a priority?" Is it keeping a deal together by managing the contract to the settlement part of the transaction? Is it attending a training event to learn about social media? Is it going to lunch with a vendor? The question reminds me of the baby bird in the Dr. Seuss classic, *Are You My Mother?* The bird is in pursuit of her mother and in the meantime is distracted by many look-alikes and potential mother substitutes.

Barbara Corcoran, who made her fortune building and selling a real estate empire, The Corcoran Group, is now known as one of the full-time investors on the reality show, *Shark Tank*. One of her key questions to the entrepreneurs before she invests in them is: "Where has your business come from so far?"

According to Barbara, unfortunately it seems most don't know. So do you know? Her fundamental rule is to first determine the source of your business. Figure out what works and what doesn't. Then you can focus your time and resources on those priorities. Pursue tried-and-true methods prior to embarking on any new ventures.

I discovered the truth of this principle a few years into my career. My most successful lead-generation activity had been mailing "just sold" postcards to my sphere. As my business focus moved from working primarily with buyers to listing homes, I decided to invest instead in glossy print advertising. The resources were not there to do both, so I stopped sending the postcards. The impact of my decision became apparent within a few months. The leads from my primary client base, my sphere, had all but dried up. It took a few months to turn the ship around and undo the damage, yet it was a strong lesson learned. Now my first priority is to know where my business comes from and keep my focus there.

The answer to the questions above lies in saying "no" to everything that isn't directly related to income-producing activities. As Barbara goes on to say: "I don't let them spend any time on anything that doesn't directly result in a sale. Because that's what you need when you're a small business." Thus, if the management of the contract can be handled by other parties, then it isn't the priority for the day. If social media is your primary source of prospecting, then attending training to improve is a key aspect to business development. If the vendor has provided leads to you in the past, then it is definitely a good use of your time to have lunch with him. That's how I answer the question daily: "Are you my priority?"

Focus first on income-producing activities that lead directly to business.

GOLF SKILLS

The well-known golf phrase, "You drive for show, but putt for dough" was coined by professional golfer Bobby Locke. While playing golf with my husband recently, it occurred to me how being a real estate professional has many similarities to golf.

The "drive for show" is the listing and marketing of a home. Teeing up the home for going on the market is in a lot of ways "show time." A golfer who shoots accurately out of the tee box can be likened to an agent who prices the home correctly for the market. It will be set up much better to sell quickly at a strong market price.

The "putt for dough" are the contract negotiations and strategy that get the deal to settlement. Putting it in the hole often requires finesse and strategy; those skills also benefit an agent in closing on a contract. The difference between an amateur and a pro in both professions often is determined by how much one practices and plays.

The middle game between the two is often the mental game. The ability to persevere through challenging situations can make the difference in finishing well. For golf, that could mean keeping one's head after landing in the sand or other hazard. For the agent, the hazards could be a title issue or a problem with the septic system.

Golf courses are designed to challenge golfer skills. And then there are the variables of weather and competition presented by the other players in the tournament. Each transaction in real estate offers a challenge to an agent's knowledge, skills, and abilities, as well. The variables that come to mind are the market conditions and the agents who are representing the other party.

Make it a practice to perfect your skills in the profession of real estate, just as you would on the golf course if a player in that sport.

Use the knowledge of golf skills as strategies for success in real estate.

TRACKING BUSINESS CHANGES IS LIKE DETERMINING A FOOD ALLERGY

Prior to introducing new foods to young children, parents or caregivers are instructed to follow a protocol. The practice is to try each new food for a period of time in somewhat isolation. The purpose of the procedure is to watch for symptoms of intolerance or other indicators like itching, wheezing, or gastro upset. It is easier to spot the symptoms if enough time lapses between each new food being offered. The ideal way to keep track is with a food diary or log.

This is an example or analogy for how real estate agents can determine what best "new" marketing strategy, lead-generation program, or business practice works. Tracking is and has always been the ideal way to identify the effectiveness of a program. An ample amount of time needs to pass before trying out a new venture. Whether this has occurred depends on the program being tracked.

Real estate agents are bombarded with many ideas, most of which involve substantial financial investment. To name a few: postcards, print advertising in local papers and glossy magazines, grocery cart ads, billboards, radio, television, sponsoring local sports leagues, pens and other collateral, moving trucks, signs, and golf tournaments. And then there are the "pay per click" and "pay for lead" and other opportunities.

Think about the ideas available to the agent that don't require as much financial commitment, but take considerable time. One could argue that time is the most valuable resource, as it is irreplaceable. Examples include social media, networking events, podcasts, blogging, lead-share programs, holding open houses, door knocking, and even time spent in training. There are so many choices, it can make a real estate agent's head swim.

Each new strategy should be held accountable for effectiveness. The amount of funds and time expended on the program should at a minimum return enough to pay for itself. Over time, it should be evident that the return on investment increases at an acceptable level. Similar to watching for allergy symptoms, there are signs a businessperson should watch for to determine if the program is a success or if it should be discontinued.

Ideally, wait to introduce a new strategy until the protocol is complete. It is by isolation that one best knows if a program works at the necessary performance level.

Institute tracking mechanisms in your business so that you know what works and can hold them accountable to success.

GETTING ASKED TO DANCE

The submission of an offer on a home is almost always an exciting occasion for sellers. It is like being asked to dance—a wallflower no more. If the home has been on the market for some time, sellers may have started to feel like no one really loves their home as much as they do. The feeling of rejection is common in both situations.

It truly is a happy day if the offer is attractive. The seller wants to dance with this particular buyer, and often everyone does a happy little jig.

The challenge is when the suitor who comes calling isn't the most handsome of the bunch. What if the offer price is low? Or has contingencies aren't to the liking of the seller? What is the listing agent to do in these scenarios?

First, still congratulate the seller on being asked to dance. Yes actually use those words and explain that everyone should be happy to no longer be a wallflower. There are benefits to finally having an interested party. It means that the list price is now within striking distance of receiving offers.

Second, as "everyone wants what everyone wants," it often happens that as soon as one buyer gets on the dance floor, invariably others who have been sitting on the sidelines reconsider and join in. A good agent will actively contact all those agents and unrepresented buyers who have shown interest in the home to be sure they have been given an opportunity to dance.

Third, as statistically the first offer is the best offer, many times a strong negotiator can get the parties together. Professional agents have been known to employ some creative steps to get buyers and sellers to come to an agreement, even if they start on opposite sides of the dance floor.

Should none of those strategies work, being asked to dance is still a good thing. There are several opportunities to reframe the situation. One is that the seller could do some things to become more attractive to the market, thereby increasing the home's appeal to future buyers. Receiving an offer that doesn't work out often is just the catalyst for change that a seller needs.

And finally, a top-notch agent can use the situation to the advantage of the seller client. Once a client has received an offer, then the agent can tell people that they've been asked to dance. The low-offer strategy has been tried and was not successful. So to have a reasonable chance of acceptance, please bring your best steps and most respectable offer to the floor.

Incorporate "getting asked to dance" scripts
with your clients and customers.

IS AN APPRAISAL FAIR MARKET VALUE?

JULY
27

The technical answer is an appraisal is not fair market value. It is helpful for agents to understand the process in order to be able to explain it to clients. According to the dictionary, the definition of appraisal is: "A valuation of property (e.g., real estate, a business, an antique) by the estimate of an authorized person."

There are three means appraisers typically utilize to arrive at real estate value: the cost approach, the sales comparison approach, and the income capitalization approach.

The most common approach for an appraisal in the purchase of residential real estate with cash or with a mortgage is the sales comparison method. It is based on the principle of substitution. That is, an intelligent buyer will pay no more for a property than it would cost to purchase a comparable substitute property. The more homogeneous a property is and the more stable the market conditions, the easier it is to obtain comparables, and thus the closer the appraisal will be to fair market value.

There is a delayed reaction that occurs with this approach, as it requires the appraiser to look in the past at settled transactions and those currently under contract. Fair market value (FMV) occurs in the present, in real time. Substitution relies on the assumption that if buyers could purchase another similar property, they would. That is the best indicator of what buyers would pay for the subject property. Since the most unique factor of real estate is its location, which fundamentally cannot be changed, true substitution can never really occur. What occurs is an estimation of value based on many factors put into a formula, which is not the same as fair market value.

True FMV of any commodity is arrived at when a buyer and seller agree to a price with specific terms and consummate the transaction. Additionally, neither party is under duress, the parties are unrelated, and thus at an "arm's length." The commodity has had adequate exposure to the open market and financing terms are typical.

In some cases, sellers have an appraisal from a refinance or when they purchased the home and want to know if that can be used. This is when it is helpful to explain the time factor in the validity of an appraisal. Typically it needs to be within six months of the transaction. Further, there is often a distinction between a refinance and a purchase money appraisal; consult the lender or other industry professionals, as requirements can vary.

The only real way to "test" whether an appraised value of a property is FMV is to expose it to the market. If a ready, willing, and able buyer purchases it for that amount, then it has met the ultimate criteria.

Educate clients on the distinctions between an appraisal and fair market value.

CONNECTORS OF PEOPLE AND HOUSES

Like a lot of boys, when our son was young he was passionate about any toy that connected things together. One of his all-time favorites was the K'NEX Amazin' 8 Coaster Building Set. The instructions and photos provided a visual for one way to connect and build a roller coaster. Drew was occupied for hours as he followed the instructions to put it together based on the information. It didn't take him long though to visualize creative "out-of-the-box" ways in which he could connect the pieces.

Real estate agents are connectors of people and houses. One way of doing so is to follow traditional strategies, or more "inside-the-box" strategies. For example, an agent can take the specified criteria provided by a buyer and set up a search that is delivered to the client automatically. The buyer then would tell the agent which houses he may be interested in and coordinate to view the houses.

Then there are the creative and more "out-of-the-box" ways to connect buyers with houses. One I follow is to set up the criteria and deliver it to myself. Then I actively view those homes. In this way, I can tell the client from personal experience the property's attributes; this is my unique value proposition. Also, on a consistent basis, I view homes and think of people while in the process. To connect people and houses is always on the top of my mind. Like Drew and the roller coaster, I'm always thinking creatively of, "Who would this house be great for?"

Another "outside-the-box" strategy is to look in the shadow markets. That is, homes that had been for sale and withdrawn or expired. In many cases, the owner would still be willing to sell the home. Then there is always door-knocking and letter-writing campaigns. These strategies tend to be most effective when the agent promotes the actual buyer need to the homeowners.

Reach out and network with agents who have completed transactions in the desired market segment. Often they know of a seller who will be coming on the market or with whom they have gone on a listing appointment. Perhaps the owner would be able to move the process forward if a real buyer was procured.

Real estate agents new in their careers often follow in the steps of a more experienced agent, coach, or mentor. This is like following an instruction manual to achieve success. Clearly this is a tried-and-true course. The next level is to connect that knowledge with creative thinking to build and achieve your vision of the business.

Think today of ways you can connect people
and houses to build and grow your business.

QUESTIONS AND OBJECTIONS ARE BUYING SIGNALS

Questions are buying signals! So are objections! Objections are questions in disguise.

When a customer takes time to inquire or states an objection, it often means that there is something about the home that is of interest. It is the agent's job to first provide the answers as she is able. If you don't know the answer, then by all means obtaining the information is your job too. Keep in mind that often there is a question behind the question. This is when probing by going five deep can gain insight into the customer's motivation.

An example dialogue between customer and agent:

Agent: I just wanted to follow up with you on your visit to our open house on Sunday. Do you have any questions I could help with?

Customer: What is the vacant land behind the home?

Agent: It is parkland. Is that something that is important to you?

Customer: Well, we wanted to know if anything would ever be built back there.

Agent provides valuable information: Actually, that is a great question! Not only is it parkland, but it is contiguous with the Potomac River, which means that all of that land will remain protected into perpetuity. Would that be important to you?

Customer: Yes, we like to hike on the weekends.

Agent: It is a wonderful area to hike. There is a private trail behind the home that is accessed primarily by the adjacent properties. And there is a public community trail at the end of the next street over; I would be happy to show you how to access it. At certain times of the year when the water is low it is possible to "river walk." It is in effect a "hike" across the river from the Virginia side to Maryland. It is a fantastic experience and if you are interested I could let you know about the next planned outing.

Customer: Yes, that would be great. Do you know if we can cut down any trees in the back of the property to make more open green space?

Agent: Well, because the land is adjacent to parkland, often the county has rules about that. The best thing about that, though, is the privacy provided. These rules practically guarantee that the land will stay in the similar state the way you see it now. In other words, you won't see another home being built behind you. My recommendation would be to contact the county to find out directly.

Note that all of these questions are buying signals. The agent engages the customer in a conversation that sells the benefits of the home and property. Further, he connects the solutions to the needs and wants of the customer.

Objections can be buying signals, as well. Successful agents have found it is best to treat objections as questions. Then work together with the customer to find a solution or benefit that meets her needs.

Questions and objections are buying signals that agents use as opportunities to convert customers to clients!

DEATH BY A THOUSAND CUTS

The origin of this phrase is from the time of Imperial China. The more contemporary usage is in the investment world. It means one small cut won't kill you or the situation. Yet at some point, with enough cuts you will bleed to death, and it will be painful along the way. It is the cumulative effect of the chain of events that ultimately is worse than if one had taken more decisive action earlier in the process.

The relevance of this is with price changes. Sellers who make insignificant price adjustments relative to the value of the property and market often end up in a worse situation than if they had made a significant cut in the first place or earlier on. The reasons sellers give for insisting on smaller cuts is that they are fearful of "giving their home away" or "leaving money on the table." The market, though, sees the change for what it is: not enough to have a material impact.

The greatest danger in this approach is when the market is shifting downward, or even just unstable. Insignificant price adjustments in these situations often end up following the market down without actually selling the home. The better strategy is to get ahead of the market. Influence sellers to adopt correct pricing by demonstrating the benefit to them and their situation.

The next question often is what does it take to make an impact on the market? Experience shows that a 10 percent reduction, in most cases, moves the property into the next pool of buyers. If the 10 percent is on the border of a significant price point, like at any $100,000, $50,000, or $25,000 mark, then it is recommended to go to or below that number. If a seller can't stomach a 10 percent reduction, then push for at least 5 percent. A 5 percent reduction at least opens up another bracket of purchasers, albeit a smaller pool.

Another course of action that moves the market along is to make adjustments more frequently. Particularly in the age of the Internet, buyers active in the market to purchase often put an alert on a home. Frequent changes in price are a sign the seller is serious about getting to market and sold.

At some point, the buyers will get on the bandwagon. This is how many homes were sold during and after the Great Recession when short sales represented a huge portion of the market. Every week or two weeks, the price would be adjusted down by a certain percentage or dollar amount. Many relocation companies employ a similar strategy. It is clear as agents when we have "found the market," as the phone begins to ring off the hook.

Explain the concept of "death by a thousand cuts" to influence seller clients to follow a pricing strategy that benefits them.

CHANGING BEHAVIOR

Our children are now in their mid-twenties, yet I remember well as new parents how inadequate to our responsibilities my husband and I felt. To improve our knowledge, skills, and abilities, we enrolled in a parenting class at our church. Decades later we remember but one important lesson: "If you want to change the behavior of a child, then first you have to change your behavior." It seems so very simple, yet profound. The only person who truly anyone can change is themselves.

There are numerous applications to real estate, particularly as it relates to the agent's time. The industry has become active 24/7 with the advent of the Internet. This can make it seem that the real estate agent is in effect "on call" all the time. The sense of urgency is compounded by the fact that studies have shown that the quicker and more proactive the response to a new lead, the greater the conversion rate. Further, with technology, smartphones and tablets make it so easy to be connected all the time from anywhere.

In addition, most real estate contracts contain a "time is of the essence" clause. According to the legal dictionary, "time is of the essence" is a phrase in a contract that means that performance by one party at or within the period specified in the contract is necessary to enable that party to require performance by the other party. Failure to act within the time required constitutes a breach of contract.

It is a good business practice to establish professional standards and expectations with clients and customers early on in the relationship. At the first appointment with a seller or buyer, share how you work, as well as other team members' roles and responsibilities if applicable. Keep communication on a business level by following up all conversations with an e-mail summary for mutual understanding.

Clients tend to mirror the agent's style. With the use of e-mail, the agent subtly affirms that ordinary business will be conducted during normal office hours. Yes, deadlines still have to be met and emergencies do occur that require attention. By following this process, they become the exception rather than the rule.

Set expectations with clients early in the relationship
so that everyone is clear on standards and expectations.

YOU CAN START AT ANY TIME

The day most people start a new habit or activity is New Year's Day. The calendar change promises a new beginning. Studies show only 8 percent of people actually achieve the resolutions established then. The secret is that you can start at any time by thinking success and then doing those activities on a daily basis to build a sustainable habit. That is how I have achieved my success vision and you can, too, by starting today.

I became a licensed real estate agent in July 2002. My broker at the time encouraged me to contact people on a daily basis to tell them I was now selling real estate. Nothing unusual about that process—it's what most brokers tell new agents.

The difference is that I created a means of personal accountability to keep track of how many people I contacted every day. I used a very low-tech, spiral-bound notebook that conveniently had twenty-five lines on each page. Every Monday I numbered a new page from one to twenty-five. I knew exactly where I was in completing the work I set out for myself each week.

I still have that notebook from my first year in the business and show it to new agents as evidence that I really did what I recommend that they do. Out of the twenty-five of that first week in the business, I converted three leads into actual transactions that year. The stories are a testimony to how a commitment to daily prospecting can lead to success.

One of the contacts I made was a friend who was going through a divorce. I sold her a small home for herself and her children. She remarried a few years later, and I sold that house and sold them a much larger newer home. A number of years later, her husband sold his company and they upgraded to an upper-bracket home and our team sold their current property. With that one lead, my team sold more than $6 million in real estate.

Another couple I met that week also stands out because of the multiple transactions through the years—six in total, plus one referral. I met them via a sign call, not the easiest lead-conversion opportunity, particularly for a new agent. As newlyweds, they were ready to buy their first condo. When she became pregnant a couple years later, as often happens they needed more space so moved up to a town home. And of course I sold the condo. Well, I'm sure you can imagine the rest of the story. As his career progressed and they had more income, each child then translated into a larger home, which meant selling their smaller abode. That one lead has resulted in almost $4 million in transactions. The secret I found is to track the business source and stay in touch with past clients. Both are keys to success in building and growing a business.

This proves that you can start at any time. It was the middle of August, nothing particularly special about that week other than I decided to begin.

Commit today to lead generation and track the sources of business.

COMPETENCE HIERARCHY

The four levels of competence theory have applications to the real estate profession. The hierarchy is set up in the form of a triangle. The broadest base contains the most people and narrows as the level of achievement becomes more challenging. In the real estate industry, the stage frequently corresponds with an agent's confidence level.

The first base level is the newly licensed agent. The stage of unconscious incompetence is when the agent doesn't know what he doesn't know. The duration in this state depends on the willingness to learn. Surprisingly, many agents are confident at this stage as they enter the field after years of wanting to "try" real estate.

The next level in the hierarchy is known as conscious incompetence. This is when it becomes apparent to the agent that there is so much that she still doesn't know and has yet to learn. Awareness may be due to having made a mistake or the agent just realizes the magnitude of the responsibility of representing a client with what is most likely their most significant asset. At this juncture, the new agent often seeks out more experienced agents to obtain wisdom on how to manage a difficult client or complicated transaction. Training really becomes impactful at this level, as the agent is now more open to learning. Actually, confidence wanes here, as agents often become discouraged at how hard it is to prospect, sell, and manage transactions. Sustaining the activities presents an ongoing challenge. This is when many become disillusioned and leave the industry.

The next step is that of conscious competence. A considerable knowledge base has been established, yet it still requires great effort. In my experience, agents who make it to this level are likely to achieve success. The reason being is that they have overcome enough challenging situations to understand what it takes to sustain productivity. At this juncture, the agent really benefits from engaging with a coach or mentor. By learning and incorporating systems and processes into their business, they move more quickly to the next level. Confidence begins to rise again, as the agent has renewed faith in his ability to achieve success and work with all types of clients.

The highest level, unconscious competence, is attained by only a select few. At this stage, the work becomes "second nature" for the professional. The tasks can be completed swiftly and at a high level of understanding with the least amount of effort. Confidence is at its highest, as well. Overconfidence can be the agent's Achilles' heel if she stops paying attention to the activities that first led to success. As the industry constantly changes and adapts to the market, it is paramount that the agent who achieves the pinnacle of success stays there by continuing to do the same.

Determine what level you are on today and
take steps to move up to the next one.

STEP AWAY FROM THE KNIVES

In difficult conversations, there are occasions when it is best to step away from the situation if it becomes volatile. Consider that the parties may be under duress and stress. In normal circumstances, people would behave differently. It is a secret to success in real estate to not take these occurrences personally.

Early on in my career, I called a seasoned agent to share that I had an offer to present on behalf of my client on one of his listings. We reviewed the offer over the phone, and he was so upset at the terms that he expressed that sentiment to me with foul language. It seemed like the appropriate response on my end would be to sign off on the call as quickly as possible, which I did in a professional manner. This allowed him to compose himself, which he did and afterwards we were able to carry on the discussion with more business-like decorum. I did go on to sell that house, and at the settlement the agent even hugged me. Handling the situation as I did was the best outcome for my client and my standing in the Realtor® community.

A course of action that is helpful is to evaluate what my personal contribution to the situation is. Being calm can actually be a super-power. Whenever possible, seek to follow the medical oath approach of "first do no harm." The agent who freaks out only contributes to the volatility of the situation. Take responsibility for the atmosphere in crucial situations and be mindful of how you can help mitigate any problems. Figure out where the high road is and take it.

There are occasions in which it can be helpful to obtain the counsel and perspective of an objective third party. In real estate transactions, the agent's broker of record should be informed if a challenging situation occurs with a client, customer, or another agent. One such scenario was a case in which I represented two adult children who were in the process of selling the family home. The daughter attended settlement and signed all of the documents as scheduled. On the day of settlement, the brother refused to cooperate. After advising the broker of what happened, he scheduled a conference call for the parties to visit. The broker calmly explained the options and encouraged the client to consummate his contractual obligation. In that situation, it was the calm demeanor of the broker, I believe, that led to the resolution of the issue.

When people are volatile, another useful strategy is to gently probe with questions. In this way, you can create perspective while managing emotions and reactions. The words of Ambrose Speirce ring true in these situations: "Speak when you are angry and you will make the best speech you will ever regret." Many times people just feel a need to vent some steam; let them have that space to do so. Just step away from the knives.

Implement strategies in your business and life
to handle volatile situations.

LEVERAGE ON THE MACRO LEVEL

Macro opportunities for leverage are limited only by the agent's ability to visualize possibilities. Anything that allows for exponential growth of one's time, energy, resources, capital, intellect, ability, and people is leverage. Other leverage opportunities build as they cross over into those that take on a broader scope.

Success begets success in that buyers and sellers want to work with agents with a proven track record. Experience is a form of macro leverage, as knowledge builds on itself.

Strong professional relationships with colleagues, other agents, and brokers are an effective means of leverage. Staff members and allied resources can help an agent keep the business running smoothly, as well as are invaluable to be able to use time and talent to success. People have strength zones, and an environment in which everyone is at their highest and best use is a fantastic way to leverage talent.

Training, experiential learning, coaching, and reading can all be forms of macro leverage. *The Millionaire Real Estate Agent*, by Keller Williams co-founder Gary Keller and Jay Papasan, addresses what happens when people hit an achievement ceiling. Many top producers obtain results from natural ability and a strong work ethic. At some point, it will only take them so far, as they hit the top of what they can accomplish on their own. To break through to the next level almost always requires new knowledge, skills, and abilities.

At higher levels of success, many agents strive to build and grow a business that is beyond what they are capable of achieving on their own. At this juncture, one has the opportunity to take the business to the next level by leveraging staff and agents. There are those who leverage the entire operation, such that it succeeds even when the original principal is no longer involved, either through pursuing other endeavors, retirement, or even death. In *The Millionaire Real Estate Agent*, this is known as the "Seventh Level Concept."

That is the vision Sue Huckaby, my business partner, had when we entered into a partnership in 2006. She sadly passed away in 2008. I then had the opportunity to leverage her work, life, and stellar image going forward. Sue had the foresight for success beyond herself, which included me. I am richly blessed, indeed.

Identify current macro-leverage opportunities,
as well as ways to take your business to the next level.

"CATCH A WAVE"

The Beach Boys' classic summer song proclaims the words of every real estate agent's dream come true: "Catch a wave and you're sitting on top of the world." This phenomenon takes place most often in extreme market conditions. A client sells in a market of rapidly rising prices and strong demand. The buyer enters the market when there is a lot of supply with many choices and not much demand. It is the professional agent who recognizes how to manage the opportunity when these markets occur and advises clients accordingly.

The seller client is "sitting on top of the world" when the home price is competitive for the market and there is low supply. As a listing agent, it is evident this has happened when my phone rings off the hook. Buying agents in these occasions open the conversation with queries such as, "Is the home still available?" and "What terms are the seller looking for?"

In the scenario where multiple offers are likely, the strategic listing agent establishes a date and time deadline for the submission of contracts. Additionally, it is beneficial to provide to all parties the desired terms and conditions for any offer(s), and when a decision will be made by the seller. The challenge in these circumstances is for the seller to be happy when he catches this wave and not get too greedy.

The buyer side scenario of "sitting on top of the world" frequently plays out much differently. In most cases, there are a lot of homes to choose from, which means the buyer agent has invested considerable time showing properties. Homes typically are on the market much longer, so the listing agent also may be weary of the length of time and energy invested in the client and property. The seller may feel beaten down on price as the buyer strives to get the best deal possible. Buyers often remain concerned of overpaying and so typically are only cautiously optimistic.

Either pure-seller or extreme-buyer market conditions rarely last forever. It is truly like "catching a wave." It is in retrospect that clients recognize that they were glad they sold or bought when they did. As an agent, it is a valuable skill to understand these market conditions and be able to explain the dynamics and adapt accordingly to the benefit of the client. In the words of professor and acclaimed scientist Jon Kabat-Zinn: "You can't stop the waves, but you can learn how to surf."

*Recognize market conditions and use your knowledge,
skills, and abilities to benefit clients.*

MEN ARE FROM MARS, WOMEN ARE FROM VENUS

The book *Men Are from Mars, Women Are from Venus*, by John Gray, is a guide on the relationship between the sexes. It has become a mainstay in American culture to quickly explain that the most common differences in communication styles, emotional needs, and behavior patterns between men and women. The concept is that men and women are unique creatures, so much so it is like they are from different planets.

As any professional agent will tell you, the distinctions become evident in the process of buying or selling a home. Women have an instinctual desire to nest, to make a house a home. This is particularly the case when pregnant or children are involved. The focus is on how the members of the family will live in the spaces. A woman is more likely to consider the emotional ramifications of the decision, which are left-brain functions. She is in tune with people's feelings, and how the move will affect everyone.

For men, it typically becomes a business transaction. The financial and logistical areas are his domain. He more often focuses on the systems and infrastructure upgrades. Decisions are made using the right brain, which is logical thinking.

The majority of real estate agents are women. The most common reason they enter the profession is that they are attracted to working with people and love the idea of looking at houses. Many enter into the profession because they want to put the two together. Women also are drawn to the possibility of a flexible schedule, as they manage child-care responsibilities.

The reason I have found that men enter the real estate profession is the opportunity to make a lot of money and to be a business owner. The focus is on the transactional aspects of the business and on getting things done.

It is interesting to note that although women represent the majority of agents, there is an income gap between the sexes. Women's earnings as a percentage of men's are 66 percent. The fact that many women only work part-time could attribute to that statistic. It is my experience that when men enter the industry they automatically set it up as a business. Those women who do operate it like a business are just as successful as men; there are just not as many of them. By my estimation, women run 20 percent of the megateams in the United States. Many are run by husband-wife teams that are a blend of the two.

Some of this information may seem stereotypical. Yet, it is still helpful to understand the dynamics of the industry. There are truly benefits to all of the attributes, the relational and emotional as well as the logistical and financial. A balance of all of these provide for a strong agent and team.

Use the concept Men Are from Mars, Women Are from Venus *to understand and influence clients, as well as run a successful business.*

THE MARKET CAN BEHAVE LIKE LEMMINGS

The video game "Lemmings" was popular in the early 1990s. The premise of the game was that lemmings will commit mass suicide by marching into traps or off a cliff unless someone does something to stop them. The player who was able to stop the behavior moved on to higher levels of play. It is actually a misconception that the lemming, in real life, will commit mass suicide. Rather, critters follow the instinctual drive of migratory behavior, which causes them to take risks that are beyond their physical capabilities.

It is interesting to think about how markets can follow behavior similar to lemmings. Rationally, people know to buy low and sell high. However, when prices are low and everyone is selling, it is more common for the majority of the market to follow suit. The same happens when there is high demand and prices are high. That is a scenario when everybody wants what everybody wants. This is the other extreme of rationalization—that all those other people couldn't possibly be wrong. Often it contains an element of "irrational exuberance."

The movie *It's a Wonderful Life* is set in the 1920 era of stock market crashes. There is a scene in which there is a run on the bank and the Bailey Savings and Loan. The character played by Jimmy Stewart states to the people who come to take all their money out of the Bailey S&L: "Potter isn't selling. Potter's buying! And why? Because we're panicking and he's not. That's why. He's picking up some bargains."

The best way to ward off a case of lemmings mentality is to evaluate the market with objectivity. That can be challenging in the purchase and sale of residential real estate because it usually carries with it deeply held emotions, in addition to the financial consideration. The behavior to be protective of one's home is instinctual, as much as it is for lemmings to follow their migratory behavior.

Just as with the lemmings game, the real estate agent is in a position to recognize the true nature of the market. In the words of economist Edward R. Dewey: "Cycles are the mysterious forces that trigger events." The key to success as a professional real estate agent is to be informed on the macro market cycles in order to advise clients accordingly.

Use market data to provide advice to clients on buying and selling real estate during extreme market fluctuations.

WHO YOU GONNA CALL?

"Who you gonna call?" is a line from the lyrics of the 1980's movie *Ghostbusters*. It has one of those crazy tunes that can get stuck in my head. The application to real estate is that by the creation of brand awareness, when people have a real estate need or referral, they will think of you. It should come as no surprise that if people do not know you are a real estate agent, they aren't going to call. This is a key objective to real estate success, to not be a secret agent.

It often is the case that most people know several real estate agents. This is true for other professions, as well. For example, we are friends with several CPAs, insurance agents, financial advisors, attorneys, restaurant owners, car dealers, and numerous other service providers and professionals. Marketing gurus have metrics on how to create top-of-mind awareness. It is a key component to build and grow a business that sustains long-term success.

There is a part of the brain known as the reticular activating system (RAS). It is the portal through which nearly all information enters the brain. It serves as a filter for incoming data and affects what a person focuses on and thus remembers. People are bombarded constantly with messages, so the RAS is like a bouncer that determines what is important and what should be stored away. It files away what may be useful later on. This is when being top-of-mind as a real estate agent becomes important. The idea is that when people have a real estate need or question or knows someone who does, they will think of you as an agent who can meet that need.

An example of the phenomenon is when people begin the process of buying a new car. All of a sudden, it seems they see the cars they are considering everywhere. They start to pay attention to advertising and media and are pleasantly surprised when in conversation that other people also have information and interest in the car purchase. This is the RAS at work. The marketing presence more than likely was always there, they just didn't notice it. To achieve success as a real estate professional requires being relevant all the time to the public. Then when the occasion arises, the customer will think of you. An inconsistent message is not as effective.

There are countless marketing, advertising, social media, promotional, public relations, and lead-generation platforms for creating top-of-mind brand awareness. The important message to the agent is to do something and to do it on a consistent basis in order to build and grow a successful business.

Establish top-of-mind awareness platforms on a consistent basis for strong name identification in the marketplace.

HOW SELLERS DETERMINE VALUE

Sellers will often state that they need to get a certain price in order to be in a position to sell. This is when being curious is a helpful strategy. I always ask why this number is important to them. The reasons tend to fall into one of three categories.

Some sellers base their price on the amount of money that they have invested into the home. This number includes the amount they paid for it, plus any improvements and settlement costs. In many cases, the value of improvements is vastly exaggerated, much like a fisherman telling the story of a big catch. And often the owners include maintenance items that are not really considered capital improvements. This approach is like adding the maintenance and oil changes to a car value and expecting the next owner to pay the previous owner for those "wear-and-tear" expenditures. It can become particularly challenging when the owner has refinanced and taken money out of the home, expecting the market to pay for that as well.

The second group bases the value on the evaluation of other homes in the community that have sold, gone under contract, or are available to purchase. Access to public tax records and estimating sources such as Zillow have increased the number of sellers who use this approach. The interesting phenomenon is that the sellers tend to always give more value to their homes, even if indicators show otherwise. Often they will use the highest sales ever, even if the market has not ever been at that level since. Further, they usually disallow or substantially downplay any low sales in the community.

The third group computes the number based on the projections of what they will come out of the home with after selling. This correlates to what they need in order to be able to buy their next home. The challenge with this approach is that just because a seller needs a certain number, there is nothing that compels the purchaser to pay it for that reason alone. If this were the case, then there would have been no short sales or foreclosures. Purchasers would have paid what the seller "needed" to get out of the home.

All of these approaches provide indicators about value and are helpful to consider. Understanding what matters to clients is important for knowing their motivation and what it will take for them to actually be a seller. The objective in the conversation is to explain that market value is actually the amount of money that a buyer will pay that a seller will accept at any given point in time. It is more like the stock market than any other financial vehicle.

Understand how seller clients determine value to best know how to meet their objectives in the marketplace.

LEVERAGE WITH MARKET KNOWLEDGE

A professional real estate agent leverages market knowledge by preparing an effective comparative market analysis (CMA) for both sellers and buyers. Both types of clients can have what I call "itis," which is a tendency or state of mind. In other words, they only see their perspective. The CMA is a key tool for agents to help clients view the situation through the market's lens.

An agent's market knowledge is key when working with sellers to price a home correctly for the market. Further, when a seller receives an offer, the ones who are prepared in advance with information about the market and expectations are more likely to recognize the value of the offer and respond accordingly.

There are situations in which the home will receive an offer, or multiple offers very quickly, because it was well positioned. The sellers can develops a case of "itis," believing that the home has been underpriced or that they are "giving it away." Some think they should wait, following the logic that if there is one offer there may be more potentially out there. In a few situations, these scenarios can occur and of course it benefits the sellers. In other cases, though, the market responds as the CMA indicated and the parties should celebrate that thorough preparation was the reason and be happy.

When the agent is strong in market knowledge, it transfers into writing successful offers for buyer clients. Buyers also are known to get "itis" and require counsel about the market conditions they are operating under. When the market is robust, then it can be a challenge to influence a buyer to be aggressive enough to win the contract. And when the market is sluggish or declining, buyers often have to be "talked off the ledge" in order to make confident decisions.

There are times when clients listen to the agent's counsel and reap that reward. There are other times when they don't listen. In those cases, they learn from the market, which can speak volumes.

Become a market expert in your area and use that knowledge to influence both buyer and seller clients in making good decisions.

TRACK YOUR WAY TO SUCCESS

In the movie *The Martian*, the main character, played by Matt Damon, is left behind on Mars. The circumstances in the story were the antagonist, as there were limited resources. This made survival virtually impossible. When he realized the gravity of the situation, he began a video journal as both a chronicle and a means of thinking his way to solutions.

Keeping a log or journal is a time-tested way to discover what is and isn't working. To think about and reflect on collected information often reveals solutions not previously considered. Adjustments can then be made and further evaluations provide even more enterprising solutions.

In the beginning of my real estate career, I kept a log of all the people I talked to about real estate. At first, this was primarily a means of personal accountability. In order to keep a record of all of the information I gathered, I moved it into a database. After I touch someone, I input any updates into the database. It makes for a much richer follow-through when you actually remember everything you talked about the last time you connected. The database also allows me to better track key metrics, such as the source of leads and when next to follow up with customers.

To take my business to the next level, I began to work with a business coach. She encouraged me to keep a journal—five minutes a day of reflection. When first recommended, I am embarrassed to admit I proclaimed I did not have five minutes a day to spare.

Then I considered the fact that I was paying her to help me break through mindset and practices that were keeping me from achieving a higher level of success. So I told her I would "try" it. For more than one year, I have written one page per day in a journal. The amazing thing is that great truths have been revealed in the process. It has helped me make changes in my business and life that I want and need to do.

High-producing agent, podcast host, and author Pat Hiban, in *6 Steps to 7 Figures*, shows a photo of all the journals he has kept in his career. Clearly it demonstrates that success leaves clues. Solutions are clearer and new ideas are revealed—no need to be stranded on Mars to track and journal your way to success in real estate here on earth.

Keep a log or journal to track and reflect on solutions
to take your business and life to the next level.

HAVE YOU READ THE CONTRACT?

The jurisdiction in which I practice real estate provides forms for agents to complete on behalf of clients. When I was a new agent, I had many questions about the contract. The law is very clear that the agent is not to practice law and thus cannot provide legal advice, unless of course the agent is also licensed to practice law in that jurisdiction. As the majority of transactions have similar components, the purpose of the standard residential sales contract is to provide a format to facilitate the process.

The fact that I had many questions is not surprising, given my inexperience. The response from my broker was always the question, "Have you read the contract?" After a few times, it became clear to me that I should read the contract prior to presenting him with my question. What I learned very quickly is that when I read the contract, often I would discover the answer myself. Reading the document that thoroughly meant that I knew well all of the clauses and addendum to the agreement. In this way, over time I developed a much stronger base of knowledge.

There are times still that I am unsure about what the contract terms mean or what the intent is, so I still seek counsel from my broker and others as the situation warrants. Reading the contract first, though, always makes the conversation that much richer. Given that the laws and forms change frequently, even as often as every year, reading the contract is an ongoing process. There is no "one and done" in real estate in contract mastery.

The movie *Joy* is the true story of Joy Mangano, the woman who invented the Miracle Mop. She endured many trials and tribulations along the way to success. One of the failures she experienced early on was that she signed a contract she had not read. At a key juncture, she took responsibility by taking the time to read the contract. It empowered her to take the action she needed to save her business. Joy went on to found a business dynasty by selling the mop and other inventions to great success on the QVC cable network.

There are jurisdictions in which the real estate agent does not prepare standard form contracts. Even in these situations, having a strong knowledge of standard practices will serve clients well.

Now as an associate broker myself, when I work with new agents and they come to me with questions, I answer them with, "Have you read the contract?" Once they have shared their understanding, I share my experience and counsel.

---

*Read the contract frequently to stay abreast of changes
and how you can best serve clients.*

ALL I REALLY NEEDED TO KNOW I LEARNED FROM DR. P

I have learned many things from my clients over the years. Dr. P is one client whose profound observations still ring true. The lessons learned resonate much as those from the famous book of essays by American minister Robert Fulghum, *All I Really Need to Know I Learned in Kindergarten.*

Dr. P taught me that it is important for the agent and the client to be on the same team. Take the client's perspective and be certain that message is communicated clearly and frequently to the market. In effect, Dr. P was affirming these lines from Fulghum: "When you go out into the world, it is best to hold hands and stick together."

It was a tough market for sellers when Dr. P's home was for sale. There was a point when sharing the honest feedback from the buyers and their agents was not helpful. We could not change the real estate market. Further, we had reached a juncture where there weren't the funds and ability or motivation to change the house or the price.

So what's a real estate agent to do? Dr. P taught me to find the value and to proclaim it. It was my job to actively promote the positive aspects of the home, property, and community. Even if it took more time to sell, I was to stay committed throughout the entire process. It was tempting to "slack off," as the sales process became a marathon rather than a sprint. Yet Dr. P was right in so many ways.

A paradigm shift took place in my mind and then my heart. I took up the gauntlet of the value and truly believed in it. That message was conveyed to the buyers and agents in a way that hadn't been happening before. Yes, I did sell Dr. P's home and the profound lessons learned continue to carry on.

***

Be open to learning lessons from clients and implement them in your business and life.

COOPETITION

Coopetition is the economic principle whereby cooperation and competition are merged. Imagine the combination of peanut butter and chocolate and the combined taste those two ingredients provide. The origin of the concept is based in the scientific field of game theory. John Forbes Nash wrote about it in the book, entitled *Theory of Games and Economic Behavior*.

The concept is integral to the consummation of the majority of real estate transactions in the US. Real estate brokers agree through multiple listing service portals to offer a commission to the "cooperating" or "co-op" broker. This system is a very efficient means of exposing properties for sale to the broad market.

And yet, every broker and real estate agent is, in essence, in competition with all the other brokers and real estate agents in the marketplace. Most real estate agents are independent contractors and thus paid on commission; therefore, payment is tendered when a settlement takes place. So competition usually is and can be fierce.

And yet, without cooperation, the majority of real estate transactions would not take place. Ultimately the free market system of the multiple listing services is of benefit to seller clients for exposure and for buyer clients for access to a broader market selection.

Thus, much like the invention of peanut butter cups, the merging of the two concepts of cooperation and competition has improved the real estate market as we know it.

---

*Find ways to embrace the dual benefits
of coopetition in your business.*

JUST KEEP SWIMMING

As the summer comes to a close and the Labor Day holiday is upon us, it seems a good time for this topic. Those with young kids in their lives will recognize "just keep swimming" from Dory's song in *Finding Nemo*.

If I were to write a letter of advice to myself as a newly licensed real estate agent, Dory's wise words would be at the top of my list. The area in which agents need to "just keep swimming" the most is in prospecting. If you are a swimmer, remember when you first learned? To perform the strokes correctly felt awkward and were difficult at first. And yet over time, as you perfected a stroke, you began to feel the power of moving through the water with speed and ease. That is the way it is with lead generation. Commit to learn the strokes of business development and over time strength and skill will build and grow so that you will flow through the process with ease.

Another lesson from "just keep swimming" is to stay on task. To constantly switch up strokes can cause a swimmer to lose momentum. Professional athletes concentrate on the perfection of one or two strokes to achieve the best results. Real estate professionals should hone one or two lead-generation methods before pursuing the mastery of others. Concentration of effort makes for a much stronger and more impactful connection than a scattered effect does.

It can be beneficial to have a new agent observe and shadow a more seasoned professional. Training and role-playing are valuable also. But at some point, the agent has to get in the water. Standing on the side of the pool is the metaphor for the agent who spends all of his time in training, thus attempting to learn to swim by sitting on the sidelines. Nothing replaces jumping in the water. The learning is in the doing and then you "just keep swimming."

Barbara Corcoran, in her book *Shark Tales*, shares the story of how she landed on the show *Shark Tank*. She was selected in the initial round to be one of the "sharks," but then at the last minute discovered she was cut for someone younger. Rather than getting discouraged and quitting, she sent an e-mail message to the producer with the subject line: "still swimming." Even when there are sharks in the water and the barracuda attacks, the professional "just keeps swimming."

"Just keep swimming" in lead generation to maintain persistence in developing and growing a business.

WORK-LIFE BALANCE

The ideal to somehow achieve work-life balance sounds to me that it is an either-or dilemma. This worldview is like a teeter-totter on a playground—when one side goes up, the other is down. The goal from this perspective is to achieve balance.

As Gary Keller states in *The One Thing*, it isn't really balance, but counterbalance. To go back to the teeter-totter analogy, when the weight becomes heavier on one end, to get it into balance a weight has to be placed on the other end. Another way to achieve balance is to lighten the load, or take something away on one or both ends.

A paradigm shift from that perspective could be one of a both-and opportunity. What if one's work brings satisfaction and happiness in life? And what if life is more meaningful because of one's work? Adding and expanding in one area doesn't necessary mean that something has to be taken from the other. Instead, it enhances and makes those relationships that much richer.

As I passed over the half-century mark, I began to embrace the worldview that everything is life. My work is a rewarding component of the whole. A Venn diagram is another way to consider this worldview. There is an almost complete overlap in the illustration, like an eclipse. From this perspective, work is not drudgery to finish and escape quickly in order to have a life.

Helping people buy and sell homes is its own reward. Just think, as a real estate professional you can be part of the joy a first-time homeowner feels when she achieves her dream of having her own place. The work enables a family to sell their home to move near loved ones after they retire. It helps a young couple create their own "nest" to raise a family. Even in challenging situations, the real estate professional is there to be part of the solution and ability to move on.

Consider today your perspective on work-life balance.

COOKING APPLIANCES
AND DECISION-MAKING

The chef and the mainstream cook alike have many choices for preparing food. The microwave is fast and easy. The other end of the spectrum is the crock pot for slow and steady cooking. The middle ground options include the oven, which offers both broiling from above for quick searing, as well as the heating element from below that can warm up, bake, and roast food. If an appliance includes the cooktop and the oven, then that is known as a stove. The cooktop feature utilizes pots and pans to warm up and boil food and liquids.

Skillets and similar kitchen equipment are to sear, fry, stir-fry, and more. Convection oven appliances are a hybrid of the microwave and the traditional oven. Trivection ovens were introduced by General Electric into the oven appliance category. They combine three means of customized cooking: radiant heat, as well as convection and microwave. According to GE, the trivection oven cooks food five times faster than the traditional oven.

Then there are the ancillary appliances, such as a warming drawer that doesn't cook the food, but keeps it warm, as the name implies. The toaster oven is a small version of the broiler feature in the traditional oven.

A real estate agent is familiar with all types of kitchen equipment and appliances, as the room is a central feature in all residential homes. The further application to real estate is the corollary to how cooking methods are like decision-making styles.

The microwave thinkers are quick on their feet and can make decisions like popcorn in a microwave. There are situations when it is best to not belabor a choice; this is when sharp wit thinking is best utilized. There are decisions that benefit from being like a slow-cooker, to be certain that one considers every morsel of the situation from all angles before proceeding forward.

There are clients whose decision-making styles are mixed. The husband may be expeditious when arriving at a conclusion, which would utilize a broiler style, whereas the wife may need to warm up to the idea, and in that situation that component of the oven is engaged. On other occasions, the decision needs to be cooked on one side and then turned over and looked at from another perspective—the searing style of decision-making benefits from this. Ideas sometimes need to be stirred up, just as with stir-frying.

People can engage in one level of decision-making speed and style in work and another in personal decisions. That is when the use of hybrid appliances works best in this analogy. Maybe the client would come to a decision if the agent applied two or three ways of considering the decision, like the convection and trivection ovens.

Like ancillary appliances, there are occasions when the decision has been made and thus cooked thoroughly, and it just needs to be warmed up. The professional agent achieves success by being knowledgeable of all the cooking methods and decision-making styles.

Apply cooking appliance methods to understanding the decision-making styles of clients.

PERSONAL BEST

The idea of a "personal best" performance was first introduced to me when our daughter was on the local swim team during elementary school. The coach urged each swimmer to use her own record as the barometer of what to beat. The idea was to leave it all in the water, to give it everything you had every time.

In real estate, there are numerous levels of achievement. Brokerage offices, local and national Realtor® associations, as well as entities such as *The Wall Street Journal* all present awards to agents, teams, and brokerages for production and number of units sold.

To break records year after year is a worthy goal. Yet there are some markets in which that just isn't achievable or practical. To push agents, staff, and teams in difficult markets can discourage morale. At the extreme, it can result in the slippery slope of success at any cost. This can lead to corruption as portrayed in *The Big Short* by Michael Lewis. That is why I believe the personal best yardstick of achievement is a standard every agent can use in any situation and market.

The 2003-2006 real estate market in most of the United States experienced double-digit appreciation year over year. It was easy to expect agents and teams to exceed past performances. It was a period of incredible expansive growth. Truly, if an agent found it a challenge to be successful during that time period, then it was a clear indicator to pursue another profession.

The market was then flat for a couple of years until the financial market crash in 2008. The correction continued for several years. Even the most seasoned professional found it extremely difficult to complete transactions during those years. In practically every deal, a seller was losing money, bringing considerable funds to settlement, or in distress in some fashion. Buyers were hyper-concerned that there was more correction on the way and thus fearful of overpaying. To get and then keep a deal together meant the agent had to bring his personal best to the job every day.

Thus, in many ways the personal-best barometer is the better indicator of achievement. If day after day, month upon month, and year after year an agent puts forth a full measure of effort, then one can be confident that she has met a worthy goal.

Give your personal best today and every day in your real estate business.

"BREAKING UP IS HARD TO DO"

There are instances in real estate when the title and lyrics of this song by Neil Sedaka ring true: "Breaking up is hard to do." The song chronicles a romantic relationship as it comes to an end. In real estate, when a contract voids it also comes to an end and not just legally and financially. There often can be considerable emotional baggage associated with the outcome.

One scenario is when a purchaser has buyer's remorse and voids the contract. Regardless of the reason and the validity of the situation, the seller often has the "wish that we were making up again." On occasion, there are bitter sentiments and the parties insist on never seeing each other again, yet every once a while there is still a glint of love. If the sellers can think of all they went through to get to that juncture, perhaps they might be open to give it another try and encourage the purchaser to find a way to work it out.

The scenario in which the seller has second thoughts is not as common. The instance this occurs in real estate most often is when another buyer presents a back-up offer. The contractual remedies depend on the circumstances, so be certain to verify jurisdictional requirements. Remember, though, that "breaking up is hard to do" for a reason.

The relationship between the broker and the client can go through breakups as well. In the case of the seller clients, they may no longer think that the listing agent represents them as well as presented at the original appointment. The agent may not be meeting the clients' expectations or they no longer "feel the love." This happens also with buyer clients, when they in effect want to "shop around" for an agent. On occasion, buyers meet up with an agent by visiting open houses. Others prefer to call each listing agent and work directly with them to set up showings. It can be similar to a romantic breakup. One or both parties want to take some time off to date other people.

At times, both jilted romantic partners and parties involved with real estate transactions discover the grass isn't necessarily greener on the other side of the fence. In fact, it could be greener because it is over the septic tank. Although pretty, it comes with a residual odor. And then they want to come back.

My husband has a saying: "Love isn't love until it is set free." What that means in the real estate world is that people enter into contracts and business relationships freely. If it no longer works for them, then perhaps it is best to let them go. Do your best to break up graciously and keep the door open; there may still be contractual and financial obligations associated with the decision.

True love, though, cannot be forced. It may be hard to break up, but sometimes that is the right thing to do for the people involved.

Apply the lessons in "breaking up is hard to do"
and take action accordingly.

THE EMERGENCY ROOM IS FOR TRAUMA

One of our nieces is an emergency room surgeon. She has shared tales of the emergency room and says that people end up there for a reason. The definition of an emergency is one that is an unexpected and serious situation that requires immediate action. In the case of a medical emergency, it is often a matter of life and death or significant trauma. The staff and physicians are prepared to handle true emergencies. What happens, though, is that people arrive who are not having true emergencies and sap energy and resources from attending professionals.

In real estate, there are rarely life-and-death decisions. Yet many aspects to the transaction are very significant to the parties involved, due to the financial and legal ramifications. Add to that the emotional and logistical components, and trauma can soon become an issue.

The professional real estate agent recognizes the distinction between a true emergency and situations that are just a lot of drama. It is important to save resources for real emergencies. I vividly remember a transaction in which it seemed the agent on the other side was sounding the fire alarm daily. It began to feel a lot like the "boy who cried wolf." At some point, it was hard to believe all of these things were actually happening. The deal went to settlement by our side remaining calm and composed and being careful not to contribute to the drama of the occasion.

A way to keep issues from becoming a crisis is to be proactive. Just as in medicine, preventive measures have more impact for long-term health than emergency treatment. Take time at initial and subsequent listing appointments and buyer consultations to set expectations and discuss processes and outcomes.

The diligent agent follows through on all the contingencies and details associated with the transaction. Checklists are vital in the medical field, as well as the real estate industry, to assure systems and procedures are followed per protocol. Keeping all the parties informed goes a long way in maintaining goodwill. Then if a situation truly does warrant extraordinary treatment, most people are reasonable in coming up with solutions that work for everyone.

Take preventive, proactive measures to keep trauma
and drama out of your real estate transactions.

AUGUST
21

MARKETING IS LIKE AIR COVER

Marketing is like air cover—the purpose is not to replace troops on the ground. Effective defensive and offensive maneuvers include both. In the case of real estate sales, there is still the need for an agent in the field person-to-person with customers. The purpose of marketing and advertising is to create brand and name awareness. The increased exposure can make the salesperson's job easier, yet it does not replace the person!

In my first year as a real estate agent, all I had were simple business cards that weren't even professionally designed. No branded website, no print advertising, and no social media. What I did was simple belly-to-belly prospecting. I contacted the people who would recognize my name—my sphere of influence. At the time, I didn't even know what "sphere of influence" meant. I just knew that in order to sell houses people needed to know that I was now a licensed real estate agent. I called and wrote personal, handwritten notes. My message was simple: I am available to assist with your real estate needs.

Frequently I hear a conditional response to the idea of prospecting from new agents and those who want to ramp up their business. That is, they will start contacting people once _____. You fill in the blank. What I see most frequently in the blank is the perception that marketing has to precede prospecting. It is proven that people want to work with people they like and trust. This is the case more so for residential real estate sales, because buying and selling a home has a significant emotional element to it. There is value to marketing and advertising for the long-run real estate career. It provides base awareness and tells the agent's story. It reinforces the professional's unique value proposition to the marketplace. The value of advertising is that it lends credibility in the eyes of the public.

One challenge with leads from marketing is that there often is not as strong of a connection. When a prospect comes from advertising or marketing efforts, in almost all cases the agent competes for the business. On the other hand, when the agent works with people from her sphere or referrals, even if the customer is visiting with other agents, the relationship starts at a higher level of trust. In *The Seven Levels of Communication*, author Michael J. Maher refers to this process as going from marketer to communicator.

Almost all marketing and advertising efforts require money, whereas most in-person business development activities do not. Person-to-person prospecting includes phone calls, in-person meetings and events, networking, door knocking, holding open houses, and writing notes. Social media can qualify as well if it's personal.

As a general rule, person-to-person prospecting is time-driven and advertising and marketing are money-driven. In most cases, the two work best as a combined force.

Ramp up and increase real estate business by combining the effectiveness of marketing and in-person lead-generation strategies.

CAR MODEL: BENTLEY VERSUS MINI

Recently I was stopped in traffic behind a car that from the rear had the look of a Bentley. As the car was a convertible and because I drive a Mercedes convertible, it made me take a closer look. To be honest, I am not a car aficionado, so please bear with me if you are. The car was a Mini and I was taken by surprise, as the emblems appear to be so similar at first glance. Both have wings that spread out on either sides of a circle. On the Bentley, there is a "B" in the center of the circle, and on the Mini, there is the word "Mini." Bentley Motor Limited is a subsidiary of Volkswagen, and the Mini is manufactured by BMW. From a distance, it was very difficult to discern the distinction, yet up close it was more evident.

In home construction and design features, this same phenomenon plays out. For means of comparison, the Bentley is the custom-built home and the Mini is the tract or production-built home. At a distance, it may be hard to discern the distinctions. Up close and over time, it becomes evident which is which. This illustration works well with buyer clients I've found. All vehicles offer the form and function of four wheels on a chassis and transportation. The difference becomes apparent when one compares models and upgrades.

In a custom home, construction elements and features are top grade relative to a tract home. One of the first clues a buyer can use to discover the level of quality is the hardware for doors and cabinetry. In a custom home, knobs are solid and often made or finished by hand. In a tract home, the hardware is often plated rather than solid, which means it will wear off and is likely to peel over time.

Another clue about the quality of the selections is to examine the cabinetry in the kitchen, bathrooms, and built-in features. Is the construction solid wood or is it veneer over particleboard? Is the finish lacquer, which does not wear well over time, or is the wood varnished or hand-finished in some fashion? Are the parts joined with concealed screws and glue, or do sections of the cabinetry stick out to catch on items? Dovetail joinery withstands daily usage better then cheaper, less labor-intensive construction methods. Pull the drawers out to determine if they fully extend so items can be reached in all sections. Verify whether they close softly, and if so it guarantees smooth and long-lasting glide function. Do appliances fit into the cabinetry, or do they stick out like they were not part of the original kitchen design?

Tract homebuilders sell value for square footage. Professionally decorated models showcase and feature the homes in the best light. The décor often draws the buyer's attention away from the construction details and instead toward items that do not have lasting market value.

The point of this analogy is to make one aware. Just as I thought I was looking at a Bentley at first glance, on closer inspection I realized the car was a Mini. One wouldn't want to pay a Bentley price for a Mini, no matter how cute the car is! The same applies to home construction.

The professional agent remains knowledgeable about the differences and is able to successfully illustrate them to clients.

———— ༄ ————

Apply the car model analogy to explain the differences in the quality of home construction to clients.

CHECKLIST EMPOWERMENT

As a private pilot, my husband is a man of checklists. Even routine items are verified before takeoff. He is adamant that the checklist is a key tool in safe flying. The communication between the pilot and copilot also assures that the responsible party has completed his assignments. Checklists empower the pilot with the confidence that all steps have been taken prior to flying the plane.

There are many benefits to using checklists in a real estate business. The majority of the details from listing a home to contract to settlement are repeatable processes. Following checklists for these routine aspects of the business assure that clients receive a consistent and professional standard of service. Also, it increases communication among team members. It can be frustrating to clients when they tell the agent something and then find out that no one else knows what's going on, or vice versa. Team members and agents can get "up to speed" quickly on the file if everyone follows the same systems by use of time-tested checklists.

The checklist actually empowers people. It instills the confidence that routine items are dealt with in a timely and consistent manner. It also creates a strong sense of accomplishment as duties and responsibilities are literally "checked off." In this way, the agent and staff members are free to focus on more critical aspects that require a higher level of thinking. I have found that when the client observes through the agent's actions that the process is being managed at a professional level, they usually are not as anxious. In other words, there is less micromanaging.

Checklists enable the agent and staff, if applicable, to handle multiple clients and transactions simultaneously. In my first year as a real estate agent I sold twelve homes, which was a nice, steady one per month. I remember vividly my first broker telling me that I was totally capable of selling one house per week. At the time I couldn't visualize how that could be done. Now that I have had experience with checklists and systems, it is truly no longer challenging.

In the *Checklist Manifesto: How to Get Things Right*, Dr. Atul Gawande provides countless examples of how checklists are beneficial for greater efficiency and consistency in the business world and medical profession. It is a great resource for the power of the checklist.

Establish checklists to manage routine aspects of the business.

KNOWLEDGE TRANSFER

A few years into my career as a real estate agent, I was asked to serve on the board of a local charity. As a member, I agreed to chair the annual fundraising gala, even though I had never attended one previously. This meant I had to rely on those who had attended before to paint the picture for me of what the gala looked like. Thankfully everyone pulled together and we put on a top-quality event. It raised more money in one night than ever had been previously achieved, and the event was deemed an overwhelming success. Not surprisingly, I was asked to do it again the next year.

People asked how I knew what to do when I hadn't ever attended one of the galas before. I shared that I had been to galas for other charities and organizations, so had a vision of what a quality event looked like. Next, I worked back from there, establishing the steps of what would need to happen. Then I recruited volunteers to oversee the different components. At that juncture, I took on the dual role of manager of the process and cheerleader of the people.

You have done this as well, I'm sure. The process of taking skills in one area of life and using them successfully in another area is known as knowledge transfer in the organizational management world. Real estate agents new to the profession rely on skills they learned and developed in previous work and life experiences. Perhaps you were on the committee for the PTA carnival or led an event at your place of worship. Logistics and people skills developed in other areas often transfer well into the real estate world.

Many times agents enter the field because they have bought and sold a number of homes themselves. Those experiences are like my having attended other galas. I had enough knowledge of what that type of event looked like that I could visualize the evening and work back from there.

Knowing where one is going often means getting there faster. Thus, it was much easier to chair the second gala than the first. I didn't have to stop at every juncture to see if we were on track. And even though different issues arose, I was more confident the next time around. This also happens with real estate professionals. Each transaction increases one's knowledge base.

Pursue training and mentoring from those who have gone before. Develop relationships with those who can point the way to a successful career in real estate for you. These are secrets to success in real estate.

Use your prior knowledge, experiences, and mentor relationships to transfer to success in real estate.

AGENT AS REAL ESTATE FORE-CADDY

The insight, advice, and moral support of a professional caddy have the ability to markedly improve a golfer's game. I had the pleasure to play for the first time with a fore-caddy at the Turnberry Isle Fairmont property in Florida. Correlations to the business of a professional real estate agent quickly became apparent to me.

The fore-caddy provides a description of the hole to the players and then goes ahead, thus the distinction of "fore." By virtue of being on the course, the fore-caddy can spot the players' shots as they come off the tee box. A good agent also gives a description of the current market environment to her clients and then goes out ahead to project what is likely to occur. For buyers, the agent explains the offer-writing process, as well as how the seller might respond For sellers, it includes how the market is likely to react to a list price. Once the shot is taken, the fore-caddy gives recommendations on how to correct if need be to stay on the course and to obtain the best outcome. The professional real estate agent also "listens" to the market for clients and provides guidance given current conditions.

The fore-caddy evaluates the weather and other variables continuously. For example, the direction and strength of the wind may affect a shot. The agent also stays constantly on top of current market conditions, such as which direction interest rates are projected, the supply and demand of competitive properties, and advises clients accordingly.

The professional fore-caddy has intimate knowledge of the rules of the game and instructs players accordingly on their options. The agent also stays current on the laws of the jurisdiction and customs of the market area. The fore-caddy typically does not take the place of a marshall or official, just as the agent does not necessarily assume the position of the broker, an attorney, or settlement agent. Yet the professional fore-caddy and agent both are well versed in the fundamentals and can refer one to other experts as warranted.

The challenges and obstacles of the golf course are well known to the fore-caddy. If asked, she will make suggestions about which club to use and how to read the green. The agent also will make recommendations during contract negotiations on how a client might respond, as well as how to "read" the responses of the other parties.

The fore-caddy is a professional, on the course daily, and plays with golfers of varying levels of skill. The dedicated agent is in the marketplace daily, stays in close contact with other agents, and provides counsel accordingly. The professional agent is knowledgeable of the inventory of homes and properties available to purchase both in the active and shadow markets.

Develop the attributes and skills of a fore-caddy
by being proactive on behalf of clients.

ACTION TRACTION

Newton's first law states that an object at rest stays at rest, and an object in motion stays in motion. One of the distinctions between those who just barely make it in real estate and those who are successful is related to this fundamental law. In effect, an agent at rest stays at rest and an agent in motion stays in motion. By getting into motion and taking action, the agent gains traction that then gains forward momentum.

This is particularly true in the case of lead generation. Consistent, active prospecting becomes a self-fulfilling prophesy. If an agent is in a slump, there are a number of things that she can do to get productive. They all involve action.

One is to go see houses. Many agents become Realtors® because they love houses. So viewing homes should be a positive activity for the agent. While looking at houses, the agent should think about people they who know might be interested. If they know anyone who lives in the neighborhood or community, this is a great chance to connect, as well.

Door knocking is another lead-generation method that immediately gets agents into productive activity. One of the agents on our team recently door knocked in her mother's neighborhood. Nothing immediately came of it, but within weeks one of the neighbors was ready to put his home on the market. He thought of this agent because of the flyer she left at the home. He wanted to hire a proactive agent who didn't just sit around waiting for the business to come to her.

Community events, charity fundraisers, children's school functions, and sporting outings are all opportunities for the agent to meet and network with people. Even when you don't feel like getting out, just doing so is a positive motion. The words of self-improvement author and speaker Dale Carnegie attest to this: "Inaction breeds doubt and fear. Action breeds confidence and courage. If you want to conquer fear, do not sit at home and think about it. Go out and get busy." Gain some traction to your action!

*Get into action today and stay in action to support
your lead-generation objectives.*

BUYERS ARE LIARS—A BUYER'S TALE

The idiom "Buyers are liars and sellers are, too" is one of the mainstay quotes in the real estate industry. Richard Courtney wrote an entire book on the topic with that exact title. As with most idioms, there is a kernel of truth embedded. And yet in almost all cases, something much deeper is going on.

It is helpful first to consider the context. The buying and selling of a home, on average, only occurs once every five to seven years for people. Combine that with the emotional, logistical, and financial aspects that make for an even more challenging situation. When people are under stress, they often respond out of character from their normal behavior.

Our team has the philosophy that when clients are under stress, we mentally surround them in a cloud of grace and forgiveness. A lot of times they don't know what they are doing. Many times it is because they don't know what they don't know. When the agent projects a calm, self-assured professional manner, clients usually relax as well.

Next, keep in mind that many people do not know what they want. Buyers often have basic parameters or a vague idea of what a home means to them. Yet, until they actually go out into the marketplace, many are clueless about what is available in the area in which they want to live.

One such example I recall is when one of my ministers shared the desire that she wanted to live in a "cute little house across the street from the church." I took on the task of looking and after I showed her a number of houses, she decided to call off the search, indicating to me she was too busy. Viewing homes fell flat, I'm sure, because nothing she saw felt like home to her. I could have declared that this "buyer was a liar." Later, when I came across what I thought met her definition, I sent it to her and she immediately fell in love. Turns out the home reminded her of the home her husband grew up in. She was immediately enchanted with memories of their courting years swinging on the front porch.

Many people often want more than they can afford, so part of the agent's duty is to manage expectations. That may feel like the buyers aren't being truthful or up-front with expectations, when in fact they are just engaging in wishful thinking.

Sellers have their tales, too, which will be presented in another daily reading in the book.

---

*Seek first to understand when working with buyer clients
to help them navigate the process.*

DOWNLOAD A NEW OPERATING SYSTEM

There are situations in which one is faced with change. On one end of the spectrum is that of a refresh or update. And in the use of the computer analogy, the other end requires downloading a completely new operating system. Those who have been in the real estate industry since before the year 2000 operated in an industry prior to the Internet. To name a few of the changes that have occurred in the industry in the last fifteen-plus years: online multiple listing services, e-mail, online contract preparation programs, and digital signatures.

The future is certain to hold more change, many beyond the mind's conception. The question is, do you embrace or resist the change? A personal example involves Venmo. Our twenty-something son encouraged me to try Venmo as a way for him to reimburse me for money he owed. Honestly, I was resistant, at first claiming I didn't need one more thing in my life to do. Couldn't he just give me the $100 he owed me in cash or a check? At first, it seemed like a fine idea for him and other millennials, but I couldn't personally see the value or benefit in the digital wallet. Finally, I decided to give it a try, as it looked like it was going to be the only way I going to get paid back.

Then it occurred to me that the tenants of our rental properties write a check every month to pay the rent. There are delays involved, including the tenant mailing the check, taking receipt, and then the time to go to the bank to deposit it. Venmo to the rescue! Now our tenants issue a Venmo payment electronically on or before the first of the month. The value truly was realized when we were cruising the Danube in Europe right around the first of the month. The rental income appeared in the Venmo account and—voila!—the transfers were made from across the globe into our bank account.

Our family now has a philosophy of, "Maybe it will be better than before, maybe it will be like Venmo!" The application required me to experience the downloading of a completely new operating system. Yet what a significant improvement it has made to my business and life. What will be next?

Embrace a new operating system today!

DO YOU HAVE AN OPINION?

As a professional real estate agent, when showing homes sometimes buyer clients ask for the agent's personal opinion. It is most helpful in this situation to share how the market perceives the value of the home. The reason being is that ultimately that is what matters, not the agent's personal opinion. There is a house for everyone and because each person's situation is unique, to project an opinion can muddy the water. Reference the market to facilitate the best response.

Still, some people can be persistent. I remember a situation when I was working with a couple to build a new upper-bracket home. There were numerous consultations with the builder on selections. Whenever the buyers asked my opinion, I responded with a recommendation along the lines of, "The market likes this, or the market places value on that. Or I think this choice might not be market friendly."

The wife was of British descent and with her marvelous accent proclaimed that she wanted my personal opinion and not the market's! My response was that that I already had a home that I liked and which met my needs. As a professional, my role was to help them build a home that met their needs. And in the event that they would ever want or need to sell the home, that they were fully aware of the value the market would place on the features.

A stumbling block that can trip up agents is when they personally don't prefer the location or style of a home. Remember, when working with buyer clients the objective is to let them buy the house that meets their needs and desires. It might not be the right house for you or for many people, yet if it is for them, it is best to not let your own opinion get in the way.

Keep the focus on the buyer's needs and wants
and provide relevant market information.

TOP GRADE

A real estate professional has the ability to apply the principle of top grading in numerous arenas. The definition of "top grade" means to trade up, to improve one's circumstances.

For the real estate professional, top grading is one of the key benefits of a strong lead-generation program. With an overabundance of leads, the mega agent can cherry-pick the best. The other leads can be assigned as appropriate to team members. In the case of a single producing agent, the overflow leads can be referred out for a commission.

This is how many top-producing agents are led to form teams. Once a steady stream of leads has been generated, often there are too many for one agent to convert and manage. Another way for a successful agent to top grade is to hire support staff to handle many of the transactional aspects. In this way, the agent can focus on income-producing activities.

This leads to another area that benefits from top grading—people. In the book *Top Grading: How Leading Companies Win by Hiring, Coaching, and Keeping the Best People*, by Bradford D. Smart, Ph.D., the author states: "You are proactively doing whatever it takes to pack your team with all 'A' players." The best at their respective profession literally do rise to the top. With staff and agents, the top producer can focus on her highest capabilities. The most common business model is that the top agent is the rainmaker with buyer agents, using listing coordinators and staff to run the day-to-day operations of the business. The beauty of top grading is it allows everyone to perform jobs that are in tune with their abilities and skills.

Real estate clients also can benefit from the principle of top grading. For sellers, listing the home at a strong market price often generates multiple offers. This allows the seller to select the offer with the terms that are the strongest. For buyers, when there is an oversupply of inventory, that is an occasion when one can purchase up, to top grade their housing options.

Everyone has the ability to top grade their habits, their mental life, their goals, their skills, and their physical and financial health. It occurs in thinking and attitude when one moves from a lack mentality to one of abundance. Successful agents are on the road to perfection. It is the healthy striving that comes from an internal drive to want to be the best professional and person that they can be. The objective is, in the words of American singer and actress Judy Garland: "Always be a first-rate version of yourself, instead of a second-rate version of somebody else."

Strive to top grade your business and life
wherever and whenever possible.

WHY SELL NOW?

The primary reason that sellers should sell their home is because it works best for them at that juncture of life. It is rarely possible to perfectly time the sale of real estate. Sellers want to understand their options if the market is not in their favor, and yet they still need and want to move. Most sellers want to optimize what they will realize on the sale of the home, or at the very least minimize losses. Thus, they wait in hopes the market will improve, and they will ultimately end up with a higher net. An option many contemplate is renting the previous residence until the market "comes back."

This scenario presents several challenges. First, there can be tax consequences for converting an owner-occupied home to a rental property. It is important for the clients to obtain counsel from a qualified tax advisor about how that would impact their financial situation. Then there is the management of the property, which includes both logistical and financial ramifications. For the most part, tenants are respectable citizens and care for the property at an acceptable level, but rarely at the level of an owner. It is the ones who don't that can cause considerable headaches. Is the client prepared for what it means to be a landlord? If the move takes the owner out of the area, it becomes even more challenging and expensive to manage.

How to time the tenant move-out to put the home back on the market is another issue. Although most leases require the tenant to provide access for showings prior to the end of the term, it is rarely in the owner's benefit to do so. To wait until the tenant leaves means the property will be vacant for a time and no income will be generated. In almost all cases, a home that has been a rental property requires freshening up prior to being placed on the active for-sale market. At a minimum, the home has aged during the time frame and that almost always has an impact on market value.

The issues that hold back the value on the property typically don't change. For example, if it is location, age of property, and style of home, those issues don't change with time. A house on a busy street will always be harder to sell. The predominate situations in which it can work to the owner's advantage of renting for a while is when they are returning to the area and will need a place to live at that time.

This scenario played out frequently during and after the Great Recession. Looking back over the ten years that followed that period, there were very few cases in which the owner came out ahead by renting in the attempt to wait out the market. In the cases where the sellers accepted the reality of the market, they were able to get their money out that was locked into the property and perhaps make that money work better somewhere else. Or at the very least, they were able to stop the madness and truly move on without the constant concern and outflow of funds on a property that they no longer resided in.

Use these points to influence clients to make the decision about whether it is the right time to sell or if it would be better to rent and wait out the market cycle.

GOOD SCHOOLS CAN EQUATE TO HIGHER RESIDENTIAL MARKET VALUE

School is back in session for most students in the fall in the United States. One of the key factors that contributes to the market value for residential real estate is the quality of the public schools. The local public school can be an even larger factor than style, age, and size of the home. Public school districts fall into the category of location, because in the majority of cases the school is location-dependent. Test scores, which translate into ranking, are the indicator that many people rely on to determine whether a school is considered good. So even if the owner does not have a personal need for the public schools, it is still important for parties to be informed when making a real estate decision.

According to CNN Money in 2012, good schools had the potential to translate into an extra $200,000 in home value. There are several reasons cited: higher percentage of home ownership, homes on average are larger, and annual housing costs are higher.

Owner-occupancy rates translate to people who value where they live. As a general rule, tenants do not care for a home the same as an owner who resides there does. Absentee landlords may not have a vested interest in the community. On average, owners who live in the home invest in improvements and upgrades, and spend more money on maintenance than landlords and owners of vacant homes do. Larger homes and higher annual housing costs correspond to a higher tax base. As most public schools are funded primarily from property taxes, this correlates to better schools.

The question is often raised, "If an owner could purchase more house for the money in a neighborhood that doesn't have as strong of schools, what harm is there in that?" The short answer is that it becomes a self-fulfilling prophecy. If the base price of homes starts at a lower amount, then it will appreciate at a lower rate. And higher-priced homes often appreciate at a higher rate, all things being equal.

School districts can change boundaries and that can affect value. And school rankings can be impacted due to school board and administration changes. Thus, it is not a guarantee. It is best to verify all of the available relevant data prior to committing to the purchase of a home. It could also play a key factor when an owner wants to sell. One of the sources many people cite for public school rankings is the *U.S. News & World Reports'* annual ranking of best high schools.

Advise clients on how public schools impact residential values and recommend sources to reference for pertinent information.

LEARN TO THINK

EPTEMBER 2

My undergraduate degree is from Stephens College, which still predominately educates young women in the liberal arts. The practical side of me concentrated my coursework in mathematics and business, yet the breadth of learning turned out to have the deeper and more long-reaching positive effects.

One poignant memory is of a professor who shared that truly she was not there to teach us "how to do" anything. Rather, the objective of the college was to teach the students "how to think." The philosophy is along the same lines as the proverb: "Give a man a fish and you feed him for a day; teach a man to fish and you can feed him for a lifetime."

As at the time I was looking for hard and employable skills, my focus was on learning computer program languages—COBOL, FORTRAN, and Basic. I realize that I am dating myself, but these programs used individual punch cards that we would then take to the University of Missouri computer building and input them for programming and analysis.

Think about how far computer programming has come since the late 1970s and early 1980s. There is probably more computing power in my iPhone than there was in the entire University of Missouri mainframe computer thirty-five years ago.

What if my learning had stopped? What if I didn't adapt to technology changes? What if I just learned how to do the program but didn't think of "how to think about programming" and thus achieve the intended result?

This is one of the main purposes of this book: to teach real estate agents how to think. Because like computer programming, if I were to share "how to" sell houses and run a real estate business, what happens when the industry and market change? Just in the decade plus I have been in residential sales, we have seen the explosion of the Internet and multiple-listing services. Contracts are now prepared digitally and documents are executed by electronic signatures. The fax machine has seen the rise and fall as a means of transmitting documents. The transition has been made to the use of e-mail, scanning, and secure site access.

From a market perspective, the successful agent adapts to those changes, as well. Truly the best in the business stay ahead of the market, anticipating changes and responding accordingly. It is thus better and more powerful to understand strategies rather than just tactics. Learn frameworks and ideas that then can be used to address whatever situation the future may present.

Learn how to think about real estate to succeed in the business.

THE WEIGHT OF WAITING

There is a cost associated with not taking action, for waiting. It is the weight of waiting. In business, it is also known as the opportunity cost; that is, the loss of potential gain from other alternatives when one alternative is chosen. In this case, the party chooses to do nothing. There are both buyer and seller "waiting" stories that illustrate this point.

Some buyer clients who choose to wait think that the market is going to go down. Or sometimes they are waiting to save more money for a down payment or for an increase in salary so that they can afford a larger home. Another scenario is waiting for their current home to go up in value.

Markets also appreciate, and there are opportunity costs that correspond to this approach, the lost potential increase in value by waiting. Or if interest rates rise, the purchasing power actually may decrease even if the borrower has more income. And while the buyer waits for the market to go up to sell their home for a higher amount, it is usually going up where they want to purchase as well, which may nullify the increase. Buyers can actually be priced out of a market because they waited too long.

The seller client who decides to delay doing anything is almost always waiting for the market to improve. There are sunk costs that the seller is trying to recoup. It may take years for the market to improve and when it does, then other sellers also may decide to enter the market at the same time. This floods inventory, thus putting downward pressure on prices. Also interest rates could increase, which decreases purchasers' buying power, thus causing them to not be able to pay as much as before. Some sellers wait for the market to improve for years, all the while not being able to move on with their lives. There are life events as well that sellers wait for, such as for the children to move out or retirement.

In the Dr. Seuss book *Oh, the Places You'll Go*, there is a section on the "waiting place." The people are "just waiting" for something to happen. Seuss proclaims on the next page that "No! That's not for you! Somehow you'll escape all that waiting and staying." The secret I have found is to help people understand the true weight of waiting. That is, what are they losing out on by not taking action? This paradigm shift often helps them move on.

I have seen agents get stuck in the "waiting place" too. Examples include waiting for the market to get better, or for a deal to close, or for this one lead to pan out. The best course of action is to follow Seuss and take action to make something happen.

Use the "weight of waiting" to help clients understand
the opportunity cost of not taking action.

EVERYBODY KNOWS SOMEBODY

There are over one million Realtors® in the US, according to the National Association of Realtors®. It goes without saying that most people will know several real estate professionals, some of whom might be a friend, relative, associate, or neighbor. The situation presents over and over that some people select me as their agent and others don't. People have very valid reasons for the choice they make.

One of the key reasons people select an agent other than one they know is because of concern that being in a business transaction will possibly damage the friendship. This is an opportunity for the agent to take the high road. If doing business together becomes a problem, it is contractually based and not a true friendship. This is the perspective I share with people when this objection comes up. My friendship with them is the priority and I want them to do what is best for their situation.

The other concern people voice is that if a difficult situation were to arise during the transaction, they wouldn't want to have to "fire" or have to confront someone they know. This more often happens with sellers, and typically involves the pricing and marketing of the home. The best response to this situation is to keep the communication on a professional level at all times. Establish the protocol to follow standards of service and procedures uniformly with all customers and clients. This is important even if the client is a friend and seems to prefer a more casual approach. In this manner, the client recognizes that you as the agent treat transactions as business, not personally. This conveys the assurance by your actions and demeanor that you are "on the job," watching out for their interests.

The strongest reason buyers and sellers give for selecting an agent they know to represent them is that they want someone who cares about them at a personal level. As the home is most people's largest financial transaction and the buying and selling of it can be emotional, many find it to be helpful to have a friend on their side. Agents have the fiduciary and ethical responsibility to provide a high degree of service to all clients. From my personal experience, when I work with people I know, I put in that extra effort and energy because I am additionally motivated by the relationship. There is a stronger mutual interest that goes beyond the monetary aspects to the transaction. It is very important to me that my friends be happy with their decision and our continuing friendship.

Another scenario is what happens if they know several agents; how do they decide who to hire? When I am presented with this question I recommend selection based on performance criteria, as past results often are the best indicator of future outcomes. Everybody knows somebody—use these scripts and dialogues to achieve great success!

Practice your response for when people you know bring up the concern of whether or not they should work with a friend.

REAL ESTATE AND REALTORS® ARE REAL

The most basic element of real estate is that it is real and that it is stationary. Its most essential characteristic is that it is in a fixed location and cannot be moved. A building can be attached to real property, which technically means it is movable or removable as the case may be. Anything attached to real property is not essentially real estate, but chattel. Chattel is personal property and thus can change locations.

The first line of the National Association of Realtors® preamble to the code of ethics: "Under all is the land."

As author Mark Twain eloquently put it: "Buy land, they're not making it anymore."

This is why "location, location, location" is the mantra of understanding real estate value. If it can't be moved, then the location is the most important factor that goes into property value.

An acronym for REAL is: Realtors® Empowered Action Leads to Transactions.

It is the real estate professional who serves as the change agent.

The key to true value of real estate is in the land and location, and it is the REAL estate agent who makes the transaction happen!

DO I HAVE TO READ THE BOOK?

For a number of years, I have led a business book club in our office. It surprises me how many people want to know if they have to read the book in order to attend. The reasoning seems to be at the level of high school thinking, rather than that of a professional. Of course, one could read the Cliff Notes or watch the movie to get the condensed version. The person who invests the time to read the book, however, will have a much richer experience. Further, as a real estate professional, reading should be part of a long-term personal and professional development program.

The response I share is: "No, you don't have to read the book to attend. However, just as in attending any training or self-improvement program, if you have read the materials, you will get considerably more out of the message." The deeper question is, "In what ways do you invest in yourself?" In order to move beyond one's comfort zone, it requires stretching into new knowledge areas into one's learning zone.

According to *Entrepreneur* magazine, wealthy people do not watch as much television as poor people. Instead, they spend that time reading. In "9 Success Habits of Wealthy People that Cost Nothing," it states that 86 percent of the wealthy love to read, with an impressive 88 percent claiming that they read for self-improvement for thirty minutes or more per day.

This reminds me of weight training. In order to improve muscle strength, one has to use heavier weights or do more repetitions. Those exercise programs are proven to build muscle. The same is true for intellectual strength and capacity. It is expanded by the actual use of the brain muscle. In the words of exercise guru Jack LaLanne: "You will not get strong by watching me exercise; you will get strong by doing the exercise yourself!"

This is the beauty of *Real Estate Success in 5 Minutes a Day*. The dedication of just five minutes a day to reading the daily tip from a top agent and then applying the take-away into action is a proven method for powerful results.

Read something for your professional development today and every day!

THE SOFT AND HARD SIDES

Traditionally the Sears, Roebuck and Co. department store was best known for hardline goods such as tools, equipment, and appliances. In order to attract more women to the store, the advertising campaign, "Come see the softer side of Sears" was introduced. The campaign was designed to change customers' perceptions of the mercantile. Residential real estate sales have a soft and hard side as well.

Commercial real estate transactions are entirely business-oriented; there is very little emotion involved unless it is a family-run enterprise. Whereas when people buy and sell homes there is almost always an emotional component. Some people liken it to processing from the heart. People may say that they feel that a home is right for them. Or that it feels like a good decision. A key to success as a residential agent is to be relationship-oriented.

The agent who can express empathy is more likely to be able to influence the client's decision process. Empathy approaches the situation by seeking first to understand the person's feelings. As a professional agent, it then goes beyond that to help the customer determine how best to obtain the desires of the heart. It contrasts to sympathy, which is when one feels compassion yet doesn't actually take on the mantle of doing something about it. When an agent empathizes with the client, there is a greater sense of connection.

The business side, head aspects, or hard side is just as necessary for success in real estate. For the clients, many will buy with their hearts, yet justify the purchase with their heads. One party in the relationship may have strong feelings and emotions, while the other focuses on the transactional and logistical aspects to the process of buying or selling a home.

There are myriad functions that fall into this category while overseeing a transaction for a client: preparing of a comparative market analysis, completing the offer to purchase or listing agreement, negotiating the terms of the contract, managing the details of contract to settlement, and engaging in crucial and difficult conversations with customers, clients, agents, and other professionals involved in the business. All of these require strong business acumen.

The successful agent is adept at both. It is common to find that one has strengths in one area over another. Take the opportunity to improve your skill set to achieve better results.

Use both your heart and your head when seeking to influence clients.

BOTH SIDES NOW

What is the secret sauce, the characteristics and behaviors that makes for a successful sales person? According to a *Harvard Business Review* study, it turns out that there are two key attributes that contribute to success in the sales arena: ego drive and empathy. It is the "both sides now" balanced combination that explains why some agents go on to a successful career and others do not achieve at a high level or leave the field entirely.

The DISC profile assessment is a helpful tool to identify a person's preferred behavioral style. The letters stand for: dominance (D), influence (I), steadiness (S), and compliance (C). The dominance-type person is direct, results-oriented, firm, strong-willed, and forceful. The influence-type person is outgoing, enthusiastic, optimistic, high-spirited, and lively. The steadiness-type person is even-tempered, accommodating, patient, humble, and tactful. The compliance-type person is analytical, reserved, precise, private, and systematic.

The DI and the ID personalities are the most likely to achieve long-term sustained success as a real estate professional. The dynamic relationship that is created corresponds with the Harvard study. The "D" or dominant person correlates with the "ego drive" characteristic. And the "I" or influence person corresponds with the "empathy" attribute.

Ego drive has been described in the industry as "fire in the belly" or one's "big why." This is the burning desire, motivator, aggressive, definiteness of purpose, and strong inner drive. The challenge is that if there is too strong of a drive, one can come across as a bulldozer.

Empathy in the real estate setting is the ability to understand how the client feels while not necessarily personally agreeing. The empathic agent stays objective and is able to provide helpful feedback while at the same time moving the client to possible solutions for the situation. The salesperson who is only a "nice guy" typically does not possess enough drive to get the client to take action. People like her, but often select to work with an agent who gets things done.

It is the combination of ego drive and empathy, both sides now, that is most likely to lead to success. Can different profiles be successful real estate agents? Of course they can! My profile is DC, which is more of a businessperson than a salesperson. The overriding factor is that my life purpose, or "big why," is a heart for people. It is realized when I serve people by providing solutions to meet their real estate needs. Because of my high "C," I can at times overuse my analytical side and on occasion have to be reminded that residential sales is a people business. It is helpful to discover your attributes and apply them to success.

Identify your behavioral style and take action to achieve success.

BACK-TO-SCHOOL SEASON IS ALSO
BACK-TO-SELLING-HOMES SEASON

September is the traditional "back to school" month across the US. It turns out that September can be a great month to sell real estate too.

Below are five benefits of selling a home in the fall months of September, October, and November:

1. Appraisal data tends to be stronger. In the fall months, appraisers are typically looking back to the previous six months of sales for comparables. Whereas when sales occur in the spring, the comparables from the previous six months is wintertime for the area. Typically spring sales are stronger than winter sales, so values often are stronger for a sale in the autumn season.

2. Another benefit of selling a home in the fall months is that there is typically less competition. There are frequently not as many homes available on the market for buyers to consider, which can make them less "picky."

3. A third benefit of selling a home in the fall months is that buyers are more motivated. If a buyer is in the market to purchase a home in the fall, they are usually real buyers and not just tire kickers.

4. One more benefit to being a seller of a home in September is that buyers are in a "back-to-school" frame of mind. After having the summer off from many responsibilities, buyers are ready to focus and make the move, literally and figuratively.

5. The final benefit of selling a home in the autumn months is that in many parts of the United States the season change is a beautiful time of the year weather-wise.

Use available data to influence seller clients to go
or stay on the market in the fall.

PURCHASERS ARE FROM PLUTO, SELLERS ARE FROM SATURN

"Purchasers are from Pluto, sellers are from Saturn" mirrors the differences between the sexes in the classic book, *Men Are from Mars, Women Are from Venus*, by John Gray. The basic premise follows that the sexes are different for a reason and vivá la difference. According to the book, each planet, aka sex, has its own characteristics and customs and when one explores, discovers, and embraces the inherent uniqueness, one can best understand how to meet the other's needs and wants. The correlation to real estate is that when the agent recognizes the attributes and distinctions of working with purchasers and sellers, she is better able to build a successful business.

Pluto is the farthest planet in the solar system from the Earth. Being the farthest means it has the longest orbit period, and these factors make it difficult to study and explore. Understanding purchasers' needs and wants can sometimes feel to the real estate agent that they are way out in space. There are occasions when it feels like light years have passed before the purchaser makes a decision to buy.

Experienced agents seek to list near where they live or work and are prepared to sell to a buyer anywhere they are licensed. Saturn is closer to the Earth than Pluto, which makes this part of the analogy work. Listings require servicing and attention, and just a few aspects include staging, snapping photos, installing the sign, and dropping off brochures and marketing materials. Saturn is one of the largest planets in the solar system, which translates into real estate as listing homes for sale being the greatest focus for an agent to sustain success.

"List to last" emphasizes this linchpin concept. Once an agent has successfully sold in a neighborhood, obtaining the next listing is more likely. This is a highly desirable, self-fulfilling prophecy. If the agent has listings spread out all over the place, the agent's time is spent in travel to and from the listings rather than on higher-priority functions such as prospecting and lead conversion.

Due to the fact that Saturn is located closer to Earth, more study and exploration has been performed on that planet. In real estate circles, too, more emphasis is placed on working with sellers. Saturn is a "gas giant," which makes one think of it as an energy machine. Real estate sale listings are the agent's "energy machine." One listing is more likely to lead to more real estate business in the form of other listings in the neighborhood, buyer leads, marketing opportunities, and referrals.

"List where you live and sell to a buyer anywhere licensed"
is a proven business model.

"IMPOSSIBLE DREAM"

The song "Impossible Dream" has as a subtitle: "The Quest." The professional agent on occasion works with clients whose expectations fall under the realm of the "impossible dream." It is this utopia, a place of mythical perfection, in which both buyers and sellers want to reside.

The purchaser has the agent on a search to achieve the "unreachable" home. Many times, clients have champagne taste on a beer budget. Or the buyer wants to negotiate to pay significantly under market price for a home. Some customers literally are all over the map in their quest for the perfect home; nothing satisfies. The agent in this situation deeply feels the lament in the song, "One man scorned and covered with scars" and yet the agent "Still strove with his last ounce of courage."

When I work with buyers who are caught up in a dream state, I first allow them to pursue it by attending open houses and wishful online shopping. At some point in the journey, reality comes into focus. At that juncture, often buyers are more open to listen to guidance and recommendations. The example comes to mind of a young couple whose search was literally all over the place. After countless weekends visiting open houses, they finally asked me what I thought. At that juncture, I was able to advise them in a direction that would work for their situation. Had I tried that in the beginning, I think they would have felt I was not buying into their dream.

The circumstances are on the other end of the spectrum with seller clients. The "impossible dream" is to have a buyer pay more than ever achieved in the marketplace with no contingencies and every benefit toward the seller. As in the song, the agent is tasked "to run where the brave dare not go."

In this scenario, I advise clients that I too want to realize the highest value for the property. That achievement would be an amazing marketing message for me to obtain more business in the community. Yet, market constraints of outside variables include the comparable valuation as verified by the appraiser. It is helpful to provide sellers with market studies on a consistent basis, typically every thirty to sixty days. In this way, the market tells the story of reality. At some juncture, it becomes clear to the seller what it will take to sell the home.

It does seem hopeless sometimes, and yet the brave agent continues on. It is the professional's quest to help clients realize their dreams.

Develop strategies on how to help your clients achieve
their real estate dreams.

ARE YOU A QUARTERBACK OR RECEIVER?

In high school, my husband played football. I didn't know him then, but have heard many stories. During the fall season with football in the air, I of course think of real estate applications.

In football, the quarterback (QB) is the one who directs the offensive play of the team. As the leader, the quarterback has the option to play the ball himself by running, to hand the ball off, or throw the ball to a teammate downfield. The QB position is the most visual and well-known.

In real estate, the quarterback is the lead generator or sometimes known as the rainmaker. The agent who generates the leads has control of the situation. In football, the eye is on the ball. In real estate, the eye is on the lead. As the lead generator, the agent can decide to run with the lead himself. Or the agent can refer the lead to a teammate or other agent.

The receiver is a valuable player too, often the fastest on the football team. In most cases, it is the receiver who does the happy dance in the end zone after a touchdown. The receiver combines the skills of running and outmaneuvering the defensive players, all the while keeping his eye on the ball in order to make a connection. In some cases, the receiver plays a defensive role, as in the case of an interception.

The referral agent in the real estate industry is also a key player. Passing the lead can be a strong strategy in the building of a real estate team. A professional agent who can convert the lead to settlement is equal to the player who makes the touchdown. Everyone on the team wins.

Play the best position in your business and life!

ANY OFFER IS A GOOD OFFER

This script entered into my repertoire during the Great Recession. It was taught to me by my broker, who insisted that the agents in the office repeat the mantra daily. At the time, buyers were fleeing real estate, prices were tumbling and no one knew where or when the bottom would be reached. When a bona fide written offer was presented, it was to be treated like water to a person lost in the desert.

Still today, when I present a contract to a seller client, my first words are always "congratulations." There are times when the offer is low, and my positive sentiment is not returned enthusiastically by the client. Nonetheless, I take the opportunity to make the case for why this can be a benefit to him. I have found that having received an offer changes the energy around a property. When one person wants something, it increases its desirability.

The question arises, "Should a buyer write an offer that might be perceived as low to the seller?" Many buyers and their agents fear being "shot" as the messenger of such an offer. My experience says "yes," by all means write the offer. Verbal offers for real estate aren't considered valid and thus are worth the paper they are not written on. It is the entire package, all the terms, that make up an offer, not just the offer price. One never knows what might be considered until they try.

An offer for the listing agent is an opportunity to revisit the market with the seller, to discuss comparables, and how the broader market is trending. As the market is the market study, an offer is the true manifestation of how buyers view the conditions. This is a very valuable dialogue to have with seller clients.

When working with buyers, I always encourage them to put their offer in writing. Some say they don't want to waste my time, the other agent's, or the seller's if in fact it isn't going to go anywhere. Yet there is benefit in the process. It is never a waste of my time to move a client along in the process. Going through the motions, I've found, solidifies me as the agent representation for the transaction. When a buyer writes an offer, he becomes much more committed and involved.

And then there is the tried and true "nothing ventured, nothing gained." There have been so many occasions, too numerous to count, in which I heard sellers say they would never accept a price below a certain number. They say, "I can't take anything less than x." And then there are those who did. On the flip side, countless buyers have said they would never pay more for a home than a specific amount. And then some did. I've also seen someone throw out a verbal number that was rejected and later the house sold for close to that number.

These instances tell me that you never know if it is going to work unless you try; if you don't try then there is a guarantee that it won't work. In the words of famed hockey player Wayne

Gretzky: "You miss 100 percent of the shots you don't take."

Always put the offer in writing if representing a buyer.
And with sellers, help them recognize that any offer is a good offer.

WHEN THE STUDENT IS READY

The proverb, "When the student is ready, the teacher will appear" is a profound statement used in many cultures. My experience with clients has been more along the lines of: "When the student is ready, then the lesson is learned." An example is when a paradigm shift in thinking or a certain level of brain development is required before a student can comprehend algebra. Even a superior teacher knows better than to attempt to teach the concept prior to that time. Doing so too early will not result in successful comprehension of the material.

A similar phenomenon can occur with both buyer and seller clients. The clients sometimes believe that the agent's self-interest for a quick transaction and commission is causing them to provide skewed market information. In these situations, the clients think that their understanding of the market conditions is superior and insist on having the agent follow their direction. It is the agent's fiduciary duty to represent her clients, even when she believes that the parties would obtain better results by proceeding in another manner.

With buyer clients, it can happen when they want to write an offer significantly below market value. Particularly in competitive situations, buyers frequently don't believe that there really are other offers until it actually happens. Agents knowledgeable on the comparables sometimes cannot persuade them of the folly of their plan. It can take some buyers actually losing out on getting the house that they want before they are ready to listen to the counsel of their agent. This is learning the hard way!

In the seller situation, what often happens is the seller wants to price the home considerably above market value. The reasoning often is that he wants to leave room for negotiations. What can happen, though, is that the house can languish on the market. Even when buyer and agent feedback and market data demonstrates that a lower price would make the home more saleable, some sellers just aren't ready to listen to counsel. It sometimes takes some time on the market before they are ready to learn. It could take months, sometimes even years.

When new in the business, I thought that perhaps it was my inexperience in being able to convince the client. Once I understood the phenomenon that was happening was that the client just wasn't "ready to learn," I was able to let time and experience impart the lesson of market forces.

I have learned something from watching this happen with clients. That is, I too have had occasions when I did not listen to wise counsel when I should have. It has caused me to be more open and ready for the lessons that are presented to me when I need to learn.

Recognize when it's appropriate to allow time and experiences to teach the lesson.

THE PEPSI™ CHALLENGE

Most people know several real estate agents. This frequently comes up in conversations I have when people find out that I am in the profession. Typically they tell me about the other agents they know or have worked with in the past. Whether I know the agents they are speaking about or not, I stay positive and am careful not to disparage colleagues. Either way, I share that there are more than a thousand agents in our immediate market area, over 154,000 in the international brokerage with which I am affiliated with and two million active real estate licenses in the United States. Most people are surprised at the number of people in the industry.

It is important to view this dialogue as an open door to offer your services. If people are adamant that they already have an agent, I offer my services if anything ever changes. Many times agents retire or leave the profession. Another common scenario is the agent who helped them buy the house isn't strong as a listing agent. So when people go to sell, they very likely will be looking for an agent who has those skills or a more in-depth marketing platform. To bring in a bit of humor, I share that it can be like the "Pepsi™ challenge": in numerous blind taste tests, people select Pepsi™ over Coke™. Maybe that will be the case for them.

Another script that I have had success with is the offer of a "second opinion." If they or someone close to them were considering surgery or a significant medical procedure, wouldn't they likely interview more than one doctor? Given that the sale of a home is likely their largest financial transaction, wouldn't they be interested in having more than one agent make a presentation?

A response that people will sometimes make is that they don't want to waste my time. This is when I emphasize that it is my job to work with sellers to help them in the marketing and sale of their home. It is not an inconvenience to show buyers houses, as that is an opportunity for me to observe in person how I can help them achieve their wants and needs. Neither of these activities are ever a waste of my time. These are some of the key functions of my job as a real estate agent.

Getting into an active relationship with the customer also creates a reciprocity loop. It is in the giving of time and services that customers are more likely to want to give back, as well. Once they see how eager you are to help them, it can open the door to a client relationship.

Employ effective dialogues on the services you provide as a real estate agent, particularly when competing for the business.

PIGS GET FAT, HOGS GET SLAUGHTERED

"Pigs get fat and hogs get slaughtered" is a phrase I distinctly remember my mentor in the business, Sue Huckaby, stating on more than one occasion. Sue was a top residential agent in the Washington, DC metro area for decades. Her accent revealed her southern origins, as she was originally from Ringgold, Louisiana. Whenever Sue believed that either a seller or buyer in a transaction was trying to take more than their probable due, she often would state: "Pigs get fat and hogs get slaughtered."

Recalling this memory of Sue intrigued me to research the origins of the phrase. Pigs get fed and thus are fat and happy. When hogs get fat, on the other hand, they are a candidate for slaughter at hog-killing time. Further, pigs can be considered cute; in fact, some people have pot-belly pigs as pets. And of course we all remember the very famous pet pig Wilbur, in *Charlotte's Web*. However, no one ever thinks about cuddling up with a hog—they are just grotesque.

There are numerous applications to real estate transactions. But, you say, "How does one know when crossing the line between pig and hog?" The difference between negotiating for what is one's fair due versus greed is situational, I have found. The Washington, DC metro area experienced double-digit appreciation year over year from 2001 to 2005, as did much of the United States. During that time period, it was a seller's market in most segments. There were numerous occasions in which I presented a strong contract to seller clients and they rejected it or countered too high. The buyer moved on, in effect by the action proclaiming that the seller was being greedy.

The Great Recession years of 2007 to 2009 led to several years of the market correcting. This was a time period categorized as a buyer's market. In short sale and foreclosure transactions, buyers kept pushing "how low can it go." There were times when it felt as though buyers were acting out of greed. It was difficult to watch people lose their homes or a great deal of money in a distressed sale. And still, many buyers would continue to aggressively pursue for more because they felt that they could.

A professional agent knows the market well and has studied both up and down cycles, buyers markets and sellers markets. In most cases, when the market is favorable toward buyers it isn't as strong for sellers and vice versa. The best way to be informed is to stay knowledgeable of the inventory and to track absorption rates. One of the key tenants of the National Association of Realtors® code of ethics is that the agent should be truthful and honest in all communication. Thus it is the duty of the professional to speak forthrightly to customers and clients regarding market conditions. It is up to you whether you decide to use a southern accent!

Find applications for this southern phrase when
you negotiate real estate transactions.

LEVERAGE WITH COMMUNITY ENGAGEMENT

Involvement in the community is a means for real estate agents to leverage their brand and name identification. It is a tried-and-true method of connecting with people to build and grow a business. People want to work with those who are invested in their community. This giving philosophy is illustrated in the book *Go-Givers Sell More*, by Bob Burg and John David Mann. A salesperson accrues the reputation of being a good corporate citizen by developing relationships, creating value, and demonstrating a commitment to the community.

There are countless ways to become engaged in one's community. As all real estate is local, the largest benefits typically accrue when involvement is on a micro level. And yet with social media, networking capabilities, seminars and events nationally and abroad, one can effectively expand the community to the world. People met in those instances are outstanding opportunities for referral business.

To name just a few areas that one can impact, the agents on our team and office serve at places of worship, children's schools, local chambers of commerce, as well as various local and national charities. A philosophy I have is that my commitment first is to the organization and not to personal business prospecting. In many cases, business does arise from my involvement, yet my top priority is to the welfare and benefit of the organization. People clearly know that I am a real estate agent, as I am not a secret agent. It is my experience that people have a greater respect by my assuming this posture.

As a board member of the local chamber of commerce, we found that the primary purpose for most people to participate was in order to get leads. Given that it is business-focused, that isn't necessarily a bad objective. To promote the additional benefits of being involved, though, board members shared the broader purpose as a desire to give back to and be part of the community. This objective includes being at the table for relevant conversations and decisions in order for us together to build a stronger and more vibrant business environment in which to live and work.

Once one is well known in the community, it can become a challenge to know what to be involved in. There is an abundance of opportunity. In response to this dilemma, our team established our own charity fundraiser. With this platform, we have the ability to have a greater influence and control the message to the charity constituents and the market. The local media publishes information about the events. Further, we use our own and the charity's social media portals to promote the fundraiser. It is effectively free public relations and has a broad bandwidth.

Use community engagement and giving back to increase brand awareness in the marketplace.

THE OREO COOKIE OF NEGOTIATIONS

The Oreo is the top-selling cookie in the twentieth century and a classic sweet treat in American homes. As many students return to school in the fall, I think of all the cookies packed in lunch boxes. There is a real estate message in this popular sandwich cookie, too.

First, let's recall the construction of an Oreo cookie. It is two, typically chocolate, circle-shaped cookies with cream filling "sandwiched" between these two cookie pieces.

In negotiations, think of the seller as one of the cookies and the buyer as the other cookie. What is sandwiched between these two entities is the "sweet spot." No doubt, finding the sweet spot is the desire of many Oreo cookie lovers. It is also the objective of a strong contract negotiator.

The intention of the process is to find the common ground in between. It works best when the agents connect the parties based on the unity of what people care about. The agents are in the middle, literally in the sweet spot between the two positions. In this space, they will be most successful when the focus is on shared outcomes, on how the parties can come together. Uncover the objectives of each party and come up with solutions on how they can best be achieved.

By way of example, sellers may focus on the settlement date in order to have funds available so they can purchase their next home. The buyers who are renting month-to-month have more flexibility on the actual move-in date, yet want the seller to complete work prior to settlement so that they can move right into the home. In this scenario, a sweet-spot solution could be for the seller to complete the work prior to settlement and then reside in the home by use of a post-settlement occupancy agreement, paying the buyer a fair rate for the time remaining after closing.

It has been said that when sellers believe that they have "given their house away" and buyers are concerned that they "paid too much," that is, in effect, market value. In the Oreo analogy, both parties have pushed themselves to their outer limits—outside the edge of the cookie into the cream, and that is when the sweet spot of negotiations has occurred. Success is achieved with the coming together of all of the parties in the deal!

The sweet spot between the parties in negotiations is the common ground and meets the interests of both buyer and seller.

PREVIEW HOMES AS MUSE!

I love to visit with new agents to hear their stories about why they chose the residential real estate profession. The reasons many share are that they love houses and people and thought it would be a great combination. That is the essence of my story, as well. And yet it surprises me how many agents don't actually go see houses on a regular basis now that they are free to do so at practically any time.

In most market areas, there is a day set aside for broker tours of listings. Typically these opens are for homes new to the market. So it is a great opportunity for agents to stay fresh on the inventory. Also, homes that are appointment-only often can be more challenging to view, thus the broker open tour is the best chance to see the home. I do my best to set aside this day to see as many homes as I can, as well as to network with other real estate agents.

Einstein believed that "combinatory play" was a central feature in his creative thinking process. By putting your focus on something you find enjoyable, it can release the stress from trying to force a solution. I'm sure you've had this happen to you as well. Einstein played the violin. Others practice yoga, paint, go for a walk, or listen to music as their source of inspiration. And then the answer comes like a flash of brilliance.

Previewing homes can be a great business development opportunity. For one, the action itself gets the agent out of the office and into the field. For agents with a true passion for homes, going to see houses is a form of play. The change of scenery is a winning strategy for me when I am stuck in a rut or in a funk.

It is important to not take your muse for granted. I'm sure you have heard of writer's block, which occurs when the flow of ideas has stopped. The same effect can happen to real estate professionals. In Ray Bradbury's book, *Zen in the Art of Writing: Releasing the Creative Genius within You*, the author speaks of the importance of the care and feeding of one's muse. In this way, the subconscious then goes to work on an idea or inspiration.

Previewing homes is a way to care for and feed your muse! When I preview homes I think of people. By being out in the marketplace, inspiration of potential sellers and buyers to touch base with comes to me. New information to follow through on is more evident when the agent is out in the actual marketplace. Take care of your muse and it will take care of you!

Play at viewing houses as a source of inspiration
for business development.

WHEN YOU HEAR HOOFBEATS . . .
A SELLER'S TALE

The origin of the phrase, "When you hear hoof beats, think of horses, not zebras" is from the medical field. It means to think first of the most logical and common diagnosis before considering the exotic. Dr. Theodore Woodward coined this counsel when instructing medical interns in the 1940s.

The most common application to real estate is in regard to the evaluation of the physical condition of the home. The response to the situation depends on the perspective, be it the seller's or the buyer's. There are some sellers who recognize that it is their obligation to maintain and deliver a home in a salable condition. They typically take the position "it is what it is" and don't read anything more into the circumstances. And then there are those clients who take the other extreme position in a hard and fast manner and refuse to do anything.

Most contracts provide for a spectrum of options. Once the buyer presents the inspection reports to the seller through the agents, there are several directions it can go. One is to declare the home in "as-is condition." If this is to occur, it usually happens as part of the listing agreement and full disclosure is made to the parties up front. Next on the continuum is to agree to repair, replace, or remedy the situations identified. The seller can agree as written or counter the terms. Another common approach is for the seller to offer money toward closing costs or to reduce the sales price to cover repairs once the buyer moves in. The buyer should verify that any change in monetary terms will be approved by the lender.

There are countless examples of how sellers respond when the buyer presents the home inspection addendum. However, for this purpose let's assume it is a typical laundry list of items for the seller to address. One approach is the seller who sees the list and says, "Well, it isn't a new home and we have put off some deferred maintenance. Let's get some estimates and respond with what we can do. Most of the items are reasonable and it is likely other buyers will want them completed too. We just didn't know that there was that leak in the basement pipe. Since you as our agent recommend we deal with this, let's get it done so we can move on."

The other end of the spectrum is the seller who says, "This is ridiculous! Do they think they are buying a new home? I'm not doing any of it, let them void the contract." And then there are a thousand variations in between. This is when the agent can apply the "when you hear hoofbeats" counsel. Encourage the client to listen to wise counsel for how best to address the situation. If it truly is an unusual circumstance, then the diagnosis should apply accordingly. If it is a typical scenario, then recommend a more common-sense approach be taken.

Use the "when you hear hoofbeats" strategy to influence clients to follow your recommendations.

BE PREPARED

The motto "be prepared" is most often attributed to the Boy Scouts. Our son achieved the rank of Eagle Scout, so our family has had many occasions to apply the principle of being ready in mind and body.

The first home I sold in residential real estate was within one month of obtaining my license. The lead was from a sign-call, which meant that I did not know the buyers. It turned out they were moving to the northern Virginia metro area and were just calling the listing agent off the sign for each of the homes they were interested in.

Even though over a dozen years have passed, I still remember it well. I guess you always do remember your first transaction. Before I set out to show the town home, I looked up what else was available in the same price range and made arrangements for us to see them as well. Then I prepared a very quick analysis to determine what I thought was the best value in the group.

After viewing the home they wanted to see, it was clear that it didn't suit what they were looking for. I shared with the couple my research and suggested we see what I thought was the best one available. When we were in that home, it became obvious to me that they liked it. So I just did the next thing, I asked them if they wanted to buy the home and it turned out they did. As I got to know them better through the transaction process, they shared that I was the first agent who actually did something more than just "show up" to unlock the door.

Ultimately this has led to my business practice of being prepared prior to any appointment. On every listing appointment I prepare a full comparative market analysis as well as bring a marketing brochure and agreement paperwork. On every buyer consultation, I take relevant comparables and pertinent information on the home and community the client expressed interest in. In all cases, I take whatever is the next logical step or couple of steps in the process to smoothly move the client along.

Barbara Corcoran of *Shark Tank* fame calls this "doing your homework." She goes on to share in her book, *Shark Tales*, "I have never met a really smart person who didn't overprepare." Being prepared is a secret of success. If I can do it, you can too.

Take the steps of preparedness in working with both customers and clients.

THEY HAVE TO BE IN YOUR CLASSROOM

Many real estate agents were teachers prior to entering the profession. That was the case with my deceased business partner, Sue Huckaby. I can still hear her say to me in her lilting southern accent: "Karen, they have to be in our classroom before we can educate them." She was referring to customers who have to become clients before we can influence any of their real estate decisions. When I look back, I see that Sue used several methods of instruction: inquiry, "show and tell," and experience.

The Socratic method is a classic form of inquiry. It consists of a discussion that stimulates thinking and illuminates ideas. It is based on asking open-ended questions. A frequent example would be when sellers indicate a list price that to the agent does not appear to be in line with the market. The agent could open up the discussion with: "How did you come up with that number?" Once the clients shares their reasoning, then the agent has a better understanding of what data and source they are using on which to base their decision. In this way, the agent can direct the seller to comparables and information that will likely be more relevant to buyers, other agents, and appraisers.

The "show and tell" method is where the agent shows the customer the market data and related information and "tells" the story. To reinforce, agents can take sellers to see homes that are the competition or suggest that the clients visit homes open to the public. In this way, the clients view for themselves how their home compares in the marketplace. This technique influences people in making decisions by providing them with information. For buyers, the agent would show homes to illustrate what is available that meets the client's criteria for price and location.

Experience can encompass a lot of different strategies. Most effective is to allow clients to "try" their strategy. For sellers, this might mean letting them list the house at the price they want, even if it seems too high for the market. As agents and buyers share their feedback, provide this to the client on a regular basis.

For buyers, this may mean letting them select the offer price. If it isn't accepted, then often the next time the client is more willing to listen to professional recommendations about how to handle negotiations. In these and other ways, the client "experiences" the market. The market becomes the market study for the client. I have found that I can analyze a property in countless different ways for a client, yet it is experience in the market that is often the best teacher.

New agents often ask, "Do I take overpriced listings?" My response is, "Yes, absolutely!" Are there instances when I would not take a listing? Sure, although that is rare. What I have found is that, like Sue, I have the best opportunity to influence the customer once they are in my classroom and have become my client.

The first objective is to get the client, then to influence her decisions.

COMMIT TO LEAD GENERATION

You have a choice. It has been proven without a doubt that real estate agents who enjoy a long-term successful career are those who generate leads in a consistent manner. How do they do that? I believe the answer lies in the words of Jon Congdon: "Trade in the concept of staying motivated and replace it with commitment."

Failure is inevitable for those who only make a half-hearted effort. Much like a speed governor on a car, the full power and potential of the engine is not realized. This is why agents usually don't reach their full potential. First the agents have to remove what holds them back and next implement the habits to take their business to the next level, which involves commitment.

The reality is that without proactive effort, almost everything is in a state of deterioration or decline. As a listing agent, the majority of one's clients are sellers, which means they move. In my business, about one-half of seller clients every year move out of the area, which means they are not likely to become repeat clients. Yes, of course there is the potential for referrals and the opportunity to market to the neighbors. The point is that it requires the constant replacement of the pool of past clients with new customers.

Commitment, on the other hand, is a proactive stance. People who are committed stay on task even when they don't feel like it and even when it is difficult. That's the difference between commitment and motivation. If the agent requires internal or external motivation prior to acting, then the business is at the risk of the whims of the day.

How can agents develop commitment? First, decide that it is the priority and complete it first before shiny objects or interesting projects distract your focus. Next, establish habitual routines that consistently enforce commitment. Follow the "smart" rule: specific, measurable, attainable, realistic, and timely. If stuck, try some new techniques or tools to break through to the next level of success.

One technique I follow is that every Monday I determine how many days that week I establish as "working." Next, I set up on my smartphone calendar how many houses I plan to view that week. As I see houses, 1 update the list with the street address for the property. I plan as well for the number of prospecting touches I plan to make for that week. This way the "space" to accomplish these tasks is committed to on my calendar and in my mind. Then all I have to do is go back and fulfill it with the action.

There are smartphone apps and computer programs designed to facilitate the process. One of the secrets to success is the consistent commitment to productive habits.

Commit to consistent proactive lead generation
by establishing "smart" habits.

SEPTEMBER 24

HOW HOMES ARE LIKE BLACK SHOES: PRODUCTION BUILT

What makes one property more valuable than another? To illustrate this distinction with clients, I use several pairs of ladies black shoes. One pair of shoes was purchased at a discount store for $13, another pair at a local department store for around $100, and the third at a boutique designer specialty shop for about $300. All shoes serve the utilitarian function of protecting feet from the elements. All three shoes have a similar look in terms of the color and a low heel height. However, there is obviously considerable price variation between them.

In terms of housing, all price levels serve the utilitarian function of shelter, and all homes have walls, floors, a roof, windows and doors, basic cooking facilities, and bathroom(s). It goes without saying that the costs of housing can vary considerably,

The store where the discount pair of shoes was purchased is known for styles that are knock-offs of designer looks. Most are constructed of man-made materials, and the lack of quality is evident after having worn them but a few times. The customer rummages through the stacks as the store is self-service, and the selections are usually limited. The atmosphere is typically very bare, and benches and other areas are shared spaces.

The discount shoe store of housing is the tract or production homebuilder. The term "tract" comes from the fact that a developer or builder purchases a parcel or tract of land, installs necessary infrastructure, including streets and utilities, and then builds similar homes on the lots. The scenario allows for economies of scale, which transfers into the final sales price of the homes. Often there is more than one builder in a development.

The builder usually offers a limited number of floor plans, along with different elevations (fronts). In order to obtain the economies of scale, typically there is a limited selection available to the purchaser for cabinetry, flooring, and appliances. Usually a basic package is provided and upgrades are allowed at a higher cost.

The builder uses economies of scale for materials and labor to keep the price down for the basic product. In terms of location, tract home developments are in areas where land is readily available, most often on the fringes of metro areas. Often this translates to longer commutes and fewer community amenities.

The analogy of how homes are like black shoes is useful when explaining to clients the differences between products. Economies of scale benefit the builder, which translate to price for the consumer.

Use the "how homes are like black shoes" analogy to explain value to clients.

WHAC-A-MOLE

The classic Whac-a-Mole game is always fun to play at an arcade. There is satisfaction in using the rubber mallet to bop the top of the moles' heads as they pop up in an intermittent fashion.

A similar scenario to this game can develop in a business when the same issues seem to keep rearing their ugly heads. When this occurs, look on it as an opportunity to be proactive and create systems and procedures in advance.

An example of this for our team had to do with Sunday open house procedures. The team marketing coordinator is in charge of securing an agent to hold the Sunday open houses for the listings for the team. The process involves sending out a group e-mail early in the week and as the agents respond, the coordinator makes the assignments. What transpired was such a variation in service that on Sundays I would receive more complaints from unhappy seller clients than any other day of the week.

For the longest time, all I did about the situation was in effect bop the heads of the moles with a rubber mallet! I complained about the low level of professionalism of real estate agents. I lamented about how licensed agents could not understand how important it is to provide top-notch customer service for the clients of other agents in the office. In my opinion, the behavior reflected badly on the entire brokerage firm. And yet my attitude was so poor, I was doing nothing positive to contribute to a solution.

It finally occurred to me that it was my responsibility to set the standards for customer service for our clients. I needed to be proactive instead of reactive. It truly was unfair and unrealistic of me to demand that people know our expectations without actually explaining them in advance. So we established a standards of service open house hosting agreement. In order for an agent to achieve "preferred" status and be considered for the opportunity to host an open house, that agent had to meet with the marketing coordinator and review the standards. All parties then have a clear understanding of the standards expected in order to remain in good standing and on the list for future open houses.

Once the procedure was fully implemented, the incidents of unhappy clients decreased dramatically. This is just one example of being proactive in creating effective systems, which is a key aspect of achieving success through leverage in one's real estate business.

Be proactive in setting up effective and efficient systems to change ongoing problem situations into positive outcomes.

HOW TO DECIDE?

One of the challenges that buyers face is how to decide what home will meet their needs as well as hold value over time in the market. Barry Schwartz discusses what happens to people when they have too many choices in his book, *The Paradox of Choice — Why More is Less*. The author argues that too much choice can actually paralyze some people.

When paralysis of analysis occurs with clients, encourage them to use the Ben Franklin method of decision-making. Simply take a tablet and draw a line down the middle and label one side "pros" and the other side "cons." One way to differentiate is whether something is actually a need or a want. The response to that question is unique to the buyer's individual situation.

When there is a choice, then the buyer has the opportunity to compare between the options. If there is only one valid selection, keep in mind there is always the other choice, that of no decision.

What I recommend buyer clients use as a guideline is based on three levels of value. First, consider the things that cannot be changed easily, such as location, lot attributes, floor plan, and quality of construction, as well as architectural structure. The things that can be changed, although they may be costly and time consuming, are secondary, such as major systems, roof, foundation, major improvements, additions, and renovations. And finally, consider the things that can be changed relatively easily: paint, update existing kitchens and baths, appliances, flooring selections, and anything cosmetic. The key is to identify the potential in the home and place priority on those that sustain value.

One area that many buyers request counsel from their agent is to what home improvements sustain value. Owners should realize that homes follow fashion trends just like clothes, cars, and other consumer goods. Designs and improvements that are classic and transition well over time periods are more likely to hold value for the longest duration. It is advisable to avoid anything trendy. For example, it was all the rage a few years ago to install a vessel bowl as a bathroom sink. Quickly people realized how impractical it was because it was difficult to clean and limited counter space. That type of improvement is not likely to provide a positive return on investment.

Along the lines of fashion trends, remember the rhetorical phrase, "You can't put lipstick on a pig." Well, actually you can, but it doesn't change how ugly the pig is. Nor does it increase the pig's value. An example that agents see all the time is when an owner installs granite countertops over original dated kitchen cabinetry. Most people can see it for what it is and realize it does not really add sustainable value.

Provide guidelines to buyer clients to assist in making good purchase decisions.

WHAT A WONDERFUL CAREER

SEPTEMBER 27

The infamous song by Louis Armstrong, "What a Wonderful World," has inspired millions through the years. The words cause me to think to myself what a wonderful career real estate is. Agents are at the touch point in the lives of people in the purchase and sale of a home, as it is people's most precious asset. Many customers and clients have become close friends through the years. It is truly meaningful when up close and personal you see on people's faces what their home means to them and how, as their agent, I have been able to help them.

The profession requires a variety of skills, including proficiency in terms of customer service functions: marketing and sales, finance, contract negotiations, construction, decorating and staging, psychology, and personal relations. It also offers the opportunity to be an entrepreneur. The business owner aspect incorporates the knowledge, skills, and abilities of finance, staff and associate relations, as well as management and growth of the enterprise. A successful residential real estate agent business owner possesses a heart for people and the head for business.

In tribute to the profession, I have taken the liberty to rewrite Armstrong's words to express what being a real estate agent has meant to me.

I see houses of colonials, bungalows too
I see them as homes for me and you
And I think to myself, what a wonderful career.
I see clients of buyers and sellers too
Lead gen fills my day, the contracts by night
And I think to myself, what a wonderful career.
The settlements of the deals so pretty in the bank
Are also on the faces of people agents help
I see clients becoming friends, giving referrals to you
We have a home, saying I love you.
I built a business, and I watched it grow
I've received much more than I've ever given
And I think to myself, what a wonderful career.
Yes, I think to myself, what a wonderful career.

Even on the most difficult days and challenging transactions, being a real estate agent is a wonderful career. People do their best work when passionate about their purpose.

Find the inspiration for why you have chosen the profession of a real estate agent and remember that it's a wonderful career!

Real Estate Success in 5 Minutes a Day | **301**

BUYERS ARE LIARS AND SELLERS ARE TOO—A SELLER'S TALE

Agents have heard the idiom, "Buyers are liars and sellers are too" or perhaps the version that concludes with "Sellers are yellers." Digging deeper, one can uncover the kernel of truth embedded in the saying. Ultimately, though, it is important for agents to remember that these are people's lives and it is our job to be of service and meet the client's needs and objectives as the professionals we are called to be.

One of the reasons for negative behavior is often due to the stress of the situation. For sellers, the sale of the home involves, in most cases, their largest financial asset. Obtaining top dollar is important in order to be able to move on to their next phase in life. The sellers' perspective is one of the financial and transactional outcomes that they can expect. And when those expectations are not met, then it is understandable for them to become upset. A lot of times that frustration is directed at the agent. If there has been poor service and communication, that can exacerbate the situation. Even if the frustration is at circumstances beyond everyone's control, such as the market, the agent often can be caught in the crossfire.

The most common areas of potential issue between seller and agent are price and condition. There is a trifecta in real estate that is achieved between location, price, and condition relative to the market. It is, in many cases, more art than science to determine that sweet spot. A professional Realtor® will provide wise counsel and it is up to the seller to accept or reject the advice. Agents, including myself, have been known to take a listing on the seller's terms. In those cases, I'm clear that I will provide feedback and periodic market updates. Then we set times to meet or visit so that the client is in the best position to "listen and respond to the market" as recommended.

It is most helpful to set expectations up front at the listing appointment and subsequent meetings. At the first meeting, I explain our value proposition, and what the team offers in terms of marketing. Further, I also describe how the team works and our standards of service. Whenever I fail to take the time to go through the process with the seller, invariably it results in annoyance and even anger on behalf of the client at some point. Then I remember to apply the techniques and strategies shared throughout this book. These tips and techniques go a long way to alleviate tension and move the seller relationship into a more professional space.

The buyer perspective is for another tale; be sure and read that story in another section of this book.

Consider the situation when working with seller clients to help them navigate the process in a productive and professional manner.

RIDE UPHILL FIRST

SEPTEMBER
29

Cycling outdoors is one of my favorite activities. When my husband and I map out a ride, we always strive to do the hardest segment first. This typically means riding uphill. The benefit of following this plan is that once we reach the half-way mark, it almost always means that the second half is predominately downhill. On long rides, we reward ourselves for doing the difficult work first by stopping for lunch or a cup of coffee and small treat. This is smart from an energy standpoint, as well, as clearly we are strongest at the start of the ride and fatigue sets in as we rack up the miles.

The reason why many coaches recommend that real estate agents commit to lead generation in the morning is based on the same principle as riding uphill first. As consistent prospecting is fundamental to success as an agent, it is important that those duties be conducted when the agent has the most energy and is fresh. According to the American Psychological Association, studies have shown that willpower is a limited resource. It is more difficult to focus on challenging tasks later in the day, when a person is fatigued.

Experienced agents establish consistent business development habits, just as we do with our "uphill first" biking rule. For example, an agent could have as a habit to not check e-mails until she has made five phone calls to follow through on leads. Most people benefit by having a reward at completion. Follow this guideline to create an anchor: "After I call five people, I will go for a brisk walk and get a cup of coffee." This simple tool makes it easier to be consistent, which creates a framework for building a business.

In the words of Robert Collier, "Success is the sum of small efforts, repeated day in and day out."

Of course, there are situations in which it isn't always possible to ride uphill first. I would still bike ride, though. The same applies to completing lead-generation activities. The purpose of the guideline is for my benefit. The beauty is that when you establish strong habits, after you've done the hard work, it is often downhill from there.

Establish lead-generation habits following the anchor guideline.

HOW DO YOU SELL A HOME THAT'S NOT YOUR PERSONAL STYLE?

It is generally assumed that it is easier for a salesperson to sell when she "believes" in the product. This leaves one wondering if the opposite is true when it comes to real estate. Is it difficult for an agent to sell a home that's not her personal style?

The Washington, DC metro area serves as the nation's capital and attracts people from all over the world. This broad cultural influence has created a virtual melting pot of home design and style. This diversity provides the advantage of there being more choices of housing styles than in most metropolitan markets in America.

If you recall the history of this nation, Virginia was on the southern side of the conflict. There are still many remnants of this in home design; the market preference is still the colonial. Trending toward the "land of the colonial" means other styles tend to stand out. Standing out in the crowd can work in the owner's favor or it can be a disadvantage; it just depends. The times it works as an advantage is when the unique style is rarely available and yet highly desirable. The times it works as a disadvantage is when it is so taste-specific that it attracts a very small pool of potential purchasers. The seller may have to wait a longer time to find an interested buyer for a uniquely styled home.

In the southwest, one sees predominately adobe architecture. On the west coast, many homes are of the California contemporary model. In the mountains, cabin style and rustic architecture abound.

My response to purchasers who ask whether I like a home they are considering buying is that I already own a home that I like. My job is to help them find a home that meets their needs and that they can be happy living in. Thus I keep my responses focused on what the market value is for a property, rather than on what my particular tastes might be.

The key for the agent to selling a style of home that is unusual for the market is to discover its unique value proposition. One successful strategy is to visit with the owner to uncover what attracted them to the home. Figure out how to apply that knowledge to the broader market. Another technique is to locate a similar property that sold. Determine what those conditions were and the price relative to the market at that time. Agents in other market areas can be a valuable resource in gleaning information about how they successfully marketed a unique property.

It often requires having an honest conversation with the sellers. Explain to them that either the home has been over-improved for the market or they built something that the market does not appreciate or desire. A competitive price will overcome just about anything.

Develop scripts and dialogues to share with clients when queried about your personal opinion and keep responses focused on market value.

OPTICAL ILLUSION

The illustration at left is an optical illusion. One's focus determines whether it is seen as either a young lady or an old woman. The secret of the illusion is to know where one should direct their eyes. The chin of the young lady is the nose of the old woman. It fascinates me that both images exist simultaneously. It does not change; what changes is a person's perspective.

To be successful as a real estate professional requires the ability to be able to adjust focus as necessary. It requires mastery of two functions simultaneously: being an agent and being a businessperson.

To be successful, an agent must be a consistent lead generator, as well as be able to consult customers into clients in the buying, selling, or leasing of real property. As the industry is predominately commission-based, until a sale occurs the agent merely completes ministerial and administrative functions, essentially for no income. This is one side of the illustration.

The other side is that of the business owner. Most agents are self-employed and thus are treated as independent contractors. To build and grow a business that is successful and sustainable requires the professional to focus on those aspects as well. This includes building and working a databank of prospects and clientele, making connections to maximum advantage, and leveraging on the micro and macro levels. To do otherwise, the agent is only as good as his last deal.

At the intersection of the above attributes is where the sweet spot of real estate success resides. It is not an optical illusion! It is surrounded by success thinking, activities, and vision. As you incorporate the lessons learned herein, you too can achieve at this high level.

Focus on the sweet spot of success.

AUTUMN STORY

In autumn, the leaves on the trees of the Shenandoah National Park in Virginia go through an amazing change of colors. As temperatures cool and days shorten, the deep, rich green leaf color of summer begins the transition into yellows, oranges, and reds. The colors at peak season are a magnificent sight to behold. In the words of Anne of Green Gables: "I'm so glad that I live in a world where there are Octobers."

As is nature's plan, next the leaves begin to fall. Thus, the synonym of the autumn season is fall. Homes on the market for sale often go through a similar process. When first on the market, the newness of the listing is green and vibrant with life. As time progresses, interest in the home starts to cool and the number of visitors tends to decrease.

The home can experience some rich activity at public open houses and agent showings when first on the market. Next is the season of color change. In the yellow and orange period, there is still movement, yet signs are that interest is tapering off. Once the red cycle arrives, that is a sign that the peak has passed and interest is likely to fall off dramatically.

Our family loves living in northern Virginia, where we can observe the progressive color change of fall foliage. Peak season, though, is difficult to time. Many factors contribute to when it is best to observe autumn color: weather conditions, elevation, and amount and number of days of sunshine, to name a few. The Virginia Department of Forestry park system provides reports and frequent updates about the status of the fall colors. Without careful planning, one can easily miss the peak season, as it typically only lasts one or two weeks.

The analogy holds true for marketing a home for sale. Price, existing competition, demand for the type of home, absorption rate of comparable homes, interest rates, and economic market conditions, as well as myriad other factors, determine the salability of a home. The real estate agent can serve as the "reporter" on these conditions, much like the forestry service. A professional real estate agent advises seller clients on how to capture the "peak season."

Influence clients to market and sell when the market
is in peak season by using the autumn story.

LEAD GENERATION REQUIRES DISCIPLINE AND HABIT

Oscar De La Renta believed the secret to glamour and style was discipline. He went on to say: "And if you don't dress well every day, you lose the habit. It's not about what you wear, but how you live your life." The same premise holds true with the real estate agent. The secret to success is discipline and habit. To paraphrase the words of De La Renta: "And if you don't generate leads every day, you lose the habit. It's not about what your lead-generation activities are, but how you live your life."

Agents can become paralyzed about whom to contact about real estate. It is like a fashion designer who stands in front of a closet full of clothes and accessories and proclaims there is nothing to wear!

Start with what you have. Open up the contact list in your phone and call all the people who will take your call. Look on Facebook to see who is having a life event and might be ready to make a housing change. Things to pay particular attention to are engagements, weddings, a new baby, children leaving to go away to college, or a mother-in-law coming to live. Peruse LinkedIn to see who has changed jobs or been promoted recently. The idea is to get into conversation with people.

The benefit of working with people the agent already knows is that there is a built-in trust factor. In fashion, stylists suggest that people build their wardrobe around a few classic pieces—the clothes they know and love the best. The same can be true for an agent who builds her business on a core sphere of influence. Many agents have found that a successful practice can be sustained by working with "A"-level clients. This approach also often leads to a strong referral business.

Business development for the professional real estate agent is a consistent, disciplined effort that becomes a habit. It is how these agents sustain success in the long term. It is not a "one and done." Rather, it is how they live their lives.

Establish the habit of consistent lead generation every day.

"WHEN YOU WISH UPON A STAR"

"When You Wish Upon a Star" is the Disney song originally written for the movie *Pinocchio*. It is famously known as the opening tune of the Walt Disney Company television series for those who grew up watching it in the 1950s and 1960s. The beginning stanzas of the lyrics are:

> *When you wish upon a star*
> *Makes no difference who you are*
> *Anything your heart desires*
> *Will come to you*
> *If your heart is in your dream*
> *No request is too extreme*
> *When you wish upon a star*
> *Like dreamers do*

In real estate transactions, sellers often "wish" that the price and exact terms that they want, their "heart's desires," will come true. And for buyers, "no request is too extreme." It can be helpful to imagine with clients what their dream-wish fulfillment would be. If I had a magic wand and could wave it to make things happen, what would need to occur to make their dreams come true?

I conduct this imagination exercise with clients, because if their dreams are achievable, even a portion of them, then their wish is my command. I would love nothing more than to be recognized as the granter of their every wish. For sellers to obtain top dollar for the market would be a great bonus for my reputations as a strong listing agent. For buyers negotiating to obtain the hard-to-get best house is a badge of honor of a proactive agent.

However, if what they desire is not realistic, this is an opportunity to share market information. Then we work together to come up with an outcome they can be happy with. Just knowing that their real estate agent cares enough to give them her very best is in a lot of ways their true "heart's desire."

For your personal life and business, have you wished upon a star lately? If not, what is your heart's desire, your dream?

Take the steps to help make your clients and your own dreams come true!

WHITE WATER LESSONS

White water rafting on the Upper Gauley River in West Virginia is an extreme adventure challenge with intense nonstop action, ranked high in the world and in the United States. It is recommended for only serious whitewater enthusiasts, as it requires precise maneuvering, skills, and attention as you navigate challenging tight technical rapids. These include steep drops, narrow chutes, rock ledges, and crashing white water. The fall is the ideal time to raft the Upper Gauley, as the dam at Summersville Lake is opened after Labor Day, thus creating the most exhilarating rapids experience.

One of the professional rafting guides on the Gauley River is a high school friend of our son's. He has many stories to tell of adventures on the river. It reminds me of my real estate transaction stories. It seems we both remember well the most challenging ones, the people involved and the lessons learned. The guide also makes sure you enjoy the journey, pointing out scenery and parts of the river that one may not notice.

The first lesson is that you don't want to raft the Gauley River alone, particularly in peak times. The guide is there for safety, as he has traveled the river many times and knows the danger spots and the techniques to navigate them. And should you fall out of the boat, the guide is there to pull you back in or to take other action as required. Given that people have been known to die rafting the Gauley, why they wouldn't want the advice and skill of a guide is surprising. The same holds true for the real estate transaction. Given that one's home is a significant financial asset, why wouldn't sellers and buyers want a knowledgeable agent? During particularly challenging markets and transactions, it is more important than ever to be represented by a professional who can get it done.

One such scenario comes to mind when representing a seller client. The title work revealed that part of an addition the owners had constructed for their handicapped daughter had been built over the setbacks allowed by the county. This meant that the home was effectively uninsurable unless rectified. The buyer still wanted to purchase the home and allowed the seller the time for the county to approve the addition retroactively, which we were able to achieve. This very unique situation required a high level of diligence and ability to navigate.

Before setting out, the guide provides instructions on how to get down the river alive, in one piece, and with all of the equipment. The parties in the boat must use rhythm to their advantage to steer and navigate the roller-coaster ride. The real estate agent also pulls together those parties who play their part in the purchase and sale of a home. All work together to assure the transaction arrives safely at settlement. If there are difficulties, like rapids, these professionals possess the skills and knowledge to provide wise counsel.

Develop the knowledge, skills, and abilities of a top-notch professional to navigate the transaction for your clients.

DO YOU BELIEVE IN THE PRODUCT YOU SELL?

Do you believe in the product you sell? If so, then do you own real estate as an investment vehicle? Over time, investments in real estate are a proven means of wealth creation. And it can become a key component to diversification as the professional transitions from agent to business owner.

A popular Chinese proverb states: "The best time to plant a tree was twenty years ago. The second best time is now." The correlation to owning and investing in real estate is: "The best time to have bought real estate was twenty years ago. The second best time is now." In other words, it is never too late.

In 2015, home ownership levels were at a fifty-year low according to Lawrence Yun, the National Association of Realtors® senior vice president of research and chief economist. This correlates that the pool of potential tenants is increasing. Further data revealed that rents were rising.

Consider the standard investor scenario, in which the purchaser puts 20 percent down and finances the balance. If the rental income covers the payment of principle, interest, taxes, insurance, and homeowner's association fees, then in effect the investor purchased 100 percent of an asset with only 20 percent of funds expended. What other investment is there in which someone else actually pays for the majority of the expenses of ownership?

As rents rise and the mortgage is paid down by the tenant, the return on investment becomes even sweeter. According to US census data, the median monthly gross rent paid has increased every decade for more than fifty years. Thus, it is with confidence when projections are that rents will rise over time.

Yes, it is prudent to plan for vacancy, maintenance, and upgrades, and there are transactional costs. Keep in mind that all investment vehicles have transactional costs and risks associated with them. Residential real estate is unique in that housing is a core human need; people have to live somewhere. Combine that fact with scarcity, and owning property as mentioned previously is a proven wealth builder. The principle of scarcity reminds me of Mark Twain's wise words: "Buy land; they're not making it anymore."

It correlates that if you believe in real estate enough that it is part of your portfolio, you will be able to sell it as an investment vehicle to your clients.

Invest in real estate yourself as a proven means of wealth creation and influence your clients to do the same.

THE "BLIND SIDE" TO BUYING AND SELLING REAL ESTATE

The movie *The Blind Side*, starring Sandra Bullock, is based on the extraordinary true story chronicled in the *New York Times* bestselling book with the same title by Michael Lewis. The tale is about football, yet as a real estate agent there are parallels to the buying and selling of real estate.

In football, the blind side for quarterbacks occurs when they can't see over their shoulders what may be coming to block them. It became a common phrase when New York Giants All-Pro linebacker, Lawrence Taylor, altered the environment and forced opposing coaches and players to adapt. As Taylor said afterwards, when imagining himself as the quarterback whom he had knocked from a game: "We all have fears. We all have fears."

The purchase and sale of a home is statistically the largest financial transaction that most people enter into. The proactive agent blocks the client's "blind side." Perhaps the buyer or seller has fears about the process; that's where the professional agent comes into play. The agent often serves the dual role of coach and key player.

There are numerous steps to go through as the agent facilitates the process, including but not limited to providing and interpreting comparables to establish property value; determining terms for an offer and negotiating the contract; obtaining homeowner association documents and delivering them per jurisdictional law and review; following up with the purchaser to be sure property insurance has been secured and the earnest money has been deposited; working with the settlement company and attorneys on necessary documents such as a survey, title information, and insurance and resolving any issues; coordinating inspections (home, radon, well, septic, wood-destroying pest, mold) and negotiating outcomes between parties; working with the appraiser on the market value of the property; following through with the lender on securing financing and providing required documentation; preparing paperwork for warranties; working with all parties to complete the walk-through and settlement according to the contract; and finalizing the process to prepare parties for closing and consummate settlement.

Outlined above are the majority of the standard steps in the process to purchase and sell real estate, yet there are thousands of other issues that can crop up, literally hitting people on their blind sides. That is when a buyer or seller *really* needs a diligent agent to navigate the process.

After Taylor altered the football scene, the second highest-paid position on a team became the tackle who protects the quarterback's blind side. That position serves as the "insurance policy" for the quarterback. All lenders require borrowers to obtain property insurance for homes with a mortgage, and there is a reason why. It is to protect the asset. In a real estate transaction, the best assurance a buyer and seller can obtain is to follow the guidance of an informed real estate agent.

Take action to protect the "blind side" for clients as their professional agent.

PEOPLE ON PARETO

The Pareto Principle, also known as the 80/20 rule, is the theory that the vital few (20 percent) comprise the largest portion of the output (80 percent). This means that the majority of an agent's business (80 percent) is generated from a relatively small number of people or activities (20 percent). It follows, then, that when an agent is deciding on where to invest her time and resources on lead generation, the focus should be on the 20 percent that has proven to achieve the greatest results. This is one of the key secrets successful agents apply to build and grow a business.

The most efficient way for an agent to know where his business comes from is to track lead sources and conversions. There are numerous database programs available to facilitate the process. The important thing is to do it consistently and to evaluate periodically so that you know where your business comes from and where to focus your time.

Let's use, as an example, an agent who holds open houses as her primary method of lead generation. In this case, it would be prudent for that agent to determine how many open houses she held the previous year and schedule on the calendar the next year an equal or greater number. It would not be advisable for the agent to decide to take the year off from holding open houses. This actually occurred with an agent I know. After her best year ever, she decided to switch prospecting strategies and effectively took the next year off. It was several years before she recovered the momentum lost from making that change. And guess what got her back on track? She started consistently holding open houses, Sunday after Sunday.

The Pareto Principle also applies to allied resources, staff, other agents, brokers, vendors, and others who contribute to the agent's success. It is proven that focusing time and energy on those people who contribute the greatest return on investment leads to success.

This principle applies to real estate agents, as well. Brokers will affirm that 20 percent of the agents produce 80 percent of the sales. What are you doing to assure that you are part of the select few who achieve at a high level?

Focus time and resources on the people who
result in the most real estate business.

CONSIDER THE KIDS WHEN MOVING

The professional agent frequently is involved in helping parents with children make personal decisions about buying or selling the family home. A lot depends on the age of the children and if the move will be local or out of the area. There are some professions and careers, such as the military or large corporations, which move people frequently. In my experience, those children often become resilient and seem to adapt easily to change.

Parents of children often place school selection as one of the top priorities when selecting a neighborhood or community to live in. In my experience, schools are often the second leading indicator to real estate value after location. This is primarily due to the fact that in the United States public schools are jurisdictional and thus location-based. Scheduling a school visit and meeting the principal are ways to ascertain if it would be a good fit for the student and if the educational platform and atmosphere meets the family's goals.

When visiting homes, involve the kids in selecting their bedrooms and determining where they will place their furniture, toys, and personal belongings, as is age-appropriate. The yard or other outdoor spaces for both the home and the community can be key aspects to whether the neighborhood will be a good fit.

One way to get to know a neighborhood is to take a relaxed walk around the community and visit with residents to learn about why they like to live there. That is actually how we selected our first home when we moved to McLean from Dallas. We narrowed the choice down to two homes, and our real estate agent wisely suggested we take a neighborhood walk. There were a number of people out working in their yards and playing with children and pets in the neighborhood we selected. In the other neighborhood, it seemed that people weren't quite as friendly. To this day we still have many friends in that first neighborhood and are so glad we employed that strategy for getting to know the community.

Communities frequently offer sports and swim clubs, parks, music, and cultural and recreational opportunities for children. Explore these different venues as part of the moving process, as it can help assure that the transition will be a positive one for all the family members. To get to know an area, set aside time to visit a new venue every month. One of our son's teachers commented that she could tell we were new to the community because we were still acting like "tourists." We had a good laugh. Our family is glad we took all those tours, as it helped us get to know our community. It also gave us many new "finds" and suggestions to share with visiting guests.

Experts have found that children adjust best when parents are positive and optimistic about the future and focus on the benefits of the move. Involving children as is age-appropriate in the process is a great strategy to follow.

Provide these and other strategies to help families with children navigate a move for a positive transition to a new home.

BLUE-SKIES THINKING

As everything begins with thought, success thinking is a core aspect to the life of a professional real estate agent. "Blue Skies" is analogous with happy days, as in the song title by Irving Berlin that opens with the words:

Blue skies smilin' at me

Nothin' but blue skies do I see

Some may say that is not realistic, that agents need to keep their feet on the ground. The buying and selling of a home is serious business, and the client relies on the agent to stay on task. There is validity to this perspective, as the ground is solid and foundational. Being able to accurately understand the current circumstances as they actually are is a valid way to visualize how one can turn the situation into a positive. This applies to the client as well as the agent's own life and business.

Often the skies are not blue, but rather full of dark clouds on the horizon. It is a professional who can look at the horizon and be able to make predictions on what the future may hold and how best to act accordingly. The market constantly changes, and it is the agent's responsibility to interpret the conditions for clients. Keep in mind that trained meteorologists often are only able to predict accurately about 50 percent of the time, yet that doesn't stop them from providing counsel.

Clouds are not always a sign of bad weather; they are positive indicators as well. Who hasn't looked for a "silver lining" in the sky and in the situation? Rainbows also are a sign of hope at the end of a storm. There are points along the way in which it is helpful to stop and take note. For example, remind the client that you were able to negotiate to have the important items on the home inspection report repaired by the seller. Or note that even though the economy is still uncertain, interest rates are historically low, which keeps purchasing power for buyers in an affordable range.

After every night, there is day. A shining sun breaks through the darkness and casts light on the situation. It is the convergence of the two that creates perspective. As an agent, when your business is in a slump, it is often difficult to see when the sun will shine again. The same can be true for clients who suffer a financial or personal loss. Keep the focus on the rays of sunlight that do appear and the activities that are known to lead to success.

If in need of motivation and inspiration, breaking into song is known to do just that. And the tune to "Blue Skies" just might be all you need to change your thinking to one of success.

Sing a success-thinking tune as inspiration for yourself and clients.

THE OTHER PERSPECTIVE

It seems obvious that buyers and sellers of real estate almost always have a different perspective about the same situation. And yet this is one of the most profound insights I have observed after having been a part of more than one thousand real estate transactions. Truly, the circumstance is what it is, and yet the orientation is unique to the party's viewpoint.

It is especially interesting to observe this phenomenon while working with the same client simultaneously as a buyer on the purchase of a home and as a seller on the sale of a home. Just as a two year old typically exhibits the behavior of a child that age, I've found that buyers exhibit certain responses that match their situation, and the same holds true with sellers.

The challenge and opportunity for the agent lies in helping the parties see the other perspective. The reason why that is so difficult in a real estate transaction is that most outcomes have significant positive or negative consequences. This can practically shut out the other viewpoint. And in many cases, it is expressed to the extreme with creative justifications on why one feels and thinks the way he does.

A strategy on how to shift perspective is by the use of an optical illusion. You may remember the sketch on the October 1st entry of an old lady that, when looked at from a different perspective, shows a young lady. Once people know where to put their focus, the other image becomes clear. The purpose of the exercise is to realize that both perspectives can and do exist simultaneously. There are two equally meaningful interpretations. There are a couple of strategies I have used to help clients make a paradigm shift.

One is to ask clients what they would do if they were in the other person's situation. Using the illustration, what if they were the young woman, or what if they were the old lady? Then expand that by asking how they would want to be treated. In many cases, I've found that people will rise to the occasion and do the right thing.

A second technique is to direct the focus into another area of the negotiations. This is what one does to see the other perspective in the optical illusion. By moving attention to the nose on the illustration, one sees a old woman, and by looking at the chin, one views a young lady. The same can be done when parties are stuck on one point—encourage them to look at another area. Then the negotiations can return to the first issue later.

There are skills involved in being able to bring together people who are on the opposite side of a transaction. And since it is a skill, it can be learned and improved with practice and experience.

Utilize the optical illusion strategy to help people see the other perspective.

CONVENIENCE PRINCIPLE

The convenience principle is based on the premise that it is easier to sustain a habit if it is convenient to do so. For the athlete, it means running shoes and exercise clothes at the ready for scheduled workouts. For the chef, it means a well-stocked kitchen with equipment and ingredients close at hand. For the lifelong learner, it means materials stored by the coffee machine to read during her morning quiet time. And for the real estate agent, it means routinely scheduling activities for lead generation.

For real estate professionals, consistent prospecting is at the core of sustained success. Examples abound of how to use the convenience principle to one's benefit. One technique I employ is to set aside one day per week to go through my database. I do this on Sunday evenings to prepare for my week's activities. As I go through the calendar and note birthdays, home anniversaries, and so forth, I prepare a list of touches to make to past clients during the coming week. If I plan to send a card or note, I address and stamp it then and stash it in my briefcase. When I have some down moments in my day, such as waiting for an appointment, I use that time to write a quick message. All that is left to do is drop it in the mail.

In our market area, most brokers opens houses are held on Tuesdays around lunchtime. Thus, I devote that day to preview houses if I am not hosting my own listing open house. In this way, I can see quite a few homes in a short period of time, while also networking with other agents to find out what else may be coming on the market. Viewing homes is part of my lead-generation process, as I actively think of people when I'm in a home. I use the knowledge to touch base with owners who live in the community and whom I know might be interested in what is going on in their neighborhood or perhaps considering a move to upgrade or downsize. It is more convenient to see houses on Tuesdays; thus I take advantage of that opportunity.

Getting started is half the battle for many people in lead generation. That is why a secret to success is to make it as convenient to do as possible. If it is part of your scheduled activities for the week, it becomes a routine habit. In the words of motivational speaker Jim Rohn: "Success is nothing more than a few simple disciplines practiced every day."

Establish lead-generating activities so they are convenient to complete on a routine basis.

THE LIFECYCLE OF SHELTER

Real estate agents witness first-hand a form of lifecycle that people fall into in terms of housing choice. Young people, after completion of their education, at some point move from the family home and typically seek an apartment, condominium, or town home. Their housing selection frequently is in a more urban environment near shopping, restaurants, nightlife, and transportation. Access to employment centers is greater, so that commute time is usually minimized. Further, many of these communities offer amenities that people in this stage of life desire, such as an exercise room, swimming pool, and club room. In exchange for the convenience, the trade-off is often a smaller dwelling in square footage and limited or no land.

As one matures, many enter into a committed relationship or marry. At that point, couples start to think about owning a pet and having children. It is interesting how many young people and couples get a dog as preparation for family life. Some urban areas have designated dog parks in response to this phenomenon, which is interesting because most parks in cities were originally designed for family recreation. What this stage turns to in housing choice is more interior living space and a yard! If children are part of the long-range family plan, then school consideration usually moves to the top of most people's list in terms of housing location.

The next stage of life often reflects the expansion of the family unit. As that occurs, many people run out of space—what with the stroller, the high chair, all the toys, and other related paraphernalia. People frequently desire a yard and outdoor space for a child to play, quiet neighborhood streets to learn to ride a bicycle, and sidewalks to exercise the family dog.

Typically at this stage, most people move into their peak earning years, thus they usually have the income to qualify for what will probably be one of the largest home purchases they will make. If not at this point, it will probably occur sometime during the next seven to ten years as they enter middle age. This is when many people move up and out to the suburbs, in order to gain the most living space and land for the money. Many are in the sandwich stage, caring for children and aging parents. This may require the conversion of a basement or other space in the home as a separate apartment for multi-generational living.

We are now at the top of the bell curve in terms of size and expense for the primary residence. What happens on the downhill side is typically the reverse of the stages it took to get to the top. Next in line is the gradual emptying of the nest. As children pursue their own lives in college or careers, often a couple will look at each other and say, "What do we need with all this space?"

The yard that was so much part of the family life, with the swing set and pool, now has become the weekend noose—requiring more work than anyone has the time or desire to attend to. Sometimes this stage is accelerated by the fact that one of the couple is deceased or there is a divorce. Regardless, most arrive at this juncture at some point. Others choose to "age in place."

This leaves to the heirs the task of cleaning out a lifetime of possessions and memories.

Where do many of these empty nesters go to downsize? Into town house or condominium living, where there is less exterior maintenance demands and a more turn-key lifestyle so that they can travel and spend time with the grandchildren that are coming along. Some move in with family members who can tend to their personal needs. Others move directly from the family home into a retirement community or an assisted-living facility.

It is interesting to note that community living in the later stages of life often mirrors those in the early stages. Think of how college dorm life compares to a retirement center—social opportunities abound in both and three meals a day are served in a cafeteria. This brings us full circle in the lifecycle of obtaining shelter.

Actively participate in the process as clients transition through the lifecycle of shelter.

WHAT WOULD "X" DO?

In the 1990s, bracelets with the letters "WWJD" were popular with Christian youth. The letters stand for "What would Jesus do." The idea of the bracelet was to be a top-of-mind prompt for youth to influence them to make good decisions. This principle can be applied when an agent confronts challenging situations in business by thinking, "What would other successful agents and business owners do in this situation?" Gary Keller, the co-founder of Keller Williams, in *The Millionaire Real Estate Agent* (MREA) discusses the concept that there have been those who have gone before, and success leaves clues.

The father of personal achievement, Napoleon Hill, refers to this as the principle of the mastermind alliance. It borrows and incorporates the education, experience, influence, and capital of others in order to advance one's purpose. Many people are familiar with the networking aspect to the principle. The combined forces generate more energy and power than when they are separate. It is like chemistry: hydrogen and oxygen combined creates water.

The beauty of this principle is that inspiration can come from anywhere, and it can be applied at any time. An agent can benefit from someone's experience and knowledge without being with or knowing the influencer personally. Just asking the question can cause your brain to elicit a response. An example of this in my business was when the market began to shift in 2007. I was conflicted about bumping up advertising to increase listings. Then I remembered the wise counsel of the experienced agents in MREA: when in doubt, hold expenses accountable by using the principle of red light/green light. Stop spending money if there is no money coming in. All of a sudden, I knew what to do and made adjustments to the marketing program, going from expensive glossy advertising to more proactive and focused prospecting. I truly was a leader in my market in making that shift early on, and it was due to the collective guidance in the MREA book.

My business partner and mentor, Sue Huckaby, passed away in 2008, and yet she still influences my decisions. She was wonderful at empowering the agents on her team to productivity. Sue would focus on the agents who were consistently performing the activities that led to production, prospecting, and converting to sell and would coach them to even greater success.

For greater impact, create a top-of-mind technique, just like the WWJD bracelets. This could include a reminder on your smart device, screensaver on your computer, or other such trigger. Remember that there are those who have gone before us that you can draw on today for success. It is a powerful form of leverage!

Use the wisdom of others for discernment in your business and life.

MAINTENANCE-FREE DOES NOT EXIST!

Practically everything in the world is in a state of deterioration. Human bodies are in a state of deterioration, relationships are in a state of deterioration, cars are in a state of deterioration, and houses are in a state of deterioration. All require time and effort in order to stop or slow the normal or natural decay and then proactively work for improvement.

A body requires exercise, a healthy diet, regular doctor and dentist appointments, as well as rest and relaxation. Close relationships deserve active listening, quality time, words of affirmation, gifts of service, and meaningful touch. A car requires gas and oil, air in the tires, and regular servicing. And a house requires painting, gutters kept free of debris, and HVAC and other systems regularly serviced. Even vacant land requires mowing, trash removal, and erosion control.

It is commonly accepted that a new car's value drops significantly the second it is driven off the car lot! So it amazes me when homeowners assume that once they have bought a home, they are done, that from then on they can live there happily ever after. Part of this misconception, I believe, is that advertisers often represent home products as being "maintenance-free." How can that honestly be?

For example, gutter companies that sell gutter shields or guards lead one to believe that the homeowner will never have to get up on the roof again. Even the gutter covers require maintenance. If they get clogged with debris, the entire system will jam up and not let water flow freely. Instead, the water finds its way into the attic and down the interior walls of the house. Yes, the system can help keep larger debris out, but that still doesn't mean it never requires service again.

I recommend that a property owner budget on an annual basis between 1 percent and 3 percent of the value of the property toward maintenance and updating of the home. For a $500,000 home, an owner should budget on an annual basis $5,000 to $15,000 for maintenance, systems, and features upgrades. This is a tidbit I share with even new homeowners.

When meeting with owners about the marketing and sale of their home, we work with the clients on preparing a features and improvements list. This list includes all additions, remodeling, and renovation work, and any appliance and system replacements with the dates they were completed. Generally, any capital improvements as defined by the IRS should be included. Appraisers use this information for evaluating the property, as well. Well-kept maintenance records also help reinforce the value of a home.

It is important to also note that the real estate agent's business is not maintenance-free. Proactive effort is required to generate leads, convert customers to sell, and consistently connect to build and grow.

Impress upon clients the value in maintaining and improving their property annually.

KEEP YOUR EYE ON THE PRIZE

When a kid opens up a box of Cracker Jacks™, what do you think he goes for first? The prize! It would be totally out of character for a child to eat the caramel-coated popcorn and peanuts one by one, patiently waiting until the prize appeared at the bottom of the box. The same hunger and desire for the prize, the fire in the belly, is the level of urgency with which professional real estate agents should view lead generation. She wakes up every morning with lead generation as her top priority.

What does this look like in reality? It means that prospecting activities take precedence over reading and answering routine e-mails. It means calling past clients and others in her sphere of influence until the agent has scheduled the requisite number of appointments for the week. It means delegating transactional-management responsibilities to other parties whenever possible.

The biggest shift occurred for me when it became an automatic process. I set up my routines and habits such that business development is the focus. That way I don't have to think about what I am going to do first and inadvertently get distracted by other shiny objects or activities.

The agent who is successful over time generates leads with the enthusiasm and drive of a kid who has just been given a box of Cracker Jacks™. He is a "crackerjack" real estate agent: a person of marked excellence.

The agent's enthusiasm influences buyers and sellers to take action. In the words of author and speaker Eleanor Doan: "You cannot kindle a fire in any other heart until it is burning within your own."

Be a "cracker jack" agent and keep the eye on the prize—
lead generation is your priority today!

WHAT IS A COMPARATIVE MARKET ANALYSIS FOR A HOME?

A comparative market analysis (CMA) attempts to look ahead at the market, whereas an appraisal looks back at the market. Clearly there are many different factors that determine value in real estate.

The Realtor® is typically the person who prepares a CMA for real estate. First, evaluate the actual property. When did the current owners purchase the home and were there any subsidy or closing cost credit paid for by the seller? If a tax assessment is available, include it with the report. Next, review the relevant details of the home that can be ascertained from previous listings of the property for sale. Often it is helpful to drive by, particularly if not familiar with the location, to know whether there is anything unique that should be considered in the evaluation, such as surrounding parks, retail, or commercial properties.

Next, look for real estate that is most like the subject property that has sold recently within the market area. Typically, sales from the most recent three to six months are viewed because that is the range that most appraisers will use to obtain comparables. The market area can be described in many variations. Typically it is a one-mile radius, the zip code, the school district, the subdivision, the county, or some other defining factor. The idea is to find comparables that are the most similar to the subject property in these areas: housing style, number of bedrooms, bathrooms, square footage of the house and the land, as well as features and improvements.

The CMA also includes homes that are under contract or some jurisdictions refer to as being in escrow or pending. That means the property is no longer actively available for sale; a specific purchaser and seller have agreed to price and terms. This is important information because it shows trends about how fast homes are selling, as well as whether price adjustments were necessary in order to obtain an offer acceptable to the seller.

Next, the CMA includes those properties active and coming soon on the market for purchase. A balanced market is when, in the most recent six-month period in any given market segment, the number of homes that have sold and gone under contract is the same as what is active and available. One can determine the absorption rate by dividing the number of sold plus under contract by the number of months. If the inventory is greater than six months, then it is a buyer's market; if the inventory is less than six months, then it is considered a seller's market.

(# Homes Sold + # Homes Under Contract)/6 = Absorption Rate
Homes Active and Available/Absorption Rate = Months of Inventory
Months of Inventory equals 6 months = Balanced Market
Months of Inventory greater than 6 months = Buyer's Market
Months of Inventory less than 6 months = Seller's Market

Other data points that can be beneficial in determining where the area is in the market cycle are to view high and low sold prices for the street and neighborhood. Look for trends of whether prices are increasing or decreasing over time. Are there any market anomalies? View the parameters provided in the chart and take all of these factors into consideration.

Use a comparative market analysis to determine the best pricing for real estate.

"SORRY SEEMS TO BE THE HARDEST WORD"

Elton John recorded this soulful song, "Sorry Seems to Be the Hardest Word." To the real estate agent, the apology often comes from a customer who decides not to use your services to buy or sell a home. People have reasons that seem valid to them at the time. Regardless of the reasons, the rejection can seem very personal to an agent; I know it does for me. The question is, what will be the agent's response? Will they no longer be friendly with the person? The approach that has the best long-term outcome for the relationship and the agent, I have found, is to take the high road.

Often, it is helpful to look at a situation from another industry's perspective. Mindy Kaling is an American actress, comedian, and writer. In her book *Why Not Me?*, she shares the story of when she found out that she was not nominated for an Emmy. Couple that with her prior engagement to be the hostess for the awards, which meant she would be reading the names of the winners. Surely if ever there was a situation in which someone had a right to take rejection personally, it was an actress whose own show was not selected.

Mindy had a choice. One option was to cancel her participation, which would have been unprofessional and potentially a public relations disaster. The other was to keep her commitment with grace and aplomb, so people would continue to think of her as being mature and classy.

To overcome her feelings of rejection, Mindy realized that as an actress she could "act as if" she was fine with the decision and visualize that outcome. Once she was able to distance herself from the actual circumstance, she was able to genuinely be happy for those who did win. To do otherwise really was no better than being a poor sport or a two year old who throws a temper tantrum.

In the case of the real estate agent, do you really want to get the reputation that you are only friends with people because they use your services to buy or sell a home? Do you want people to head in the other direction when they see you at the grocery store, the health club, on your kid's sports field only because they are concerned you will be offended if they select another agent? I choose the high road because, like Mindy, I want to live a life of grace. That is a strong foundation to build and grow a successful business. And who knows, you might be the second or third agent they decide to use who ultimately sells the house.

When people you know select another agent, choose to accept with grace and professionalism by taking the high road!

OFFENSE VERSUS DEFENSE

While in the process of buying and selling a home, client requests of real estate agents often can be reduced to this question: "What have you done for me lately?" And that question, I have found, has two key aspects: offensive endeavors and defensive maneuvers.

On behalf of purchaser clients, proactive tasks by an agent include researching homes that are on the market and those that are in "shadow inventory." There was a time when purchasers did not have access to home listings unless they worked with a real estate professional. With the advent of the Internet, a lot of real estate information is available to the public. What the agent provides in this environment is discernment of that information.

When I work with buyers, I set up for myself searches that meet their criteria, rather than bombard the client's e-mail in-box. When a home hits the market that looks like it might be of interest, I take the time to go see it personally. Online photos will make a property look its best. An example is a home that looked wonderful online, yet once at the actual property, I realized there were a number of steps up a steep hill to get to the home. That was not apparent in the listing photos or on Google Earth. If after checking out the home I believe there will be some interest, I call the agent and get information on the seller's situation. After doing this groundwork, if I still believe that my buyers might have some interest, I send it to them and offer some times I have available to show the home.

To be on the offense for seller clients includes both pre- and active marketing of the property; showing the property and following up with feedback; negotiating on behalf of the client's best interests; and assisting with the maintenance and care of the property. An example of being offensive on behalf of seller clients is when buyers write an offer with a home sale contingency. It is my practice to go see the home referenced in the contingency, meet with the agent to get a better handle on the pricing relative to the market, and share that knowledge with the client.

Both buyer and seller clients benefit from an agent who proactively works to obtain the best outcome possible in negotiations on purchase price, inspections, financing, and appraisal contingencies.

The other side of the game is defensive actions, which include similar functions; it just depends which perspective the agent is representing. These include following through on all deadlines and obligations; advising clients when issues are beyond the scope of the agent and recommend when to seek additional counsel or expert advice; and providing options in difficult negotiation situations. One task unique to listing agents that can be a defensive maneuver is mitigating any "disparagement" of the property on behalf of seller clients. It is a key to success that the professional agent assumes the position as the situation warrants.

Take both offensive and defensive action on behalf of your clients.

THE STRENGTH OF WEAK TIES

There is a pool of buyers and sellers ready, willing, and able to take action to move at any given point in time. The pool may be deep and wide, or it may be shallow and narrow. Yet it does exist. Even in the market crash of the Great Recession, there were still buyers and sellers in the marketplace. Experts refer to homeowners who are considering selling and officially haven't yet done so as "shadow" inventory.

Do you believe that? If you do, then you will stop waiting for the perfect client to call or walk in your office, and will instead go out and find the motivated. You will take the steps to influence people and move them along in the process if they aren't yet motivated. As an agent, you will love and appreciate the clients you have and take full advantage of the opportunities presented. Listen closely to clarify what their next real estate decision might be.

The truth is that the perfect client is rare. It is as valuable as a precious gem and meant to be treasured. The mining of leads is more like the mining for gold; there is always more debris than precious metal. This is where the value is in "the strength of weak ties" concept.

Many successful agents earn a good portion of their business from their spheres of influence. This includes family, friends, neighbors, and business associates. Agents should have a proactive and consistent method to both stay in touch with those folks as well as market their value proposition as an agent. This is the mining of the databank.

The next levels of influence are known as the weak ties. You will likely not have a direct connection with this person; it is more distant. Yet studies have found that many times this is where the opportunity lies. The visual is of concentric ripples that develop when throwing a rock into a pool of water. That's where the weak ties lie—out at the edges. It is the friend whose neighbor is thinking of putting her home on the market. It is your husband's business associate whose daughter wants to buy her first condo.

Another way to strengthen this network is to get in touch with acquaintances with whom you have lost touch. A college friend whom you haven't thought about in a while may be a gold mine of contacts. Expose yourself to other networks by attending events and social occasions that are outside your current sphere. It is in the outer circles of influence where you are more likely to engage with buyers and sellers ready to make a move.

Social media such as LinkedIn and Facebook are tremendous platforms for connecting and reconnecting. You just never know who knows whom you know!

Grow and build your network of leads by strengthening both strong and weak ties.

WISDOM COMES FROM
EXPERIENCE IN REAL ESTATE AS IN LIFE

It is considered common sense that wisdom comes from experience. The book by Michael Lewis that later became a movie, *The Big Short*, addresses the real estate market and credit bubble of the 2000s. Many believe that period of rapid growth led to the financial market crash of September 2008 and the Great Recession. In hindsight, the wisdom gleaned is that the market was overinflated. Some would say that it was a self-fulfilling prophecy, that most of the appreciation in the market of 2004-2006 was not sustainable because of the exuberance, that what happened next with the market correction was inevitable.

Which came first: the exuberance over the appreciation or just the exuberance that threw out sound judgment and common sense? What was learned presents the bigger question of the current market environment.

The rise and fall of the last real estate cycle was similar to the one that occurred in the 1990s. After a time of rapidly rising markets, the economy was officially declared a recession. What was learned from that period is that it took seven to ten years from the peak of appreciation to get back up to the top levels of value again.

Author and humorist Mark Twain said: "We should be careful to get out of an experience only the wisdom that is in it—and stop there—lest we be like the cat that sits down on a hot stove-lid. She will never sit down on a hot stove-lid again, and that is well; but also she will never sit down on a cold one anymore."

Should one wait to sell because of the fact that there were so many people who lost their homes in short sales and foreclosures during the down market? What if a buyer continues to wait so long that she actually misses a golden opportunity? That would be like the cat that would never sit down on a stove-lid again for fear that it may be hot.

Good houses priced correctly sell in every market. Successful agents operate in the market they are currently in, taking care to not reminisce about the past and not overcompensate in the other direction. Use wisdom and experience to help clients determine where the current market is and how they can apply that knowledge to make decisions that are the best outcome for their situation.

Provide wise counsel to clients on real estate market cycles.

CREATE A PLACEHOLDER

OCTOBER 22

There are several definitions for a placeholder. One is mathematical and is the symbol in an expression that may be replaced by the name of any element in the set. In other words, it holds a place for that number. The technique in sales is very similar. It is like setting a table for a dinner party and leaving a space for the guest. When a salesperson creates a placeholder with a client, he creates the vision of possible outcomes. This allows the idea to germinate and take root in the client's mind. If done well, the client then comes around to the agent's way of thinking, perhaps even coming to the conclusion that the idea was his all along.

Market studies can be an effective way to create a placeholder for value with clients. In review of the comparables with the client, discuss other homes that have sold, are under contract or active that have similar attributes. This is an opportunity for the agent to share where she thinks the market is going. Should the trends actually occur in the way predicted, the client is not taken by surprise when it happens. It may help a client to sell or buy now instead of waiting a year or two.

An example when I used this recently was at a listing appointment. There was a home under contract the next street over. We discussed that once that property went to settlement, it would set the new standard for the neighborhood. Depending on the final selling price, we might find that the list price for my client's home was no longer a relevant market price. By discussing in advance, most sellers are more open to price adjustments in the future, thus being more responsive to the market.

A situation in which the strategy might come into play when working with buyers is negotiating the home inspection. Set the expectation ahead of time that the best outcome usually occurs when buyers don't "nickel and dime" the seller. Go on to create the placeholder that reasonable requests include plumbing, electrical, safety, and other key items. Having this conversation ahead of time can be more effective than waiting until the inspection report is provided, when emotions may run high.

It is a key success strategy to make a place for future likely occurrences with the client early and often.

Find opportunities to use the placeholder technique with your clients to set the stage for future conversations and decisions.

A CAREER IN REAL ESTATE IS A MARATHON

The Marine Corps marathon is a race held in the Washington, DC metro area in October annually since 1975. It is known as the "People's Marathon," as there is no prize money. My husband and I proudly watched our son compete with more than thirty thousand other runners, all with the hope to complete the route.

A career in real estate is best run as a marathon. There are times when it can be a good strategy to up the pace and sprint, for example during the launch phase. Yet most have found that pace isn't sustainable for the long run.

As this was our son's first marathon, he joined a team. It is not advisable to run a marathon without training properly. There are those who have run the race before who have mapped out how to achieve the best results. The training schedule provides a plan to run certain lengths with rest in between so that the runner builds up endurance for race day. Failure to train properly can lead to poor performance on race day and possible injury. The same applies to real estate agents. The license is just the beginning, like signing up to run a marathon. The training and running is when the real work begins.

The team concept provides camaraderie, encouragement, and accountability. Training and learning with and from others is significantly more motivating. Even though they run their own race, having others alongside makes the journey more empowering. A real estate agent is often a solo practitioner. Yet many professionals who enjoy long careers have found benefit in connecting with other agents, brokers, and those in related industries.

Those who have run multiple marathons attest to the runner's high and sense of accomplishment that spurs them on to run yet another race. This also occurs for the successful agent. There is a deep sense of professional accomplishment in completing a challenging transaction. There is an emotional high of helping a first-time homeowner realize her dream. There is pride in building a business that helps people in the buying and selling of their most prized possession. And there is the celebration of working alongside agents on the team who reach their annual sales goals.

It is said that no one quits running a marathon at mile twenty-five. Once they see the crowds cheering and the light at the end, they get a burst of energy and power through. That is how it feels as an agent as a deal gets to settlement. All the challenges and difficulties pass away as the agent pushes through and gets another deal done.

Repeat marathoners tell new runners not to stop, but rather to run past the finish line. Do more than it takes to complete the race. That's a great message for the agent as well. Your team will be cheering you on!

A secret to success in real estate is to run your business like a marathon.

FRAME THE ARGUMENT

To influence people requires framing the argument from their point of view. The strategy succeeds best when the agent uses language and examples that will resonate with the client. Uncovering the kernel of truth in the outcome often has the most impact.

An example of how to frame an argument to influence a seller client occurred early in my career. After several years of appreciation at a double-digit level in our market area, the initial signs of softening started to appear. Buyer activity slowed down considerably and inventory levels were rising faster than demand. In addition, it was early fall, which meant if the home did not sell soon it would probably be sitting vacant through the winter months, as the owners had already moved to their new home.

I explained the market dynamics to create a sense of urgency. Instead, the seller assured me that he was in no hurry and in fact it was fine to wait for spring, when he felt the market would be better. That was when I recalled he was in the tech industry. I asked him what happened during the dot-com bust. All of a sudden, it was like a light bulb went off in his head. By using his lingo, he immediately understood what was happening in the real estate market, priced his home correctly, and sold in a timely fashion for a fair price. Later he thanked me for my wise counsel.

A scenario that impacts buyers frequently is how to manage the risk associated with buying and selling at the same time. Many have the financial capability of bridging between the two and yet would prefer to have the assurance of having their home sold before buying another. This places the burden on the sellers, because in effect they are taking their home off the market while the buyers sell their home. If the sellers' house has been on the market for a while, many are more open to the idea. However, if the house is new on the market and likely to sell quickly because it is a great house, then the buyers are putting their offer at a disadvantage.

The way to frame this argument is to ask them where they see themselves living in the future—and of course it is in the new home. Next, ask which is more important to them: knowing they would live in a home they love for many years, or getting top dollar for the house they are selling. At that juncture, most are ready to focus on the future and remove the contingency in order to get the best house.

The secret to make the sale is to uncover what would be meaningful to the other party. In the words of author Seth Godin: "Even when people making an argument know this, they don't like making an argument that appeals to the other person's alternative worldview." That is the challenge: to take on the other's perspective and by doing so help them make the paradigm shift to see the benefits of heeding wise counsel.

Frame the argument from the other party's perspective
in their language to make the sell.

LEVERAGE ON THE MICRO LEVEL

Micro opportunities for leverage for the real estate agent include most frequently technology and systems. The use of a smartphone leverages communication and allows for the agent to read, respond, delegate, and forward e-mails, texts messages, and phone conversations in a timely fashion. Use of technology for document preparation and digital signatures increases efficiency and effectiveness and are forms of micro leverage.

Checklists and color-coding of charts and files are examples of transactional systems that allow professional real estate agents to leverage time by simplifying routine processes. Document storage in the "cloud" creates ease of access for all parties, as well as eliminates the need to send various forms back and forth from multiple devices.

There are also myriad systems for lead capture, generation, and follow-through to sales conversion. Effective prospecting leads to more business, which then spills over into macro leveraging.

The agent who previews and shows homes can be a form of micro leverage. The activity increases the agent's market knowledge so when talking with buyers she can more quickly "connect the dots" with available inventory. When preparing a comparative market analysis for a potential seller client, market knowledge is a beneficial part of the process. And when meeting with the seller to determine pricing, the agent is more effective actually having seen the comparable homes. All of these are micro forms of leverage of one's knowledge and experience, which impacts confidence and professionalism.

On a personal level, agents can also use leverage to increase efficiency and effectiveness. Shopping online for essentials and having groceries delivered are time-saving strategies that anyone can utilize. Establishing systems for the storage of personal items such as keys often eliminates last-minute delays and frustrations. Schedule coordination with a master digital calendar helps assure that family members and friends are connected.

Essentially anything that allows for exponential growth and use of one's time, energy, resources, capital, intellect, ability, and people is leverage. Many micro-leverage opportunities cross over into those that are macro.

Take small steps to increase leverage on the micro level in your life and business.

RENTER NO MORE

One of the factors to consider when deciding it is time to buy a home is how rent compares to the expenses of home ownership. If the cost to rent is less than the cost of home ownership, it can make financial sense to continue to rent. If the cost to own a home is less than it is to rent a comparable home, then it is seriously time to buy!

There are statistics available to determine the financial advantage. It varies based on interest rates and cost of housing for the market area. Home ownership has long been valued as being a good investment in many cultures. There is a scene in the classic movie, *It's a Wonderful Life*, in which people who have been longtime tenants in pauper housing are finally able to purchase their own homes. It is a celebrated day, as there is pride associated with home ownership. Renting is temporary and owning is more permanent.

Another way to view the distinction is that renting is essentially consumption. It is trading money for the use of someone else's property under certain terms. For some, there is more freedom associated with being able to pick up and move. Yet there is risk with that as well. And that is that rent paid to a landlord does not build on anything, and thus the tenant has nothing to show for years of payment. One way to distinguish between consumption and investment is to ask, "Is the long-term payoff worth the initial outlay now?"

Once one becomes an owner, then every dollar applied to principal has the potential to add value to the asset. In the beginning, if the home is mortgaged, primarily interest only is paid. The equity in the home continues to increase as the homeowner consistently pays down the mortgage year after year. Compared to renting, home ownership is an investment that often leads to wealth creation.

It is important that people not disturb the equity by treating it as a cash register by refinancing and taking out additional loans on the collateral. Homeowners who held onto their properties and paid them down consistently year after year have found having that asset is a benefit in their later years of life. In most instances, the personal home is one of the best long-term financial vehicles for most people.

Consider the words of financial author and columnist Jason Zweig, as they are important to remember: "A home is more than an investment. It is the place that helps shape who we are."

Determine the benefits to owning versus renting for your market area and use that information to influence tenants to invest in home ownership.

"REUNITED AND IT FEELS SO GOOD"

When I hear the song "Reunited" by Peaches & Herb, I think fondly of clients with whom I have had the privilege to work on multiple transactions. The lyrics resonate my sentiments: "Reunited and it feels so good; reunited 'cause we understood, there's one perfect fit." Past clients are a core component to the long-term business success of a professional real estate agent. And it truly does feel so good when a client comes back for help with another real estate need.

There are ways that an agent can nurture the feeling and increase the likelihood of repeat clients. Some professionals host community events and client parties. On a monthly basis, our team sponsors a community charity fundraiser dinner at a local restaurant in conjunction with vendors and other allied resources. Past and current clients are invited to attend, which gives us an opportunity to stay in touch with them while at the same time giving back to the local community.

What one appreciates is known to appreciate. Show gratitude to your clients for their business in small and big ways. Examples of small ways to stay in touch include sending birthday and home anniversary cards. Stay current on the market area and apprise past clients with sales data updates, as well as any trends or new developments that would be of interest. Send items of value on a consistent basis.

Don't play hard to get or find! Be sure to romance your past clients and sweep them off their feet with customer service. Take it to the next level in Nordstrom fashion and provide a customer experience. Offer recommendations for contractors, vendors, and other related resources that would benefit them. Show them that you care and that you want to be in a relationship with them. When I receive referrals from clients, regardless of the outcome of the lead, I send a gift card for coffee or treat at their favorite café, as well as a note thanking them for thinking of me.

Another scenario is the seller client who decides to take his home off the market for either better conditions or personal reasons. And there is the buyer client who had to put his search on hold. Stay in touch, as this is potential business. In a way it is like a political incumbent; you have the best chance of getting rehired if you stay in touch and deliver good service. The best and easiest client is one who already knows you, so be certain you stay top-of-mind. This is how many top real estate professionals achieve the sweet spot of success.

---

*Stay top-of-mind with past clients for repeat
business and sustained success.*

HOW HOMES ARE LIKE
BLACK SHOES: CUSTOM HOMES

Custom homes are like the black shoes offered in upscale departments stores and boutique specialty shops. The agent who sells upper-bracket homes understands what unique features and attributes distinguish and attribute to value in this niche.

The shoes purchased at a department store are often designer brands, albeit a less expensive grade. The materials are mixed, constructed with leather uppers, yet in many cases the soles or other materials are man-made. At peak times, the salesperson may wait on several customers at a time. The environment is comfortable, and there is a varied selection. The salesperson is likely paid on commission, so is motivated to offer additional services such as checking the storeroom for other sizes and styles and other stores for availability, if requested.

The department store of housing is the mid-level neighborhoods and builders. Materials are of a higher quality, a level above "builder grade." Buyers have more selections and can make the home their own with more variations; often it is referred to as "quasi-custom." The location is preferable in some way, for example: proximity to employment, transportation, schools, parks, and other recreational facilities. The builder employs economies of scale for materials and labor, yet there is still considerable individual and special attention to the product and client.

The black shoes from the boutique store are constructed entirely of high-grade leather and quality materials. The designer emblem is evident and the look chic and fashionable. The product has a classic and timeless nature to it, and will remain a well-loved fashion staple for many years. Or it is a trendy style that shows the owner is on the cutting edge of fashion. A visit to the boutique is a pleasurable experience, as service is of the highest caliber. The shoes elicit compliments and project the statement that the owner has style and taste.

A true upper-bracket luxury property conveys the sentiments of the shoes from the boutique store. The architecture is unique, yet timeless. Or it is on the cutting edge of design. The materials are of the highest grade and quality available. From the lead architect to the craftsman, each practice at the top of their respective fields; this is a true custom home. The landscape design complements the contours of the property and accentuates the best features of the locale. Often these estate-style homes are gated or have additional security and privacy.

Geographic attributes of custom homes increase value: any water view, be it ocean, river, lake, or creek; mountains or other scenic properties; unique city views; and a golf course or similar club in the neighborhood. The professional upper-bracket agent is knowledgeable about market attributes and features that contribute to a property and truly distinguished as a custom home.

Apply the "how homes are like black shoes" analogy to illustrate the variety of upper-bracket home attributes to clients.

FACTOR TRANSPORTATION COSTS INTO HOUSING CONSIDERATIONS

For most metropolitan areas, the most expensive residential real estate is that in closest proximity to the city center. The reason is obvious: land values are typically higher and there is usually greater density. Many homebuyers venture to the suburbs to get more land and greater interior square footage. The country beckons on a Sunday drive and seems so lovely—at least until Monday morning or Thursday evening, when the dreaded commute looms.

The Center for Neighborhood Technology (CNT) provides reports based on census data, coupled with income and local transportation costs, which are good guides to share with buyers. CNT president, Scott Bernstein, was quoted in the *Washington Post*: "The farther out you get, the cost of transportation can double. Somewhere between eight and twelve miles out from the center . . . housing costs drop precipitously, but transportation costs go way up."

One aspect to transportation costs that is more difficult to quantify is commute time. Consider the time as an opportunity cost, the lost opportunity of doing something other than sitting in and navigating traffic!

It is worth noting that the combined cost of a home that requires a longer commute by car might exceed that of a more expensive home located closer to transit or employment center. The work week for most is Monday through Friday, with weekends as personal time at home. That means that the commute affects five-sevenths of one's life. In one year, accounting for holidays and two weeks of vacation, that translates into the average worker spending 90 percent of his days with that commute.

As an agent who works with buyers locating to a new area, it is helpful to have them drive the commute during high traffic times before making a decision on an area. What seems like a reasonable drive on the weekend can become torture when the roadways are clogged with other commuters. Keep in mind, too, that most people who telecommute one day a week tend to select Friday. Midweek days, particularly Wednesdays, are often the peak traffic day in most metro areas. Keep in mind also that during summer and other vacation seasons, traffic often decreases significantly. Thus the true barometer to check a commute is on anticipated full traffic days.

Assist buyers in factoring in transportation costs and commute time into housing selection.

I SEE LIVE PEOPLE!

In the movie *The Sixth Sense*, the main character, Cole Sear, proclaims: "I see dead people." In real estate, "I see live people." I constantly think about people when I view homes. Who might want to live in that particular home or neighborhood? Which investor is in the market to take on his next property? What family is ready to upsize or what couple is ready to downsize? Which young professional is at the stage to purchase the first place to call her own?

The character in the movie goes on to explain that the people he sees are "walking around like regular people. They don't see each other. They only see what they want to see. They don't know they're dead." It is much the same way for how I see live people in real estate. They are "walking around like regular people" and often do not even know that they are ready to or need to make a move.

The professional agent develops a finely tuned sixth sense, an intuitive feeling that the time might be right for people to make a move. The couple that recently married will soon be ready to "build their nest." For the parents whose last child recently left for college, empty-nest syndrome may soon be on their minds. The investor who is ready to acquire the next rental property for his portfolio might be interested in the deal of the day.

Often the people in an agent's sphere "only see what they want to see" and don't have the vision on timing a real estate sale or purchase and the value of a particular property. People "don't know what they don't know" and that is why a good agent helps people catch the vision.

Another way to put this principle into practice is ask agents at broker's open houses: "Do you have someone in mind for this home?" If the answer is "no," encourage the agent, now that she has seen the home, to "review all of her buyers to think of who the home might would work for." This is a way to help agents "see live people" when marketing a home.

A successful agent in our area peruses the market daily for the best deal available. And when he finds it, it empowers him to contact all those people he knows who might be in the market for a "good deal." This is one additional way to "see live people" when thinking about real estate.

Think about what their real estate needs might be when you "see live people."

CHANGE AGENTS—
SUPERMAN AND WONDER WOMAN

Halloween is celebrated today in many countries. One of the best parts is the parade of kids trick-or-treating in costume at our door. I love when children take on the characters of superheroes. Think of Superman and Wonder Woman! Superman transforms from Clark Kent, a mild-mannered reporter, into a superhero who defends truth, justice, and the American way. Wonder Woman heralds from a blend of many heroines and protects people in danger with the use of truth as one of her weapons.

Real estate agents have many attributes of superheroes. A professional agent uses his super abilities to help the buyer and seller navigate the complicated process of change. She protects her clients with truth and knowledge. Paramount is the ability to use vision and enhanced listening skills to help maneuver clients through periods of uncertainty and challenge. Agents and superheroes both use overt and covert efforts to achieve their mission.

Christopher Reeve, who played Superman, shared these inspiring words: "What I do is based on powers we all have inside us; to make the best of what we have—and you don't have to be Superman to do it." As real estate professionals, we may not save people from burning buildings, yet we are helping them to buy or sell their most valuable asset in life.

Not sure if you are up to being a superhero? According to research by American social psychologist Amy Cuddy, strike the physical pose and you will take on the characteristics. For Superman strength and Wonder Woman boldness, stand tall with your fists on your hips. In the words of Cuddy: "Fake it until you become it."

Yes, change can be stressful, but with the Superman and Wonder Woman real estate agent on duty, everyone lands safely with their feet on the ground, smiles on their faces, and a place to call home!

Incorporate superhero attributes when working with clients to navigate change!

ALL IN THE FAMILY

All in the Family was an American sitcom in the 1970s. As the purchase and sale of a home has such significant ramifications, I've found that in almost all cases there are peripheral people involved—usually family! Sometimes there can be financial advisors, close friends, neighbors, and business associates as well. All seem to have an opinion on what the client should be doing.

With experience, I have come to realize it is best to assume that there are other people who will be involved or will influence the client's decision-making. Recently I was coaching an agent who was working with clients on the purchase of a new home. She was dismayed that the brother-in-law came along for many of the appointments with the builder. It felt to her that he was acting as the "bad cop," bringing up problems and concerns that weren't even issues just to show that he was adding value.

On average, most Americans buy and/or sell a home only once every five to seven years, so it isn't surprising that the process is overwhelming for many people. Even if one has done it more frequently, laws and practices often change, as does the market. Perhaps this is why many people seek outside counsel from trusted friends, relatives, and associates. One of the strategies I have employed to great success is to follow up on all conversations and meetings with an e-mail synopsis of what was discussed. In this way, the clients have written clarification that they can then forward to whoever is advising them or from whom they are seeking counsel. Then if that person has a question or desires more information, the clients usually just forward it to me directly.

At that juncture, I have a better understanding of anyone else involved. In the case of a newly widowed woman, it was her financial advisor who was reviewing everything. In the situation of a first-time homebuyer, it was her lawyer father who was weighing in. In the case of a young married couple, it was her sister, a real estate agent in another state, who was sharing her opinion. In the case of the out-of-state seller, it was his neighbor who was watching over all the comings and goings of the house and reporting back.

Now I proceed with every transaction with the assumption that someone else is watching or listening to everything I'm doing, albeit through my client's eyes. It has been my experience those parties' intent is for the best for the person. Thus, I can be the most helpful by not assuming a defensive posture. When I convey through my words, message, and actions that I also am seeking the best for the client, most people relax and are open to my counsel. Just remember, it is "all in the family."

Recognize that most real estate transactions have others involved;
embrace the situation by providing professional service and
counsel to the client.

PLATINUM RULE

The Golden Rule, "Do unto others as you would have them do unto you," has its origins in the Bible. In my life and business, I have discovered that people don't necessarily want what I want. In those cases, to make the experience personal for the individual, I embrace the platinum rule: do unto the others as they would have me do unto them. The Golden Rule creates an environment of reciprocity, which is a fundamental means of exuding influence. The platinum rule creates a spirit of service and meeting needs. There are valid occasions for both.

One way to apply both of the rules is to use the DISC™ behavioral assessment. The tool helps the agent to both understand and know herself. It also provides insights into the behavior of others. The DISC™ profile has four categories of behavior: dominance, influence, steadiness, and conscientiousness. Everyone has a little bit of all of the styles, but most people have a predominant as well as a secondary style.

Clearly it would be awkward to deliver an assessment to a customer or client. Instead, use clues to determine why a person behaves and reacts in a certain way. Some of the indicators I use that provide insight into what client preferences might be are: profession, décor, management of the home, and demeanor.

A "D" is a results- and action-oriented person and includes most CEOs and businesspeople, as well as high-level government officials. The "I" profile is enthusiastic and collaborative and includes most sales professionals and others who work with people in a proactive manner. The "S" person seeks stability and is most often in the role of support functions and includes school teachers and administrative staff. And the "C" person focuses on details, accuracy, and precision, and includes accountants, engineers, and many doctors and lawyers.

A real estate example: the agent is an "I" and the client is a "C." If the agent follows the Golden Rule, she would exude enthusiasm about herself, accomplishments, and all of her marketing platforms. To follow the platinum rule, the agent would provide the client with details on the market as well as an extensive analysis of comparables and other relevant information. This is a real-life situation. I was hired and the "I" agent was not. The client later shared the reason was that I supplied the data he requested plus more, and the other agent did not, so I won the business.

Determine your DISC™ profile and use those insights to
understand clients to meet needs at a platinum level.

FEATURES OF WORLD-CLASS CITIES

There are key similarities to world-class cities. First, many are located on a river or major waterway. Ten European capitol cities are sited on riverbanks. London is on the Thames; Paris is on the Seine; Rome is on the Tiber River; Dublin on the River Liffey; Budapest on the Danube; Moscow on the Moskva River; Amsterdam on the Amstel; Berlin on the Spree River; Prague on the Vltava River; and Madrid on the Manzanares River.

The United States capitol of Washington, DC is located on the banks of the Potomac River (this occurred in 1846, when the portion that was deeded previously to be part of the District of Columbia on the west side of the Potomac River was retroceded to Virginia).

Other prominent US cities are adjacent to bodies of water as well. New York City is on the Hudson River; Chicago is on Lake Michigan; major cities such as Los Angeles and San Francisco on the West Coast are on the Pacific Ocean; New Orleans is on Lake Pontchartrain; and Miami is on the Atlantic Ocean. The waterways provide opportunities for commerce and recreation.

Another primary feature of a beautiful city is its parks and gardens. London has the magnificent grounds of Hyde Park, and Paris offers Champ de Mars parks around the Eiffel Tower. High on the hill overlooking the Danube, the Prague Castle has magnificent gardens.

In Washington, DC there is green space between the Washington Monument and the White House, known as the Ellipse. The National Mall is an open area with the US Capitol banking the northern end, the Washington Monument on the southern, and various Smithsonian museums flanking both sides. All of the major European cities boast fabulous museums, too many to mention.

New York City has the iconic Central Park, which serves as the hub of outdoor life in the largest city in the United States. There are walking, jogging, and biking paths. There are carousels for children and those young at heart to enjoy in the warmer seasons and ice rinks in the winter. Art and architecture, history and culture, nature and sports events all are offered in the park, which was designed decades ago by Frederick Law Olmstead.

It is a key to success for a professional real estate agent to understand the core fundamentals of value to real property. Knowledge of the key features that makes a city world class is part of the repertoire.

Promote the amenities and features of your community that accent quality of life for residents, visitors, and potential buyers.

KEEP YOUR EYES ON THE BALL

Any sport with a ball will have this as one of the primary mantras. If the objective is to move the ball down the field, court, or course, then the focus has to be on the ball. Coaches will say, "Don't let the competition get into your head, but rather play the ball!"

In business, the idiom means to pay attention to the situation. It is easy to be distracted by what the competition is doing or to get involved in the minutiae of the day. The professional real estate agent knows that the game is played in her head first. She must decide that the priority is to generate leads.

The population of people in the market to buy or sell a home generally falls into three categories. One-third will immediately select the agent and move forward with the process. Another one-third will contact other agents to consider doing business with. And one-third will delay their decision.

The easy play for the agent is the low-hanging fruit of those ready, willing, and able to buy or sell a home. By all means, convert those leads. Take that ball and run with it! Remember, though, that the sweetest fruit is often the hardest to reach, which falls into the other two categories. Be sure to pursue those leads as well.

The group that selects another agent should remain in your pipeline until the actual sale takes place. I put a "watch" on the listing. In about one-third of the cases, the agent is not successful in getting the house priced to market and sold. When the listing becomes either withdrawn or expired, I circle back to the owners.

Keep in mind this is not the same as prospecting withdrawn and expired listings, as many programs advocate. That is an entirely other form of generating business. This is a ball that you had in your hands and was intercepted by another player. Just as in sports, the agent can make a comeback. Remember to honor the Realtor® code of ethics; I am not advocating going behind the sign.

The third category includes those sellers who delay their decision for myriad reasons. It also applies for buyers who haven't found a home and were in the second category; perhaps now they are ready to try another team—me as their agent! The system I follow is that every one of these potential leads has a file with an alert to follow up periodically. Every day I am in the office, I contact five of these prospects with the idea to move the ball down the course.

By going after the other two-thirds, agents can increase their lead-conversion ratios above typical numbers. Just remember, the guaranteed outcome of not trying is certain—zero conversion. Put in the effort and keep your eye on the ball for a successful outcome of customers converted to clients.

Keep your eye on lead-generation activities to
convert customers to clients.

"FIRST-MOVER ADVANTAGE"

The "first-mover advantage" is most commonly referred to in the technology industry. It is the concept of being first to enter the market. Technology is such a fast-pace environment that there is often much to be gained to be the first one in. This isn't always the case, as there are situations in which lessons can be learned from watching those who have gone before and making adjustments accordingly. Not surprisingly, this is known as the "second-mover advantage" scenario.

In buying a home, many purchasers wonder whether they should be the first ones to make an offer on a property. This most often occurs in situations in which there may be multiples offers submitted. The concern is that the listing agent, by request from the seller, will "shop" the offer, increasing the likelihood of even more competition and perhaps a bidding war. This is possible and very likely, as the listing agent is required per the listing agreement with the seller to represent that party's best interests. And it is in the seller's best interest to have multiple options of buyers.

The idea of "waiting" for other buyers to become interested in a home is counterintuitive. Why not be first? Sometimes other buyers decide not to compete and being first could mean that it will discourage others from writing an offer. Also, there is a "halo effect" around the first offer. Sellers and agents generally give it greater consideration by being first.

Another scenario is in regard to the timing of listing a home for sale. Often sellers know that others in their neighborhood or community are planning on going on the market too. Being first can reward the seller by not having as much competition. It can set the stage before the market gets flooded with inventory. In this way, the "first-mover advantage" is a marketing strategy.

Utilize the "first-mover advantage" strategy to benefit your client, whether buying or selling!

MARGIN APPLICATIONS

The margins on a page provide for white space around the edge. Think what it would be like if the text were to cover the entire page. That would make it very difficult to read. It is the white spaces that provide the necessary break for the eyes to absorb the content. Further, there are minimal professional standards for margin width. By following protocol and providing the appropriate amount of white space for the visual dimensions of the page, it implies a level of trust to the reader.

The concept of "margin" in one's time applies to the business and life of a real estate professional. Scheduling each day to the outer edges often leads a person to the brink of burnout. Provide for a pleasing level of "margin" during the day to allow for time to deal with emergencies and unplanned events, as well as time and energy to absorb the content.

Personally, I operate at my best when I schedule no more than four appointments, events, or meetings per day. In this way, there is ample time in between for an appropriate beginning and conclusion without running over the edge. Any more than that and I can feel my tension levels increasing. This has become my professional standard in order to continue to be pleasing to those who work and live with me!

Another context in which margins are utilized is investing. An investor "buys on margin" when borrowing money in order to purchase. The business owner should be mindful of the true costs of borrowing. Gary Keller, co-author of *The Millionaire Real Estate Agent*, stresses that money spent should return, at a minimum, the invested amount. If not, it is actually an expense.

Time, money, and investments should all be held accountable for an appropriate return. As with equity investing, at some point there may be a "call" and you will have to "pay up." The professional agent sustains success by being aware of the true costs of margins professionally and personally.

---

*Take care to apply sufficient margins in your schedule,
finances, business, and life.*

PARADOX OF CHOICE

Buyers face the challenge of purchasing the best house they can afford that meets their needs and wants in terms of location, size, and a whole host of other parameters that are important to their unique situation. The first consideration is almost always financial. Practically everyone is on some kind of a budget. Those with unlimited resources are a scarce few—and even they care about buying the most house for the money. The next determining factor is location, which is driven by work commute time and often school choice. As location is the one aspect of real estate that uniquely cannot be changed, this is logical. Once a buyer narrows down neighborhoods, the next objective is to discover what housing options are available. This is when the professional agent is instrumental in providing guidance.

A key aspect for a buyer to remember in the search process is that architectural styles, floor plans, and finishes all change with the times. Consider a few fundamentals in order to buy well. It is best to not buy the most expensive house on the street or in the neighborhood. The reason is that neighborhoods have "ceilings," a maximum value that is difficult to break. Significant price appreciation over peak levels typically only occurs in very robust seller's markets with high demand. Thus, if one owns the most expensive house, there is very little room for appreciation and upside potential.

Next, the buyer should be mindful of any fatal market flaws. Both being on or backing to a busy street can be serious issues for the resale of a home. If the road has speed bumps or other traffic-calming device, those are signs that it will likely be difficult to sell. Other issues that cannot be changed by the buyer yet impacts value of residential real estate are power lines and locations adjacent to high-density areas, such as retail shopping and commercial buildings.

The other factor buyers should consider prior to a home purchase has to do with functional obsolescence. This is a principle appraisers apply and means anything that reduces the usefulness or desirability due to outdated design features. It primarily applies to items that cannot be easily changed. For example, many homes in the 1940s were built with only one full bathroom on the bedroom level. In recent decades, that is considered a functional obsolescence. The question arises: "How easily and at what expense would it be to add an additional bathroom so that it keeps current with market trends and living standards?" The answer determines if it would be a good decision to buy the home and improve the value or not.

On rare occasions, functional obsolescence also applies to the other end of the spectrum. This is the house that is too good or "super adequacy." In these situations, the home has been over-improved for the market. It can become difficult to sell because it is too unique. There just aren't enough buyers willing to pay what the home costs with the improvements.

Apply the "paradox of choice" tool in order to advise clients to buy well.

NATURE VERSUS NURTURE

The nature-versus-nurture discussion focuses on the age-old question: how are human personality and traits determined? Is there inbred in DNA the predisposition to certain attributes that lead to the behaviors that shape one's life? On the other side is the concept that attributes are encouraged and thus can be shaped and molded with time and influence by others and the environment.

The same debate occurs with buyers and sellers of real estate, whether are not they are conscious of the fact. The wise real estate agent recognizes the possibility and distinctions.

When nature drives buyers to purchase a home, there is something inside them or their family dynamics that causes the urgency to buy. Examples that come to mind are when a couple is expecting a child; there is an internal drive to "nest" and prepare a home to welcome the new one. In the case of sellers, when a couple is going through a divorce or there has been a death of a family member, internal urgencies cause people to move the process of selling a home along.

In terms of nurture, external situations can create urgency. One is interest rates and how that affects buyer purchasing power. That factor impacts sellers as well, because if the buyer cannot afford or qualify for a mortgage, it limits what one can pay for a home.

For both buyers and sellers, supply-and-demand dynamics influence external urgency. Buyers experience more urgency when there is less available to buy. Sellers experience more urgency when homes in their area are selling for top prices for the market conditions. Other external factors that can affect both buyers and sellers that are out of their control include: broad-based economic policy, the stock market, and the availability or lack of strong employment options.

Real estate agents can increase external urgency by being proactive in locating a home that meets the buyers' needs and desires. Perhaps the buyers indicate they would move if the "perfect house came along." That is a case in which the agent can externally drive motivation. Help that buyer "fall in love" by making the match.

In the case of sellers, agents can use effective marketing and feedback to nurture the sale. Proactive education on market conditions helps sellers correctly position the home, increasing the likelihood of them becoming "real sellers." Agents who recognize the nature-versus-nurture scenarios achieve greater success with their clients and business.

Use the nature-versus-nurture concepts to assist buyer and seller clients to make real estate decisions.

"WITH A LITTLE HELP FROM MY FRIENDS!"

The words of the Beatles hit are a key to my success. Truly no one succeeds alone. Even if they did, it would be quite lonely. In the words of the song, friends act as accountability partners, telling you if you are singing out of tune, as well as encouragers when you need a little help, or are sad and worried.

Most who choose to become real estate agents are independent, free-spirited types. Like many entrepreneurs, they repeatedly fall victim to the "superhero syndrome" and attempt to do everything on their own. To ask for and receive help can often be difficult.

On a recent family trip, our son decided to purchase a new laptop. At first he was all pumped up about his new technology. It quickly spiraled into frustration about the time it took to get it set up. Then he hit a wall; even after hours on the phone with tech assistance it just wouldn't connect to the Internet. His father and I made suggestions that were not embraced, so we decided to give him some space. Finally, at dinner his sister offered her assistance. As I had the same type of computer that we knew worked, she suggested using it as a guide to verify that his was set up correctly. He released his need to fix it himself and quickly the situation was solved.

Note that he had to accept the help when it was offered. This meant he had to let go of his need to control the situation. This scenario plays out frequently in business. New agents arrive with creative ideas on how they will make their mark in the industry and some do succeed, but most don't. There are others who have gone before who can offer vision and wise counsel on how to get into productivity quickly and sustain achievement. Yet, all that help is for naught if the person doesn't accept it and make it their own.

Agents who have been in the business for some time can benefit from outside counsel too. Over the years I have had a number of productivity and business coaches. The one thing that has become apparent is that there is little benefit in me paying for and participating in coaching if I'm not going to listen to their counsel. To continue to do the same things in the same way only results in the same outcomes as before. To break through to the next level of achievement requires thinking and doing activities differently and to have the vision to see what needs to occur. There is the added challenge of discernment, as there are a lot of voices offering counsel. "Success begets success" is the best determining factor over the long run and how I decide who to pay attention to.

Also, think of the people who are your friends in the industry. Allow them to be there as encouragers and also accountability partners to help you take your business to the next level.

Ask for and receive help from friends, coaches,
and others who can lead you to success.

BITE-SIZE CHUNKS

The process of buying and selling a home is often overwhelming for clients. As most people move on average once every five to seven years, it is difficult at best to keep up with all of the industry changes. Many are on information overload, receiving advice from others as well as what is available on the Internet and in the media.

One of the professional real estate agent's primary roles is to guide the client through the process, particularly the logistical details of contract to settlement. The agent should follow a checklist of all the key aspects to the transaction. In order to minimize overload on the client, it can be helpful to deliver information in bite-size chunks.

Early on in the process, provide an overview of what the client can expect to happen in order to meet deadlines and consummate the transaction per the contract terms. The classic book by Heidi Murkoff, *What to Expect When You Are Expecting*, is a good guideline for how to do this. To correlate to real estate, a suitable name is: "what to expect when you are buying or selling a home."

Start with providing an outline of critical dates and deadlines. Bite-size nuggets are easier to consume and focus on. Group items according to category—for example, all inspection contingencies, or all financing-related requirements. People process information chunked together more efficiently. Think of the ten-digit phone number as being broken down into three-three-four.

Next, follow through with a more detailed explanation on an as-needed basis. Maintain the ebb and flow of the transaction in this way. In many situations, a certain outcome can generate several possible scenarios. For example, if the property is on septic and it passes inspection, then it is time to pass "Go" and move on to the next item on the list. If the inspection identifies issues, then the agent takes the client through the options at that juncture.

Another strategy to keep everyone on track and informed is to have periodic check-in points at key junctures. Once all the inspections have been completed is a good time to review what remains in the process.

These techniques, as well as others, keep clients engaged in the process while not overwhelming them with "too much information." Just remember, bite-size chunks are easier to consume.

Implement bite-size chunking to navigate the process with your clients.

NATIONAL MEDIA VERSUS LOCAL REAL ESTATE MARKET

The national news headlines are sure to grab the attention of anyone considering buying or selling a home. Most news media regularly provide information on the state of the real estate market. The reason is that the real estate market has a huge impact on the economy. Not only is the residential home in almost all cases the most expensive asset people own, the purchase and sale of a home translates into other considerable purchasing opportunities. There is a saying among economists: "As goes real estate, so goes the economy."

Some reports come out monthly, such as the S&P/Case-Shiller home price index, which covers twenty major US markets. Others are produced quarterly or annually. What appears to be good news for buyers could be perceived as bad news for sellers of real estate, and vice versa. These statistics do not take into consideration that all real estate is local. Otherwise, why would "location, location, location" be the mantra most often repeated when people discuss real estate values?

There is often "fine print" in the articles, as well. It is critical to notice what the statistics are actually based on. Is it year over year or month over month? The distinction makes a world of difference. One key aspect I observe is trends and which direction the market is headed.

The informed professional has a battery of media sources to stay abreast on the industry: *The Wall Street Journal, Inman News*, local and national Realtor® association feeds, and magazine and local publications.

Potential purchasers and sellers read media headlines in an effort to get their own interpretations of the local market conditions and how the market will affect their situations. It is critical to success that the professional agent stay attuned to the media. Serve as the expert of choice for clients by translating the headlines and make recommendations based on the local conditions.

Stay knowledgeable with media reports to understand local market conditions and share relevant information with buyer and seller clients.

"BAD HAIR DAY"

To have a "bad hair day" means that every once in a while nothing seems to go right. Just let it go. In 2015, Disney released a movie about prom night—and all of the pressure placed on having a magical experience can make it overwhelming. The lesson the main character came away with is that being perfect is overrated, and for everyone to just enjoy the night and have fun.

The process of buying and selling a home can be very overwhelming for the parties involved. There are a lot of moving parts, and a great deal of money is often at stake. Further, emotions at times run high because people are experiencing other changes in their lives as well as the move.

In order to not let the negative energy impact me and my business, I have found it helpful to step back and consider that perhaps when someone does not behave well, they might be having a "bad hair day." This is an opportunity to consider that if that person were not under all the stress of the situation and change, her behavior and response would be different. On our team, we use the phrase that someone is having a "bad hair day" as a way to relieve the stress of the situation.

Adopt positive affirmations to replace potentially negative situations. Remember the words of Eleanor Roosevelt: "No one can make you feel inferior without your consent." When you wait for someone else to do something or allow his emotions to influence you, in effect you have given him the power. Instead, get into action and take control. The brain can and should immediately see opportunity and abundance.

When things are going well and there is a great deal of business in the pipeline, it is easier to shake off people who are having a "bad hair day." When each deal is a struggle and the agent needs the commission income to cover expenses, then it is more difficult to let it go. The solution is to generate leads and get into a productive mode. When the agent has an overflow of business, she is no longer tied to each individual deal and often in a better position to ride out bumps and setbacks.

The word "emotion" is comprised of 80 percent "motion." Thus get into motion—it truly is the best way to overcome anything that stops an agent from being motivated and successful.

Deal with people who are having a "bad hair day" by letting it go and focus on doing successful activities.

"HOME IS WHERE I WANT TO BE"

The line, "Home is where I want to be," from the song "This Must Be the Place," by the Talking Heads, expresses the sentiment of many people. There is a basic human need for shelter, which can be met by a house. What makes a house a home are themes throughout history in literature, movies, and music such as this one.

The house is the bricks and mortar, the actual physical structure. A home is where life is lived and memories are created. How can you tell the difference when working with buyers? The clues are in the words of the song: "It is where the person wants to be."

One significant buying signal is how long the parties stay in the home, either during an open house or a showing with the agent. If buyers are "in and out," that is an obvious signal that it isn't the place for them. Returning for a second time and wanting to show family and friends are good indicators of interest. Another sign to look for is "eyes that light up." There is a sparkle in the eyes of someone in love and that applies equally to falling in love with a home.

On the selling side, the paradigm shift on when the home has become a house is often when the owner has already moved. It can occur also once the sellers know where they are going, in particular if they have bought another home or put one under contract. That is often when the focus is more on the future and the new home than on the past and the house they had lived in. In real estate jargon, they have become "real sellers"; until then, they are just "listers."

The American Thanksgiving holiday is one in which many people are drawn to be home with family and friends. It is a good reminder to start with heart and connect there first.

Start with heart to help clients make the move that is right for them—from house to home.

EXECUTIVE FUNCTIONS

The executive functioning part of the brain is the area that performs the manager role. It includes problem solving, planning and execution, working memory, reasoning, and the ability to switch tasks. As with any attribute, people are born with different levels of strengths and weaknesses in executive functioning. In the sales profession, the ability to influence others is often considered one of the primary characteristics of success. The skill to consult to sell is absolutely a key aspect to the profession.

Once a transaction is under contract, though, there are still numerous details to get it to settlement. There is nothing more frustrating and exhausting than selling the same home over and over again because a contract voids. This is when the skills of executive functioning are valuable.

In 2008, at her passing, I assumed the legacy of the business began by Sue Huckaby in 1977. As a real estate agent, Sue was well known for her charming southern personality. She could persuade anyone with her lovely accent and personable demeanor. As often happens with highly successful salespeople, keeping track of details was not one of her strengths, and she was famous for lost keys. Her husband, Jerry, came aboard and took over the management functions, which freed Sue to do what she did best, sell houses. Having someone assume the executive functions is when her sales career became a business.

Many other agents have found that matching one's weaknesses with another's strengths to be a strong strategy for success. This can be achieved by hiring staff, partnering with other agents, building a team, or various other combinations. It takes self-awareness to achieve, yet it often makes the difference.

There are two directions with many variations that the agent can employ. One is to have vision and project into the future the business model and then pursue talent and build out the plan. This is how city planners operate. First they determine infrastructure needs into the future, like airports, schools, road systems, and public operations. Then they put into place the timeline and funds to achieve the plan. The other strategy is more reactive. Once roads, schools, and infrastructure are full to capacity and even overflowing, then the planners manage the immediate need and strategize on long-term changes from that vantage point. The agent also can follow this course and after growing to a level she no longer can sustain alone, go out and pursue talent to fill the void. One is proactive, the other reactive.

*Assure talent is operating from their strength abilities
to take the business to the next level.*

WHAT IS AN OBJECTIVE SALES PRICE FOR A HOME?

The seller wants to sell for the highest price possible and not leave any money on the table. The purchaser wants to buy the real estate for the lowest price possible, for certain never more than the current market will bear. The real estate agent is the objective ambassador of the transaction.

There is an adage that states: "A person who represents himself at a trial has a fool for a client." Adages become part of common usage because they contain a ring of truth over time. The primary reason most sellers do not sell their own real estate is because deep down they realize that they cannot be objective. It truly is, in the words of Shakespeare, a case of "love is blind" and thus not rational.

Many times, owners will obtain an appraisal and wonder why the home doesn't sell for that price. The reason is that an appraisal looks back at the market. Past results are really the only indicator that can be used to project future outcomes, yet just as with the stock market, there is no guarantee. The agent instead utilizes a comparative market analysis (CMA), which looks forward to where the market is going. Clearly there are many different factors that determine value and being objective in the market analysis is even more critical.

Ilyce Glink and Samuel J. Tamkin, in the real estate section of the *Washington Post,* discussed this very question: "Why am I not getting the asking price for my home?" The closing remarks best sum up the answer to the question: "You must overcome the feeling that you 'must get a certain price for the home' . . . it isn't what a seller must get but what a buyer wants to pay for a house."

The story of the market is actually being on the market. Thus the answer to what is an objective sales price is: "What is fair market value?" Fair market value is defined as "what a buyer is willing to pay that a seller is willing to accept at any given point in time, given that it is an arms-length transaction and there is no duress."

The additional challenge is that the market is constantly moving. Every day, homes are going to settlement and under contract and coming active on the market for sale. It is a dynamic process. A professional real estate agent in the particular market area is best able to assist sellers and purchasers in understanding current conditions that determine value.

Use market analysis and knowledge to understand the factors that determine value.

LOOKING FOR STUFFING

A couple days before Thanksgiving I was at the local supermarket purchasing groceries for the special meal. The store had been renovated recently, so I was having difficulty finding my way around. On top of that, I only cook stuffing at this one holiday meal, so I was unsure where it was located in the store.

Thankfully, one of the employees saw that I was having trouble and offered to help me locate the item. He could have directed me to the aisle, but instead took the full-service approach and walked with me. Along the way we chatted about the frustration associated with infrequently buying something. Even though I'm sure he was very busy, he made me feel as though I was not a bother at all. In word and deed, he conveyed that it was his pleasure to be of service.

This made me think of our clients when they are buying and selling a home. The national average is that people move once every five to seven years. In that time frame, there are many changes to the process and transaction. Most notable recently are associated with the lending environment and settlement procedures. Legislation is frequently enacted that amends contractual and disclosure aspects to the sale and purchase of real estate. Further, the real estate market is constantly fluctuating, all of which can make the process challenging for clients to navigate alone. These are all important areas where agents can be of service to clients. It is the responsibility of the professional to stay abreast of all these changes and to inform clients as appropriate.

Further, the service-oriented agent is constantly proactive about anything that could potentially impact the client. A home we have on the market for sale for one of out-of-town clients is vacant. The heating system had not been operating properly and extreme cold weather was predicted for the area. So a staff member met the HVAC contractor at the home for the service call.

Just as the grocery employee should know where the stuffing is located, the agent should be informed about the industry. The professional recognizes the client's needs before the client is perhaps even aware of them. This can be accomplished much like the grocery store employee: walk with the client through the process step-by-step. The professional agent sells her service as she exceeds client expectations.

Adopt protocols to deliver top-quality service to
clients today and every day!

THE GOOSE THAT LAYS GOLDEN EGGS IS THE ONE THAT IS VALUABLE

The Aesop Fable is actually titled, *The Goose that Laid the Golden Eggs*, meaning it is past tense. The story is told of a couple that was not happy and satisfied with the daily provision of one golden egg per day produced by the goose. So in order to obtain all the gold, they killed the goose, only to discover that by doing so they also ended the source of their sustenance. The tale is one of greed and impatience. The moral of the story is that the old couple should have nurtured and kept the source of their sustenance alive and well.

This is first a lesson in generating and nurturing leads. In real estate, leads are like the golden eggs. For a successful agent, prospecting is an active process. Until an agent has a lead, truly there is nothing for her to do. Once the lead is obtained, like the goose, it must be nurtured in order to produce a golden egg. Both are required in order to build, grow, and sustain a business.

For many agents, the source of leads is from a rainmaker or team leader, particularly those new to the profession. After some success in nurturing and then converting leads into sales, some agents become dissatisfied, like the old couple. They think that it is the work they performed in nurturing the lead that led to the business. In these situations, seeds of discontent can grow. The rationale is that the agent shouldn't have to give as large of a portion of their commission to the lead generator.

This scenario has played out in teams across the industry. At this juncture, the rainmaker may feel the buyer agent doesn't appreciate the efforts expended to provide leads, and in a way it "kills" the relationship. In some cases, the agent learns how to generate leads and provides her own sources. Still other agents are on the proverbial search of alternative golden-egg-laying geese and move from company to company, thinking that if only they could find another one, this time they would not "kill" off the source.

Another application of the fable is that of treating referrals like the golden-egg opportunity that they are. Agents should take care of and nourish those who refer business. It is a great way to assure a steady source of future leads!

Cultivate and nourish the source of leads to your business!

GPS IS NOT A THINKING PERSON!

Many remember when we navigated the old-fashioned way — with a paper map! When global positioning systems (GPSs) became available as units mounted on the dashboard, it changed the way real estate professionals navigate. GPS has become a critical tool for the practice of selling residential real estate.

A GPS is particularly helpful in those areas where the streets change names or they stop and start in different sections of the community. Arlington, Virginia is one of these communities in which the GPS is extremely helpful. Before having a GPS, often the buyer client would be in the front seat trying to navigate, instructing the driver on where to turn. With a GPS, the buyer can focus on neighborhood features, points of interest, and community amenities.

The listing information often includes directions to the home; however, those are frequently written assuming the driver is starting from a central location. Typically when agents are out showing buyers homes, they probably are not starting at a central location, but rather coming from another home in a residential neighborhood. Sometimes navigating back to the main roads and then figuring out where one is and getting to the next location can be a nightmare! The GPS allows the driver to focus on driving, rather than worrying about getting lost.

However, a GPS is not a thinking person! A GPS device is known to take a driver in what a resident of the area would know is an out-of-the-way direction. Also, even though some GPS systems alert users about traffic and construction sites, often there is such a delayed reaction that the feature isn't very helpful. So it is still imperative that a thinking person be involved in the navigation.

Even with a GPS, it can still be useful to have a map to identify the properties to view and to lay out a plan for the order in which to see the homes. Buyers moving from out of the area often appreciate having the full perspective of the community where they are looking to purchase real estate. Once perspective is obtained, then use a GPS as a tool by plugging in the addresses for the home tour. If the client decides to change the order of homes to view from what had been mapped out, or a seller has requested the arrival time be different than what was originally planned, those changes can easily be made.

Just like any technology, though, remember that GPS is a tool. It still requires a thinking person. This is one reason why I believe technology will not replace the real estate agent as it did the travel agent. Given that it is a complicated and highly valued transaction, most people want the guidance of a trusted professional.

Use technology to your benefit, being mindful that it is still important to have a thinking person involved.

GOT HOLIDAY DECOR?

NOVEMBER
19

For many people, the holiday season begins at Thanksgiving and extends through December until after the first of the year. Many sellers who have their homes on the market wonder if they should decorate for the holidays.

Holiday trimmings can contribute to a home feeling warm and friendly. Further, special decor can show different uses for spaces and features of the home. Lights accent areas that may be "lost" to darkness and cheer up the front of a home in the bleak mid-winter season.

Many top agents concur that the client should proceed with what the family normally does and wants to do. If the homeowner normally strings exterior lights, then by all means use it as an opportunity to showcase the property. If a tree is a centerpiece to the living room, then continue with that tradition.

Stagers frequently urge owners to "depersonalize" the home when it is on the market for sale, and that still is a valid recommendation. However, some personal touches of unique character keep a home from feeling too cold and uninviting.

A strategy employed by many professional agents is to have the home photographed prior to decorations going up. In this way, the presentation of the home is not tied to one particular look and season.

In some situations, putting up holiday decorations is an additional burden to the already overwhelming task of keeping a home in show condition. In that case, sellers are certainly free to opt out for the season. If the timing is such that everyone is busy packing and making plans to move, then including the burden of decorating for a holiday may be just enough to send them over the edge. In those cases, perhaps it is a good idea to take a rest from decorating for this particular holiday season.

Some select a happy medium approach, placing a wreath on the front door and some greenery around the mantle to convey the holiday spirit with minimal effort. The home will exude warmth and an inviting atmosphere. Remember to continue the focus of keeping the home in show condition for buyer visitors and open houses.

Consider the client's situation and market dynamics and advise accordingly regarding holiday décor.

A RED LIGHT IS FOR STOPPING

It seems obvious that the red light is for stopping. If pressed for time, on occasion it might make sense to speed up to power through the traffic light. There are risks associated with that course of action, some of which are immediately apparent—such as if the action causes a crash. At other times, one doesn't know the price for running the red light until the ticket comes in the mail. What seemed like a good idea in the moment becomes clearly evident later that a better decision would have been for the driver to stop.

How does this apply to real estate? It seems simple: when faced with a situation like a market shift, rather than power through, maybe one should just stop and take time to evaluate. Perhaps it is an opportunity to change directions, to turn a corner or make a U-turn. In *The Millionaire Real Estate Agent,* author Gary Keller discusses in agent expense management the useful tool of "red light, green light."

In the market shift that led up to the 2008 financial market crash, many in the real estate industry were faced with this very dilemma. Thousands of clients and potential customers were directly affected. In order to sell, for many homeowners it meant taking a substantial loss. At the same time, the volume of transactions decreased significantly. Essentially that equated to less business available. Business that did exist was difficult to obtain, as well as challenging and time-consuming to get to settlement.

At the time, the primary source of my business was from expending thousands of dollars on glossy print advertising. The only impact it was making on the bottom line was decreasing it. Although the business had been built on the upper-bracket market and glossy advertising, in order to survive I had to change directions.

First I employed the "red light, green light" method and stopped that form of print advertising. If I had "powered through" the light, the company would have experienced negative cash flow. Next I masterminded with other top agents in similar markets across the United States to find out what they were doing. With that input, I navigated the current market conditions by changing directions. This involved more active prospecting, such as contacting my sphere and past clients. It also meant targeting a more salable lower price-point of homes in our community.

Viewed correctly, market shifts can be an opportunity. If an agent has been proceeding in the wrong direction, it is a good idea to stop and gain input to correct the orientation. Seek guidance from those who have navigated that road before. Perhaps you will discover that you were heading in the right direction all along and get back on the road, this time with more confidence.

Evaluate market shifts by first stopping; obtain counsel on course direction before proceeding.

THE OVERSELL DILEMMA

The adage: "under-promise and over-deliver" has as its roots the dilemma of the oversell. By their very nature, salespeople tend to be optimistic, tend toward emphasizing the positives, and open to expansive possibilities. As income is commission-based, it is imperative that the agent "makes the sale" in order to be successful. In order to secure the listing, an agent may be tempted to exaggerate the potential sales price of a property. On the other side, the agent can be too eager in selling the benefits of a home to a buyer.

Early on in my real estate career, my mentor, Sue Huckaby, cautioned me to be careful of over-promising with clients. I can still hear her drawling Southern accent: "Careful, Karen; if it doesn't sell for that, you may make them mad at you." At the time, the market was robust and accelerating at such a rapid manner that it quickly recovered any over-price enthusiasm. As the market began to correct, these words stuck firmly in the back of my mind.

And yet, there have been cases where the market did respond and a home did sell for an amazing price. Experience shows that these occasions are the exception rather than the rule. The market truly is the market study. If agents possessed the ability to manipulate the market to pay higher or lower, as the case may be, then wouldn't they do that? Maybe that was possible pre-Internet. With data so readily available, the market determines what the value of a home will be, not the agent.

How is an agent to win the business and at the same time not oversell on the price? In these situations, I incorporate the "both/and" technique. Tell them the truth about the market. Be honest about recent comparables, what the current experience is, and what could potentially occur in the future. Affirm the positive attributes of the property and how it may be possible to achieve the client's objectives.

One way to accomplish this is to attribute the honest, negative feedback and outcome elsewhere. In conversations, be careful to say that it is the "market" that is behaving irrationally. When sharing feedback with sellers, convey in a manner that reflects what buyers and their agents are saying about the home, not personal sentiments. The relocation company, short sale, or desperate neighbor who sells his home for a low price is the challenge. Demographic shifts, changes in political administration, higher interest rates, or new lending guidelines are the culprit, not me personally. Proactively communicating the factors and concerns in advance can help the client better understand when the market doesn't respond.

Another script relates to the appraisal process. An agent could negotiate an amazing price for the home, yet with the strong lending guidelines the appraiser does not validate the value, the buyer may have difficulty obtaining financing. The point is always that as the agent I believe in the home and the value potentially inherent. That is what I can promise: I will do everything in my power to obtain the highest price the market will bear if representing a seller and the lowest for a buyer.

Use "both/and" scripts so that you "under-promise"
and "over-deliver" with clients.

PAUSE TO EXPRESS THANKS!

Thanksgiving is a special holiday in America, although other countries also have adopted the concept of a day of gratitude. In a desire to live a more purposeful live, I take the time during the week to pause and express thanks! And I encourage you to do the same.

First, I thank all of the clients and customers over the year with whom my business partner, Lizzy Conroy and I, the agents on our team, and staff have been given the privilege and pleasure to work. On an average annual basis, it is usually around one hundred families, and over the years has grown into the thousands. It is because of clients that I have the Keller Williams motto: "A career worth having, a business worth owning, and a life worth living!" Our team believes in long-term relationships, treasures repeat clients, and considers all that we serve to be "customers for life."

There is a scene in the classic movie, *It's a Wonderful Life*, in which the father shares with the son, played by Jimmy Stewart, a profound statement. There is a fundamental human need for shelter and, in their own small way, when they as a business help people satisfy that need it can be very meaningful. That to me is the core reason I give thanks this week—I have been so richly blessed with this opportunity of a profession. It is so noble to help people with one of their most important decisions—thank you.

Thanks also to those I work most closely with on a daily basis. My business partner, Lizzy Conroy, makes every day a pleasure with her smile and positive can-do attitude and spirit. Our support staff keeps the team organized and on track, happy to be of service. The associate agents in the group are always there to hold an open house or to take care of a potential customer or client. The group is a "team" and "together everyone achieves more."

A real estate agent or business would not be successful for long without a strong broker and capable back-office support. The Realtors® community network is a key aspect to successful transactions and includes local cooperative agents, as well as referral agents near and far. Allied resources and vendors provide ancillary services that are paramount to meeting clients' needs during the buying and selling process. All contribute in their way.

As you can see, it is difficult to be inclusive, as there are so many to thank. There are those whom I'm sure have made a contribution to the success of your business and life as well. Take the opportunity to pause at this special time of year and express your thanks.

Pause to express thanks to those in your business and life
who contribute to your success.

HAVE YOU DONE *EVERYTHING* ?

This is a common phrase around our house, as my husband Andy has been in the trade association industry for many years. To represent his constituency, he frequently asks staff and colleagues: "Have we done everything to promote the product and industry? Have we done everything we can to stop the disparagement of the product and industry?" In the real estate industry, there are numerous applications as well.

On the promotion side of the equation, the agent is being proactive on behalf of the client. Questions to ask include: "Have you done everything you can to find a house for buyer clients? Have you as the agent done everything to promote the listing that you are charged with selling? Have you done everything to get the parties to come to an agreement in a negotiation? Have you done everything to educate and inform both buyers and sellers of the market conditions?"

By way of example, I was representing a seller client of an upper-bracket home. Unbeknownst to me, the buyers wrote a letter to the seller personally outlining in great detail why they would pay only a certain amount for the property. The seller was quite offended and proclaimed that he would never sell the home to those people or for that amount. As time went on, those buyers remained interested, but he stood steadfast in his conviction. Soon we approached a time crunch for both parties. In order for the buyers' children to enroll in the local schools, settlement had to occur in thirty days. I went back to the owner and explained that this would be his last opportunity to sell and move within a thirty-day timeframe. No other buyers had come forward, so no matter what his feelings were about these particular people, this was his best option. He agreed and later expressed his thanks for me being up-front and doing everything I could to get his home sold.

From the stop disparagement perspective, the situation is more of a defense posture. The questions to ask include: "Have you done everything to prevent the client from harm? Have you done everything to provide wise counsel and counseled with expert advisors as necessary should a problematic situation arise during a transaction? Have you yourself as an agent sought wise counsel and advisors, including the broker of record when the occasion calls for it? Have you kept track of all contingencies and stayed current of deadlines and contractual obligations?"

Often agents find there is "one more thing" they could do to benefit the client or make certain a client does not get into a precarious situation. This is the reminder! Ask yourself the relevant questions and take the necessary action.

Affirm daily that you have done everything you can to benefit and protect your client to achieve a successful transaction.

KEEP YOUR KOOL

To be KOOL is to be a "Keen Observer of Life" according to one of the top Keller Williams trainers, Dick Dillingham. Some might call it intuition. Malcolm Gladwell refers to it in his book, *Blink*, as those people who know in an instant what is really going on. Following are a few ways in which I applied the ability to be "KOOL."

In order to best understand buyers' unique needs and wants, I discover the most by showing them homes. Rather than acting as a "tour guide," I watch and listen. This means I do not point out the kitchen and other obvious features. There are signals all around when KOOL radar is up.

An example early in my career was a young couple interested in buying a town home. We had been through about one dozen and there was no interest; the experience was just dead flat, no emotion. All of the homes were "okay," but neither of them could really articulate why they didn't like any of them. Until we were in a town home with a walk-out basement—the husband practically lit up. Thank goodness I was paying attention and didn't miss it. I probed deeper as to what about the walk-out basement he liked. He shared the story of Sunday afternoons at his uncle's home watching football in a basement like that. At half-time the kids would go out back with the adults and throw a ball around. He still had many happy memories associated with that experience. Needless to say, the couple purchased a home with a walk-out basement soon after.

In many social settings, real estate is a conversation of personal interest because almost everyone wants to know more about the market. A KOOL agent pays attention to responses and questions because often there can exist a lead-generation opportunity. One such occasion was at a business dinner with my husband. The gentleman seated next to me asked about how Zillow worked, and my opinion and experience on its validity. It turned out the couple was considering downsizing when their youngest left for college, so I was able to turn that conversation into a future listing appointment.

Being a "Keen Observer of Life" is a key to success.

Keep your KOOL by becoming a Keen Observer of Life!

"YOU GET WHAT YOU PAY FOR"

This common phrase is actually part of a quote by Kurt Vonnegut from his novel, *Cat's Cradle*. The entire quote is: "In this world, you get what you pay for." And so it is in the real estate world. In most cases, buyers and sellers "get what they pay for."

Many times buyers will tell me that they only want to buy a home if it is a deal or a steal. It seems that unless the home is so undervalued in terms of price, they don't want to consider it. This strategy can make sense if the purchase of the property is for investment purposes. Then price and other financial considerations would have significant weight. However, if one is purchasing a home to live in, then "stealing a home" may not be the best strategy. A better approach is for buyers to pursue homes that have strong value relative to the market. The reasons follow.

First, a home is shelter, a place to live. A home is where the buyer, family, and friends will spend the majority of their time. A home is not an investment vehicle. It can be, yet it is not the primary purpose. Stocks, bonds, and certificates of deposit are investment vehicles and not considering the return on investment would be illogical. Purchasers should buy a home because that is where they want to live. To consider a home based only on if one can get a deal or a steal seems illogical in light of the core purpose. Do you want to live in a "steal" or a home?

Second, if a home can be bought for a "steal," then that probably means other potential buyers have rejected it as a place they want to live in. If others in the marketplace don't want to live in the home except for at a very low price, then there could very well be fundamental flaws in the property or location. Those very attributes are likely to hold the value back in the future, as well. So one literally gets what one pays for: something of low value.

A car that is cheaply priced often turns out to be a lemon. The expenses associated with owning a "lemon" often begin to outweigh any savings at the outset of the purchase. A home that is cheaply priced often has issues as well. The old axiom, "Something that is too good to be true probably is" became a well-known saying because there are kernel of truths embedded.

Professional real estate agents concur that purchasers should not overpay relative to the market conditions. There is a certain goodwill that occurs when a sale is a win-win for all parties. A win-win scenario takes place when the purchaser buys at a fair market price and the seller receives a fair market price. A steal isn't necessarily the best deal.

Use scripts and dialogues with clients to influence
them to make good buying decisions.

TO BE FIRST OR LAST

There is a strategy associated being first. In graduate school, whenever given the opportunity I frequently chose to be first up to present. In that way I would set the standard and the stage for all future presentations. Everyone was in essence compared to those who had gone before. The material was fresh in my mind, and I was less likely to get a case of the jitters. Also, it meant I stuck with the script and plan for the presentation rather than take a chance on other presentations influencing me.

There are those who prefer to be last. The reasoning, I've been told, is that they gain knowledge and learn from others about what works and what they could improve. Also, it often gives them more time to prepare. People remember best their most recent experience, so logic follows that the last presentation would be the most memorable.

In many cases, prospective sellers will interview more than one real estate agent, the most common number being three. It can be helpful to know where one is in the "lineup" and respond accordingly. On occasions when I haven't been first, I have had sellers call and cancel the appointment because they hired one of the agents who presented prior to my scheduled time. This gives further credence to choosing to go first if given the option. However, being the last one can also be an advantage, because by that time the sellers have seen all the other presentations. Often at that juncture they are ready to make a decision on the spot and don't take the time to circle back to those who presented earlier.

The other scenario that may come into play is when a purchaser writes an offer on a property. Many share that they don't want to be the first offer in because of concern that the listing agent may use their contract to "shop" around and try to obtain better offers. This can be the case and actually illustrates that the listing agent is doing her job. I urge purchasers to not let this dissuade them from making an offer if the home is their top choice. Why would they want to wait until other people have written an offer and then be in a competitive situation? In situations of multiple offers, being first in can have a positive effect on the seller if the selling agent presents it as such. The reason is that the seller may remember the first purchaser more fondly; it has a halo effect. Subsequent offers will never be "first," just like there is always only one firstborn child.

The opportunity to be first presents itself in the broader application to one's life, as well. Be first in line to achieve your dreams and vision!

Strategize on when best to present in business opportunities and life.

"NO FAULT DIVORCE" REAL ESTATE SCENARIOS

The principle behind "no fault divorce" is that the parties seek dissolution of the marriage and there was no misconduct by either partner. The couple is no longer compatible. In some ways, the commitment of a listing agreement between a seller, buyer, and the broker can be likened to a short-term marriage. And the concept of "no fault divorce" can occur in real estate scenarios as well.

On some occasions, actual misconduct occurs on the part of the agent or broker. All jurisdictions in the United States have recourse options available to people who have been wronged by the actions of a real estate agent or broker.

There are circumstances when the seller just isn't happy with the manner in which the agent provides service. It may turn out that it is not a good fit and the client doesn't realize it until they work together for some time. Or the buyers discover the agent isn't familiar with the area where they want to purchase and want to find an agent who has more experience in the community. Promises could have been made that weren't kept. Expectations could have been implied that didn't come to fruition.

These are possible situations in which sellers or buyers may want to seek a "no fault divorce" with their agent and broker. Just as with a marital divorce, even if there is no contest, there may still be costs associated with the act. And that can be the case as well in the dissolution of an agency agreement with a real estate broker. Be certain to "read the fine print" in the agreement to determine any specific obligations in the case of separation. These may include reimbursable expenses or compensation allocated for time and effort.

In my real estate business practice, I want to work with people who want to work with me and I want to work with them. My husband has a saying: "Love isn't love if it isn't set free." This is the essence of the relationship I strive to maintain with clients. Even though as the agent I may possess the contractual right to charge a termination fee, I have found that it does not benefit to do so over the long term. The bad will that often develops over those fees significantly overrides any good will created with marketing and advertising.

There is the rare occasion when the agent or broker seeks to terminate a relationship with a client. In those situations, agents may decide to declare that they cannot meet the needs of the client and request to be released from the agency agreement. The agent who mindfully handles challenging client relationships possesses a key to sustained success in the real estate arena.

---

*Apply the principles of "no fault divorce"
to navigate difficult client relations.*

FEEDBACK SANDWICH

One of the key functions of a listing estate agent is to obtain feedback from selling agents and buyers on their impressions of the home. Feedback comes from public open house visitors, as well. Although important, the most valuable feedback is that which comes from real buyers in the market who are ready, willing, and able to make a purchasing decision. This feedback typically comes via their real estate agent. And it is a key component for helping sellers to "listen to the market."

Some listing agents use automatic feedback systems. Other agents rely on staff to follow up with agents. I have found that I glean the most information by having one-on-one conversations with the buyer's agents. In that visit, I ask if there is any interest and what thoughts the buyer has to share that would be helpful for the seller to know. Dr. Stephen Covey's habit "Seek first to understand" is good counsel to follow before selling the benefits of the home.

Often questions and even objections turn out to be buying signals. The conversation allows me to address relevant concerns. Further, I can apprise the agent on any other interest, anticipated offers, or contracts that have been received and didn't come to an agreement. If there truly is no interest in the home, then I probe about what other homes the buyers saw so that I can understand the competition. Additionally helpful to know is if the buyer has written an offer or is planning on doing so for another home. This information helps me to better explain the market conditions to the seller.

When presenting the feedback to the seller, I share it in a "sandwich" format. First, I find something positive to say about the home. This opens up the seller to then hear the constructive part of the feedback. Next, I offer the meat of what the market is saying—what the seller really needs to hear and yet may be difficult to share. To close the sandwich, I inform the seller about how questions and objections were handled in order to promote the best attributes of the home and property. The reason for the sandwich approach is that sellers need to hear that the agent believes in their home, and that the agent is doing everything she can to sell the positives, not just focusing on the negatives of what the market may be saying.

From there, I move into feed forward, which are recommendations on what the seller could and should do in order to be responsive to the market information provided via the feedback. When buyers continuously focus on the obvious, that means they are "stuck" on the things that cannot be changed. For example, many older homes have low ceilings. If that keeps coming up in the feedback, then what the buyers are really saying is that they want a newer home for that price. For a lower price, they might be willing to accept lower ceilings. If there are things the seller can address and change, such as a new roof, then that of course is an option. In most cases, though, the best action the seller can take to find the market is to adjust the list price.

Apply the feedback sandwich and feed forward techniques in working with seller clients to understand the market's response to their home.

IN THE DARK AND HEARING THE SOUND OF CRICKETS

There are times in a real estate agent's career when it seems that everything has gone dark and that all one hears are crickets. People say that "no news is good news." Yet that isn't always the case. When the phone doesn't ring, that can be a bad scenario for a real estate agent's business.

Many agents base the interest level in a home on the number of showings in a certain time frame. There are rules of thumb experienced agents employ that depend on the price range and the market. Some agents advocate that six showings in six days or one dozen showings within one month are indicators the home is priced at market. For the upper brackets, the entire market may be six buyers, and that may take six months to occur. What is clear is when there are no showings; the silence can be deafening to the sellers and their listing agent. The market is the market study. Little or no interest sends the message that the home is not priced correctly for the current market.

Another situation of "hearing crickets" can occur when clients don't like the news being delivered by the agent. The news may be a low-ball offer or it may be that the agent recommends a price adjustment. It may be buyer and agent honest feedback that is just too hard for the seller to accept.

Buyers also can "go dark." This may occur if the agent hasn't been able to find a home that meets their needs. Some go offline to evaluate their plans for going forward. On occasion, that includes hiring a different agent to represent them in their purchase.

The darkest time of many agents was during the years of the Great Recession. The real estate market crashed along with the financial markets. It then went through a significant correction and extensive recovery. Many agents left the business, unable to manage the shifting market. There were many dark days during that time period.

Fortunately, the darkness is usually short-lived. Thankfully, day always follows night. But the darkest night can be challenging. This is when a professional agent gets out her flashlight and shines some light on the situation and the client. If the market or the client is in a dark place, it is the professional who doesn't take it personally. Rather she takes action to proactively move the situation forward into the light.

Shine light into the dark situations with clients and your business.

FOLLOW THE DIRECTIONS

Our family has a recipe for scratch pudding that is affectionately known as "Mimmie's Stuff." It has been handed down through the generations. At some point in my adult life, I realized that I had to learn how to make the fluffy concoction myself. Even though I watched as my mother and grandmother made it through the years, it wasn't until I did it by myself the first few times that I came to realize the complexity of the recipe.

The individual steps by themselves seem simple enough; however, it is imperative that each one be followed to the letter and in the order provided. A chemist or experienced chef could explain why one has to first beat the cold whip cream and then wash all of the equipment prior to beating the egg whites; and yet that must be done or it will not come out smooth and fluffy. What I learned is that to be successful one must follow the directions as written. This is not a time to be creative. There are several real estate applications that come to mind.

One is in the use of standardized contract forms, which the agent completes as allowed by jurisdictional law and practice.[1] In these situations, the agent should first read the contract, just like reading the directions. This may need to be done several times for comprehension. Before I begin the process of making the pudding, I read the instructions and make certain I have everything I need. Then I set myself up for success by preparing all the equipment and ingredients. The correlation is to follow the same process in managing the real estate transaction from contract to settlement.

Our family tradition holds that Mimmie's Stuff is a special treat enjoyed only once or twice a year. This keeps it special, but presents a challenge as one gains skill from frequent practice and application. This can occur in real estate transactions, as well. Some situations present themselves so infrequently that it is difficult at best to build up a knowledge base, skill level, and best practices on how to handle them. This is when it may be advisable to seek expert counsel. The first few times I set out to make Mimmie's Stuff, it meant phone calls to my advanced counsel—my mother. Resources an agent can reach out to include the broker, agents with more experience in the company and association, settlement attorneys, and legal counsel.

A key strategy for success in cooking, as well as real estate sales, is to follow the terms and requirements as set forth in the directions and contract.

*Apply the principle of following directions for success
in your real estate business and life!*

This is not designed to be legal advice or counsel; please seek that for yourself and client as appropriate.[1]

"JUST DO IT"

Twice my husband and I have had the privilege to visit the Mayan ruins at Chichen Itza, a UNESCO World Heritage site in Mexico. Our first visit was in the 1990s when people were still allowed to climb the Mesoamerican step-pyramid known as El Castillo. It didn't occur to me that at some point climbing the pyramid would not be an option. But a couple decades later, on our second visit, it was no longer allowed.

Like many people, I have a fear of heights. Deciding on whether to climb to the top of the pyramid presented a challenge: could I overcome my fear enough to take advantage of the opportunity? Doing so turned out to be an exhilarating once-in-a-lifetime feeling of achievement. The climb up actually wasn't as bad as I had imagined; it was the descent that proved more difficult. In retrospect, I came away with a few lessons: the experience was not as hard as I had anticipated; what I had perceived to be difficult in advance turned out not to be the challenging aspect; and the sense of accomplishment was significantly satisfying. In effect, in my mind I made it worse than it was while simultaneously diminishing the gratifying aspects. Truly, if you argue for your limitations and think you cannot do something, that is exactly what you will get.

Chichen Itza is the site where one of the most memorable Nike "Just Do It" commercials was filmed. And why the famed ad slogan resonates true for me and countless others. If I hadn't climbed the pyramid two decades ago, the opportunity would have been lost. And because I did, the experience is now stored as a great memory to draw on when future challenges present themselves.

When it comes to lead generation, the best strategy to overcome negative inertia and procrastination is to "Just Do It." Take the first step and keep in mind that once you "Just Do It," then at least you have that accomplishment to celebrate. Rarely is it as bad as imagined. Doing nothing doesn't lead to anything. Activity always generates some result.

Real estate applications have to do with situations that are challenging to deal with. Perhaps the appraisal comes in lower than the contract price, the buyer elects to void the contract, structural damage was found at the termite inspection, and so on. Clients are served best when an agent professionally faces these challenges head on with a "can do it" attitude.

The video clip of insurance executive and top salesperson Art Williams' famous speech, "Just Do It" is fantastic inspiration for anyone who needs encouragement. Successful agents "Just Do It" in business and life.

Apply the "Just Do It" motto today!

FIRST, SPEND NO MONEY

This principle is taken from the Hippocratic Oath in medicine: "First, do no harm." The application, "First, spend no money" applies to writing an offer on behalf of buyer clients. The objective is to first pursue any outcome that is at no or low cost for the client. In a competitive situation, it makes the offer stand out among the others. Even if the offer is not in competition, anything that benefits the buyer's position without spending money is a good thing.

It is of utmost importance that the buyer be preapproved or qualified by a preferred local lender, preferably with whom you have a relationship. It is even better if the lender will contact the listing agent directly to affirm the qualifications of the client. If the purchaser already has a lender relationship, then introduce yourself to him. Offer your assistance to expedite the lending process. Should it be a cash transaction, obtain verifiable documentation.

Take the time to get to know the listing agent. She has a direct relationship with the seller and will honestly be the one "selling" your client's offer. Make the effort to meet her, either at a public or broker's open house. Even in this day of e-mail, recently I had a buyer's agent personally appear at my office to deliver his client's offer and to sell the terms of the offer. That made a favorable impression and led to an agreement between the parties. Romance the agent! At the very least, be polite and professional—good manners go a long way. Provide a thorough outline when submitting the offer to the listing agent and explain the reasons for any special terms. This makes it easy for him to present it to his client.

Take the steps to remove contingencies as rapidly as possible. Have a home inspector pencil in the inspection to show good faith that the buyer intends to remove contingencies in a timely fashion. In hot markets, agents have been known to have the buyer conduct pre-inspections prior to submitting the offer. Keep in close communication so that if there are any issues or hiccups, the agent is not taken by surprise or caught off guard.

Have the buyers write the seller a heart-felt letter and include photos. Unless the seller is an investor, he probably cares about the people who will be buying their home. The agent should be mindful not to violate any fair housing laws and to advise her client accordingly. Negotiate with trusted vendors for quality service such as inspectors, contractors, title insurance, settlement companies, and attorneys.

Give the sellers the "easy" terms, which often include the settlement date that works best for them, earnest money in line with market parameters, and minimum contingencies that the purchaser really needs. Time may mean money for the seller, so consider agreeing to a post-settlement occupancy or rent-back. The objective is to give the seller as many things as the purchaser can that don't actually cost money. Then the purchaser can focus on obtaining the best home in the market for her needs.

Follow the "first spend no money" principle with buyer clients in writing offers to present and obtain the best terms the market will bear.

YOU KNOW HOW TO TAKE A LEAD

In a famous *Seinfeld* episode, Jerry is frustrated that a car rental company took a reservation for a car, yet didn't actually hold a car for him to pick up. This hilarious skit reminds me of what happens with agents who take a lead, yet don't convert the lead. In Seinfeld's words: "You see, you know how to 'take' a reservation, you just don't know how to 'hold' a reservation. And that's really the most important part of the reservation, the holding. Anybody can just take them."

It takes a system along with knowledge, skills, and ability to hold the lead and convert it to a sale. It is proven that what one tracks gets done, so first start with a system. My business partner, Lizzy Conroy, uses a simple spreadsheet. On it she has the contact's name, housing need, level of urgency, and the approximate dollar volume she expects to earn off of the lead. Her objective is first to take the lead and then to hold onto it until it actually is converted into a sale. No one has to follow up with Lizzy to be sure she is working her leads, although we do meet on a regular basis to coach on conversion strategies. She recognizes that each lead can be vital to her success as an agent.

Sometimes the leads are a fire hose and sometimes they are a drip. An agent starts with what he has at hand. In the words of businessman and motivational speaker Nido Qubein: "Your present circumstances don't determine where you go; they merely determine where you are." One of the lessons I have learned with experience is that, in looking back, I can see what happens in variable market conditions. Houses sell in all types of markets. The times when it is good for sellers often means that buyers don't achieve everything they want. When the market is good for buyers, then sellers typically do not get top dollar. The point is that there are transactions in all market cycles. The secret to success isn't a secret: it is to work all leads until they convert to a buyer or seller.

I recall vividly my mentor Sue Huckaby sharing a story about selling homes in the 1980s. Mortgage interest rates topped out at 18.45 percent, and at the time her husband was a congressman from Louisiana. She implored him to have the federal government do something about interest rates so that she could sell more houses. He said that she was going to have to figure out how to sell houses in spite of high mortgage interest rates. At this time, in 2016, thirty-year fixed interest rates are less than 4 percent. Sue clearly did not allow high interest rates to keep her from selling homes, as she went on to achieve great success with the rank of number ten in the nation a couple of decades later.

The moral of the *Seinfeld* story is no excuses—when you take a lead as a real estate agent, you hold the lead until it is converted to a sale.

Take a lead and hold it until the sale!

MAGIC WAND

If I could have one thing, it would be a magic wand that could grant wishes for my clients. With a flip of my wrist, my magic wand would make sellers' homes sell for the price they want, with all the terms that benefit their situation. And for buyer clients, I would magically make appear the perfect home that meets all of their needs and heart's desires at a price they could afford to pay. Perhaps markets work that way in a fairy tale; alas, that is not how markets operate in the real world. It can be a useful exercise to consider possibility thinking.

In many situations, sellers want to defy market conditions and predictions. They want to be the "exception" to the rule. This occurs frequently when the sellers believe they have a unique home and all it takes is "one buyer." The reality version is that being unique in a lot of cases is like trying to find a needle in a haystack. Waiting for that one person to come along can just accumulate days on market. Rather than wait, the "real world" approach that is more likely to be successful is to find the market by adjusting the price periodically. There will be a point when the buyer finds you, instead of you trying to find the buyer. That's when the magic comes in. Once demand has been created, then sellers sit in the best position to make their wishes come true.

To create some magic for buyers, an agent can sprinkle some creative fairy dust in the home search efforts. Work with the buyer to tweak the search parameters a bit. Often this will open up entirely new markets to explore. For example, in our area the school boundaries cross over several zip codes. An informed agent will know that there are other areas that the buyer could consider and still realize the objective of being in the desired district.

Agents who proactively preview homes and network with other knowledgeable professionals spread a little magic by finding out about homes before they hit the market or at least early on in the process. As the best houses sell fast, buyers benefit by having a dedicated agent working on their behalf. Even though information is readily available on the Internet, being ahead of the curve can create some magic for buyer clients.

Isn't it interesting that these strategies do not involve changing the market? Rather, all are designed to help people change or adjust their expectations. Is it even possible to change the market? The real estate market is an extremely powerful force of its own. Supply and demand are like gravity. What an agent can do is help their clients understand the dynamics and to exert the appropriate influence in order to best obtain their goals and objectives.

Create a little magic for your clients by utilizing some new strategies.

USE STATISTICS TO YOUR ADVANTAGE

The statistic "80 percent of the sale is made after the fifth contact" has been imprinted on my brain such that should I ever consider quitting before five contacts, I would soon be overruled. The numbers come from an authority that should know, the National Sales Association:

- 2 percent of sales are made on the first contact;
- 3 percent of sales are made on the second contact;
- 5 percent of sales are made on the third contact;
- 10 percent of sales are made on the fourth contact; and
- 80 percent of sales are made on the fifth to twelfth contact!

This is good news! It means that if you are persistent, your chance of success improves dramatically after the fifth try.

There is even better news, found in the classic study of sales calls made by Dartnell and McGraw Hill. It determined that:

- 48 percent of all salespeople give up after the first contact;
- 25 percent give up after the second contact; and
- 17 percent give up after the third or fourth contact.

The above data illustrates that 90 percent of salespeople give up before they even get to the point where 80 percent of the sales are potentially made. This leaves a lot of business on the table for those agents willing to put in the time and effort.

The benefit of tracking is that one knows what works and can replicate those activities that lead to success. Since becoming a residential real estate agent in the summer of 2002, I have kept a log of all the contacts I have made. First it was kept in a spiral bound notebook and later in a database program. New agents are fascinated to hear the stories of all the business I have earned through the years from the contacts I made during my first weeks as an agent. Of course, there are many touches that did not turn into opportunity. But the validity of having those numbers supports the premise that an agent can use statistics to her advantage.

There is a lot of opportunity for success—it goes to those who do not give up.

Use the power of statistics to your success at prospecting!

RECHARGE YOUR BATTERIES

How do you recharge your batteries? For me it is outdoor biking; my husband calls it "air in my helmet." There is something about being outside in fresh air with the wind in my face that clears my head. Some of my best ideas and productive thinking occurs when I am out riding my bike and not directly focused on a situation. Others paint, run, practice yoga, or meditate. The important thing is to have an outlet to release tension and to get your mojo back. What brings you joy?

The process of buying and selling a home is often stressful for the involved parties and frequently agents receive the brunt of the frustration. In these situations, agents can experience what is known in the mental health professions as "compassion fatigue." This occurs in fields where one is continually dealing with people who live in denial, don't want to listen to wise counsel, or the situation is difficult and challenging. Secondary trauma is projected onto the person who is actually trying to help the one in distress.

There are those agents who thrive on a challenge and rise to the occasion when a demanding situation is presented. These can be wonderful opportunities to achieve at a high level and demonstrate professionalism while under pressure. In my business, whenever possible I strive to use these scenarios to serve clients and earn repeat business.

An example of an actual transaction was when I represented a client being transferred out of state. The owner moved and the relocation company took over the property. As the home was vacant, the company required that I hire someone to have the home winterized. Upon completion of the winterization, the licensed contractor failed to properly turn off one of the exterior faucets. Weeks later, when the technician turned the water on for the home inspection, no one thought to check the exterior faucets.

The home was located in the country with no nearby neighbors. The basement had flooded by the time we realized what happened. The relocation client expected the contractor who performed the winterization to be held accountable, which was understandable. As I refer the contractor a great deal of business, he fully rectified the situation. The outcome was that the purchaser did go forward to buy the home. Due to the way our team handled the crisis, the relocation company added me to their preferred agent list for the market area.

Professional agents face challenging clients and situations throughout their careers. The ones who thrive find a way to recharge their batteries so that they have the energy to achieve and sustain success.

Engage in activities and pursuits that recharge your batteries
so that you are of service to clients.

PEOPLE ARE AUTOBIOGRAPHICAL

It seems obvious, yet true, that people view the world from their own unique perspective. Their perception is reality to them. Due to the highly personal nature of buying and selling a home, this phenomenon is even greater in the case in residential real estate. Leadership guru Dr. Stephen F. Covey, in *The 7 Habits of Highly Effective People*, espoused as habit number five the principle of "seek first to understand." By using this approach, clients are more likely to feel that the agent has their best interests at heart.

One way to uncover customers' stories is to get curious. Peel back the onion to find out what is important to them. Once clients feel that the agent cares enough to understand their situations, they are more likely to be open to hear alternative scenarios and ways to view the situation. Philosopher Blaise Pascal eloquently said: "People are usually more convinced by reasons they discovered themselves than those found by others."

The sellers' perspective is most typically that their home is more valuable than others in the marketplace. The tendency is to recognize the fatal flaws in other homes that have sold or are on the market. At the same time, sellers discount the issues in their own homes while magnifying the virtues. One strategy to employ is to encourage self-discovery. Provide a market study at a minimum of every thirty days. Include previewing any new-to-market competing properties. If the sellers are open to the idea, encourage them to visit public open houses. The agent also can offer to take them to see the competition first-hand. This can be particularly enlightening, as being present in the home together may yield insight into what the clients are thinking and feeling.

The buyer's story is similar, yet most often the mirror image. The agent should stay in curiosity mode about the client's perspective. A dialogue an agent could use is: "Isn't it interesting that one of the homes on your list you thought was overpriced went under contract so quickly?" It is a key strategy for success to wait for and listen. The answer will tell a great deal about the client's perspective.

There are situations when, as their agent, you may have to give clients permission to change their minds. I've heard many clients state that they will "never sell for less than a certain dollar figure" or "won't pay any more than x amount," only to agree to do so later. A dialogue that helps people get unstuck when this happens is: "At this time, I can understand how you might feel that way. Other people have felt that way before too. What we have found is the market constantly changes and those who successfully achieve their objectives are responsive to the market." This approach recognizes the validity of their perspective, while at the same time helps them move forward.

Stay curious to uncover clients' perspectives to help them achieve their objectives.

DO IT MYSELF

The phrase "do it myself" is often heard from the two-year-old child. One recognizes this behavior, whether as a parent or by observing the children of relatives or friends. The reason why two year olds go through this phase of development is so that they can declare their independence. It seems obvious to adults that the child is stretching their identity muscles. As long as the environment is safe and age-appropriate, then it can be empowering to allow the child to "do it myself."

Those who choose real estate as a profession tend to be entrepreneurial-minded. In many cases, real estate agents are independent contractors. The agent maintains a great deal of freedom of action and practice, though under the supervision by a broker of record as required by jurisdictional law. Being self-reliant may possibly hold an agent back from growing to her full potential. Learning from others is often what it takes to advance a business to the next level.

One way to achieve at a higher level is to create alliances with other professionals in related industries. A mastermind effect can be created by building a team of people who are your go-to vendors, such as lenders, title and settlement companies, attorneys, inspectors, contractors, stagers, and other real estate agents. Leverage essentially means using something to maximum advantage. This is the principle of connect to build and grow a business.

December is national business planning month and a prime time to evaluate the next steps to take in the new year to achieve the next level of success. Schedule now for regular training, mastermind sessions, and coaching with other agents and professionals in the industry to stay fresh on best practices. There are frequent changes in technology and the industry that the agent must stay current on to stay relevant.

Maintain a growth mindset by proactively engaging and learning from those at the next level and above. Success leaves clues. Follow them to build a career worth having, a business worth owning, and a life worth living.

Take the steps today to connect to build and grow a business and to achieve a life worth living.

YOUR MANNERS ARE SHOWING

In real estate, there is the potential for difficult transactions. Remember, you are dealing with people's money and most prized possession. There is frequently a tension between the parties, as sellers almost always think they have given their house away and buyers are concerned about overpaying. It is the law of reciprocity that people will behave toward you in the same manner as you treat them. This is why I have found it helpful to maintain the decorum of good manners in all situations. No one knows what the future holds; perhaps there will be a need for something from the other side as the transaction progresses.

The first introduction sellers usually have to buyers is from the feedback provided by the listing agent. I have found it helpful to include something positive the buyer says about the home. On one occasion, the feedback from the buyer seemed heavily weighted to all the things wrong with the home. When the buyer wrote an offer, the sellers considered it with a bad taste in their mouth. This reminds me that the spirit of the message delivered can often be more important than the actual words. The parties came to an agreement, yet unfortunately at every turn it seemed to be very contentious.

Another area in which to maintain good manners is that of negotiations. It is important for all parties to bargain in good faith. Sellers often bristle at what they deem to be a "low-ball offer" and don't want to have anything to do with the buyers who write them. If no other offers have been forthcoming, then perhaps the buyer reflects the current market conditions. Use a dialogue like this to calm sellers in this situation: "You may feel this offer is low. Know that other sellers have felt this way before too. What we have found is that even if you believe the buyer is having a case of bad manners by presenting a low offer, we should act in good faith to see if we can come to an agreement."

Keep a spirit of good manners throughout the transaction. What goes around comes around. Remember, something could occur and the client needs goodwill from the other party. For example, there was a major storm just one day before settlement and a tree fell on the seller's house. As we had maintained a positive professional relationship with all parties, thankfully we were able to come to an acceptable arrangement to deal with the situation.

The acronym THINK is a useful guide to maintain a professional environment among parties. The letters stand for: true, helpful, inspiring, necessary, and kind. Real estate professionals can be instrumental in setting the tone for the transaction—remember to THINK before responding.

Encourage a spirit of good manners among all parties in a transaction.

LEADS ARE ALL AROUND ME

The surprising thing about the real estate business is that one never knows where the next lead is going to come from. In fact, my husband reminds me of this every time one comes from an unusual place. This then makes me think of the lyrics in "Christmas Is All Around" from the movie *Love Actually*: "Christmas is all around me and so the feeling grows!" I've taken those words and changed them to: "Leads are all around me and so my business grows!" I've found that when I increase my awareness and believe that something is possible, it happens.

There are the obvious sources of leads: past clients, spheres of influence, friends, neighbors, associates, neighbors of current and past listings, open house attendees, and now the Internet. The uncommon ones are the stories that are the most memorable.

While on a business trip in California with my husband, I was taking a shuttle bus from the golf course back to the hotel. As I often do, I struck up a conversation with a lady who was seated near me and also attending the conference. It turned out that she lived in the area where I sold real estate. At the time, she was going through a divorce and planned to get her own place as soon as she returned home from the conference. Soon after, I represented her on the purchase of a town home.

Another great story comes from my business partner. She was putting out a Sunday open house sign when someone stopped and they struck up a conversation. The buyer wasn't interested at all in the house that Lizzy was holding open, but was in the market to buy. Lizzy was able to help her purchase another home in the community.

On the seller side, another story comes to mind. An agent on our team had been proactively previewing homes to stay current on the market. She had gone to see a home listed by another agent. A few days later, the owner contacted her directly. The couple was quite impressed that she would go to so much effort to be knowledgeable on the market. Needless to say, they soon made the decision to change agents and hired our agent, who sold the home for them.

These stories illustrate that by raising your awareness, you too will find that leads are all around. And when you tap into that, your business grows.

Look for leads all around you today and every day!

CAN'T NEVER DID DO ANYTHING

It is difficult to admit, as an author of a book that has a considerable motivational component, but I have a tendency toward pessimism. Whenever I am lamenting that I can't do something, I am sure to hear from my husband: "Can't never did do anything." It means, "Karen, you have given up before you even started. And of course it goes without saying that if you don't even try, how will you know whether you can or cannot?"

Usually by this point I have provided a laundry list of excuses on why I "can't" do it. This is where the words of success author Jonathan Budd convince me: "Prepare to let all of your useless excuses for why you can't do something go, and instead find a way to do it." As Budd said, the lesson I've learned is that when I focus my energy on what I can do, amazing things happen. The best way to describe the paradigm shift is like a light switch—it is either on or off. Turning on the "can" turns off the "can't" at the same time.

This experience transpired while writing this book. For many years, people have told me that I should write a book, as I have great stories about real estate and sales techniques. In the fall of 2014, I met with executive coach Moira Lethbridge. We discussed my journey, my business, and my goals, as well as my "futures" list. At that time I shared with her the idea of writing a book.

Fast forward one year later, to fall 2015. Another year had passed and I was no further along in writing a book. Moira hosted a weekend "deep dive" retreat designed to delve into implementation of one idea. Of course I selected once again to explore writing a book. All of the participants created a magazine cover story to be published one year later that visualized the success of their idea. In my "cover story" presentation to the group, all of a sudden I could "see" how it could actually happen and how I could do it. It was a flash of inspiration, and my "can" light came on because I turned off the "can't" switch.

The next weekend, I had a trip planned to Dallas to visit friends. I brought the book *Big Magic* by Elizabeth Gilbert to read on the plane. The book convinced me even more that not only was the universe telling me that I was supposed to write this book, but that I was supposed to write it *now*. The "can" switch came on even brighter and whatever doubt remained was switched off. As I moved forward into action, the pathway became clear on how I could write the book.

The subtitle to *Big Magic* is "Creative Living Beyond Fear." Truly, fear was holding me back from living the life I was created to live. And if I can do it, you can too!

Turn on the "can" switch and turn off the "can't"
in your business and life.

FOREVER HOME

On occasion, clients will speak longingly of a "forever home." When sellers bring up the topic, it is usually when they have built a home that they thought they were going to stay in for quite some time, had circumstances not changed. When buyers bring up the concept of a forever home, it is for them the ideal as they look into the future "out there" somewhere. Either way, there is a connotation that it is the "dream" home, in which every desire they have for a home exists. It reflects a family or person's unique living style and design features.

According to the National Association of Realtors®, the average American moves once every seven years. The definition of "forever" is: without ever ending, eternally, continually, and always. Thus, the concept of a "forever home" literally is an oxymoron, as it is a rare occurrence. As a professional agent, it is wise to recommend that people consider the future market when they purchase, build, or renovate.

Dominique Browning, the former editor-in-chief of *House & Garden* magazine, in the June, 2011 issue of *Realtor®* magazine, shared some of the pitfalls of the "forever home." One situation to avoid is being too trendy. An example that comes to mind is bathroom tile. Colors and designs that reflect the current fashion typically have a short life span. For longevity, it is better to select neutral, timeless palettes and patterns.

Second, Browning recommends that homeowners avoid floor plans and spaces that are too unique. Build a structure that follows classic design principles. One can then update with décor more easily and at lower cost. Suggestions for this strategy include the use of paint, wall hangings, window treatments, pillows, rugs, and the like.

Finally, she says to plan for the everyday and not for a once-in-a-while event or even those few times a year entertaining. Guest room space is expensive real estate when one can easily host the occasional guest at a local hotel. Holiday entertaining for twenty probably happens only on special occasions. Most homeowners rarely have a daily need for two kitchen sinks and a formal dining room. Use these tips and others to advise clients on home and real estate attributes that sustain value.

Advise clients on home and real estate attributes that sustain value.

"SAME TIME NEXT YEAR"

The movie *Same Time Next Year* spans over two-and-a-half decades of American life, starting in 1951. It is a romantic comedy in which a couple meets and carries on an affair at the same country inn every year. The place stays the same, but the characters and society change dramatically through the years. It is like returning repeatedly to a time capsule. Thus the title, *Same Time Next Year,* reflects the theme.

The movie opens in the 1950s. Ramblers and ranch-style homes were the most popular architectural structure of homes in America. There are many variations of the theme, including split-levels, bi-levels, and split foyers. Many homes reflected the influence of Frank Lloyd Wright.

This style transitioned into the mid-century modern architectural motif. In the 1960s, residential homes featured a more contemporary look, with straighter lines and a boxier feel and larger windows. Conservation became important in the 1970s and materials utilized most often were natural woods to reflect a return to nature.

The decades showcased in the movie reflected change in architectural style, even though the movie didn't reflect that part of American history. Some homeowners choose to keep their homes true to the era in which they were built, which can have the effect of feeling like one has entered a time machine. Others retain the core architectural elements while updating to remain current with modern living. And of course, there are many variations in between.

There are agents whose advertising and marketing materials seem to be from another era. Clients share that it feels like misrepresentation when an agent doesn't look like her photo. It is human nature to want to present one's best self in promotional materials. Photo retouching and other techniques can make a tremendous impact on the presentation.

Keep in mind that puffery tactics of real estate marketing border on misrepresentation, the same as when promoting one's own brand. If the purpose is to achieve name and face recognition, then it seems obvious that it is important to look like the photo. The public respects agents who are in tune with the market, both professionally and personally.

Time moves on and those agents who achieve and sustain success do so as well.

Apply the lessons of Same Time Next Year *to marketing homes and your personal brand.*

FIRST CLASS VERSUS ECONOMY CLASS

There are several levels of service one can select from when flying. Whenever it is available, like most people I prefer to fly first class. The reasons are probably obvious: more leg room, better food, and of course there is the service. The flight attendant hands me a warm towel to freshen up and cheerfully serves my every need. My favorite is the warm mixed nuts! All of the travel class options arrive at the same destination; the travel experience is the differential.

There are now more levels of service available for buyers and sellers of residential real estate than ever before. At one time everyone had one choice—the traditional brokerage model. Just as with other industries, like travel and the purchase and sale of stocks, there are now more options available to the consumer.

The distinction between the big-box retailer and the local corner store is played out in the movie *You've Got Mail*. The big box store offers low prices. To achieve that, the experience is impersonal and there is a low level of customer service. The corner bookstore knows your name and the genres you love to read. The staff is knowledgeable and helpful without being pushy. Now both are in jeopardy of being put out of business by digital downloads and free delivery of books direct to your door, with no shipping charge.

In the case of books, perhaps one could argue that the service of a well-read intelligent person to recommend a purchase isn't necessary. Can the same thing be said for the purchase or sale of a home, one's most significant asset and financial investment? Real estate agents must provide a service that differentiates them from being merely an order-taker; otherwise their profession will be next in line to be replaced by the Internet and service-provider door openers.

The real estate professionals who serve, not sell, are the ones who meet their clients' needs first and foremost by providing wise counsel. One could argue that it is even more important with the overwhelming level of information available and the ease to which it is obtainable. It is the agent who can discern the data and interpret it in a meaningful way that will always be in demand. Yes, all levels of service might get me to my destination, but I prefer first class when available.

The flight attendant role is significantly more than that of beverage and nut server. The purpose is to assure safe and pleasant travel to the destination. What if there is turbulence or other such emergency? Wouldn't you want an attendant who is trained and prepared to handle it in a calm and professional manner? Absolutely! This is one of the primary purposes of the real estate agent that is often overlooked. That is, to assure that the transaction is managed professionally, resulting in a smooth settlement.

Provide professional service as the differentiator in the marketplace.

DO YOU BELIEVE?

Entry into real estate sales is relatively easy, given the earning potential and the fiduciary responsibility to facilitate the purchase and sale of what is most people's largest financial asset. Yet only 20 percent of agents survive after the first year. Almost anyone can do it, yet clearly so few actually do. Everyone starts with high hopes of providing a valuable service and making it in the business. No one goes into real estate thinking they will be in the 80 percent that drops out. What is the secret sauce that makes the difference?

In her book *Shark Tales*, real estate mogul Barbara Corcoran shares that aggression is the attribute she looks for on *Shark Tank*. When people present their ideas, she "tests" for the trait by confronting the person with: "I don't believe you are aggressive enough." And then she waits to see how the person responds. The reaction in itself is the answer.

Not to second-guess the success of Barbara Corcoran, but I think that there may be more to achieving success in the business. The secret sauce, I believe, is passion. Passion is emotion and energy with a purpose. People who are passionate have a "big why" according to Gary Keller, founder of Keller Williams. These people are driven to achieve, put in the hard work, and care about the people and the outcome. If you are passionate, you not only believe it with your heart and mind, you also do everything in your power to make it happen.

In the words of famed chef and author Julia Childs: "Find something you're passionate about, and keep tremendously interested in it." When a person stays tremendously interested in something, then she plays to win rather than to lose. Instead of holding back, she makes things happen. I've found that if one argues for her limitations, then she gets to keep them. If, however, you believe that you are capable and worthy, then that outcome can happen too. Confidence is gained through competence and vice versa.

How do you know if you can do it if you don't try? Author Ayn Rand said: "Every man is free to rise as far as he is able or willing, but the degree to which he *thinks* determines the degree to which he will rise."

The beauty of the sales profession is that there is always demand for people who perform well. Success is truly the ultimate job security. Do you believe? If I can do it, you can too!

Embrace your passion and take action to achieve great success!

THE POMODORO TECHNIQUE®

The Pomodoro Technique® developed by Francesco Cirillo is a time-management method that uses a tomato-shaped timer. The simple idea is to set a timer for twenty-five minutes and focus on one task to completion. Then take a well-deserved five-minute break, during which time you could get up and walk around, do some stretches, or complete a quick housekeeping task. It follows how good hockey players skate: full speed, then stop.

The beauty of the built-in timed breaks is that it reduces burnout. Some people never get started because they become paralyzed by how to tackle several hours of work. Procrastination is the archenemy of the real estate agent. It is tempting to put off prospecting, particularly when you are busy. In effect, this will eventually stop the flow of business in the pipeline. It is better to consistently engage in business development every working day rather than wait until the well is dry and struggle to generate leads.

There are other strategies that employ the use of a timer. James Clear, author of *Transform Your Habits*, advocates the two-minute rule to combat procrastination. He maintains if a task can be done in two minutes, go ahead and just do it. The physics principle discovered by Sir Isaac Newton kicks in: "An object at rest tends to stay at rest and an object in motion tends to stay in motion." In this case, the object is the real estate agent staying in motion by doing something to break the inertia.

Gretchen Rubin, in her book *Better than Before*, advocates the use of a "power hour" to tackle challenging or undesirable tasks. The term "power hour" for prospecting has long been part of the lexicon for salespeople in many industries, not just real estate. The idea is to employ full engagement, to bring your full attention and focus to the task at hand.

So if it is two minutes, twenty-five minutes, or a power hour, incorporate a timer to your advantage. Whether a tomato-shaped timer or one on a hand-held device, the success key is to commit to practice. In the words of Aristotle: "We are what we repeatedly do. Excellence, then, is not an act, but a habit."

Set a timer to prospect and accomplish other key activities that lead to success.

BALCONY AND BASEMENT THINKING

The view from the balcony is far-reaching. With height, it allows one to obtain perspective and see beyond the immediate situation. The basement is at the core of the foundation. A solid one is crucial to the integrity of the structure. Thus, there is a place for both balcony and basement thinking in an agent's business and life.

The real estate stories that resonate over time do so because they have core elements embedded within. This one shows the lesson of balcony and basement thinking. A friend referred me to one of her neighbors. This friend is influential in the community and with her husband owns a well-regarded high-end landscape maintenance and design/build firm. Our son took their daughter to prom. The listing was for an upper-bracket home that was being sold via a relocation company.

The market was cooling for this price-point home and so when an offer was presented from buyers relocating from the West Coast, I encouraged the sellers to come to an agreement. During the home inspection negotiations, the buyers requested that the owners clean the carpet. According to their agent, the buyers' young son was susceptible to allergies, and they were particularly concerned about the fact that the owners had cats in the home. The sellers agreed to correct the other material items on the list, and in a spirit of moving the deal forward, I agreed to have the carpets professionally cleaned at my cost.

As is the practice, the relocation company took over the property prior to settlement. All receipts for work performed were delivered to the buyers' agent in a timely fashion, including that of the professional carpet cleaning. At the closing table, the father of the husband was present, as he made a significant contribution to the down payment. After reviewing everything, he asked if the carpet was treated for cat urine prior to cleaning. Truly, at that time I was not aware that was necessary or even an option. Someone on my staff coordinated the work, so I was not involved. He refused to go forward with the transaction unless someone could guarantee this was done and if not that it would be completed prior to his family moving into the home. His exact words resonate in my mind: "You have a moral obligation to deliver a home that is clean for my grandson to live in."

Thinking from the balcony, I could see into the future that these folks were soon to be the neighbors of my influential friends. Looking forward, I wanted them to feel good that I did the right thing. And at my basic foundation, I wanted to be known as an agent who fulfills her "moral obligations" to all parties. In the words of John D. Rockefeller, Jr.: "Every right implies a responsibility; every opportunity, an obligation; every possession, a duty." Thus, I agreed to have the carpet company go out the next day and treat all the areas for cat urine. This opportunity cost me several thousand dollars and imprinted on my brain the responsibility of "moral obligation."

Consider both the balcony and basement views when faced with moral obligations with customers and clients.

KNOWING "WHEN"
IN NEGOTIATIONS

Real estate negotiation strategy often involves having a strong sense of what the parties are capable of and their limits, much as in a card game. Kenny Rogers sings in the classic "The Gambler" about "readin' people's faces" and "knowin' what the cards were, by the way they held their eyes." Just as in cards, negotiating ability is often more intuitive than scientific and usually acquired through experience. Even the old card player laments that this knowledge was achieved over a lifetime.

There are several moves open to a negotiator and to a card player alike: hold firm; fold, which is to stop making concessions or bets into the pot and see what the other players do; and move on or walk away. The song paints the picture with these words: "You've got to know when to hold 'em, know when to fold 'em, know when to walk away, know when to run." Negotiators in real estate also have in their hands the options of accepting the terms and countering.

A key lesson for real estate agents is in the last line of the chorus: "You never count your money when you're sittin' at the table, there'll be time enough for countin' when the dealin's done." There are numerous reasons for the agent to "not count your money" too early in the process. One is that it can cloud your judgment when the focus is primarily on the money. When that happens, agents often become overly vested in the outcome.

Second, deals can fall apart. A deal isn't done until it has gone to settlement and the commission has been paid. Living on "the come" or money before it has been earned and cleared the bank is a precarious way to run a business.

Another reason is if the parties, in particular your clients, sense that you are in the deal only for the money, then often they have concerns about whether your interests are for their benefit or merely your own. Finally, focusing on the money might cloud judgment and cause the agent to miss clues and key aspects to the negotiations that would be beneficial for their client or harmful if not addressed, which could jeopardize the deal.

The professional agent maintains focus on the client's situation and needs throughout the transaction.

Focus on the client's needs in the transaction, rather than how much commission is to be earned.

SCHEDULE POWER

There is power in a schedule, as it creates natural deadlines. Getting started is often the most difficult part of the process. A schedule builds in the activity and applies to working with clients as well as the business side of being a real estate agent.

The most effective way for sellers to get their home ready for the market is to create a timeline. I do this with sellers when I meet with them to execute the listing paperwork. First, we start with the date that they want to go "live," then work back from there. Our team engages a professional photographer and that firm prefers to schedule out about one week in advance. It is particularly critical to schedule early in the busy spring season.

Once we have the photography date penciled in, next we work backwards to schedule the stager consultation. Depending on the punch-out list of items established by the stager and the time it will take for the seller to complete, that gives us the next date to aim for.

Next, we work forward from the go "live" date to schedule the first public open house and the broker's open event. If the sellers start to feel pressured, I am clear that we can adjust the schedule; however it is rare that we have to. Most sellers rise to the occasion to meet the deadlines. I have found that the sellers who say they will call me when they are ready frequently take considerably longer.

Schedule power works just as well for buyer clients. Once a home is under contract, project out a timeline for the contingency removals. Examples include scheduling all inspections, completing the loan application, title insurance, homeowner's insurance, and appraisal. To view the entire process at once may overwhelm the client. This is when the agent can serve as advisor to help navigate and prioritize the deadlines. In the words of productivity coach Sally McGhee: "It's a cinch by the inch, and hard by the yard."

A moving company that is a preferred vendor also uses schedule power with clients. Once the company determines the number of boxes that the client is likely to need, she counsels them to work backwards from the move date to pack a certain number of boxes per day. It is rare that someone does not achieve the plan. People don't have to think each day what they are going to do; they just work the schedule.

Examples of schedule power in a successful agent's business abound. An example from our team is the system we use to provide feedback to seller clients. A staff member pulls listing lock box reports on Tuesday. Over the next couple of days, the listing agent calls the buyer agents for feedback. A report is sent to sellers by the close of the business week. Adjustments can be made to respond to market conditions. Good habits break the inertia of when routine processes are to occur.

Use schedule power with clients and your own business as a key success activity.

REALITY TV ISN'T REAL

Real estate is real. Reality TV is not, even if it has a real estate or home renovation theme. The genre creates expectations that on so many fronts aren't realistic. In reality, buying and selling a home cannot happen in a thirty or sixty-minute segment. Remodeling a home is costly, time consuming, and very messy.

As a media segment, reality TV has become more like fiction than nonfiction. Nonfiction reflects the "true" aspects of the situation. Any thinking person quickly recognizes the outcome achieved in reality TV clearly did not occur in "real time." Perhaps the appeal of the shows is that it is human nature to want to suspend reality for a time.

In *Why Reality Television Isn't Real*, Phillppa Warr, an arts and entertainment writer, states: "In reality television, as in life, it seems we prefer the edited version of ourselves—the one where the story on television plays out like the one we might secretly harbor in our heads."

In many ways, putting a home on the market can feel like appearing on a reality TV show. Professional photographs created into virtual tours and video are often part of the marketing platform for the property. To achieve top dollar for the market, most agents advise sellers to stage a home to make it look like a "set." The home should be kept in "show condition" for when buyers and agents visit. Keep in mind the distinction between puffery and misrepresentation as specified at the jurisdictional level; consult a broker for clarification and advisement.

Sellers often proclaim that the way they live normally is not the same as when their home is on the market. It isn't "real life" and can be difficult to maintain at show level if the home doesn't sell quickly. In reality, though, no one really wants to see the warts and blemishes in a home. A bit of fiction in real life isn't such a bad thing if it makes reality more appealing and thus salable.

There is the "show of the transaction," too. The buyers and sellers are the leading actors. Agents are the directors and the broker functions as the producer. The lender, home inspectors, and settlement company representatives play supporting roles. As an agent connects to build and grow her business, it is critical to have the best in the industry on stage and part of the production.

As a professional real estate agent, it can be beneficial to watch the shows so that one is aware of what customers and clients in the marketplace are viewing. Just be cognizant of the difference between reality and fiction.

Understand how reality TV helps clients prepare
their home for show condition.

BUILD A BUSINESS

DECEMBER 21

The process of building a business that lasts is similar to that of constructing a home. It starts with an architect to create a design and plans. There are countless variations along a continuum. One can build custom from top to bottom, all the way to tract home design that is extremely repeatable. In business design, it begins first in one's mind by employing success thinking and vision. Success activities are key for implementation of construction; otherwise they become merely "best-laid plans."

The master builder first prepares the site and lays a solid foundation. The foundation is essential in home construction, yet often agents are so eager to start their business plan that they begin with what truly are the decorative elements. Next is the rough framing construction. This too is a crucial step in the process for the agent, as the framework becomes the structure that the agent connects with leverage and efficiencies. These systems include lead generation, database creation, and ongoing training.

The home elevation vision is paramount, as it is the external view that people see. The agent's elevation, if you will, is the branding. Just as in home construction, it is important for the exterior design to be congruent with the interior decor. That means being authentic to one's true self that you can live with day in and day out.

Ways to increase leverage and to take the business to the next level is to partner with another agent, join a team, employ staff, and work with a coach or mentor. Just as in the leap-frog game on the children's playground, these strategies can propel an agent forward at a faster rate than what would occur organically. With collaboration, "we becomes more than just me." Strategic thinking is enhanced by "two brains are better than one."

Keep in mind that once the home has been built, there exists opportunities to remodel, incorporate additions, or retrofit as circumstances change. Remember when a one-car garage was sufficient for a family's needs? Now the three-car garage has become the trend in many markets.

That also can happen as the agent builds his real estate business. What once was appropriate and right for the situation may require adaptation for the current market demands. In visiting with all the people who have built a new home or completed a significant remodel, there still is a list of items they wish they had done and will do differently "next time." That also is likely to happen as you grow a business. There is always room for improvement and opportunity for growth.

*Create today the vision to build your real estate business
and as the master builder does, start with a solid foundation.
If a vision is in place, review and remodel as necessary.*

FULL EMPLOYMENT

Insights frequently come to me from sources outside of the real estate arena. One such occasion was a speech by a well-respected leader in another industry. She proclaimed that professionals in the field should embrace objections and issues. The reason she expounded upon is that it is problems that provide "full employment." If there are no situations to resolve, then the client would have no purpose or little need for the services of a professional.

This thinking caused a paradigm shift in the manner in which I practice real estate. Rather than view questions and objections as annoyances and problems, I now view them as opportunities to provide value and solutions.

In the current and likely future of the real estate marketplace, buyers have access to a great deal of readily available information. It is the true professional who looks at this as an opportunity to provide wise interpretation of what can feel like a tsunami force of data.

It is the intimate and breadth of knowledge of the real estate market that provides sellers with guidance on establishing a market list price. As a listing agent, when buyers express the factors that keep them from making an offer, then it is the professional's job to demonstrate the positive features of the property. When parties are far apart in negotiations, it is the agent's expertise that finds a way to bring them together.

The agent has "feet on the street" and is proactive and knowledgeable about the market. The professional seeks to continuously improve her skills by pursuing training, continuing education, and coaching opportunities.

In other words, all of these situations and others are how an agent earns the commission. If it was easy, then anyone could do it and it would not require the services of a professional. There are those who propose that, due to the Internet and proliferation of information available, parties at some point will no longer require the services of a professional real estate agent.

The National Association of Realtors® 2015 statistics indicate that 87 percent of buyers and 89 percent of sellers chose to employ a real estate agent. Most said they would do so again when provided the opportunity. The solutions-based approach illustrates how an agent can demonstrate and sell value.

Embrace the "full employment" philosophy to create value for your customers and clients!

SUCCESS VISION

Wisdom literature states: "Where there is no vision, the people perish" (Proverbs 29:18). The wisdom translated to this industry is: "Where there is no vision, the real estate business perishes." Along with success thinking and activities, vision is a core principle to achieve the sweet spot of success.

First, determine your unique sense of purpose and mission. All agents essentially sell the same service of helping clients in real estate transactions. What is special about you? That's your vision! Think big! Southwest Airlines could say that they are in the transportation industry, specifically airline travel. Southwest Airlines asserts that their mission is much bigger than that; the company is in the freedom business. People are free to move about the country, employees are free to be their very best. That is a very empowering vision! Markets and business strategies can change, but the purpose and mission at the very core transcends those fluctuations.

Motivational guru Jim Rohn states: "Success is something you attract by the person you become." To sustain success, one is always becoming. Aim for progress rather than perfection. Decide on your definition of success and prove it to yourself by doing the activities.

To keep your vision at the forefront, establish activities that support it. One of the key components to achieve our team's goals is to always have twenty-four listings. To visualize that objective, we have a board on the wall in our common area for all the agents and staff to see the "slots" for twenty-four listings. Each slot either has the brochure cover for one of our team's listings or a placeholder for "listing coming soon—it could be yours." The listings we currently have stay front of mind and so consciously and unconsciously we are all strategizing on how to sell that home. For the placeholder slots, it is a reminder that we are to always be looking for the next listing opportunity.

December is promoted as national business planning month. It is a natural time to set aside to prepare your vision for the coming year. Every year our office holds a "vision board" party for agents. Poster board, materials, and magazines to inspire are provided for agents to create their vision of what they want for their lives. The vision can be both personal and professional and some areas it can include are financial and productivity goals; health and physical; personal and business development; education and training; spiritual growth; relationships, family and friends; and travel, leisure, and relaxation. The professional agent achieves the sweet spot of success by having vision.

Establish a vision and set into place thinking
and activities that keep it front of mind.

THE HOLIDAY CHRISTMAS CLASSIC HOME SWAP

The Holiday is a movie about two ladies who are both coming out of bad relationships and decide to "home swap" as a means of getting away. One is a society column editor from London and the other is a movie producer from LA. The homes are stereotypical for the locale. The London home is actually a "quaint cottage" in slow-paced Surrey, and the Los Angeles home is top-shelf glamour among Hollywood stars.

The movie portrays that homes take on the owner's personality—or perhaps is it the other way around? House swapping in the movie thus turned out to be more than just homes and location, but lifestyle, as well as friends and associates. By discovering their new locales, both ladies "found themselves" and were able to "move on" in a way that they couldn't before.

Moving to a new home offers a new setting and many times a new life. As a real estate professional, I have watched scenes like this play out. The empty-nester couple trades a large home in the country on several acres with a luxury town home with an elevator in town. The changes associated with this home swap are from exclusive and private evenings and weekends and an at-home lifestyle with urban pursuits of walking to shops and restaurants, as well as nights out at the theatre and museums. There is a trade-off as well, from high maintenance and free time spent doing yard work to freedom where one can travel with ease.

The real estate agent often is a strong influence in helping people visualize what a new home, along with a new lifestyle, would mean for them. Some people take a short-term rental to "try it out," much like the home swap in the movie.

How can you use the "home swap" story to help your clients visualize a new lifestyle?

IT'S A WONDERFUL LIFE AND PROFESSION

It is a tradition in our family every year during the holiday season to watch the Frank Capra classic, *It's a Wonderful Life.* In fact, I've seen it so many times that I can quote word-for-word many of the scenes. Perhaps it is because of all the real estate lessons contained within!

The heart of my core "big why" for being a professional real estate agent is played out in a scene in which the family is at the dinner table. As George Bailey is leaving for college soon, he shares his dream with his father that he wants to be an architect and see the world. He just can't imagine being a part of carrying on his father's dream of running the Bailey Building and Loan. George sees the enterprise as small and penny-ante and he wants to create and build on a grand level.

> **George:** Oh, now Pop, I couldn't. I couldn't face being cooped up for the rest of my life in a shabby little office. Oh, I'm sorry, Pop, I didn't mean that, but this business of nickels and dimes and spending all your life trying to figure out how to save three cents on a length of pipe . . . I'd go crazy. I want to do something big and something important.

> **Pop:** You know, George, I feel that in a small way we are doing something important. Satisfying a fundamental urge. It's deep in the race for a man to want his own roof and walls and fireplace, and we're helping him get those things in our shabby little office.

As a professional agent, I echo Mr. Bailey's sentiment. In small and big ways, we are doing something important, satisfying the fundamental desire of home ownership. As agents. it is rewarding to assist purchasers in finding a home that meets their needs and walking them through the myriad steps to make that happen. It is our privilege as well to work on a daily basis with sellers on what is typically their largest asset, to walk clients through the maze of both marketing and selling their home.

Another scene has to do with connect to build and grow a business. In the movie, there was a financial run-on at the institution as frequently occurred in that era. After satisfying all the Building and Loan customers who wanted to withdraw their money, there was just $2 left. George says with great ceremony: "A toast! A toast to Papa Dollar and to Mama Dollar, and if you want this old Building and Loan to stay in business, you better have a family real quick." Business development should be part of every real estate agent's core practices. To take one or two leads and multiply them real quick into transactions that leads to more clients is another lesson from this classic movie.

Apply the lessons of It's a Wonderful Life *to your business.*

CONSULT TO SELL

The successful agent converts seller and buyer leads to sales. It requires strategy and effort to first obtain and then market and sell a listing. It takes time and skill to convert a buyer to a client who writes, ratifies a contract, and thus purchases a home.

On a family ski trip when our kids were young, the conditions were very wet and cold. The time off the slopes was spent in an attempt to dry out our gear. Our son had an idea to put a hairdryer in his boots to both dry and warm them up at the same time. This led to the creation of a business plan to install boot warmers at ski resorts. Coincidentally, I worked for a company that owned the Ski Chalets in the Washington, DC metro area. Drew met with the owner, Wilbur McBay, to "pitch" his idea. He was very conciliatory to Drew, as Drew was a teenager at the time, yet Wilbur did not have high hopes. He shared that it is not enough to have a good idea; you must be able to sell the idea.

This same situation can occur in the real estate industry. The agent takes the listing and goes about figuring out how to sell the property. If the home is priced correctly for the market, it will sell. If the home is not priced correctly for the market, the person the agent next sells is the owner. The challenge is that the owner may feel the agent isn't on his side and doesn't see the value in the property. The owner feels like he is being "sold." There is the added challenge of confirmation bias, which is the tendency to focus on the beliefs that support your position. Confirmation bias is strongest when the stakes are high. This is why it is commonly thought that attorneys should not represent themselves, as they cannot be objective.

In these situations, remember the lyrics of the song "Anthem" by Leonard Cohen: "There is a crack in everything— that's how the light gets in." In sales, the "crack" is the factor that matters to the client. An effective agent uses that as leverage to illicit change. For example, a seller prices his home at what seems to be market value at the time. What happens if soon after a neighbor lists his home for substantially less? Even though they may be two completely different houses, it still changes the market dynamics. If the seller is anxious to move, or has already purchased another home, it has let the light in for a price change.

A buyer scenario was when I worked with a couple who were both CPAs. The couple fell in love with a home that had recently come on the market, and there was a lot of interest. To win the home would require moving quickly and aggressively on an offer, which was not their nature. They were the type who wanted to spend time analyzing the situation. I used the accounting inventory method of "last in, first out" to sell them on writing a compelling offer. It is just like with the inventory method—the best houses sell quickly because they are the best houses. As I spoke their language, a light bulb came on and they wrote the winning offer and happily moved into their dream home!

To consult to sell, use the client's language and situation to sell the idea.

Consult to sell by using the factors that are important to the client as leverage.

POWER THROUGH THE DIPS

The real estate industry is like a roller coaster. The market rises and falls; what goes up also can go down. The good news is in the United States, the trajectory is generally positive in most markets. The challenge is that no one knows for sure how the market will behave the next quarter or the next year. The seasons also create natural cycles that can cause dips throughout the year.

When an agent has a buyer client who is truly an "A" client and ready to go, all is well. When the agent has a listing that is priced and positioned correctly for the market, that too is an occasion when the agent is at the top of her game. Contracts are in escrow at the settlement company and deals are in the pipeline, the phone is ringing for listing and buyer appointments—these are all signs that the agent is successful. Those are all top-of-the-roller-coaster highs, arms up in the air, a big smile on the face and perhaps even some happy screams.

Then there is the other end of the roller-coaster ride. Since real estate agents are almost exclusively paid on commission, there can often be a great deal of work to be done before any money comes in. When a transaction goes to settlement, then the fee can be substantial, yet a lot of times there is quite a bit of time in between. When the agent doesn't have anything in the pipeline, when there are no listings or active buyer clients to work with, when the phone isn't ringing, those are all the down parts of the cycle. On top of that, the real estate professional has ongoing expenses of maintaining licensure, as well as marketing and other reoccurring costs, including staff and office expenses.

It is easy and fun to be at the top; it is not so at the bottom. So how do you power through the dips? When I'm in a dip or predict one is on the horizon, I immediately get into action. Specifically, I double all my prospecting efforts. The momentum that I gain by action helps the cogs catch to start propelling me back up. The effort to get back up the other side is always greater than it is to coast down. So I know that going into the dip I don't coast, but rather I peddle and gear up so I can power through.

How do you know whether this is a dip you should push through? According to Seth Godin in *The Dip*, it is when the long-term benefits are worth the short-term pain and effort. Further, he goes on to say: "In a competitive world, adversity is your ally. The harder it gets, the better chance you have of insulating yourself from the competition."

After having experienced a few market dips in my career, I now actually enjoy the thrill of the roller-coaster ride. If I can do it, you can too!

Power through the dips in your real estate business by increasing lead-generating activities.

HOUSING "BLACK FRIDAY"

The holiday season is now in the past and the New Year is fast approaching. While many are still in celebration mode, active professional real estate agents are busy. It happens that "housing Black Friday" is often the Friday following Christmas. Realtor.com® 2014 data supports this phenomenon: "So what is the true Black Friday of the housing business? Here's a holiday shocker: December 28 was actually one of the busiest days for real estate searches in the entire year." That's right, immediately after the Christmas holiday people began actively searching for homes. I have several theories for why this is so.

People have either been entertaining guests over the holiday season or visiting relatives and friends. All of the flaws of the home they currently live in have become very apparent. They decide that next year is the year they are going to do something about it. Moving becomes the family's New Year's resolution!

Others may realize that the home has become too big. Finally, they come to the conclusion that they don't want to own and maintain the property through another winter season. For those whose homes are bursting at the seams, they realize they really do need more space and are ready to make the move to a larger place.

During the holiday season, more people have time off from work responsibilities. Many companies shut down or require only a limited work schedule. Because of this, people have more time to spend on the Internet to explore housing options.

End-of-the year bonuses have been dispersed and can go toward a down payment. Families often make decisions about gifting money during the holidays, which can also contribute to a purchase.

Many sellers begin the process of preparing their home for the spring market after the first of the year. This often includes contacting a professional Realtor® for a free comparative market analysis. This is the time of the year agents are called to view homes for sellers to help them determine what work should be done in order to sell quickly in the spring market. What are you doing to get ready?

Prepare for housing Black Friday in your market area!

CROSSOVER

The real estate agent makes the crossover into business owner in order to connect to build and grow. Some recognize this early on and set up the systems and processes as such. Others transition as they sell more houses and realize that to take it to the next level they must have operations in place to sustain the business. Some just wing it. And there are those who are clueless.

There are touchstones to the process of transforming from sales agent to business owner. One of the first crossovers for me was when I hired a bookkeeper. This occurred when I came to the realization that I could earn considerably more selling than I could spending the time accounting for income and expenses, writing checks, and balancing accounts. Having a professional handle the books has paid for itself in spades, as reconciliation against the broker accounts has meant catching discrepancies early on in the process.

This transition freed up the time to focus on cash flow and the pipeline of business that creates it. Since I was no longer mired in the weeds of the details, it further highlighted the need for me to read the profit-and-loss and balance statement more thoroughly. The process taught me the wisdom in the words of Benjamin Franklin: "Beware of little expenses. A small leak will sink a great ship."

The activity of knowing the numbers goes beyond just accounting, which looks backward, and into lead tracking and conversions, which look into the future. Once the business owner knows the value of a lead, follow-through on each and every one becomes paramount. To do otherwise is just allowing money to slip out the back door. This process goes hand-in-hand with lead conversion. Tracking this data point helps identify the agents who are capable, the ones who need more training, and the others who should be counseled to pursue other opportunities. Keys to long-term sustainable success in any business are to know your numbers and how you stand in the industry.

The agent who builds and grows a business recognizes that to take it to the next level requires leveraging people, in the form of agents on the team or staff. This is when you cross over into being a business owner. December is national business planning month and thus a prime opportunity to determine if it is time for you to make the crossover. Schedule now to plan for the new year and your future success.

Take the steps to cross over from sales agent to business owner.

TO STAGE OR NOT TO STAGE, THAT IS THE QUESTION

Builders with model homes touted the benefits of staging long before it went mainstream in the resale community. Often the furnishings "sell" the home. The attractiveness halo has significant power to influence a buyer's decision. This is the reason that the best houses sell so quickly. It is in effect the law of attraction. Buyers are drawn to the homes that stand out in the marketplace. It follows, then, by the contrast principle that those homes that do not show well will languish on the market.

There are a number of certification and accreditation programs for the staging profession. The question presented here is to what extent a home should be staged prior to going on the market for sale. The purpose of staging is different than decorating for living, which takes into consideration the owner's tastes and lifestyle choices. When a home currently lived in is staged, it is to create a setting that invites those who visit to imagine their lives there.

Another way to think of it is the home is "on stage." The showings are dress rehearsals for the performance. If it "shows well," then there will be the standing ovation as everyone raves about the home. If it doesn't, the unfavorable and even bad reviews are feedback delivered by buyers and agents.

Along with the principle of "everybody wants what everybody wants," attractive homes are the most sought after and receive the most interest. Buyers then are more likely to experience "FOMO"—or "fear of missing out"—as they compete for the best houses.

According to the National Association of Realtors®, 87 percent of buyers who used the Internet during their home search said they found the photos to be a key aspect of the process. Photo quality is more important than ever and that is achieved best when a home is presented in show condition.

The question then becomes to what extent. For certain, almost everyone benefits from decluttering. If buyers have the sense that the current owners are stuffed to the seams in the home, then they too become concerned that they won't have enough space to live and store their possessions. A stager I work with says that people expand into whatever space they have, and I have found that to be true. So the first order of business is to store away any unnecessary items. Next, most professionals will encourage homeowners to depersonalize so that the buyers can visualize living there.

The most effective steps to take, which are also low cost, include paint; cleaned carpet or buffed hardwoods; and yard cleanup. For the touches that take a home from ordinary to extraordinary, consult the professionals.

Incorporate staging in your business practice to increase the attractiveness factor of homes on the market.

ADVANCE ONE GRADE

Studies show that only 10 percent of learning is transferred to on-the-job experience. Retention and application after one experience, such as one training session or reading a book on a particular subject, is minimal.

Just as with a musician practicing an instrument or an athlete in training, it is with multiple repetitions that skills are first learned, developed, and then built on. Thus, participating in the same training on multiple occasions and rereading the same book have the potential of exponentially increasing the learning and application of the principles and practices into one's everyday business and life.

As a paradigm shift, consider that every time one has completed a particular training program or read a book, it is like advancing one grade in a school system. This philosophy embraces the idea that each time one experiences the material it becomes richer, deeper, and more meaningful. It provides more occasions for application and breadth of learning. In the case of rereading the same book, one will often gain new insights the second time around. Further, the trainee has had more experience "out in the field," so the examples will be more readily apparent and correlations to "real life" will be easier to make.

Organizational psychologist Dr. Eduardo Salas stated in *The Wall Street Journal* that by the time a person returns to her job after training, most have lost 90 percent of what was learned. This training attrition increases in situations when one doesn't use the skills right away. The retention has, in effect, a "half-life" and decays soon after if application processes aren't implemented and reinforcements set into place.

In his book *The Outliers*, Malcolm Gladwell postulates the "10,000-Hour Rule." It follows that it takes around ten-thousand hours to achieve world-class expertise in any skill. The path to success is paved with repetition and implementation. And one key to that success is to reread valuable books such as *Real Estate Success in Just 5 Minutes a Day.*

Experience great success by multiple readings of
Real Estate Success in 5 Minutes a Day.

About the Author

Karen Briscoe is principal owner of the Huckaby Briscoe Conroy Group (HBC) with Keller Williams, headquartered in McLean, Virginia. The HBC Group has been recognized by *The Wall Street Journal* as one of the 250 Top Realtor® teams in the United States. Further, the team has ranked in the top one-hundred teams with Keller Williams International every year since 2009, when the group joined KW.

Karen regularly speaks on a national and local level on the "Best of 5 Minute Success." Further she is the host of the weekly "5 Minute Success" podcast which has an amazing array of guests who achieve success at a high level in business and life. Karen also is a frequent guest on other podcasts that focus on entrepreneurial, success and motivation, as well as real estate related topics. She has completed the John Maxwell Team Certification Program for Coaching, Speaking and Training.

Karen is the creator of the "5 Minute Success" series. Further, she is a contributing author to real estate media outlets *INMAN* and *Real Trends*.

Since 1977, HBC Group has sold more than 1,500 homes valued at more than $1.5 billion. The team consistently sells over one hundred residential properties annually, ranging from multi-million-dollar luxury estates to condominiums and townhomes. Primary market areas include Northern Virginia, suburban Maryland, and Washington, DC. The group consists of Karen, her business partner Lizzy Conroy, Karen's husband Andy as Vice President of Operations, staff of four and two associate agents. As a real estate professional, Karen is a member of the Institute of Luxury Home Marketing, FIABCI International Real Estate Federation and Women's Council of Realtors®.

Karen began her real estate career developing residential lots with the Trammell Crow Company in Dallas, Texas. In Northern Virginia, she worked in commercial real estate with The Staubach Company prior to entering residential sales. Karen earned a Master's degree from Southern Methodist University in Dallas, Texas and received her BA from Stephens College in Columbia, Missouri—her hometown.

Through HBC Group, Karen and Lizzy launched Community Charity Champions to raise funds for local nonprofit groups and organizations and were awarded the Social Corporate Responsibility Award by the Greater McLean Chamber of Commerce. In addition, Karen has been a board member for Lift Me Up!, a therapeutic horseback-riding program for children and adults with disabilities in Great Falls, Virginia, since 2006. Her family is actively involved at Trinity United Methodist Church in McLean, Virginia.

She attributes her life worth living to God, her husband Andy, children Drew and Callie, her family and countless friends and business associates.

Karen is available to speak to your organization, group, company or association. You too can achieve success at a higher level in business and life by investing just 5 minutes a day!

Made in the USA
Columbia, SC
22 January 2019